THE SYNAGOGUE

AND

SOCIAL WELFARE

A Unique Experiment
(1907-1953)

by

SIDNEY E. GOLDSTEIN

Published for
STEPHEN WISE FREE SYNAGOGUE
and
HEBREW UNION COLLEGE—
JEWISH INSTITUTE OF RELIGION
by
BLOCH PUBLISHING COMPANY
NEW YORK
1955

Dedicated

WITH

GRATITUDE AND AFFECTION

TO

The men and women with whom I have served
for half a century
and whose association and cooperation
I have cherished throughout the years.

PREFACE

In this volume, "The Synagogue and Social Welfare—A Unique Experiment," I have endeavored first, to describe the experiments we conducted in the Social Service Department of the Free Synagogue in order to meet community needs; second, to relate our experiences in selected areas of social action and the results achieved; and third, to state what I believe to be the laws of social organization as derived from the experience, teachings, and ideals of the Jewish people. It is our conviction that the synagogue is, by virtue of its origin and development, not only a house of worship and a seat of education, but also a religious center for community service and social action; and that as such it must do its utmost in accordance with its resources to improve community life, to advance social movements, and to further social causes in the interest of social welfare.

I am deeply grateful to all the men and women with whom I have been associated in this unique experiment; and I am especially so to Mr. Ira Frank, president of the Stephen Wise Free Synagogue, Mr. Frederick L. Guggenheimer, and Judge Joseph M. Levine, former presidents, to Mr. Alfred Yankauer, for many years chairman of the Social Service Board, and to Dr. Nelson Glueck, president of the Hebrew Union College—Jewish Institute of Religion. These men have not only aided me with their encouragement and counsel; they have generously made available the funds for publication of this volume.

A word about the period covered. In 1907, when the Free Synagogue was founded and its Social Service Department organized, I became executive director of the Department. In December, 1953, I retired as director and as associate rabbi of the Stephen Wise Free Synagogue, at which time Rabbi Edward E. Klein, Dr. Wise's successor in the rabbinate of the Free Synagogue, added the direction of the Synagogue's reorganized social service program to his other responsibilities, ably assisted by Rabbi Gerald Raiskin, Mr. I. Joseph Harris, executive secretary of the Synagogue, and Mr. Philip Heimlich, chairman of the Social Service Board.

S. E. G.

FOREWORD

There is a dearth of literature on the functions of the rabbi and synagogue in the changing American Jewish scene. There is, however, a vast outpouring of data from social and psychological sources which we must consider. We face the task of evaluating and analyzing this data, particularly with reference to our traditional religious insights about man and his needs, and with reference to services and programs offered to our community by our religious leaders. What is the role of the synagogue in meeting the cultural and social needs of individuals, beyond the more commonly accepted role of educational and religious center? What is the role of the specialist in human relations, in community organization, in social action, in counseling, and in social and national problems? Is it possible to establish lines of communication between the rabbi and others professionally active in the contemporary Jewish scene? What is the relation between the ethical imperatives of Judaism as a source of creed and practice and the newer techniques of human relations? Our need for insight into these problems lends an urgency and a timeliness to a published study in the field of synagogue and social welfare.

This new volume by Rabbi Sidney E. Goldstein supplies answers and stimulates an intelligent reflection upon these issues. It includes a history of the synagogue as well as an analysis of its multiple role, and suggests a program for translating Judaism into everyday experience of the contemporary Jew. Both the rabbi and professional social worker will be interested to learn of the pioneering role of the Free Synagogue in initiating projects of community service. The personal experience of Rabbi Goldstein may well be an example for the American rabbinate which seeks to make Judaism a living reality in the life and total experience of the Jewish community. Few rabbis might succeed in emulating the rich career of Rabbi Goldstein and few congregations might be privileged to undertake so ambitious a program as is recorded in this study. No rabbi or communal worker can read this book without being greatly stimulated by the many creative projects and original programs described.

Rabbi Goldstein wisely stresses the need for competence and understanding on the part of rabbis who minister to social needs. He who would assume the role of social prophet and social engineer is wisely cautioned regarding the complexity of our present social order and the need for thoroughness and intelligent understanding. It is significant that Rabbi Goldstein stresses the role of the rabbi as community organizer, as a social pioneer, and as a dreamer of visions of social welfare. In Rabbi Goldstein's view, the synagogue looms large as a catalyst of social welfare. The fact that several of the major projects developed by the Free Synagogue have now been assimilated into the larger Jewish welfare organization of New York City, may be taken as a tribute to one who envisioned these projects, helped inaugurate them, and made sure that they found their proper place in the total community pattern. While the structure, personnel, and program of the synagogue do not enable it to provide for all of the human services with which it properly concerns itself, the synagogue stands at the center of Jewish life as a creative and guiding spirit.

A young man ordained at the Hebrew Union College in 1905 saw visions of a revitalized synagogue drawing strength from the ethical imperatives of Judaism and shaping its program in the light of the rapidly developing science of man and society. In nearly fifty years of blessed service, Rabbi Goldstein has already given American Jewry a splendid example of creative rabbinical work. His alma mater, the Hebrew Union College-Jewish Institute of Religion, takes seriously the task of training rabbis in the problems and tasks outlined by Rabbi Goldstein. In the Department of Social Studies (now entitled Human Relations) our student rabbis continue to be prepared for their role in reinterpreting the message of Judaism and in defining and implementing the place of the synagogue in social welfare as well as in religious faith and religious education. We are all deeply indebted to Rabbi Goldstein for this stimulating addition to the study of the role of the synagogue in relationship to the totality of the aspects of modern American life.

NELSON GLUECK
President, Hebrew Union College,
Jewish Institute of Religion

TABLE OF CONTENTS

LIST OF ILLUSTRATIONS

INTRODUCTION

Back in 1907, Sidney E. Goldstein, a young man of foresight and vision, was invited by Stephen S. Wise to pioneer with him in the founding of a liberal, Reform synagogue that was to be unique among the congregations of the land—unique in that it would truly and faithfully and democratically interpret the ethics and teachings of our fathers. Such a synagogue, they said, would establish as major policy the voluntary membership contribution, the unassigned pew, the freedom of the pulpit. Moreover, they insisted that it be what the synagogue originally was and has been at its best, not only a house of worship and a seat of education, but also a religious center for community service and social action. Religion, they urged, dictated that prayer service be reenforced with and supplemented by human service to be truly divine service. Their fervid Jewishness, their lofty idealism, their social consciousness, their love of and concern for their fellowman, stirred their conviction of what religion is at its highest, and inevitably brought about the establishment of the Free Synagogue of New York, and with it, what has made the Free Synagogue richly and religiously unique—its great Social Service Department.

It is the story of the Free Synagogue's Social Service Department that is now unfolded in the illumined pages of this volume, and described with the authority of its own architect, organizer, and director. For more than forty-seven years now, from the day of the founding of the Free Synagogue, until his retirement a few months ago, Dr. Sidney E. Goldstein presided without interruption over the Department's vast, blessed program of human service. At long last, during his days of retirement, days that should have been given over to richly deserved rest, he undertook the important task of recording in this book, "The Synagogue and Social Welfare," for all to know—the laity, the rabbinate, the welfare worker—how the social or human service program of the Free Synagogue functions as a department equal to and coordinate with religious observance and religious education; how a whole congregation lends its talents and its resources in following a leader who demonstrates how dedicated people can join in meeting the social and welfare needs of its community.

"The Synagogue and Social Welfare" is in fact the autobiography of Sidney E. Goldstein. Everything he describes is a narrative of his own life's work, a work that meant continuing self-sacrifice and unending days and years of anxiety and labor inherent in the study and solution of the social problems he elected to attack. He yielded pulpit prominence and public acclaim to the much less glamorous involvement to which he gave himself with such intensity. Thousands of men and women, young and old, whom the constituted health and welfare agencies were neither prepared nor sufficiently equipped to serve, came to him and his staff of trained and expert coworkers, for healing and health and hope—and they received care and comfort and courage—warmly, sympathetically, understandingly. Some of today's important "Federation" institutions in New York City came into being because the Social Service Department of the Free Synagogue demonstrated the need and showed the way. In fact, Federation, which for many years assisted the Social Service Department financially, spoke of it as "A laboratory—without test tubes and without chemical compounds—but a laboratory nevertheless, where experiments are conducted to meet the unmet social and welfare needs of the Jewish community."

In "The Synagogue and Social Welfare," Dr. Goldstein speaks with the voice of the teachers in Israel. He reveals their passion for social justice, their kinship with all mankind, their vision of a better world. His contributions of heart and mind and soul and strength covering a lifetime of consecrated labor will, we trust, rouse communities everywhere to the realization that in the Kingdom of God social action and religious observance go hand in hand. The rabbis and officers and members of the Stephen Wise Free Synagogue earnestly hope that this record of our achievements will serve to stimulate and encourage congregations throughout the land so that their synagogues, too, like the Free Synagogue, may become religious centers for community service and social action.

IRA FRANK
President
Stephen Wise Free Synagogue

I

PERSONAL BACKGROUND

SIDNEY E. GOLDSTEIN

PERSONAL BACKGROUND

In this opening chapter I have endeavored to answer the questions often asked me: Why did you not accept a pulpit when you were graduated from the Hebrew Union College? What moved you to spend so many years in developing the social program of the synagogue? How did you equip yourself for this venture in an unexplored field? Long before I entered the seminary I was convinced that the preaching of the pulpit and the teaching in the school must translate themselves into social practice; that social service, service to society, is not only a legitimate, but that it is a necessary, an inevitable, expression of the religious spirit.

Hence, when I was graduated from the College in Cincinnati in 1905 with the degree of rabbi, I decided not to enter the pulpit. Instead, I determined to enlist in the field of social welfare and social reform. This decision was a surprise and disappointment to my family, to the faculty of the College, and to my friends, for I had spent eight years in preparing for the rabbinate. But it was the natural outcome of my own deepest desires and the result of a series of personal experiences. I was interested in theology or the credal element in religion only as an intellectual or academic expression; and I was attracted to the ritual of religion or to ceremonies and symbols only as an esthetic formulation. The element of religion that moved me most was the moral mandate and the passion for social justice.

My experiences I can trace back even to childhood. One of my earliest recollections is marching at the side of my father in Chicago in a parade of protest against excessively long hours of work. I shall never forget the pride I felt in taking part in this protest, for I was permitted to carry one of the banners. My father was a cutter in the clothing industry and worked hard with a long-bladed knife

3

that cut a high pile of goods marked according to pattern. When I was graduated from grammar school, I entered the same industry —in fact, the same factory—in which my father worked. In the course of time I also became a cutter, but not with a knife. I learned to run a machine operated by electricity which cut through piles of cloth fifteen to twenty layers high. This was hard and hazardous work. It was so hot operating this machine during the summer months that I kept a pail of cold water and a metal chain constantly under the table, and from time to time dipped the chain in the water and hung it about my neck. But in this factory and this industry I early became acquainted with the problems with which the laboring man must wrestle and also something of the grievances and injustices that the laborer suffers. In the evenings I attended classes and in this way secured my high school education. During weekends, which then meant Sunday, I listened to sermons in the morning and went as often as I could to lectures and concerts in the afternoon and evening.

I am not, however, a native of Chicago. I was born in the state of Texas, in what was then a very small city called Marshall. My mother was also born in the Southland, in Louisiana, and never quite recovered from her southern customs and southern prejudices. She was a well-educated woman, priding herself upon her command of the English language; to the very last year of her life, when she died at eighty-three, she wrote prose and poetry in odd hours in some way discovered during the day or night. She was in fact widely read in English literature and had a vivid and romantic imagination.

My father was born in Odessa, Russia, and came to America when he was a young man. He must have had a cultivated and socially developed family, for his interests were always wide in range and his activity in the advancement of social movements was persistent and bold. My maternal grandfather, born in Holland, was Dutch to the core. He looked Dutch and acted Dutch. My maternal grandmother, on the other hand, began life in Ireland. How my maternal grandparents met I never learned, but I do recall that my childhood was filled with tales and legends of the "little people" with which my grandmother entertained us whenever we visited her. I was the oldest of six children, and as I look back now, I think we had a perfectly normal life and were as comfortable as most of the families in our neighborhood. We lived at that time on the West Side of Chicago, in a modest little frame house. My mother, a good manager, worked late in order to keep us well-clothed and well-housed. The neighborhood was cosmopolitan, like the city as a whole, and I do not recall that we suffered at all from what is now called national or religious or racial tensions. We all seemed to be Americans.

Our childhood pastimes and recreations were utterly unsupervised. There were many open spaces in the district, and the little group of boys with whom I played spent a good part of their leisure time in digging caves in the earth, and in appropriating apples and sweet potatoes that we roasted in bonfires and ate with secret relish. We learned to secure fruit and vegetables without great risk; usually we had long broomsticks with nails at the ends. The techniques I see boys employing today look crude compared with what we mastered in our time.

One form of recreation I recall clearly was hoop-rolling. We generally secured our hoops from barrels of wood; but one day I decided I wanted something better, and succeeded in prying a metal tire off a wagon wheel as tall as myself. This hoop, which I propelled with a metal rod, was long the pride of the neighborhood. But my most vivid recollection was of the long trips I took, alone. I loved adventuresome walks, and one day decided to skate on the Desplanes River several miles west of Chicago. Somewhere down the river I ran across thin ice and fell into the water. It was late afternoon and there was not a living person within sight. In some manner I managed to scramble out of the river and to climb the bank. Then I skated as fast and as hard as I could in order to dry my clothes and save myself from pneumonia. It was surprising that I did not develop even a cold, for up to my fifteenth year I went to bed with what was then called "lung fever" every spring and every fall, probably the result of a bad case of whooping cough I had developed as a baby.

My early school life I always found enjoyable and at times even exciting. The work was not difficult for me, and I was able to do

well in almost all subjects. Now and then there were little eruptions, which I now recall with some amusement. On one occasion
the teacher left the room for a few moments. I was sitting in one
of the front seats. For some reason I have never been able to understand, I sprang to the top of my desk and began to lead the class
like a bandmaster, with a long ruler for a baton. When the teacher
opened the door she stood startled. I shall never forget the expression upon her face. She was a young, sweet-looking woman with
light skin and pale blonde hair, dressed in a green suit with shiny
brass buttons down the front. When she recovered from her first
shock, she walked with great dignity to her desk, sat down, and
looking straight at me said, "Sidney, I'm astonished." I answered,
"Yes ma'am; so am I." The class began to laugh, and despite herself she had to smile and merely ask me to remain after school.

We had another teacher especially for calisthenics, a young man
who had evidently been trained in a military school and who always
stood as straight as a martinet. He was known throughout the
school for his one command on all occasions: "Sit—erect!" The
word "erect" always came out like a rifle shot. One winter afternoon when our group was skating in Douglas Park, this teacher
joined us. He lost his balance and fell flat upon his back. I looked
at him, and without a moment's hesitation cried out, "Sit—erect!"
The whole group went into an uproar. The teacher struggled to
his feet and skated off, much humiliated. When I look back upon
this period I can understand fully what my mother meant years
later when she said to me, "Do you know why you never became a
juvenile delinquent?" I said, "No, why was it?" She smiled and
answered, "Because they had not coined the term in those days."

I have always regarded it as a fortunate circumstance that I lived
in the city of Chicago during the plastic years of my adolescence.
For here in the last decade of the nineteenth century lived a distinguished group of men and women whose social vision greatly influenced not only local legislation, but national and international
movements. This group included Jane Addams of Hull House,
Newell Dwight Hillis of Central Church, Frank Gunsaules of
Armour Institute, and Emil G. Hirsch of Sinai Temple. They were
then at the peak of their power and all aflame with the white heat

of social justice and social passion. Jane Addams was always less concerned with what we now call the techniques of social work and more with the spirit of social service. She taught me the meaning of service in terms of personal experience, and the need for changes in community life in order that men and women and little children might grow into normal human beings. Dr. Hillis and Dr. Gunsaules, with their historical interpretations, aided me to understand the meaning of social progress and to appreciate the advancement mankind had made through social movements and through the emergence of new social ideals from age to age. They were both brilliant preachers, illumining every topic they undertook to discuss. But the man from whom I learned most was Emil G. Hirsch. He was a profoundly learned scholar, an eloquent and impressive preacher, a master in many fields of knowledge, but most of all he was a man of truly prophetic insight and ethical feeling. As a youth I listened to Hirsch not only every Sunday morning in Sinai Temple, but whenever he spoke or preached at public meetings or at conferences. He was at times witty, at times caustic, at times deeply moving, but he never spoke without content and power.

Dr. Hirsch had his own method of preparing an address. He always began with a proposition; he would state the arguments against his position, and usually do so better than could his opponents; and then he would marshal all the arguments in favor. His range and mastery of material was so great that by the time he concluded there was nothing to do but say "Amen." I recall some of his greatest sermons and most powerful addresses. One year when Chanukah and Christmas fell upon the same day, he opened his address with this statement: "The coincidence of Chanukah and Christmas this year invites a comparison and emphasizes a contrast." It was in this sermon that he coined the phrase so often quoted: "The Greeks stressed the holiness of beauty; the Jews emphasized the beauty of holiness." But no words can picture the power of the man. He possessed in a most unusual degree a rare combination of qualities: a wealth of knowledge gathered from many disciplines of study; a philosophic understanding of problems; and in addition a gift of expression unmatched by the greatest speakers of his generation. Other public speakers I have known have passed through three stages. In the beginning they employ all the antics of elocution; later many develop the art of oratory; and a few ultimately reach the stage of eloquence. Hirsch never stooped to elocution; he never cultivated oratory; but he was always eloquent. His voice was thrillingly impressive; his language always accurate and compelling; his manner and his spirit, at his best, always exalted. He seldom made a gesture, but no one could escape the command he exercised over his audiences, small or great.

I was in Sinai Temple the Sunday Dr. Hirsch preached one of his most prophetic sermons. That morning the newspapers of Chicago had spread across the front page the words, "The Packers Are Stealing the Water of the City." Hirsch arose in the pulpit, stern and grim: "I have been announced to speak on such and such a theme (I forget just what it was) but I have decided to change my topic to 'Thou Shalt Not Steal.'" He not only exposed and denounced the packers of Chicago for robbing the city, but condemned them for the shame they had brought upon the community and upon themselves. Then in the midst of one of his most passionate passages, he turned to Nelson Morris, who was then a member of his congregation, and thundered, "Thou art the man!" The congregation was startled and aghast. Nelson Morris, of course, resigned, and so did a number of his friends. The next Sunday Hirsch arose and said with a wry smile, "I have this week received notice that a number of our members have resigned. I have always known that the Jews possessed at least one virtue—the virtue of resignation. But let me state that while the members are free to resign, the rabbi is also free to resign." The resignations stopped.

His power over audiences was, I recall, splendidly illustrated in the discourse he delivered at the dedication of the Haskell Oriental Museum at the University of Chicago. The audience consisted of scholars from all over the world. Hirsch opened his great address with a paraphrase of a verse from the psalm: "From the rising of the sun to the going down thereof, from the east to the west, from the Orient to the Occident, the name of the Lord shall be praised." For an hour and a quarter he held this great audience of scholars spellbound. His theme was the debt of the Occident to the Orient. It was the most masterly revelation of pure eloquence I can recall in the long line of great public speakers to whom I have listened in the course of the years.

At the University of Chicago I attended courses in the evening and enrolled as a student in the Divinity School during many summer quarters. There I studied with some of the great leaders in religion and education and sociology, among them Barton, Breasted, Henderson, Charles Merriman, Albion Small, and most important of all, John Dewey. Dewey at that time was professor of philosophy and also head of the School of Education. I heard him deliver his first lecture on "School and Society." This was the beginning of the great movement that changed the whole content and character of education not only in America but in Europe and Asia. It was in this first lecture that he told us the story of the New England miller who wanted to sell his mill. The people who came to inspect it grew suspicious because of the low price he asked. They could find nothing wrong with the mill. Finally one of his friends went to him and said, "John, I have explored the mill. The building seems to be in good condition and the machinery seems to be in good shape. What is the trouble with it that you are willing to sell it at this price?" "Well," said John, "the building is in good shape and the machinery is in good condition. There is only one trouble. The millwheel stands just one foot above the water." Dewey paused, looked out the window abstractedly, as he often did, and then turned to the audience: "That, I believe, is the trouble with the school and society. The millwheel stands just one foot above the water." The object of Dewey's program was to bring society and the school into contact. In after years I came to know Dr. Dewey better and served with him on a number of committees. To the very end he was a penetrating and vigorous thinker; a leader not only in thought, but in action.

When I decided to study for the rabbinate, I did not receive much encouragement, except from my father and to some degree my mother. Dr. Joseph Stolz, in whose religious school I studied and in whose temple I was confirmed, discouraged me. He thought my family needed me more than the rabbinate. Our doctor also opposed my choice, chiefly because of the bronchial wheezing to which I was then subject, traceable directly to my whooping cough as a baby and recurrent attacks of bronchitis up to my fifteenth year. The doctor said, "You will never be able to speak in public with any degree of comfort to either yourself or the audience." After considering the matter, I decided to overcome this handicap. I bought a pair of dumbbells, and every day, morning and night, practiced breathing exercises to expand the chest and improve the voice. It was a long and difficult struggle, but I finally succeeded in overcoming the wheezing to such an extent that it was noticeable only in very damp weather, even as to some extent now. It was also necessary for me to prepare myself in Hebrew. This I did through private lessons on weekends from an orthodox rabbi. When I had mastered sufficient to meet the entrance examination, I went for an interview with Dr. Isaac M. Wise, who was then attending a conference in Milwaukee. He graciously accepted me and arranged for me to come to Cincinnati in September.

In the Hebrew Union College, which I entered late in the century, and where I spent eight years, I found little if any understanding or appreciation of social conditions and programs and the movements for social justice. In order to satisfy my interests, I found it necessary to do extra-curricular work with Dr. Boris Bogen, who at that time was director of the Federation of Philanthropies of Cincinnati. Under his tutelage I became better acquainted with the social needs of the Jewish group and with the agencies being created to meet these needs. Bogen was a trained and experienced worker in the field of social welfare, but best of all he was a warm-hearted human being. He had a genuine interest in the people he served and in the social agencies of the community. But I must confess that I greatly missed the stimulus and inspiration of the men and women from whom I had learned and under whom I had worked in Chicago. Through association with Bogen, however, I managed to keep alive and active in the social field and especially in labor problems.

It was therefore not surprising that when Eugene V. Debs ran for President in 1904 I should support him. This open aid to a socialist at the turn of the century created excitement in the student body, startled the faculty, and scandalized the Board of Governors, at that time one of the most conservative groups I have ever met. The climax came when my turn was reached to preach a sermon before graduation. We were assigned the temple in which to preach, and the president of the College was always present. It was the Passover period; and I took as my text, "Let my people go in order that they may serve Me." I pleaded for emancipation of the great masses of men who were suffering want and injustice at the hands of the country's corporations and capitalists. I had no sooner said "Amen" than dear old Dr. Kaufman Kohler rushed to the pulpit and began to pray. He not alone repeated what I had said, but besought the Lord to save the congregation from the heresies I had poured upon them. This experience confirmed my decision not to enter the pulpit, but to engage in social welfare and social reform.

There were some men on the faculty to whom we were devoted. The most learned was Dr. Moses Mielziner, professor of Talmud and codes. He was the mildest and meekest of men, but possessed a grasp of his subject and a mastery of his material almost unbelievable. He never spoke without saying something profound. The man who was of greatest influence, however, in the lives of many of us was Dr. Moses Buttenweiser. He was a biblical scholar, but more than this a true interpreter of the spirit of the biblical books. His course on the Psalms was not only stimulating; it gave us some insight into the heart of Hebrew poetry. His course on Job was a revelation, including a full discussion of the dilemma of good and evil, one of the eternal problems of life. But his classes on the Prophets was the most serviceable and exciting of all. He was the only member of the faculty who seemed to understand and to feel the social message of the prophets. He had the gift of helping us realize the evils with which the prophets wrestled, and from him more than any other member of the faculty I learned something of the spirit of the prophetic books and the social implications of Judaism. To him social justice was a vital matter, as to the men and women I had known in Chicago. He had an amazing understanding of the evils of our own time and an abiding conviction that these evils must be corrected and overcome. I often called on Professor Buttenweiser in his home, and after every visit felt encouraged to continue my interest and activity in the field of social advance. Other men were greater scholars, but no member of the faculty was a greater influence in the life of the small group of students that met from week to week for a discussion of current problems.

The University of Cincinnati, which we attended in the morning, was at that time a small institution; but it included within its faculty three men whom I vividly recall. One was Professor Hicks, who failed me in a course on economics because I refused to accept what was then called the law of supply and demand. He insisted upon the classic formula that price is determined by demand and supply. But I had learned through experience that price is determined by demand, sometimes stimulated, and by available supply, that is, the supply made available by those who control the commodity. In the years that have passed this has come to be recognized as correct. Another man I learned to respect and admire was Professor Benedict, head of the Department of Philosophy. He knew the history of philosophy thoroughly, and the different systems; and he taught philosophy not as a system of thought but as a program of conduct. His emphasis was always upon the ethical element and the cultivation of a moral sense.

However, the man I really learned to love was Dr. Brown, head of the Department of English. Crippled with rheumatism, he came to college in a wheelchair and was propelled up a ramp to the platform in the classroom. He must have suffered constantly; but he had one of the most sensitive faces and most spiritual natures I have known. He taught two courses I greatly enjoyed, on literary criticism and English poetry. He had the power to make literature a vital subject and to present the poets as real human beings; but was most impressive when reading and interpreting the poems. His was an exquisite insight into the poetic and philosophical works of Wordsworth, Tennyson, and especially Browning. Through some miracle of voice and facial expression, he succeeded in communicating the beauty of poetry and the romance of literature. As I recall his face and his manner, I can think of only one word—"illumination." There was in the man an inward light that seemed to illumine the very atmosphere around him.

Beyond these few men at the Hebrew Union College and the University of Cincinnati my studies were uninspiring. The courses were not adequately designed to equip students for the services they were to render as rabbis in American Israel. There was no course on the origin and development of the Synagogue, one of the most important institutions developed by the Jewish people, and the center of the rabbi's activities; there was none on organization and administration of the Synagogue; and certainly no course on its programs of activities. Nor was there any instruction on the relation of the Synagogue to the community, to the social order, and to social problems. Had it not been for my extra-curricular interests and activities my years in Cincinnati would have been arid and unbearably nostalgic. Fortunately I was able to maintain contacts with men and women in Chicago, and to renew my associations during the summer quarter at the Divinity School of the University of Chicago.

The Hebrew Union College was then housed in a large residential edifice in downtown Cincinnati. It was a storehouse of material, but there was little if any effort made to acquaint us with the large movements in Jewish life and their meaning to us as religious leaders. I have visited many seminaries and have been a member of the faculty of the Jewish Institute of Religion for thirty years, and cannot escape the feeling that too many of the seminaries are little more than antiquarian museums. The meetings of the faculty are seldom vital. But if we have sufficient humor we can survive them. I recall that a friend met Dr. Stephen S. Wise in the hall of the Jewish Institute of Religion and said to him, "Dr. Wise, are you going to see the Marx brothers tonight?" Dr. Wise, who really enjoyed the brothers, looked at the questioner with a twinkle in his eye and replied, "Why should I? We have just had a meeting of the faculty."

Many people have asked me how I met Dr. Wise. This came about in a most fortuitous manner. When I decided to enter the field of social welfare, the most interesting opportunity open was the position of assistant superintendent in Mount Sinai Hospital, New York. In Mount Sinai I served under Dr. Sigmund S. Goldwater, one of the ablest and most efficient men I have ever met. He was not only an organizer and an administrator of great ability, but a man with wide social interests and a keen understanding of social problems. As an assistant superintendent it was among my duties to meet the patients as they were admitted to the hospital, to visit them in the wards, and to see them again upon discharge.

I soon discovered that the hospital was excellently administered by Dr. Goldwater; that it had a superior medical staff and a well-trained nursing service. But I also learned that there was no awareness whatever of the social problems of the men and women and children who entered as patients. This was the flagrant lack in hospital care at that time. In order to bring this need to the attention of the Board and the community, I wrote an article entitled, "The Social Function of the Hospital." The first article on this theme to appear in print, it was published in what was then called "Charities and Commons," predecessor of "Survey." This was in 1906, at the same time that Dr. Richard Cabot was beginning his great work in the Massachusetts General Dispensary. He too had discovered that hospital and dispensary patients were not isolated units but members of families, and that they all had social problems. Dr. Wise, then serving as rabbi in Portland, Oregon, having read the article, wrote that he would like to meet me upon his next trip to New York. When he reached the city he told me of his plan to organize a new type of synagogue, one that would be not only a preaching and teaching organization but also a practicing institution. He asked whether I would be interested in associating myself with such a movement. His plan to translate preaching and teaching into social service appealed to me at once. This was the beginning of my association with Dr. Wise and the Free Synagogue.

Starting with the founding of the Free Synagogue in 1907, it lasted to the end of Dr. Wise's life, a period of over forty years. I know of no other synagogue in which two rabbis have served for so long a period, and survived. I once asked Dr. Wise how he accounted for this fact; and he answered in his own characteristic manner, "In two ways:—first, my own inexhaustible patience of spirit; and second, your own incredible power of endurance." I am inclined to think there was another reason. This is illustrated by an anecdote related by a distinguished statesman in a conference at Washington. During the second Roosevelt presidential campaign, this statesman was driving home from Union Station. He turned to his Negro chauffeur: "Sam, for whom are you going to vote?" "I," said Sam, "am going to vote for Mr. Roosevelt." "And your brother?" "Same as I is going to vote; for Mr. Roosevelt." "And your uncle?" "Yes sir, he too." "Why?" said the statesman. "I thought all the Negroes in Washington were Republican." "Yes, sir, we are all Republican. But time's come when we's got to do what's right even when it's against our principles." Sooner or later we all learn that we have to do what is right even when it is against our principles.

I never lost my regard and admiration for Dr. Wise. He had his weaknesses and faults and inconsistencies, as every human being has. He had a passion for democracy, but could be arbitrary and dictatorial. We usually agreed upon most matters of importance, but even when we differed he never at any time attempted to question my complete freedom of thought, expression, and action. The most important matter on which I ventured to differ from him was Zionism. He always hoped I would accept Zionism, and I think it saddened him when I found it impossible to give the movement my coopcration or allegiance. My life-long conviction that nationalism is one of the curses of history and makes impossible the kind of world in which I believe, has always prevented me from allying myself with it. In addition to this conviction I could not believe that establishment of a Jewish State should be the outcome of four thousand years of Jewish development. I still believe in the Jewish people as a kingdom of priests and prophets and not as members of a political unit. In both the Bible and later literature the people is described as *goy kadosh,* a consecrated people. But consecrated for what purpose? The most exalted answer is, I find, in the passages known as the "Servant of God" poems in Deutero-Isaiah. Like all servants of God Israel must suffer as a witness to the truth; but through his sufferings healing will come to all men. In this age of a new nationalism the highest role to which Israel can aspire is expressed in the universalism of the poems that describe the "Servant of God."

To all these men and women and to many more I owe much, and especially to three presidents of the Free Synagogue, all my close personal friends. But the man to whom I owe most is Baruch

Spinoza. I first became acquainted with Spinoza's life and works when I was fifteen. I was too young and immature to understand the "Ethics" or the "Theologico-Political Tractate," but I was old enough to appreciate the "Improvement of the Understanding." This essay is only a fragment, as was Spinoza's life, but it impressed me deeply; and I shall never forget the hour in which I first read these lines in translation: "After experience had taught me that all the usual surroundings of social life are vain and futile, I finally resolved to inquire whether there might be some real good having a power to communicate itself, which would affect the mind singly and to the exclusion of all else; for the ordinary surroundings of life which are esteemed by men (as their actions testify) to be the highest good, may be classed under three heads—Riches, Fame, and the Pleasures of the Senses: with these three the mind is so absorbed that it has little power to reflect on any different good. When I saw that all these ordinary objects of desire would be obstacles in the way of a search for something different and new— nay, that they were so opposed thereto, that either they or it would have to be abandoned—I was forced to inquire which would prove the most useful to me." In these lines Spinoza seemed to sum up the aim of life and to express clearly the aspirations I had dimly felt. This was not merely the idealism of youth; it has been a conviction that has grown and matured as the years of my life have increased. In my seventy-fifth year I am more convinced of the validity of Spinoza's conclusions than I was at fifteen.

Again and again I have returned to Spinoza for understanding and fortitude and inspiration. In spite of his literary form, that to some degree hampers his freedom of thought and expression, I always find in his writings a reinforcement of the spiritual ideals. When I went to Switzerland in 1928 to take the sun treatment, Mrs. Goldstein and our two daughters, Eleanore and Beatrice, then young women, accompanied me; and we decided to journey to Holland, chiefly in order to visit the Hague and Spinoza's home. We spent some time at the Peace Palace in which the World Court meets. But our real objective was the home of the man we had come so greatly to admire and revere. As we walked through the little garden that Spinoza must have trodden many times, as we climbed the stairs he must have climbed from day to day, I felt a sense of something like awe. When we gathered in the little empty attic in which Spinoza had lived and worked and dreamed and died, I felt that we were standing upon holy ground, more so than in the storied crypts of Westminster Abbey or the sombre aisles of Notre Dame, or when we visited the antique and austere Sephardic Synagogue in Amsterdam in which my grandfather had worshiped. For here had dwelt one of the most profound and luminous teachers of mankind. Throughout the years I have read and reread the lesson he taught, that the aim of living is not accumulation of riches nor achievement of fame nor enjoyment of the pleasures of the senses, but the search for truth and justice and the certitudes that are the essential laws of life.

In these paragraphs on my personal background I have included only such material as would indicate why I chose social welfare and the improvement of our social life through the Synagogue as my major activity. I know of course that the rabbi in America serves in a four-fold capacity; he is a preacher, educator, pastor or counselor, and leader in the field of community service and social advance. If I were to list these functions in the order of my own preference, I should put social welfare first, counseling second, education third, and preaching fourth. The reasons I may present in later chapters. Certainly there are other and minor interests I have endeavored to cultivate, among them literature, science, philosophy, and an appreciation of classical music. But these I have not had time to develop to the degree I really wished.

I have given, I realize, no details of my experiences in furtherance of the social movements in which I have been privileged to serve. In the chapters on "The Synagogue," "The Synagogue and the Community," "The Synagogue and Social Action," and "The Synagogue and Social Ethics," I shall discuss more fully the service I was able to render as chairman of two important committees of the Central Conference of American Rabbis—the Commission on Social Justice and the Committee on Marriage, the Family, and the Home; and also as chairman of the New York State Conference on Marriage and the Family, and president of the National Council on Family Relations; likewise as chairman of the War Resisters League of America and the Joint Committee on Unemployment; as a member of the City Affairs Committee of New York and of the

Planning Committee of three pioneering White House Conferences—the Conference on Children in a Democracy, the Conference on the Family, and the Conference on the Aging; and also my activity in the Birth Control movement. In rereading Who's Who, I find I have been more active than I expected to be when I chose my major field of service.

In view of the fact that these paragraphs on my background are not a biography, even in brief, I have omitted any description of the family into which I was born, and the characteristics and careers of my mother and father and brothers and sisters, all of whom had interesting developments and some of whom have made distinct contributions in their own fields. I have also omitted a description of our immediate family, including Mrs. Goldstein, our daughters, our sons-in-law Harvey Konheim and Hugo Nichthauser, and our five precious grandchildren. In a chapter as limited as this, it would be impossible to describe what all the members of our family have meant to me and to dwell upon the joys and sorrows and tragedies through which we have passed. Every member has been gifted with a positive personality and has been endowed with peculiar capacities and powers.

Nor have I spoken of my own inmost experiences. The years have been full and crowded, and in many ways richly and rarely blessed: blessed through the love of those who have been nearest and dearest to me; blessed through the kindnesses of the congregation in whose midst I have dwelt for nearly half a century; blessed in the many opportunities for service that have been granted me to improve human welfare and advance the cause of social justice. Something of the associations I have enjoyed, and something of what I have thought and felt and endeavored to achieve, will undoubtedly reveal themselves in the chapters to come, and especially in the closing pages, in which I have expressed some of my conclusions. I realize that my experience as associate rabbi and director of the Social Service Department of the Free Synagogue has been unique, and it is my earnest hope that the experiments we conducted during forty-six years will serve as incentive and pattern to other congregations, who believe as we do that the Synagogue is not only a house of worship and a seat of education, but also a religious center for community service and social advance.

II

THE SYNAGOGUE

STEPHEN S. WISE

THE SYNAGOGUE

This section merely outlines the development of the Synagogue as a social institution. The Synagogue has often been studied as a house of worship, together with its liturgy and architecture and equipment; and the Synagogue has also been studied as a seat of education with its programs of instruction for the different age groups. But the Synagogue has not thus far been studied as a religious center for community service and social action. A full treatment of the Synagogue as a social institution would require a series of studies of the social activities of the Synagogue in the many countries in which the Jews now live; and of the social programs of the Synagogue in the countries in which the Jews have lived in the course of the centuries. Such a series would reveal the Synagogue in a new light and would undoubtedly prove that it has always been central to the Jewish community; and that it has likewise been the source of Jewish community service.

1. ORIGIN OF THE SYNAGOGUE

It is surprising that no one has written the history of the Synagogue as a social institution. There are books on the architecture of the Synagogue; on the theology of the Synagogue; on the liturgy of the Synagogue; and on the music of the Synagogue. But there are only essays and chapters on its origin and development. For over two thousand years the Synagogue has been central to Jewish life. It is one of the institutions through which Israel has survived; through which Judaism has been preserved and expanded; through which tradition has transmitted the heritage of our people. In time of peace, the Synagogue has been a source of instruction and inspiration; in time of trial it has been a source of sustainment and

21

strength; in time of crisis it has been a refuge and even the funeral pyre of Israel. Both Jewish and Christian students of Jewish culture recognize the supreme importance of the Synagogue, not only for Judaism but for Christianity and Mohammedanism. R. Travers Herford is eloquent in his description: "In all their long history the Jewish people have done scarcely anything more wonderful than to create the Synagogue. No human institution has a longer continuous history and none has done more for uplifting the human race" ("The Pharisees," p. 91).

The origin of the Synagogue like that of many social institutions lies hidden in the mists of early Jewish history. Many students of Judaism and Jewish culture are of the opinion that it was born in Babylonia. George Foot Moore, Ismar Elbogen, Salo Baron, and many other men of distinction in Jewish scholarship and history assume that the Jews established the Synagogue during the Exile as a place in which to assemble and to conduct services. The assumption is only natural. The Jewish people were taken to Babylonia by Nebuchadnezzar, 586 B.C.E., and continued to look to Palestine as the center of Jewish life and to the Temple as the only sanctuary in Israel. But they needed some spot in which to gather in a foreign land, to recite their prayers, to read and expound the Law, to discuss the problems of an alien environment and a hostile country. That they did come together "in assembly" is clear from the writings of the exilic period, especially from passages in the Book of Ezekiel. That they must have established some institution in which to meet, to study, to worship, and to discuss community matters seems a reasonable social necessity. Whether this institution was the Synagogue and whether it actually originated in Babylonia is still, however, not certain.

George Foot Moore is frank in his statement: "Its origin is unknown, but it may be reasonably surmised that it had its antecedents in spontaneous gatherings of Jews in Babylonia and other lands of their exile on the Sabbath and at the times of old seasonal feasts or on fast days, to confirm one another in fidelity to their religion in the midst of heathenism and encourage themselves in the hope of restoration" ("Judaism," Vol. 1, p. 28). R. Travers Herford is of the same opinion: "I place then in the period of captivity, the appearance of the germ of the Synagogue, in simple meetings for worship and instruction. How these developed cannot be traced. But it is again reasonable to suppose that they gradually became regular by tending to associate with the Sabbath, partly because that was the holy day from time immemorial and partly because it was a day of rest from ordinary activities" ("The Pharisees," p. 91). Baron comes to the same conclusion in discussing the community organization of Babylonian Jewry: "All statements about these public gatherings are made with considerable diffidence, since little is known about what went on. At any rate it is certain that these gatherings later gave rise to the institution which became the foundation of Jewish life in the Diaspora —the Synagogue" ("A Social and Religious History of the Jews," Vol. 1, p. 102). It must be noted that these authors do not maintain that the Synagogue itself existed in Babylonia. They speak only of "the antecedent," "the germ," "the gatherings," that later led to the institution.

On the other hand, there are some Jewish scholars who question this historical assumption that the Synagogue originated in Babylonia. Louis Finkelstein, for example, is firmly of the opinion that its origin can be traced to Palestine and to Palestinian organizations existing before the Exile ("Proceedings of the American Academy for Jewish Research," 1928–30, pp. 45, 59: "The Pharisees," pp. 563, 569). His thesis is two-fold: "First, that there were prayer gatherings under prophetic guidance even before the fall of Jerusalem in 586 B.C.E.; and second, that out of these gatherings there grew imperceptibly and more definitely institutionalized synagogues that played so important a role in the Maccabean age." This thesis rests upon the biblical evidence that prophetic gatherings took place in early times on the Sabbath and new moons, and also on the history of the word *"midrash."* This is derived from a Hebrew word that means to inquire, and came to signify the place of prophetic inquiry or discussion as well as the substance of the discussion. That there were meeting places in the days of the prophets and that there were gatherings of people for prayer, there can be little doubt. But that these meeting places and gatherings in the pre-exilic period served as the sources of the Synagogue whether in the exilic or the post-exilic period cannot be established as an historical fact. Finkelstein and those who share his views may be correct; but in view of the fact that so little evidence is available, the conclusion must remain a conjecture. It must not be forgotten that the Temple with its sacrificial cult and its priesthood was also called a house of prayer and that prayer was a part of the Temple ritual.

In an endeavor to determine the origin of the Synagogue, where and when it began, we must remember that there are only two types of material that can aid us: the archaeological and the literary. The archaeological material now available does not carry us back very far. In Babylonia no ruins of synagogues have been uncovered, unless we include the one at Dura on the Euphrates, which dates from the third century C.E. The ruins of the synagogues thus far uncovered in Palestine do not date back beyond the second or the first century of the Christian Era. Nelson Glueck and others have unearthed many cities and discovered many interesting remnants of earlier periods; but no remains of synagogues earlier than the beginning of the Christian Era (Annals of "The American School of Oriental Research"). Erwin R. Goodenough, in the volumes just published, cities many inscriptions and much evidence to indicate that synagogues existed in Rome, Greece, Asia Minor, and North Africa, and that some of these date back to the first or the second century B.C.E. He speaks of one marble slab in the British Museum that was found in Egypt near the city of Alexandria in 1902. On this there is an inscription in Hellenic Greek: "In honor of King Ptolemy and Queen Berenice, his sister and wife and their children, the Jews dedicate this Proseuche" ("Jewish Symbols in the Greco-Roman Period," Vol. 2, pp. 70–100). Oriental scholars are of the opinion that the king referred to was Ptolemy the Third, 241–242 B.C.E. The word "Proseuche," while often used to refer to the synagogue, really means a place of worship, and may refer to some temple that had been built in Egypt by a Jewish community. That the Jews of Egypt did build temples in imitation of the Temple in Jerusalem is well known from the records of the Elephantine community. These, however, have a priesthood and a sacrificial cult and were not synagogues in the usual sense of the term.

Tradition, of course, ascribes the origin of the Synagogue to Abraham or to Ezra. An examination of the literary material compels us to come to a different conclusion. In the pre-exilic literature in the Bible, there are many references to altars and shrines and high places (*bamot*). These sanctuaries, scattered throughout Palestine, became important, especially in cities like Shiloh, Schechem, Beth-El, and Samaria. The Temple in Jerusalem was the great religious center. But there is no mention of an institution called the Synagogue or of an institution with its functions.

One passage in Jeremiah (XXXIX:8) is often quoted as a reference to the Synagogue: "And the Chaldeans burned the house of the king and the house of the people with fire and broke down the walls of Jerusalem." The term "house of the people," the medieval commentators Rashi and Kimchi and later writers interpret as meaning the Synagogue. The reason is an interesting and typical piece of medieval exegesis. In the Talmud the Synagogue is often spoken of as "the house of the people." The commentators naturally but incorrectly assume that because it is so called in talmudic Aramaic, the Hebrew equivalent in the text of Jeremiah one thousand years earlier must also have meant the Synagogue. It is clear, however, that the text in Jeremiah is in the form of the customary Hebrew parallelism, and that the implied meaning is a contrast. The Chaldeans, in other words, are described as destroying everything from the house of the king to the homes of the people, or as we should say in current phrase, everything was destroyed from the palace to the hut.

In the exilic literature there are numerous references to "assemblies," especially in Ezekiel. Ezekiel also speaks of a *mikdash meat* (XI:16). This the Targum freely paraphrases into the Aramaic *batai kenishta*, which means synagogues, and the medieval commentators follow the paraphrase or free translation. In other words, the Targum assumes that the prophet living during the Exile is speaking of the Synagogue. But there is nothing in the verse or the context to justify this interpretation. The verse reads as follows:

"Although I have removed them far off among the nations, and although I have scattered them among the countries, yet have I been to them as a little (or lesser) sanctuary in the countries where they are come." There is in fact nothing in Ezekiel that would lead us to conclude that he is speaking or even thinking of the Synagogue. On the contrary, every passage in the writings of this prophet proves that he is thinking primarily of the Temple with its ritual of prayer, its sacrificial cult, and its priesthood. In his religious philosophy the Temple is to be rebuilt in Jerusalem and is to be central to Israel's life. It is of course reasonable, even necessary, to assume that during the fifty years of exile in Babylonia the Jewish people would meet for prayer, for exposition of the Law, and for discussion of their problems in a foreign land. The very fact that they believed they were in exile because of their sins would lead them to gather in religious assemblies and to pray for restoration to the Land of Israel and for re-establishment of the Temple. But nowhere in Ezekiel do we find any description of the type of meeting house or the form of service or the leaders developed.

In the writings of the great Prophet of the Exile whose name is unknown to us but whose prophecies are attached to the works of Isaiah of Jerusalem (Isaiah, XL–LV) there is, strangely enough, no mention of the Synagogue. A part of one verse in Deutero-Isaiah is often quoted and interpreted as meaning the Synagogue: "For My house shall be called a house of prayer for all peoples" (Isaiah LVI:7). But a reading of the whole of this verse and the passage of which it is a part clearly proves that the prophet is speaking not of any synagogue in Babylonia or elsewhere, but of the Temple to be re-established in Jerusalem. The first part of this verse is as follows: "Even them will I bring to My holy mountain, and make them joyful in My house of prayer; their burnt offerings and their sacrifices shall be acceptable upon Mine altar." In this passage the prophet predicts that not only will the Temple in Jerusalem be a religious center for the people of Israel, but that to the people of Israel will be gathered even the aliens who keep the covenant of God. This great religious teacher, as is evident from all his writings that we possess, is firmly of the conviction that God is of all peoples, of all lands, of the universe. He is the Sovereign of all the earth and the Master of all men. Therefore all men will come to accept His covenant and worship Him upon His holy hill. But the central sanctuary he describes is still the Temple in Jerusalem. In no verse does Deutero-Isaiah speak of or describe a synagogue.

The post-exilic literature in the Bible, especially Ezra and Nehemiah, contains many references to "assemblies" of the people. That the people, both those who lived in Palestine and who returned from Babylonia, assembled in meeting places for worship and to listen to expositions of the Law, there can be no question. In what kind of place they gathered, however, cannot be determined from the passages in the literary material that has been preserved. It is surprising that the writers of the post-exilic period do not speak of the Synagogue. But it must be remembered that the chief concern of the leaders, especially those who had returned from Babylonia to Palestine, was to rebuild the Temple and to reinstitute the sacrificial cult and the priesthood. They were not concerned with any minor institutions, even had they existed. Certainly they do not speak of the Synagogue.

In Psalm LXXIV there is a verse that is frequently quoted as a reference thereto. The psalm is post-exilic, according to biblical scholars, and probably dates from the time of the desecration by the Syrians. It vividly describes the invasion of the country, the devastation of the land, and the desecration of the sanctuary. But it is clear from verses 2 and 4 that the sanctuary of which the poet speaks is a Temple on Mt. Zion. Verse 8 reads as follows: "They have burnt all the meeting places of God in the land." It is conceivable that this phrase, "meeting places of God," refers to synagogues or places of worship, but there is nothing in the psalm itself to indicate this. In fact the rest of the psalm, especially the section from verse 1 to verse 11, argues against this interpretation. The poet is thinking of Mt. Zion and of the Temple thereon. It is in this "meeting place of God" that the adversaries roar and destroy and set up their own idols (verse 4).

One of the most surprising facts in post-biblical literature is that there is no mention whatever of the Synagogue in the first and second Books of the Maccabees. These Books, in the Apocrypha, are regarded as historical; they date from the Maccabean period.

They describe in detail the conditions in Palestine during the Syrian invasion and portray the revolt of the people against the attempt by Antiochus to impose an alien religion upon the Jews. One would expect in material so current and even contemporaneous that some description would be given of what occurred in the synagogues of Palestine and of what happened to these institutions during the devastation. This is all the more true since the Maccabean revolt was so largely a movement of the Pharisees, the party of the people. The Synagogue too, we must remember, was an institution of the people and was largely developed by the Pharisees themselves. Not once, however, does it appear in these documents. The center of interest is the Temple—the capture of the Temple, the violation of the Temple, the cleansing of the Temple, and the rededication of the Temple. Even the legends of the time make the Temple the center of interest and concern. If the Synagogue was so fully developed and so widespread in Palestine during this period, if there was a synagogue in every city and town, as we have reason to assume, it does seem that some mention would be made of prayer services of supplication conducted in the houses of worship; of the meetings held there in time of national trial; of what happened to some of them in the path of the enemy. The only reasonable explanation for this omission is that these Books of the Maccabees were written by the Sadducees.

In post-biblical literature, both Jewish and non-Jewish, there are many references to the Synagogue in both Palestine and other lands of the ancient world. Philo speaks of the synagogue in Alexandria and particularly of the Great Synagogue described in the Talmud (Yer. Suk. vi). This, we are told, was in the form of a huge basilica with colonnades. It contained seventy-one golden chairs, corresponding to the seventy-one elders. The congregation was arranged in accordance with the trades of the time, and was so large that the *hazzan* on the platform had to signal with a scarf when the time came to respond to the benedictions. The description is so extravagant, however, that some scholars doubt its accuracy. When it was established we do not know, but from the terms used it is fair to assume that it was during the late Hellenic period.

The fact is that a complete description of the Synagogue does not appear in the literary material preserved up to the period of the New Testament. The earliest book in the New Testament, scholars are agreed, is the Gospel of St. Mark. Here the Synagogue is mentioned a number of times and always as an established institution in the town or city, and it appears to have had a fully developed program (Mark I:23, 29, 39; III:14; XII:39; XIII:9). The date usually given for Mark is the latter part of the first century of the Christian Era or about 90. In this Gospel Jesus is pictured as teaching and preaching in the synagogue on Sabbaths; but in addition he also heals the sick and restores the crippled. A study of the passages here and in other books of the New Testament dealing with the life and work of Jesus and his disciples in Palestine reveals the interesting and significant fact that the Synagogue does not serve merely as a house of worship and a place of prayer; it is also a seat of study, education, discussion. In addition it serves as a center of community life. In other words, in the New Testament and especially in those passages that speak of the Synagogue in Palestine, it maintains a three-fold function: it is a house of worship, a seat of education, and a community center. This corresponds exactly with the Hebrew terms that describe the Synagogue as a Beth-Ha-mikdash, Beth Ha-midrash, and Beth Ha-kenesseth. Whatever its origins, this is what the Synagogue has become when it first appears in the literary material we possess.

There were many synagogues in Palestine during this early period, how many it is impossible to determine. The Talmud speaks of 480 in Jerusalem alone (Yer. Meg. 73A); and in another place states there was a synagogue even within the Temple itself (Yoma VII:1). From the New Testament material and other literature of the time, it is clear that there were synagogues in all the principal cities not only of Palestine, but of Asia Minor, Greece, Rome, and Egypt. The historians of the early centuries of the Christian Era all describe synagogues of the period in these countries. Wherever the Jews settled they established a synagogue. This institution was not a substitute for the Temple and its sacrificial cult, but a center of Jewish community interest and community action and a symbol of Jewish solidarity. It is true that in the Talmud the foremost institution is the academy or yeshivah. The yeshivah is the place in which teachers and students gather for study and discussion and also for reaching decisions on important current problems. It is also true that in the Talmud the chief concern with the Synagogue is as a house of worship or a place of prayer. The discussions deal largely with the order of the service, arrangement of the liturgy, the teaching of the Law and later books, amplification of the Law, and its application to contemporary social life. But the Synagogue is often described and discussed in the Talmud, compiled about 500 C.E., and many parts of which date back to the first Christian century.

The conclusions we must reach are now clear. There is no mention of the Synagogue as an institution in pre-exilic, exilic, and post-exilic literature of the Bible. It appears on the historical scene in the New Testament, that is, during the first century of the Christian Era. At this time the Synagogue is already a fully developed institution, serving as a house of worship, a place of study, and a center of community service. How long it took to develop into this type of institution it is impossible to tell on the basis of evidence now available. That it had antecedents there can be no doubt; and it is reasonable to assume that these existed in both Palestine and Babylonia, in Babylonia during the Exile, and in Palestine certainly after the Exile and probably before. In other lands and especially in Egypt, Jewish groups erected temples to serve as substitutes for the Temple in Jerusalem, that is, they possessed a liturgy, a sacrificial cult, and a priesthood. Whether they took the form of places of prayer or study or community service, there is no way of determining; though it is reasonable to assume that after the destruction of the Temple in Jerusalem by the Babylonians there developed in both Palestine and Babylonia places in which the Jewish people and their leaders assembled for recitation of the prayers that formed part of the liturgy of the Temple, and for reading and interpretation the Law which served as their guide in life. And it is also reasonable to assume that the people must have gathered in some center for a discussion of the problems in their political, economic, and cultural life. The origin of the Synagogue is historically important; but for our present purpose more important is its function.

2. FUNCTION OF THE SYNAGOGUE

On the basis of evidence now in our possession, it is impossible to determine whether the Synagogue began as a house of worship, as a place of study, or as a center of community activities. But from the time it first appeared, it has served as a house of worship, and throughout the centuries worship has continued to be its primary function. What was included within the term "worship" in the early Synagogue it is difficult to determine with certainty, but we do know there was a daily ritual and that prayers were recited three times a day, in the morning, at noon, and in the evening. Special services were recited on the eve of the Sabbath and on Sabbath morning, also for the New Moon, celebrated as the beginning of the Hebrew month, for the three festivals: Sukkoth or the Feast of Tabernacles, Pesach or Passover, Shavuoth or Pentecost; and on the Holy Days, that is, Rosh Hashanah, New Year's Day, and Yom Kippur, the Day of Atonement.

Even in these earliest periods of worship, it is possible to discover how the elements of this function of the Synagogue developed, and as it prevails even at the present time in Orthodox and Conservative and Reform or Liberal Judaism. These elements include: (1) the prayer service; (2) the musical service; (3) ceremonies; (4) exposition of the Law or sermon; (5) the environment. Not all were included in each period of worship. Some periods, for example, did not include any ceremonies; and some were conducted without a reading of the Law or any interpretation thereof. But in the more important periods of worship, that is, those conducted on the Sabbath, the festivals, and the Holy Days, all elements are part of the service and together constitute the order of worship within the Synagogue.

The element that continues as a permanent part of every period is the prayer ritual. A study thereof reveals the interesting fact that sections of the prayerbook are drawn from different parts of the Bible, the Pentateuch, the Prophets, and the Holy Writings; and that other parts have been introduced from Mishnah and Talmud and even from later medieval philosophical literature. These are in addition to the prayers of supplication and praise and thanksgiving that constitute the framework of the ritual. Many parts were taken over from the Temple service, especially the recitation of the Ten Commandments, the Shema, and the Blessings. Others were not included in the ritual until the early centuries of the Christian Era, for example, the Eighteen Benedictions known as the Amidah, the 'Alenu prayer that closes the service, and also the Kaddish. Some parts were not added until the Middle Ages, such as the hymns and the penitential poems or piyyutim.

Many of the prayers included in the liturgy of the Synagogue are found or mentioned in the Talmud; but the liturgy itself did not take definite form until the ninth century, when the Gaon Amram ben Shensha (died 875 C.E.) arranged the prayerbook known as the Siddur of Rav Amram. The pattern that Amram set was followed by other men, such as Saadia and Maimonides, and it serves as precedent for both the Sephardic and the Ashkenazic prayerbooks that have developed down to our own time. In the Orthodox synagogue the prayer ritual occupies a larger part of the period of service than in the Conservative, and a larger part in the Conservative than in the Reform or Liberal synagogue.

The element of music in worship is as old as the prayer service itself. This may surprise many, but it must be remembered that in the earliest days the prayers were not recited but chanted; even the portions of the Law or the Pentateuch were sung and not read from the Scroll. The chant in the case of every prayer and every portion of the Bible was designed to express the spirit and mood of the passage. In other words, it was based upon the sense of the text and its construction. In this way it developed from musical compositions which are based upon musical modes. The entire congregation knew the chant and joined in. As music itself developed, musical modes and compositions entered into the service and became a larger and larger part of the period of worship. In Temple days a number of musical instruments were employed, as is evident from descriptions in the Bible and the verses in many of the psalms that form part of the ritual. But for a long period after destruction of the Temple musical instruments were banished from the Synagogue, partly because their playing seemed a violation of the law of the Sabbath, and partly because it seemed inconsistent to play them during the period of Exile and national mourning for the destruction of the Temple and the dispersion of the people. Within the last century, however, in the Liberal synagogue and also the Conservative, the organ and other musical instruments have been introduced, and full choirs, including both male and female voices, enrich and beautify the service. The cantorial and musical compositions by the great composers, both Jewish and non-Jewish, now form a permanent and impressive part of the period of worship. There is an ancient Jewish tradition: "There are two gateways that open into heaven: one the gateway of prayer; the other the gateway of song."

The ceremonies that now form a part of the worship have developed in the course of the centuries. The Kiddush, which is now chanted in the synagogue on Sabbath eve, was originally not a part of the period of worship, but of the service in the home on the eve of the Sabbath. The waving of the *lulab* during Sukkoth and the procession that takes place during this festival date back to talmudic days. The ceremonies that surround the reading of the Torah on the Sabbath, festivals, and Holy Days have become more and more elaborate until today the Torah service in many synagogues becomes the central point of the period of worship. Opening the Ark, taking out the Scroll, reading or chanting the portion of the week, calling up members of the congregation, and return of the Scroll to the Ark, altogether form an impressive ceremony.

The bar mitzvah ceremony also has become a part of the period of worship and now takes place during the Sabbath morning service. This ceremony, which marks the entrance of the young man into full responsibility as a member of the Jewish people, is post-talmudic, but has become in Orthodox and Conservative and in many Liberal congregations a very important rite. The blowing of the *shofar* on New Year's Day and at the close of the Day of Atonement is another significant ceremony, and an essential part of the Holy Day service. But perhaps the most impressive of all is the ceremony of Confirmation which takes place in all Liberal and some Conservative synagogues at the festival of Shavuoth. This is the time at which, according to tradition, the Law was given to

Moses on Mt. Sinai, and is fittingly the day to mark the entrance of young people into the covenant that Israel made with God at Sinai.

The environment, the fifth element, may seem to many of little significance in the period of worship, but the construction and character of the building, the lighting and the decorations, the furniture and furnishings, do create an atmosphere. The environment may be so utterly barren and empty of meaning that it contributes nothing to the mood of worship; or so dark and depressing as to overwhelm the worshipers with a sense of gloom and despair; but, on the other hand, it may be so rich and splendid and radiant as to exalt the congregation to the heights of awe and reverence.

For many centuries the interior of the synagogue was most austere, even bleak. This was due in part to fear of violating the Commandment that forbids the Jews to make any graven image or likeness of anything that is in the heavens above or on the earth beneath or in the waters under the earth. It was due in part also to the tradition that during the Exile the people of Israel must banish all adornments from their life, as a sign of mourning over the fall of Jerusalem and the destruction of the Temple. Gradually, however, the outlook upon life has changed, and with the change has come a new environment. The walls in many synagogues are richly decorated, and the stained glass windows are of great beauty. Even the structure of the auditorium is so changed as to be impressive and inspiring. The Ark that contains the Torah and the mantles of the Scrolls themselves are all designed to awaken in men and women a sense of the beauty of holiness. Without a rich and reverent environment, it is difficult to create a religious atmosphere in keeping with the current concepts of religion.

The purpose of worship may change in emphasis from time to time. It is true that some people attend religious services solely as a matter of habit; and that some attend because of respect for their parents, or because of a desire for social contacts, or in search of recreation. But there are others who realize that worship has other purposes and can serve them in other ways. The purpose of worship, as we now understand it, is not single but manifold. It can bring comfort to people who are in sorrow, and there are few who do not suffer grief at some time in their lives. It can bring men and women encouragement and strength in time of trial and disappointment, and these experiences come to most men and women. It can give guidance and counsel in hours of temptation, and temptation comes to many of us frequently. It can bring enlightenment to those in search of understanding, and certainly there are many who in these times are in doubt. It can also offer inspiration to men and women, who feel the need of inspiration in the drab and dreary round of daily life.

But the highest purpose that worship can serve is to bring us into communion with a power greater than ourselves; there are many men and women who seek communion, perhaps more than we suspect. In other words, the purpose of worship is to lift men and women above the common levels of life and to give them the insight and exaltation, the refreshment and recreation, of spiritual power that can come from the wellsprings of religion. In order to achieve this manifold purpose, however, it is necessary that the period of worship be so organized and so conducted as to express the spirit of reverence, which is the characteristic quality of religion itself.

As it is impossible to discover when the Synagogue first developed as a place of worship, so is it impossible to discover when it first became a center of study and education. It is not unreasonable to suppose that the texts of the biblical books, especially of the Torah or Pentateuch, served as a basis of study and discussion wherever the people assembled. Of this, however, we are certain, that the most ancient records we possess describe the Synagogue as a Beth Ha-midrash, or as a place of learning and discussion. It is most important to note that the earliest educational programs were not limited to children. Classes for children were organized, and they were instructed in the elementary subjects that form a part of the heritage and the culture of the Jewish people. But in addition to these there also were study groups for youth and adults and the aged. In other words, the educational program that developed within the Synagogue and with the Synagogue as the center covers all age groups, and includes elementary, intermediate, and adult education.

To what degree this program reached every member of the Jewish community, we do not know, but we do know that illiteracy was regarded as a disgrace, and was exceptional. The Jewish people have taken seriously and literally the verse: "These words, which I command thee this day, shall be upon thy heart; and thou shalt teach them diligently unto thy children and shalt speak of them when thou sittest in thy house, and when thou walkest by the way and when thou liest down and when thou risest up" (Deut. VI:6– 7). The translation of this command into social practice results in the educational program that centered in the Synagogue and that has been not only an age-old tradition in Israel, but an essential part of the culture of the people.

Educational sessions are now held on weekdays and on Sunday mornings, and in some synagogues even on Saturday mornings. Most synagogues today have sessions on Sunday morning, during which the elementary classes meet for classroom instruction and for assembly. These run from 9:00 to 12:00 or 12:30. The weekday sessions are held on Monday, Tuesday, Wednesday, and Thursday afternoons from 3:30 or 4:00 to 5:30 or 6:00. They are arranged in the late afternoon in order to accommodate the children who attend public school. In the morning the curriculum generally includes language, literature, history, religion, and in some schools arts and crafts. The weekday sessions are as a rule devoted to instruction in Hebrew. Sessions for the adolescent groups constitute the high school course, and are generally held on Sunday morning. In these boys and girls from fifteen to seventeen or eighteen meet for advanced studies in the history and literature and religion of the Jewish people and for a discussion of Jewish community life and organization and institutions. In many synagogues college groups composed of young men and women meet some evening during the week, to study current Jewish problems. In addition to elementary and intermediate sessions, classes are conducted for adults on Sunday morning, sometimes in the afternoon and evening. These classes frequently take the form of discussion groups or seminars, and are led by the rabbi or the head of the department of education. In this program of adult education, courses are given to meet the needs of the particular congregation and community. Topics in the curriculum range from the Hebrew language to contemporary problems and Jewish philosophy.

The curriculum of a fully developed synagogue department of education includes the following: (1) language; (2) literary material; (3) history; (4) religion; (5) social service; (6) current events; (7) arts and crafts. Each of these items can be taught as a subject in itself or as part of the culture of the Jewish people. Each can also be presented as an isolated subject with limited implications, or in such a way as to develop social implications and the social spirit. The Hebrew language, for example, can be taught simply as a language, with the linguistic limitations. But the language is so rich in terms of social significance that it is natural to emphasize the social implications of the Hebrew tongue. The very phrase with which Jewish men and women greet each other, *Shalom Alechem,* peace be with you, stresses this fact. The *shalom* means more than peace. It signifies the peace that exists between individuals or that should characterize all human relationships.

Another word that runs constantly through the Hebrew language is *tzedek* or justice. No word is more frequently employed, as also its derivative *tzedakah,* righteousness, or righteous conduct and righteous relationships between man and man. The word *ḥesed,* mercy or compassion, is another that constantly recurs in Hebrew. It expresses the feeling that men have for those who suffer and those who sin, which again stresses human attitudes and human relationships. The word *ahavah,* love, with all its derivatives, occurs again and again in the Hebrew language. In fact it is one of the primary words employed in describing human relationships, as exemplified in the commands: "Thou shalt love thy neighbor as thyself" and "Thou shalt love the stranger as thyself."

The literary material in the curriculum may also be presented as examples of the literature of the Jewish people; and that literature does contain all types of composition—myths, legends, essays, novels, histories, philosophies, orations, poetry, drama, tragedies, and something that is not found in other writings, what Moulton calls the prophetic rhapsody. But this material may also be presented with its social implications and significance. This is true even of the early myths and legends in the Bible, the first collection of Hebrew literature. The story of Creation that opens the Book of Genesis, for example, has its climax in the establishment of the Sabbath. The Sabbath, however, is ordained as a day of rest not only for theological but also for humanitarian reasons. It is the day on which both the master and the servant, the stranger and cattle, shall rest from labor and recover strength and refreshment of spirit.

The story of the Garden of Eden has its theological and philosophical interpretations, but also its social implications. In fact, if this story is studied carefully, it is soon discovered that the Garden of Eden is the picture of a social life such as would arise in the mind and the imagination of a people still in the nomadic stage. The Garden with its trees and shade and fruit and rivulets of water is a mirage of the desert such as would be conjured up in the dreams of desert tribes. Even the story of the Flood, a myth common to all peoples, has in its biblical form a social meaning. The world is filled with wickedness and corruption. In the minds of primitive people there was only one way in which the earth could be cleansed and purified, and that was through the medium of a flood of water which would wash away all evil and destroy all wickedness on the face of the earth. The Flood, in other words, is the earliest social panacea.

What is true of language and literature is also true of the historical and religious material, current events, and arts and crafts. All can be taught in a restricted and limited manner, but if they are taught as they should be, the social implications will inevitably appear. The history of a people is largely of their social organization and social relationships. Too frequently, however, it becomes little more than a chronicle of dates and events and episodes. By developing the social implications of history the material becomes immeasurably more interesting and vital. The same is true of the religious material. It can be limited to articles of belief and to ceremonies, or it can include the codes of conduct that apply to family and social life. In this manner the material is directly related to human experience and the life that men and women lead from day to day. Current topics may also suffer in the same way that historical material does in some departments of education. But the social meanings of contemporary experiences are so clear and vivid that it is difficult to exclude them. In truth, unless current events are given a social significance there is grave danger that they will lose their appeal. Arts and crafts have of course an esthetic value, and may be employed to re-enforce the expression of religion in terms of beauty. But this also possesses a social meaning. The homes in which the people lived during the stages of their development, the furnishings they fashioned, the games they played, the dances they enjoyed, even the music they sang—all are a part of their social life and an expression of the spirit of the people. The more intimately all this material is related to social relationships and to social organization, the more vital and meaningful it becomes.

The records now available do not make it possible to determine when the Synagogue became a community center as well as a house of worship and a place of education. But it is reasonable to suppose that from the very beginning the people of the community assembled there for a discussion of community matters, and made the Synagogue a center of community activities. It was, in fact, the center in many towns and cities and perhaps the only place in which the people could gather in large numbers. The very terms used in the Talmud, Beth Ama, house of the people, and Beth Ha-Kenesseth or Kenishta, place of assembly or gathering, indicate that it was there that the people came together. The program of activities in the early years it is impossible to describe except on the basis of the meager material still preserved. It is known that whenever important local and national problems arose the people came together in the synagogue to discuss them and to take action. It is also known that the synagogue or adjoining buildings served as havens in which to house transients and to provide them with meals. And it is also known that the two almoners, or as we should say overseers of the poor, were associated with the synagogue. They were called the *gabbae tzedakah,* distributors of charity. It was their function to collect what was needed and to serve those who were in need. In other words, the Synagogue was the center of whatever social service was required in the community. This was true of all synagogues in Palestine and Babylonia and also of many, perhaps all, in other countries.

The synagogue meetings described in all the books of the New Testament, in truth, were not only for purposes of prayer nor altogether for purposes of study. The people gathered there to discuss current and urgent questions in their community life, whenever men of importance came to the city. These men appeared in the synagogue and there addressed the people. It is also clear from other sources that when danger threatened the community, the people met in the synagogue to decide what action to take. Josephus speaks of a synagogue meeting convened even on Sabbath morning. Commissioners had been sent from Jerusalem and the people were called together to hear them and their message. The subject of discussion was altogether of a political character (Vita LIV:277 and 300). The city council, it is also stated, met in the synagogue at Tiberias. In other words, the Synagogue served as a communal center in which the people assembled to discuss community problems. This was not regarded as a desecration of the sanctuary, nor was the conduct of Jesus questioned because he undertook to heal the sick within its walls. On the contrary, the only question that arose was whether these things should be done on the Sabbath. The answer of Jesus to those who accused him of violating the Sabbath was altogether correct: "Is it lawful on the Sabbath to do good or to do harm, to save a life or to kill?" Even according to Jewish law, the critics were wrong, for human life is supremely sacred in the teachings of Judaism, and the most stringent laws of the Sabbath may be suspended in order to preserve and to protect those who are ill.

During the Middle Ages the Synagogue program greatly expanded. Israel Abrahams (Jewish Life in the Middle Ages, Chapters 1, 2, and 3) describes the many assemblies conducted within it and the many services rendered through the Synagogue. During these centuries it served as a communal center with a well-developed program of community activities. The people of the town met there for discussion of community problems whenever crises arose in the life of the Jews. They often assembled for social gatherings and for recreational activities. Transients were accommodated in the house of worship, and even commercial transactions were conducted and announced therein. Weddings, and funerals of out-standing men, took place within the holy precincts.

By the synagogue, however, was understood not the auditorium in which worship was held, but the vestry rooms downstairs or the buildings adjacent to and associated with the synagogue building proper. The synagogue, in other words, was central to the Jewish community and included within the range of its influence and con-trol all those within it. This was due in part to the fact that there was no other building in the community adequate to house these activities; but it was due in greatest measure to the fact that dur-ing the Middle Ages religion and religious institutions dominated social life. It was a function of those associated with the synagogue to study the needs of the people and to arrange to meet them. Its leaders were the leaders of the community. The institution was the center of both the religious and the civil life of the people. No distinction was made between religious and secular activities. All came within the scope of religion. Religion was the way of life, and the synagogue was the center from which the forces directing the development of the community radiated.

In summing up our knowledge of the function of the Synagogue we may safely say that this is threefold. It is a place of worship in which the people gather on Sabbath, festivals, and special occasions for prayer and supplication. It is a seat of study and education in which classes meet for instruction and discussion, children, adoles-cents, adults, and elderly men. The Synagogue in fact is the cradle in which the system of Jewish education is nourished and devel-oped. It is also, and this we must not forget, a meeting house, a religious center for community service and for social action. This is not surprising, for in the smaller communities there was no other institution that would serve as a center of community interest. Religion was central to Jewish life and the centralizing influence in the community. It was natural therefore that all community life and activities should center in the Synagogue, that the Synagogue should be the central organization of the community. This was true in New Testament times, in talmudic days, and in the Middle Ages, and it has been true in modern times in every community in which the Synagogue has been true to its origin and to its traditions.

3. SOCIAL FUNCTION OF THE SYNAGOGUE

In modern times the Synagogue has continued to develop as a religious center for community service and for social action. The records of the early synagogues established in the United States all show that each proved not only the first Jewish institution to be established but that it was central in the Jewish community. The Spanish and Portuguese Synagogue of New York, first to be founded in the United States, still preserves the minutes of the meetings of the board during the earliest years. These date from 1729 and refer to a constitution of 1706, though the structure itself, known as the Mill Street Synagogue, was not taken over until 1730. The minutes are filled with items that prove the social interests and the social activities of the members. Funds were regularly collected and distributed for care of the Jewish poor, and arrangements were made to advance loans to the Jewish needy whenever necessary.

As the Jewish community of New York grew, it became necessary for the congregation to meet the needs of many groups requiring assistance. The cemetery, of course, was the first enterprise, and the remains of this earliest Jewish burial ground in America are still preserved at the corner of James Street and Chatham Square. The Jewish sick required medical and surgical care, and the leaders of the Spanish and Portuguese Synagogue and others organized the movement to found Mt. Sinai Hospital. A study of the records of this institution discloses that the first officers and members of the board were of the Spanish and Portuguese group, leaders in congregational life. Later leaders of congregations established by the German group became members, and still later representatives of congregations organized by Eastern European Jews. What is true of Mt. Sinai Hospital is also true of the Hebrew Orphan Asylum and many other social agencies, including what is known as the Family Welfare Agency. Plainly, the leaders of the synagogues were the founders of social agencies to meet growing needs in the Jewish community.

In 1885 Rabbi Gustav Gottheil of Temple Emanu-El organized the Emanu-El Sisterhood of Personal Service. This he did in order that the congregation might serve the Eastern European Jews who came to America after the pogroms that swept Russia in the early Eighties. The organization of this Sisterhood set the pattern for other congregations. In the course of a few years every important congregation in New York had organized a sisterhood for similar purposes. Each undertook to cover a geographical area, and to serve all men and women in need within that section. But some did develop into social organizations that specialized in different types of service.

The Sisterhood of the Spanish and Portuguese Synagogue, for example, under the leadership of Mrs. Mortimer Menken, becoming especially interested in the Jewish delinquent girl, made a definite contribution to the program to cover this group. The sisterhood programs in New York continued until the United Hebrew Charities, later known as the Jewish Social Service Association and now as the Jewish Family Service, decided to organize districts and to staff them with professional paid workers. Temple Emanu-El in 1905, under the leadership of Rabbi Joseph Silverman, established a settlement house under the auspices of its Brotherhood, which maintained it for many years. Thus, the synagogues of the metropolitan area undertook to develop their social service activities through their auxiliary organizations, such as sisterhoods and brotherhoods. In other communities this pattern has been followed, though in many congregations contributions for charity are still distributed by a committee of the board. The congregation itself does not take individuals and families under its care.

During the twentieth century the synagogues have developed a greatly expanded program as communal centers. Within the last fifty years a number have become interested in the social needs of the members of the community, and have developed programs and erected buildings to house them. One of the first was in Pittsburgh. Dr. Leonard Levy persuaded his congregation to build a center next to the synagogue in which social activities could be developed and the young men and women be saved from joining Christian organizations. Emil G. Hirsch of Chicago in 1912 moved his congregation to establish a large center as a part of Sinai Temple, with a full cultural program. From that date one congregation after another has followed the example set by Pittsburgh and Chicago.

The programs within these centers, however, are largely recreational, educational, and cultural. Some contain not only an auditorium for lectures, but rooms for classes and seminars and also for games; some have gymnasiums and swimming pools. The synagogue center probably arose out of two trends. One was that of the institutional church which developed in the early part of the century and was designed to meet the growing needs in the community for social activities. The Church at this time began to concern itself with social conditions and problems and needs. The Synagogue, noting this trend, was undoubtedly influenced by what was taking place in the Church. But it also came to realize that in order to fulfill its function it must become something more than a house of worship and a seat of education, that it must develop programs to meet the social needs of the members and the community. The synagogue center movement thus owes its development in large part to a growing interest in social life, and to an effort on its part to retrieve its prestige as a communal center.

In some Jewish communities, especially among the Conservative and the Orthodox groups, a new movement has developed which might be correctly described as a Jewish Center Movement. The Brooklyn Jewish Center, under the direction of Rabbi Israel H. Levinthal, and the Chicago Jewish Center under the late Rabbi Solomon Goldman, are examples. The Jewish Center is one large building that houses a multitude of activities. Its purpose is to serve as an integrating influence in the life of the community. It endeavors to bring together members of all ages for group association and cultural enterprises, as well as worship. The department of education covers the needs of children, adolescents, and adults. The social program varies in accordance with the needs of the community. Some work that is done may be correctly described as social service. The Jewish Center, through a committee, meets emergency needs of men and women in distress, and makes provision for care of the poor and underprivileged. But the largest part of the program is devoted to cultural activities. Men and women are en-

couraged to come to the Center in order to meet each other on a
social level, and the young people particularly are invited to organize groups in which they may become better acquainted. The
social function of the Jewish Center is to provide opportunities for
the members of the community to meet in social ways and to cultivate the Jewish interests they have in common. There is no doubt
that in this manner the Jewish Center develops a feeling of fellowship and solidarity. This movement, however, must be distinguished from the Jewish Community Center Movement, which has
different objectives and programs.

In all types of synagogues, those with and those without social
centers, social facilities, and social programs, there has been an interest in social needs, especially those of the Jewish people. In most
synagogues there is found at the door the *tzedakah* box, in which
men and women place their gifts as they leave the auditorium. In
some congregations collections are taken from week to week, and
appeals are made for various causes, local, national, and international. These appeals are held especially during the High Holy
Days and in times of great need. The gifts and collections are distributed to various institutions and for the support of different
movements. In this way the congregation, through its charity chest
committee, expresses its interest in social needs and in social
agencies serving both the Jewish and the general community.

During the grave periods of distress in Europe that came with
the First and Second World Wars, all congregations in Israel aided
in the collection of funds. In some synagogues large meetings were
called to present the needs of the Jewish people to members of the
congregation and the affiliated men's and women's groups. The
congregation in this manner continued the long tradition that
one of the most urgent of commandments is to ransom and redeem
the captives. The great program for the rescue and the restoration
of the Jews who have survived in Europe is a prime concern and
obligation of every congregation in Israel. In the smaller communities in which the synagogue is still the center of Jewish life, it
has been the agency through which the community has expressed its
concern and endeavored to meet its obligations.

When the Free Synagogue was founded in 1907, Dr. Wise insisted that the house of worship be something more than a preaching and teaching institution; it must be also a center of social practice and community service. From the outset we divided the Free Synagogue program into three major departments: 1) Department of Worship; 2) Department of Education; 3) Department of Social Service. This program we believed to be in accordance with the age-long tradition and purpose of the Synagogue. It is a development of the program of activities in the best periods of its history. We do not know, as is evident from earlier chapters, much about its origins. Scholars differ in regard to both time and place. But we do know that when the Synagogue first appeared on the stage of history in the first century it was already a well-developed institution with a three-fold function—a house of prayer, a seat of education, and a religious center for community service and social action.

The Synagogue rests upon the same foundations on which, according to the sages, the world is built: "Simon the Just was one of the last survivors of the Great Synagogue. He used to say: 'Upon three things the world is based—upon the Torah or learning, upon the Temple service or worship, and upon the practice of charity or social service" (Ethics of the Fathers I:2). These are the foundations upon which we have endeavored to build the program of the Free Synagogue for a period of over forty-five years. The degree to which we have succeeded is fully presented in the records, but more important, in the lives of the people with whom we have worked and whom it has been our privilege to serve.

What are the purposes of the Social Service Department? We know that the Department of Worship is to meet the ritual needs of the people, to comfort the sorrowing, to strengthen the weak, to encourage the insecure, to enlighten those in doubt, to lift all men from the common level of life, and to aid men and women to establish communion between themselves and a Higher Power. We know that the purpose of the Department of Education is to transmit to generation after generation the heritage of our people, to strengthen them in their knowledge of things Jewish, and to develop their allegiance to the teachings and principles and ideals of Judaism.

The aim of the Social Service Department is first of all to socialize the membership of the congregation. This means to widen their interests, to deepen their sympathies, and to cultivate the social conscience of those associated with us. It is not surprising to learn that the interests of most men and women are as a rule limited. They live and move and have their being in a small circle that circumscribes their outlook on life and their conduct. Through social service, this circle is enlarged and men and women come to realize that there is a social life outside their limited circle and that there are social problems we cannot disregard. Nor is it surprising that the social sympathies of men and women are all too often intermittent and shallow. It is only when an emergency arises or a crisis develops that our sympathies are called into action and continue to express themselves—and then for only a short time. There are not many men and women who live a life of deep and continuous social feeling. Nor is it surprising to discover that the social conscience of men and women is immature and sporadic. We have not yet learned how to cultivate our conscience, nor how to exercise this faculty in our social life. If our social conscience were alert and strong, we could not be silent in the presence of so much injustice and so much evil about us.

A second purpose of the Social Service Department has constantly been our endeavor to relate the Synagogue to community needs, to community programs, and to community organization. In many instances synagogues seem to be unaware that they are not isolated institutions; but a part of the community in which they are situated, one of the social agencies the community has established. Even in the smaller communities in which the number of Jews may be very limited, there are needs that the Synagogue must, by virtue of its origin and history, undertake to meet. Everywhere there are requirements in the field of health. In not one community that we know are health needs being adequately met at the present time. There are needs in the field of education. In no community that we know are the educational wants of all groups today being studied and fully met. In every community there are needs in the field of housing. But in none are all the people housed as we know men and women should be if they are to develop a wholesome social life. Slums are not limited to the large cities. In each community there are needs in the field of recreation. No community today possesses all the recreational facilities required nor are the recreational agencies expertly staffed. If they were, we should not face today's problem in juvenile delinquency. Agencies are created to meet all these needs, and in some communities agencies are created to organize for the welfare of the citizens and for the service of men and women and children. Too often it happens, however, that the synagogues are merely spectators that watch the procession of community life pass by—to paraphrase a striking passage from the writings of Jane Addams. In truth there are some so unrelated to the community that they could close their doors and disappear without memory that they had existed. Long ago Jeremiah urged his people to pray and to work for the welfare of the city to which they were to go, for in its welfare would they too fare well.

A third purpose of the Social Service Department throughout the years has been to further social movements and to advance social causes. The Synagogue is not only a religious center for community service, but also for social action. In our judgment it ought to do its utmost to further programs designed to diminish and to end social evils, and to establish social justice. The Synagogue is not only a guardian of the community, but also a source of inspiration and support to every cause that means social progress. It is our conviction, that derives from the origin and development and ideals of the Synagogue itself, that it not only has a right to interest itself in social causes, but has the responsibility and the duty of advancing every worthwhile social movement. The Synagogue should be among the first of our agencies to end such evils as incompetence and corruption and crime in the community. It should be among the first to fight child labor, discrimination, and the denial of human rights to every individual and to every group. It should be among the first to help remedy national misunderstandings, colonial exploitation, imperialistic domination, and the greatest of all evils, war. No matter how imposing the building, how impressive the service, how scientific the system of education, the Synagogue falls short of fulfillment if it fails to translate its preaching and its teaching into social action. It is even pedagogically wrong to teach people to know, and to move people to feel, and do nothing whatever to translate what they know and feel into conduct. The head, the heart, the hand, are symbols of the three-fold purpose of the Social Service Department.

The question naturally arises: Have these purposes been fulfilled? It is very difficult to determine to what degree the membership of the Free Synagogue has been socialized. In the first place we must remember that its composition has changed from year to year. And secondly, we must recognize that we have no instruments by which to measure the changes that take place in men and women. And even when we note changes it is unscientific to say that these have been due to the social program of the Synagogue, in view of the fact that men and women are affected by so many influences in the course of their lives.

But I do think it is possible to take a limited group of members who have been in the Free Synagogue for many years and to study their development. In those I have studied, not more than a hundred, I have found that in these men and women the range of social interests has increased. They are far more aware of conditions and problems than they were in the beginning. I find also that their sympathies are less shallow and spasmodic. They show a continuing sympathy with those in trouble and with social distress. But most important of all, they respond much more readily and more vigorously to appeals for social action. In other words, their social conscience is now awake and operating. We can speak to this group with full confidence that they will understand what we are saying and will cooperate with us in development of our program. This is the judgment of only one person, but I think the men and women of the group themselves would agree that these changes have taken place in their lives, and are largely due to their association with the Free Synagogue.

Another simple way in which to measure the growth of the congregation in social interests and sympathies and action is to compare the collections on Friday nights from week to week, and during the Holy Days from year to year. At every service we describe some area of work the Department is developing, and cite illustrations of the needs that come to us and the ways in which the needs must be met. As the weeks pass, the members become more and more aware of the problems and the social conditions out of which they arise. We have noted that when we have a large percentage of our own membership present at the services, the per capita contribution on Friday evening reaches its highest point. But when we have a large percentage who are not members of the congregation at special services, the per capita contribution goes down. The conclusion is inevitable that our own members respond more generously, because they are educated to an understanding of our program of service and realize that it is a function of the congregation to maintain a social program as well as a program of worship and a program of education. It seems not unfair to say that in the course of the weeks and months and years the membership of the Synagogue is socialized, that is, their social interests are broadened, their social sympathies are deepened, and their social conscience is strengthened. This is undoubtedly one result of the establishment of the Social Service Department.

There is no doubt whatever that the second purpose has been fulfilled. The Free Synagogue has become a religious center for community service, and has related itself directly to social needs and the care of groups inadequately served by existing community agencies. From the beginning the Social Service Department has been interested in children, in adolescents, and in the problems of the family. The various projects we have developed will be fully described in the section of this work dealing with the Synagogue and the Community. From year to year we have studied community needs and the groups that have not been served in accordance with their needs, and we have worked out programs designed to meet them adequately. In other words, the Social Service Department has served as a laboratory in which social needs have been studied and programs have been developed. A number of projects with which we have experimented have developed into community agencies now separately established on a community basis.

As a result of this effort to relate the Synagogue to the community, we have become well acquainted with social needs, especially in those areas we have explored and in which we have conducted experiments. In a large complex community like New York, there is always the danger that some needs will go unmet, even unrecognized. In spite of the Federations and the Welfare Councils and the great network of social organizations, public and private, there are still many unfulfilled needs and many groups inadequately served. Every well-organized and well-conducted social agency recognizes this fact, but few are able to engage in experimental projects to serve as pilot studies and indicate the ways in which social requirements can best be fulfilled.

The third purpose has also been in large part fulfilled. The Free Synagogue has again and again furthered social movements and advanced social causes, largely through the efforts of the Social Service Department. Thus we have also made it a religious center for social action as well as for community service. When child labor was an issue in America, the Synagogue did its utmost to advance the Child Labor Amendment, and sent delegations to Albany to plead for ratification of the proposed amendment to the Constitution. When the Genocide Pact was before the United Nations and presented to Congress for ratification, we did our utmost to further that cause, not only through special meetings but through direct contact with the members of Congress and of the United States delegation to the United Nations. In both we failed to accomplish our purpose. The Child Labor Amendment failed, and the Genocide Pact has not been ratified by the Congress, but the movements have grown and the Synagogue has not been inactive.

In the matter of civil liberties, the Synagogue has been an active agent not only in advocating but in effecting a change in attitudes. We have as a social organization cooperated with others in reducing discrimination and inequities, and also directly developed programs on the local, the state, and the national levels. It is not unfair to say that the Free Synagogue has taken seriously the whole issue of civil liberties and has done much to implement the programs that have led to greater social justice for all groups in the community and in the country.

Leaders in the social field, both lay and professional, have not always recognized the importance of the social program of the Synagogue. Social work executives a generation ago were correct, we believe, in establishing district offices in geographical areas with a trained and skilled staff of workers. The development of social work into a profession and the improvement of techniques required them to place it upon a professional level. The development of functional activities also made it necessary for agencies to specialize in fields of service, such as child care, delinquency, the sick, and family welfare.

But the leaders in Jewish social work, we are convinced, made a grave mistake in discouraging the sisterhoods and in eliminating the Synagogue finally from the field of social service. In doing this they not only deprived the Synagogue of a necessary and legitimate form of religious expression, but robbed the community of a large reservoir of interest and energy and support in the social field. The sisterhoods and brotherhoods and the synagogues could and should have been encouraged and guided and retrained for service. The failure of leaders to appreciate the importance of the function of the synagogue in the social field, their endeavor to exclude it from participation in social work and community service, is difficult to understand. Leaders and laymen in the field have no vested interest to safeguard. It may be that social workers themselves have made the mistake of overemphasizing professionalism. But those who are acquainted with Jewish social workers and who have attended Jewish social work conferences, as I have from year to year, can hardly escape the impression that social workers are not sympathetic to the Synagogue or even to religion. On the contrary, some of them quite openly say that they do not believe in "sectarian service." I recall one meeting in the offices of Federation, at which the Jewish social workers present frankly stated that they did not believe in "sectarian service" in spite of the fact that the agencies associated with Federation were still called the Jewish Child Care Association, the Jewish Board of Guardians, the Jewish Family Service, and that the Federation itself was called the Federation of Jewish Philanthropies.

But the synagogues cannot altogether absolve themselves from blame. Not many during the last fifty years have shown a real interest in community service and social action. The laymen have assumed, it seems, that all social problems would be covered by the existing social agencies, and have been quite willing to leave the field to professional social organizations. The rabbis and the congregations have done little to equip themselves for service and leadership in this field. They have been too busy with worship and education and practical rabbinics, so called, to take an active part in community service. But worse than this, they have not been encouraged by the faculties in the seminaries to believe that the rabbi should be trained and experienced in the social field as he is in other fields of synagogue activity. In truth, it must be admitted that the Synagogue has in large part and in many congregations and communities abdicated its leadership, or even its participation, in community service and social action. Even in those communities in which Jewish Community Councils have been organized, the Synagogue usually plays an unimportant part in the development of the Council program. At one time the Synagogue was the center of Jewish community life. Today it is relegated to the circumference. If it is to retrieve leadership in the social field, it will be necessary for the rabbis to be trained for this service, and for the synagogues to recapture the original concept of an institution with a three-fold purpose, that is, worship, education, and social service.

4. SOCIAL SERVICE DEPARTMENT OF THE SYNAGOGUE

Introduction

The chart or diagram accompanying this chapter outlines the Social Service Department as of the year 1954. This Department of the Free Synagogue has survived and developed during the last forty-five years for a number of reasons. In the first place, we have made it not an auxiliary section of the Women's Organization or the Men's Club, but a coordinate department of the Synagogue program itself —equal to the Department of Worship and the Department of Education. From the beginning we have had a faculty of men in charge of these different departments, one who has majored in the Department of Worship, one in the Department of Education, and one in the Department of Social Service. This does not mean that the men have limited themselves to their major interest or activity. Each one has minored in the other departments of Synagogue life.

Organization of Social Service Department

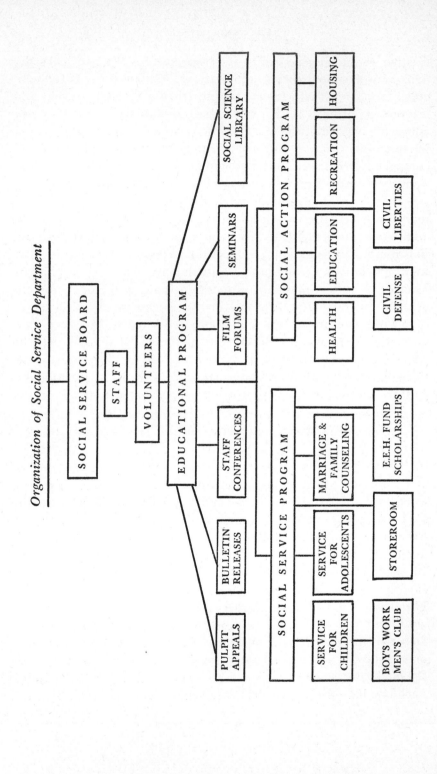

In the second place, when we organized the Social Service Department in 1907, we did not restrict ourselves to a geographical area. We decided in accordance with the tendencies of the time to devote ourselves to a functional program and to specialize in types of service. This was a carefully considered and deliberate decision on our part.

In the third place, we have developed a staff that is highly trained for the service they are expected to render, and that compares in competency with the staff of any social agency operating in the social field. We have maintained a department composed of men and women who by virtue of their training, experience, and personality are thoroughly equipped to serve those committed to their care or to whom we offer our service.

Social Service Board

The governing body of the Free Synagogue is known as the Executive Council. It has a president, two vice-presidents, a secretary, and a treasurer. Under the Executive Council serve the committees appointed by the president. These include the committees on ritual and choir and ushers, and others related to the Department of Worship. They also include the School Board and the Committee on Adult Education, that is responsible for the program of the Department of Education; and the Social Service Board, responsible for development of the program of the Social Service Department.

The Social Service Board itself, it is important to recognize, is composed of men and women who are interested in this department, those who represent the divisions of congregational life, the Executive Council, the School Board, the Women's Organization, the Men's Club, and the Youth Groups. In this way the Department brings together representatives of the major activities of the Synagogue and establishes an immediate relationship with its major organizations. The Department is separately incorporated under the laws of the state of New York. But this is done only in order that it may legally receive and dispense gifts and bequests. The Social Service Board meets once a month to receive reports upon the work on the different projects, and to consider recommendations made by the director or any member.

A sub-committee known as the Finance Committee of the Social Service Board is charged with the responsibility of preparing the budget from year to year. But this must be approved by the Social Service Board and the Executive Council and then submitted to the Distribution Committee of Federation. The Social Service Department of the Free Synagogue has been a charter member of the Federation of Jewish Philanthropies since the Federation was organized in 1917.

Finance Committee

The Finance Committee carefully prepares the budget of the Social Service Department at the beginning of the fiscal year. It is based upon the projects we plan to develop, and the items are listed line by line—salaries of professional workers, salaries of secretarial staff, stationery and postage, telephone and bookkeeping, building maintenance, relief or financial assistance, educational projects, and other items to cover minor activities. From month to month a financial report is submitted to the Social Service Board and discussed by the members. This keeps the members posted upon both what is being spent and what is being done. A voucher, made out for every expenditure, is signed by the director. It is then sent to the treasurer of the Social Service Department and a check drawn to cover each voucher. The check is signed by two officers of the Board, usually the chairman and vice-chairman. A full set of books is kept and carefully audited. Each year the auditor's report is submitted to the Social Service Board and to Federation. In this manner an accurate account is kept of every dollar received and expended. In addition to the Current Fund, the Social Service Department has also an Experimentation Fund and a Bequest Fund. These serve as a reserve out of which to cover deficits that accrue in the Current Fund.

Income

The income of the Social Service Department is derived from various sources. At every service, Friday night and during the Holy Days, we take a collection. This is in response to an appeal from the pulpit for the programs then developing. The funds thus collected are credited to what is known as the Memorial Fund of the Synagogue. Not one cent of the collections in response to the Social Service appeal is used for administrative purposes of the Synagogue. This Memorial Fund amounts to between $15,000 and $18,000 a year. At one time, during the period of greatest prosperity, our collections totaled as much as $34,000 a year.

Out of the Memorial Fund the Executive Council at this time allots to the Social Service Department the sum of $7,500. When our income was larger the Synagogue Executive Council allotted as much as $18,000. In addition to this amount the Department receives small donations from week to week, from those observing some anniversary in the life of the family or a friend. These donations now total about $1000 a year. The Department also receives gifts and bequests. These, sometimes forming a fairly large contribution, are credited to the Bequest or Reserve Fund. The Social Service Department also receives an annual allotment from the New York City Youth Board for the care of cases referred to it. The contract with the City now allots the Department $5,700 a year. The largest allotment, however, has come from the Federation of Jewish Philanthropies, dependent upon Federation's interest in the projects we are developing. When we entered Federation our allotment was nearly $17,000 a year. It has gone as high as $30,000. At present it is $13,000. The total budget for the year runs between $60,000 and $70,000.

Staff

The staff of the Social Service Department consists of an executive director, a supervisor of casework, a group of social workers, a number of secretaries, and a corps of volunteers. The executive director is also an associate rabbi of the Synagogue, who has been in charge of the Department since its organization. He is responsible for its administration and for planning new projects approved by the Social Service Board. The supervisor of casework is in charge of the social workers and also serves as intake worker, that is, for first contact with new cases.

The group of social workers is carefully selected on the basis of training, experience, and personality. They are all graduates of colleges and in most cases of a school of social work, with a master's degree. In some agencies in New York a degree from a recognized school of social work is required, but in others any man or woman with a college degree and in-service training is accepted and attains professional status. The caseworkers have always been experienced in the field to which they are assigned. When we were in Bellevue Hospital the staff consisted of medical social workers. When we were engaged in Boys' Work and Girls' Work the caseworkers were men and women who had majored in this field. In Child Adoption we selected workers acquainted with placement work and adoption procedures. At the present time the caseworkers are all mature people who have years of experience and who are especially qualified to serve children and adolescents as well as families. They are carefully observed by the supervisor and meet regularly with him for case conferences.

In addition to the director and the group of social workers and secretaries, there is also a panel of men and women organized for special types of service. This includes lawyers, doctors, psychologists, and psychiatrists. The men and women, adolescents and children, who come under care of the Social Service Department are assured of expert study, counsel, and social care. This is the least they have a right to expect of any agency that assumes to serve persons in distress. We cannot expect to engage in social service today without trained and experienced workers, any more than a school can expect to engage in teaching without trained and experienced teachers.

In the smaller communities and synagogues it may not be possible to secure an expertly trained staff of men and women, but it is possible for a small congregation in a small community to organize a social service committee composed of men and women interested in this field. And it is also possible to engage at least one worker competent to serve the cases accepted for care. It may be difficult to limit itself to one type of service or to engage in a functional field of social work, but it would be wise for the congregation or social service committee to specialize in the care of one or two or three groups. In every community there are children who are neglected and in need of service; adolescents who are confused and in danger of lapsing into delinquency; families in distress for divers reasons. These groups would serve as an excellent beginning for any synagogue eager to translate religion from preaching into practice. But we cannot emphasize too strongly the fact that social work has now become a professional procedure, and that people in distress have a right to expect of us or any agency that undertakes to serve them three things: a sympathetic approach and reception; an intelligent study and understanding of their case; and expert and authoritative social care. They may demand exactly what they expect of a physician in case of sickness, or a lawyer in case of legal difficulties.

Volunteers

One of the important contributions we have made to the social field is the corps of volunteers. We understand that social work within the last fifty years has become a scientific service with a professionally trained staff of men and women in command. Therefore the volunteer must know enough about the theory and practice of social work to cooperate intelligently and effectively with professional workers. From the very beginning of the Social Service Department we have insisted that volunteers be carefully selected, trained, and supervised. From year to year we have arranged courses and conferences for the men and women of the Synagogue that will equip them as volunteers. Their first training is a simple course in social diagnosis, social treatment, and social agencies. They must know the major causes of social distress, that is, the conditions out of which distress arises. They must also understand the modern methods of social care, which means that they be acquainted with the techniques. In the third place, they must be acquainted with the social agencies and organizations and institutions that can be called into active cooperation. Unless they possess a knowledge of the resources of the community, they are at a loss to know how to cooperate with other agencies and to arrange for proper care for their cases. In other words, it is not sufficient for volunteers merely to have a desire to aid others. We have found that not everyone who volunteers is competent to serve people in difficulty.

After the elementary course, it is not difficult to carry the volunteers forward to larger and more complicated problems and the means available to meet them. Through advanced courses and readings and conferences, the volunteer can be constantly encouraged to increase his equipment. Our position is frankly this. The volunteer can be of great service in the social field not as a substitute for, but as a supplement, to the professional worker. In the course of time he may become more and more expert through training and experience. Many of the men and women who have entered the Social Service Department as volunteers have become as expert as professional workers, and they constitute an efficient group that counts large in the community program. A number of men and women now in charge of established agencies began with us as volunteers.

For a time professional workers had little sympathy with the volunteer. At best they looked upon him as a necessary evil, but today they realize that through the volunteer they can extend their province of service and assign to him many tasks to relieve the professional worker. The Federation of Jewish Philanthropies of New York now recognizes the need and value of the volunteer, and has arranged special courses to prepare him for active and effective service in association with social agencies. This work of selecting and training and guiding and encouraging requires patience and understanding; but the results have more than rewarded us for the work done, and the volunteer has also discovered that he is not only serving others but also himself, and that service leads to an enlargement of one's scope of life.

Relation to Other Agencies

As stated, the Social Service Department is a constituent member of the Federation of Jewish Philanthropies, which we joined when it was organized in 1917. The assumption was that the Department was one of the accepted social agencies of the Jewish community of New York, and therefore should share in the program and funds collected by Federation. The Free Synagogue is the only congregation in the city that is a member of Federation. It is our conviction that Federation should encourage other synagogues to organize social service departments and to develop various projects in the Jewish community, especially those of an experimental nature. In fact, we have always looked upon the Social Service Department as a laboratory in which we have been able to study unmet needs in the Jewish community and in which we have endeavored to work out programs designed to meet these needs. Federation in its literature describing the work of its agencies used this description of the Social Service Department of the Free Synagogue: "This is a laboratory—without test tubes and without chemical compounds—but a laboratory, nevertheless, where experiments are conducted to meet social and welfare needs of the Jewish community." We in turn do our utmost to encourage members of the congregation and the community to contribute to the funds of Federation. In our judgment the Synagogue should share in this work of stimulating contributions, as well as share in the allotments for programs still desperately needed. If synagogues in different parts of the country do not take part in the Federation Fund or the Community Chest, it is probably because they are not prepared to undertake social projects. This only means that they must organize themselves for service.

We also cooperate with all other social agencies in the care of our cases. If a child comes to us who is in need of placement, we consult the child placing agency, or what is known in New York as Jewish Child Care Association. If a child comes in a state of delinquency and we are unable to cope with the problem, we reach the agency that specializes in this field, the Jewish Board of Guardians. If an aged person comes under our care and we are unable to meet the needs, we cooperate with the Central Bureau for Jewish Aged. No agency in New York is large enough or expert enough to deal with all types of problems. We act as one of the network of community agencies in New York.

Synagogues seldom function in this capacity. Even in those communities in which Community Councils are organized, the synagogue is seldom a member, and is therefore unable to be of any service in the Council. The synagogues of the country have thus frequently abdicated their leadership in community life, and withdrawn from all forms of community service outside of education and worship. They seem willing to delegate to other organizations their own social function. They do not think of themselves as we do, as a religious center for community service and social action. To us it is regrettable that the synagogues play so minor a part in the development of community programs and community life.

Educational Program

In order that the members of the congregation and the community be educated to an understanding of the program of social service the Free Synagogue is developing and the projects we undertake from year to year, we have in the course of time worked out what seems an interesting and effective technique. In the first place, at every service we make an appeal. But it is not made in vague and general terms. We describe some phase of the work we are doing and cite some case of distress that has come to us. This constitutes a concrete illustration of the program of social or human service the congregation is endeavoring to organize or to administer. The results are always interesting to watch. In fact, the members seem to be as much interested in the appeal as they are in the ritual.

Second, we include in the weekly bulletin of the Synagogue some appeal or paragraph of a social interest. We remind our members and friends of the needs discovered, the funds they are establishing, and the ways in which they can aid us in the work. From time to time we include articles that describe not only cases but projects. The Bulletin is issued not to members of the congregation alone, but also to those of affiliated organizations, the Men's Club, the Women's Organization, and the Youth Groups. Every week we reach 1500 men and women, members and their families. Our estimate is that the Bulletin is read by between 5000 and 6000 individuals, who are in this way aided to understand the purposes and the program of the Social Service Department.

In order to increase the equipment of the staff we also arrange for regular staff conferences. The social workers meet regularly with the supervisor to discuss problems that arise in the care of the cases. In addition the entire staff meets with a psychiatrist each week to discuss the principles to guide them. This conference with the psychiatrist, Dr. Thomas Hora, is of utmost benefit to the members, as it leads to a better understanding of the techniques of treating the individual human personality. The entire staff also meets from week to week with the director to discuss policies and the larger areas to be explored in order to be of greatest service to distressed persons. It is not sufficient to limit ourselves to the individual child or adolescent or man or woman. It is necessary to study conditions in the family, in the home, in the neighborhood, in occupational life, and in our social environment, political, economic, and cultural, that cause or complicate distress. We try to make the members of the staff thoroughly cognizant of the principles to guide us in diagnosing and treating trouble. And we discuss with them the social philosophy that forms the background of our program. In this way we escape the danger of limiting ourselves and the members of the staff to the mere techniques of social work.

In addition to pulpit appeals, Bulletin releases, and staff conferences, we have developed an educational program for the larger group of people who constitute the community. This includes seminars, the Social Science Library, and Film Forums. From year to year we study problems as they arise in the local community, in the nation, and in international affairs. During 1953 we discussed the subject of crime and corruption in the community, with discussion led by Rudolph Halley, then president of the City Council. We have had seminar discussions of civil liberties, conducted by a member of the American Civil Liberties Union, usually the late Arthur Garfield Hays. Another large and important national problem for discussion was the evil of drug addiction. This was led by representatives of the city and state and of the division of the United Nations dealing with the problem. When the Genocide Pact was before the United Nations, we did our utmost to persuade the American delegation to vote for ratification. We have also held seminars upon the McCarran-Walter Immigration Act and the Declaration of Human Rights, each led by an expert in the field.

We are fortunate in being situated in New York, which is the center of so many local, national, and international organizations. Each seminar consists of a lecture followed by a discussion, and at each literature bearing upon the topic is available for distribution. The literature is carefully selected; it contains the most important material. If the McCarran Act is discussed, the Act itself is distributed, and articles for and against it are assembled and made available to the audience. We follow the technique developed by the best conferences we know of.

The Social Science Library, accumulated in the course of years, is composed of books, pamphlets, and magazines dealing with such subjects as marriage and the family, social work, anthropology, sociology, economics, political science, and international relations. It is open to members of the congregation and the community free of charge. The books are carefully selected upon recommendation of departmental chairmen of several universities; and the pamphlets and magazines are chosen upon recommendation of the lecturers who come to us.

The Film Forums, presented every spring, have attracted a large number of men and women from the fields of education, social work, medicine, and psychiatry. The series of 1951 had a registration of 1700 and an average attendance of over 600. 650 of those who registered came from social agencies, 550 from high schools and colleges, the rest from the community at large. In 1952 we decided to charge a dollar for the series of Film Forums. In spite of this charge, 673 registered and the average attendance was over 400. In every series we have endeavored to discuss some current topic and to secure speakers expert in the field and films well prepared and selected. The programs that follow will illustrate the Film Forums best. Each includes not only the lecture and film but a question and answer period. The questions are always interesting and revealing.

TEN FILM FORUMS

on

MENTAL HYGIENE

MONDAY EVENINGS in MARCH and APRIL

STEPHEN WISE FREE SYNAGOGUE
30 West 68th Street
New York

PROBLEMS of PERSONALITY

MONDAY EVENING, MARCH 5th, 8:15

Motion Picture
"EMERGENCE of PERSONALITY"

Speaker
DR. ISRAEL STRAUSS
Consulting Psychiatrist

MONDAY EVENING, MARCH 12th, 8:15

Motion Picture
"FEELINGS of DEPRESSION"

Speaker
DR. SANDOR LORAND
Psychiatrist and Author

MONDAY EVENING, MARCH 19th, 8:15

Motion Picture
"EMOTIONAL NEEDS of CHILDHOOD"

Speaker
DR. SYLVAN KEISER
Psychiatrist and Lecturer

MONDAY EVENING, MARCH 26th, 8:15

Motion Picture
"SOCIAL DEVELOPMENT"

Speaker
DR. ISIDOR SILBERMANN
Psychiatrist and Author

MONDAY EVENING, APRIL 2nd, 8:15

Motion Picture
"THE STAIRS"

Speaker
DR. FREDERICK D. ZEMAN
Specialist in Geriatrics

MARRIAGE and HUMAN RELATIONS

MONDAY EVENING, APRIL 9th, 8:15

Motion Picture
"THIS CHARMING COUPLE"

Speaker
DR. DAVID MACE
of England

MONDAY EVENING, APRIL 16th, 8:15

Motion Picture
"MARRIAGE for MODERNS"

Speaker
DR. LENA LEVINE
Psychiatrist and Author

MONDAY EVENING, APRIL 23rd, 8:15

Motion Picture
"MARRIAGES ARE MADE on EARTH"

Speaker
DR. ABRAHAM STONE
Physician and Marriage Counselor

MONDAY EVENING, APRIL 30th, 8:15

Motion Picture
"IT TAKES ALL KINDS"

Speaker
DR. SIDNEY E. GOLDSTEIN
Marriage Counselor and Rabbi

MONDAY EVENING, MAY 7th, 8:15

Motion Picture
"WHO'S BOSS?"

Speaker
DR. JACOB T. ZUCKERMAN
National Desertion Bureau

You and your friends
are cordially invited
to register and to
attend these sessions

TEN FILM FORUMS
on
MENTAL HYGIENE

MONDAY EVENINGS in MARCH and APRIL

STEPHEN WISE FREE SYNAGOGUE
30 West 68th Street, N.Y.

MENTAL HYGIENE AND THE FAMILY

MONDAY EVENING, MARCH 3rd, 8:15

DR. ABRAHAM STONE
Marriage Counselor
"THE CHANGING STRUCTURE OF THE FAMILY"
Film
"MARRIAGE AND DIVORCE"

MONDAY EVENING, MARCH 10th, 8:15

DR. DAVID MACE
Marriage Guidance, England
"THE CHANGING ORGANIZATION OF THE FAMILY"
Film
"FAMILY CIRCLES"

MONDAY EVENING, MARCH 17th, 8:15

SIDNEY E. GOLDSTEIN
Rabbi and Counselor

"THE CHANGING FUNCTION OF THE FAMILY"
Film
"THE CENTRE"

MONDAY EVENING, MARCH 24th, 8:15

JACOB T. ZUCKERMAN
National Desertion Bureau

"CAUSES OF DISORGANIZATION OF THE FAMILY"

Film
"ARE YOU READY FOR MARRIAGE?"

MONDAY EVENING, MARCH 31st, 8:15

JUDGE ANNA M. KROSS
Home Term Court

"THE MARRIAGE LAW—HOW CAN WE IMPROVE IT?"

Film
"MARRIAGE IS A PARTNERSHIP"

MENTAL HYGIENE AND HUMAN BEHAVIOR

MONDAY EVENING, APRIL 7th, 8:15

DR. WILFRED G. HULSE
Psychiatrist

"PSYCHOLOGICAL FACTORS"

Film
"THE ANGRY BOY"

MONDAY EVENING, APRIL 14th, 8:15

DR. FRED U. TATE
Psychiatrist

"HEREDITARY FACTORS"

Film
"FEARS OF CHILDREN"

MONDAY EVENING, APRIL 21st, 8:15

DR. THOMAS HORA
Psychiatrist

"ENVIRONMENTAL FACTORS"

Film
"UNDERSTANDING YOUR EMOTIONS"

MONDAY EVENING, APRIL 28th, 8:15

DR. ISRAEL STRAUSS
Psychiatrist

"SOMATIC FACTORS"

Film
"CHILDREN OF THE CITY"

MONDAY EVENING, MAY 5th, 8:15

DR. LAWRENCE I. KAPLAN
Psychiatrist

"GROUP LOYALTIES"

Film
"ACTIVITY GROUP THERAPY"

Please Register In Advance

Free to Members.   Registration Fee for Non-Members $1.00

NAME_____   ADDRESS_____

ORGANIZATION_____

In the Spring of this year, 1953, we are dealing with the general topic of "Adolescence and Mental Hygiene" with the following program:

FOUR FILM FORUMS
ON
MENTAL HYGIENE

MONDAY EVENINGS IN APRIL

STEPHEN WISE FREE SYNAGOGUE
30 West 68th Street
New York

MONDAY EVENING, APRIL 6th, 8:15

DR. THOMAS HORA
Psychiatrist

"WHAT IS ADOLESCENCE?"

Film
"UNCONSCIOUS MOTIVATION"

MONDAY EVENING, APRIL 13th, 8:15

DR. RENATUS HARTOGS
Psychiatrist

"THE MORAL UNCERTAINTIES
AND
CONFUSIONS OF ADOLESCENCE"

Film
"CHILDREN OF THE CITY"

MONDAY EVENING, APRIL 20th, 8:15

DR. FRED U. TATE
Psychiatrist

"PSYCHICAL CHARACTERISTICS
AND
DISTURBANCES OF ADOLESCENCE"

Film
"OVER-DEPENDENCY"

MONDAY EVENING, APRIL 27th, 8:15

DR. LAWRENCE I. KAPLAN
Psychiatrist

"PHYSICAL CHARACTERISTICS
AND
PROBLEMS OF ADOLESCENCE"

Film
"FAREWELL TO CHILDHOOD"

Please Register In Advance
Free to Members.   Registration Fee for Non-Members $1.00

NAME_____ ADDRESS_____

ORGANIZATION_____

Social Service in the School

One way in which to present social service material in the religious school is to organize the children into what may be called a "City of Justice." This method has been tried out in a number of schools, and has served to educate children in elementary, intermediate, and high school departments in the principles of social organization. In the Free Synagogue the "City of Justice" was fully developed and maintained for a number of years. The organization included a chairman or president, a treasurer, and a secretary. These officers were elected at the beginning of the year by the students themselves.

In addition to the officers the "City of Justice" consisted of four or five departments: the Department of Health, the Department of Education, the Department of Justice, the Department of Social Service, and for a time the Department of Supplies. The chairmen of the departments were also elected and had the power to appoint their associates, usually three or five. The "City of Justice" met regularly once a month during the period of the assembly. At each meeting, with the chairman presiding, reports and recommendations were presented by the treasurer, the secretary, and chairmen of the departments. These were always carefully discussed and acted upon by the children who composed the "City." The departments were selected because they corresponded to the basic social enterprises in the city and were designed to interest the boys and girls in the programs of health, education, justice, social service, and purchase and distribution of supplies. A faculty adviser was associated with each department, but at no point did he attempt to control the action of the children, limiting himself to guidance and counsel. The deep interest of the children was evident at every meeting.

Each department of the "City of Justice" had its own little program. The Department of Health interested itself in health conditions within and about the school. Before every session the chairman visited the rooms to be sure they were properly heated, cleaned, and ventilated. He insisted upon wire baskets and a thermometer in each room, and was most conscientious in watching conditions that affected health. The chairman of the Department of Education cooperated with the teachers and faculty in many ways. The reaction of children in the classes to the textbooks, the topics studied, and the program of each assembly were the concern of this department. It was surprising to discover not only how frank the children were in their comments but how helpful their criticisms were. The chairman of the Department of Justice was charged with responsibility for correcting conditions in the school troubling teachers and principal. The problems of tardiness, of class behavior, of individual delinquency, all were studied by the Department of Justice. In fact, it was transformed into a little court that heard cases. It was most interesting to watch the way in which the children dealt with the problems. The Department of Social Service undertook to collect money and clothing and at times commodities from the children in each class. The chairman and his committee carefully studied the needs brought to their attention and the causes that appealed to them for support. In this manner the children became acquainted with individuals and families and groups and movements requiring support, and learned something of the art of giving and of sacrifice. The Department of Supplies undertook to purchase and to distribute the supplies required in the school, and learned the lesson that production and distribution should be for service and not for profit.

In 1922 Dr. Wise founded the Jewish Institute of Religion, a seminary primarily for the training of men for the rabbinate. This action was the result of a long series of discussions and several experiments. For a number of years we had conducted summer schools for social workers and for rabbis, and for many years we had invited young graduates of the Hebrew Union College to serve interneships in the Free Synagogue. Those of us associated with Dr. Wise finally decided to found a new seminary, and for a number of reasons. In the first place, we believed that a seminary was needed that would not be Orthodox nor Conservative nor Reform, but simply Jewish, and that would allow men to prepare themselves for the rabbinate and leave them free to select the type of congregation they desired. Second, we felt that the seminary should be established in New York City, the greatest center of Jewish population in the world, in order that the men might come into contact with the different Jewish groups and organizations in New York and become acquainted at first hand with the currents of the Jewish people in the metropolitan area. In the third place, we believed that a seminary should be associated with the great universities in New York and with the important seminaries of the Conservative, Orthodox, and non-Jewish groups. Lastly we were of the opinion that a new group of men should be trained in a new way to meet the new needs arising in American and world Jewish life. This decision represented realization of a plan that had been maturing for many years and of which some of us had dreamed for nearly a generation.

It is not generally known that when Dr. Isaac M. Wise died in 1900 a committee of students of the Hebrew Union College went to Chicago to plead with Dr. Emil G. Hirsch to establish a seminary there in connection with Chicago University, which was then the greatest educational institution in the Middle West and one of the outstanding universities of America. Dr. Hirsch considered the matter carefully, as he was then a member of the faculty of the University of Chicago, but finally decided not to undertake the task. We even pleaded with the Board of Governors of Hebrew Union College to move the institution from Cincinnati to Chicago. The College was then a small institution housed in an old private residence on Sixth Street. But the Board of Governors would not consider this move for a moment. They insisted upon maintaining it in Cincinnati as a memorial to Isaac M. Wise, and eventually on moving the College to the new campus opposite the University of Cincinnati.

When we decided to open the Jewish Institute of Religion, there were many protests from the Board of Governors and graduates of the Hebrew Union College. They feared we were developing an institution to compete with the College in Cincinnati. They did not realize that we had a larger concept and that our plan was not to compete nor to supersede but to pioneer in the development of a new and much needed program. Dr. Wise succeeded in bringing together as a first faculty a great group of men, Jewish scholars from England and the Continent.

Despite all opposition and skepticism and pessimistic predictions the Jewish Institute of Religion has continued. Even though I was a graduate of the Hebrew Union College, I recognized the need of this new institution and cooperated with Dr. Wise in founding the Institute (later to be merged with the College). I spent much time in travel and in building up congregations to be served by the men in training and by the graduates. Some of the alumni of the Jewish Institute of Religion now occupy important pulpits and have made a significant contribution to American and world Jewish life.

The establishment of the Jewish Institute of Religion gave me the opportunity to do something that for many years I had dreamed of, organizing courses to train men in the social aspects of the rabbinate. No course in any Jewish seminary was given in this subject. We were the first to establish a Department of Social Service in the curriculum, whereby we should attempt to aid men to understand the social tasks of the rabbi, the social function of the Synagogue, and the social implications of religion. It was not our intention to train men for social service careers. This we believed the function of the schools of social work then developing. Some of the graduates, however, did become sufficiently interested in community service to accept positions in community centers and especially in Young Men's Hebrew Associations. Other men, with strong interest in Jewish education, specialized in this field, and became leaders in it.

In order to acquaint men with the social tasks of the rabbi, as these were developing in American Jewish communities; to aid full understanding of the social function of the Synagogue, which we were stressing in our conviction that it must be not only a house of worship and a seat of education, but also a religious center for community service; and to expound the social implications of religion, as implied in the prophetic literature and the works of all the great prophets—I worked out a series of courses to be given during the four years of training. That this program may be a part of the record and illustrate the type of work I have performed in the Institute since its founding, I reproduce here a full description of the four courses and the field work outlined for each. This work we could develop only in the time allowed us by the academic studies, and by the time the men were compelled to spend in maintaining themselves through teaching or week-end positions.

COURSES IN SOCIAL SERVICE

COURSE I

The Synagogue

Origin and development; construction and equipment; organization and administration; typical programs of activity, including Department of Worship, Department of Education, Department of Social Service, Men's Clubs, Women's Organizations, Youth Groups. Relation of the Synagogue to other social institutions; place and function of the Synagogue in the changing social order. One or two hours weekly throughout the year.

Field Work

The field work in this course consists of an intensive case work study of types of synagogues in New York City and smaller nearby communities, including Orthodox, Conservative, and Reform. Each student is required to study one synagogue of each type, including its construction and equipment, its organization and administration, its program of activities. This field work is supervised and is designed not only to make the student acquainted with synagogue programs, but to develop critical standards of judgment concerning the activities of the Synagogue and the function of the Synagogue in Jewish and general communal life. Conferences with rabbis of typical synagogues. This field work requires four hours a week during the scholastic year.

The Synagogue and Pastoral or Counseling Service

Problems of the individual; methods of social diagnosis; principles of social treatment; function of agencies of care. Problems of the family; new foundations; changing structure, organization, and function of the family; special problems of the Jewish family in America. Elements of personality and factors in human behavior, including physical, psychical, and social. One to two hours a week throughout the year.

Field Work

Field work in this course includes personal service with individuals and families and groups that the rabbi meets in the course of his ministry; and is designed to introduce the students to the field of pastoral or counseling service as it is now scientifically understood. Each man is assigned to three or four types of work in the course of the year in order that each one may become acquainted with the problems that arise in the field. The types of work include service with the sick, service with the delinquent, service with the dependent, service with boys and girls and adolescents in need of care. This field work is done in agencies dealing with the Jewish group. Conferences with executives and members of the staff of social agencies. This field work requires four hours a week throughout the scholastic year.

The Synagogue and Community Organization

Development of the Jewish and general community and communal organizations; relation of the Synagogue to community needs in the fields of health, education, recreation, housing, and civic organizations. Group relationships; causes of group friction; forms of group cooperation. Types of organization of the Jewish community; relation of the Synagogue to community life.

Field Work

The field work in this course includes a study of the communal institutions that have been organized by the Jewish people and also of Jewish national organizations that have their headquarters in New York City. The agencies studied include agencies for the care of the sick, such as hospitals and health organizations; agencies for the care of children, including orphan asylums, boarding-out departments, child adoption organizations, and the Children's Clearing Bureau; agencies for the care of the delinquent, including the Jewish Board of Guardians, Children's Court, Domestic Relations Court, reformatories, and penal institutions; agencies for the care of the dependent, such as the Jewish Family Service Association; agencies in the field of education and recreation, including Jewish Education Association, Young Men's Hebrew and Young Women's Hebrew Associations, the Jewish Welfare Board. In addition, the students will visit and study such agencies as the Bureau of Social Research and other national organizations. Conferences with executives of agencies and organizations. This field work requires four hours a week throughout the year.

COURSE IV

The Synagogue and the Social Order

Problems in the economic organization, including distribution of income, unemployment, child labor, and Social Security. Problems in the political order, including civil rights and rights of minorities. Problems in the cultural system of America, including the programs of segregation, assimilation, and social adjustments. Problems in international organization, including the work of the United Nations, International Labor Office, and World Court. The relation of Judaism to current social philosophies, including Capitalism, Socialism, Communism, Fascism, Democracy. One or two hours a week throughout the year.

Field Work

The field work in this course consists of first-hand studies of special problems in the economic, political, cultural, and international life; a study of the activities of agencies operating in the fields in which the problems are found. Visits to the sessions of the United Nations; conferences with the leaders of Jewish national organizations, such as the American Jewish Committee, American Jewish Congress, the Zionist Organization, and Israel. The field work in this course requires four hours a week throughout the scholastic year.

Purpose of Field Work

The field work in the Social Service Courses constitutes an integral part of each course. Field work is just as necessary in social service as laboratory work is necessary in courses in physics, chemistry, and biology; and serves as a basis for classroom interpretation and discussion. In addition, field work brings the student into immediate contact with the largest Jewish community in the world and gives him an opportunity, under the guidance and supervision of experts, to study the ways in which the Jewish people organize themselves to meet community and national and international needs. These contacts, personal and social, prove of great value to the men in the course of their ministry and in the communities in which they serve.

5. SOCIAL PREPARATION OF THE RABBI

In studying the function of the rabbi in the American synagogue we found that he serves in a four-fold capacity. He is a preacher, educator, pastor or counselor, and also a leader in community organization and social welfare. It is important that he be trained in the seminary for the work he is to do in these different departments. As a preacher it is a function of the rabbi to interpret current problems in terms of Jewish experience, Jewish teachings, Jewish principles, and Jewish ideals. The rabbi, as we understand it, is not a book reviewer nor a dramatic critic nor an economist nor a political scientist. He speaks as the representative of Judaism, and in terms of Judaism interprets the problems with which his congregation and his community are wrestling. These may be personal, family, or community problems, or problems of our larger social life.

In addition to delivering a sermon, the rabbi also conducts worship. This means that he must prepare not only a sermon but a service, in which is included the elements of the prayer or ritual, the music, the ceremonial, as well as the sermon, and also something else that we sometimes forget, the environment. Men and women come to the service or worship with definite needs. Comfort in times of sorrow is a universal need. They require courage and strength in time of temptation and trial, and from these no man is exempt. They need enlightenment and guidance in times of doubt and confusion, and certainly this is an acute requisite at the present time. They need stimulation and inspiration in the dreary and drab routine from which we all suffer more or less. But most of all they are in need of communion with a power higher than themselves, a need that many more feel than we are accustomed to assume. This function is probably primary in the American synagogue, and requires careful preparation for its fulfillment.

The rabbi also serves as educator. It is his function not alone to organize the school and the department of education but to train and supervise the teachers and to formulate and develop the curriculum. As an educator it is his task both to transmit to the people of Israel their precious heritage, and to do what he can to develop the powers, capacities, and personalities of his members. In providing the department of education that in the modern synagogue includes all age groups, children, adolescents, adults, it is important for him to recognize clearly the objectives of religious education. When an individual comes to be enrolled in the department of education, he sees that individual in a three-fold aspect with a three-fold need—but first as a person. It is his function as a religious teacher to do what he can to awaken and strengthen the religious consciousness or spiritual life of the person. He also looks upon the individual as a member of the Jewish community, as which he wants to make the individual acquainted with things Jewish and to deepen in his heart an allegiance to the principles and ideals of Judaism. But he also sees the individual as part of the larger social complex, and here too it is important that he do everything possible to establish the proper social adjustments and to cultivate in the individual a sense of social responsibility. This three-fold objective of the rabbi as an educator is not always fully realized, nor is he always adequately prepared to fulfill that function. It is not enough to teach Jewish history, Jewish literature, the Jewish religion, and the Hebrew language. Knowledge is important, but in addition each individual must cultivate loyalties to the values and ideals of Judaism, and must learn to translate into practice what his religion teaches. To know, to feel, and to do sums up this function of education in the field of religion.

In addition to serving as preacher and educator the rabbi is expected to be pastor and counselor. As such he is expected to do more than visit the sick and sympathize with the sorrowing. Members of the congregation and the community come to him with their problems. These may be simple or difficult and complicated. For this function it is important that the rabbi be carefully trained in the techniques of counseling as we are now developing this program. He must know how to approach people in trouble; how to assemble the evidence that is valid; how to determine the cause of the trouble or make what is called a social diagnosis; how to plan out a program of care; he must know also the agencies in the community and the resources upon which he can draw.

It is not possible for the rabbi as a counselor to treat every case of distress or to solve every problem, but it is important that he know enough about the causes of distress and of suffering to determine the nature of the trouble and to decide where the person can be best served. If the problem is legal he should refer the matter to a competent lawyer. If the matter is economic he should refer it to the proper home economist. If medical, he should know enough to send the case to the proper physician. If psychological, the patient is to be sent to a psychiatrist. It is not the function of the rabbi as a counselor to become an amateur in psychotherapy, though he must avail himself of all the techniques of counseling in order to relieve distress and rebuild men and women who have broken down, and do whatever he can to remove the cause of the trouble.

The rabbi in America is also expected to serve in the field of social welfare and to assume participation or leadership in the advancement of social movements. To this end, it is necessary for him to become acquainted with the social needs and agencies and programs of his community. In order to be of service in the advancement of social movements, he must study and understand the social movements of his time on the local, the state, the national, and the international level. Without this thorough grasp of social movements, the rabbi can give no leadership to congregation or community or country. For example, if the rabbi is to aid in the ending of child labor through legislation, it is necessary for him to study the evils of the situation and the extent to which children are stunted through premature work periods in the factories and the fields and the mines. If he is to help improve the standard of living, he must study all factors that lead to a low standard, such as unemployment, maldistribution of income, and extortionate prices of commodities. If he is to help eliminate the greatest of all evils, war, it is important that he study the conditions in our national and international life that lead to conflict. It is not sufficient merely to protest against social evils; he must equip himself to understand how to overcome them. It was for this reason that we introduced, for the first time in American seminaries, the Department of Social Service. Our purpose was not to train men as social workers, but to aid them in understanding their function as leaders in the field of social welfare and social improvement.

This four-fold function of the rabbi as preacher, educator, counselor, and leader in the field of social welfare does not include his function as a scholar. At the time we established the Jewish Institute of Religion, many of us were in doubt as to the ability of the rabbi in America to set aside the time necessary to develop himself as a scholar, that is, in the field of Jewish scholarship. It seemed to us, and I still believe this to be true, that the same thing is happening in religion as in medicine and in the social sciences. Not many decades ago the physician in the community not only practiced medicine; he taught medicine if he could, and did such scientific research as his time permitted. Today, we have first the great body of practicing physicians, second the group of teachers, whole or part time, in the best medical schools, and third the scientists in medical research, as in the Rockefeller Institute.

Only a short time ago social welfare was occupied altogether by those who practiced and taught and studied. Today, we have the great group of practicing social workers, the smaller group of teachers in the colleges and schools of social work, and a still smaller group of men and women engaged in research in the social laboratories of the country, such as Columbia, Chicago, and Chapel Hill. In religion it is interesting to note that we have first the large group of rabbis, second a smaller group of teachers in the seminaries, and third a still smaller group of scholars such as are found in all the seminaries. The rabbi may not be able to become a scholar, but he must employ in all that he does the resources and the techniques of scholarship.

The courses we included in the Department of Language, the Department of Literature, the Department of History, and the others formed only a part of the larger concept of the program we planned to develop. In addition to training men for the rabbinate, we believed that the Institute could and should be made a center of Jewish influence in this largest community of Jewish life. The men and women in this community, whether Orthodox or Conservative or Reform, are in need of courses in the history, the literature, the religion, and the culture of the people of Israel. It is amazing to discover how vastly illiterate these persons are and it is encouraging to learn how eager they are to learn.

With the faculty of the Jewish Institute of Religion as now organized and with adequate resources, we could develop, as we planned from the beginning, a program of extension courses that would be the equal of extension courses in any great university. This in fact was one of the purposes for which the Jewish Institute of Religion was established, as stated in the charter. Not only did we want to organize classes that would train men for a professional career, but also programs for community education and community service. We believed we owed it to the Jews of this community to make available to them the rich treasures contained within the walls of the Institute, and to do what we could to put them in possession of their inheritance. We have a heritage of four thousand years, during which we have not only accumulated a vast amount of knowledge but come into contact with every type of civilization and every scheme of salvation. It is a history that is utterly unique. We agreed at the outset that we should not shut ourselves in and certainly that we should not shut the world out.

Our concept of the Institute also included something else. Not only did we believe that it should become a community center of learning, but that it could and should become a community center of service. I doubt whether we realize what an infinite variety of questions and problems are posed by the men and women who make up this community. I wonder whether we appreciate the fact that they are often perplexed and confused and distressed, and in need of encouragement, counsel, and guidance. They are not all members of synagogues, but they all have problems, personal, family, religious, social. What human being is there who has no perplexities in these difficult days? Think of what it would mean if these people had someone to consult, who would listen to them with sympathy, discuss their problems with understanding, counsel them with expertness and authority. No one can work in this community as I have done for forty-eight years, meeting men and women from day to day, and not realize the need for a consultation center in human problems and human relationships. What a wealth of clinical material surrounds us for a study and training course in human behavior, in the factors without and the forces within, that cause or condition human conduct and create human distress. The fact of the matter is that some of the members of the faculty are today engaged in counseling and guiding men and women either in private practice or in synagogue service. They are working on a professional level. It would not be difficult therefore to organize with the staff we have a consultation center to which men and women could come and where they would find the service they need in solution of their problems.

Another plan we had in mind and that has grown more important with the years is a series of rabbinical interneships to be arranged for men in their final year at the Institute. Instead of the present unsupervised service in school positions and small congregations, I would recommend a system of rabbinical interneships in the larger congregations in the metropolitan area. Interneships in medicine, in law, in social work, in teaching, are now regarded as a necessary part of a man's training for his profession. Think how much the students would gain in congregational experience if they could serve with men now in charge of the larger congregations in this area, Orthodox, Conservative, and Reform. This plan would not only give men experience in congregational service, but make it possible for them to acquire some understanding of Jewish problems and Jewish organizations.

New York is the largest and best equipped social laboratory in the Jewish world. But the men in the Institute have no time to meet the leaders, no time to visit the organizations, no time for an interpretation of the problems we face, no time to see and to understand and to feel the throbbing life of the American Jewish people. I appreciate fully that it is most important for men to master as much as possible of the vast storehouse of Jewish learning; but I also know something of the problems that men meet in congregations and communities, and something also of the equipment needed to meet these problems intelligently and wisely. Doctors today are not expected to gain their initial experience at the expense of their patients. In order to present this plan adequately, I have drawn up a memorandum to be submitted to the president of the Jewish Institute of Religion and Hebrew Union College, a copy of which is here appended.

Now that the Jewish Institute of Religion has merged with the Hebrew Union College, will these aims and objectives be realized? At the present time the program is being reorganized and the curriculum revised. A number of important changes are contemplated. Students will be allowed to take the first and second years either in New York at the Institute or in Cincinnati at the College. But all will be required to take the third, fourth, and fifth years at the Hebrew Union College in Cincinnati. It seems to me that it would have been better, if circumstances had permitted, to have arranged for the students to spend their first and second years in Cincinnati and their third, fourth, and fifth years in New York, the large center of Jewish life.

Also, the title of the Department in which I have taught has been changed from Social Service to Human Relations. This probably is a better name and larger in its implications. But I trust that the course will not be limited to the first and second year men, as seems probable, but continued throughout the next three years as well. The students are greatly in need of training and experience in this aspect of the rabbinate. But the most important change is one of function. The Jewish Institute of Religion has now become avowedly a seminary for the training of men for the Reform or Liberal rabbinate. The original plan was to make the Jewish Institute of Religion all-inclusive and to allow members of the faculty and the students to decide each for himself whether to serve the Orthodox, the Conservative, or the Reform group.

We are not certain how these changes will work out, but in view of all conditions, and especially the limitation of funds and faculty and facilities, the new plan should be given every opportunity to succeed. I am certain that Dr. Glueck is as eager as any one to develop a program that will serve the best interests of the Jewish people in America.

SUGGESTIONS

FOR

INTERNESHIPS IN THE RABBINATE

I

COMMITTEE ON INTERNESHIPS

In order that this program for the sixth year, that is, the program of Interneships in the Rabbinate, may be wisely and effectively developed I recommend that a Committee on Interneships be appointed at once; and that this Committee be composed of the abler men in the rabbinate and also of the abler presidents of congregations in the East, and of representatives of the Union of American Hebrew Congregations as well as representatives of the Board of Governors. This Committee I urge should be appointed as soon as possible, as it will probably take months of meetings to agree upon the different items of the program and to establish the interneships.

In view of the fact that the program is to constitute the sixth year of the rabbinical course of the Hebrew Union College–Jewish Institute of Religion, the program should be recognized as a part of the seminaries from which the men graduate and should be regarded as an integral part of their preparation for the rabbinate. This new and significant venture should not be allowed to become a subordinate activity of any other organization.

I suggest as members of the Committee, such men as Rabbi Julius Mark, Rabbi Louis I. Newman, Rabbi Bernard Bamberger, Rabbi Jacob Shankman, Rabbi Lawrence Schwartz; the presidents of three or four important congregations in the East; representatives of the Board of Governors, such as Mr. Frank Weil and Judge Joseph M. Levine; and representatives of the staff of the Union of American Hebrew Congregations. The president and his assistant and two or three members of the faculty should serve on the Committee, perhaps ex officio.

II

PLACEMENT OF INTERNES

In order that the graduates of the Hebrew Union College–Jewish Institute of Religion may derive the maximum benefit from a year of interneship, it is necessary to place these men in the larger congregations with the abler leaders and with the best developed programs. This I urge for the same reason that medical students seek to place themselves as internes in the larger hospitals with the abler physicians and surgeons and with the richest amount of clinical material. In these larger congregations the men serving as internes should have an opportunity in the course of the year to serve in the different departments of synagogue life and to become acquainted with the different aspects of congregational and synagogue activities.

This means that it would be necessary to secure the active cooperation of both the rabbis and the congregations. The rabbis would be expected to accept the internes and to guide them in their work, and the congregations would be expected to subsidize the internes during the period of interneship. This is the plan that is in effect at the Union Theological Seminary.

I realize that it will take time and many conferences to develop this program with the rabbis and the congregations. But in and around New York there are a number of important congregations and a number of able men who probably will be willing to cooperate in this important experiment. I am thinking particularly of Rabbi Julius Mark of Emanu-El, Rabbi Louis I. Newman of Rodeph Sholom, Rabbi Bernard Bamberger of the West End Synagogue, Rabbi Jacob Shankman of New Rochelle, Rabbi Lawrence Schwartz of White Plains, Rabbi Jacob Rudin of Great Neck, and Rabbi Edward E. Klein of the Stephen Wise Free Synagogue. But I am not sure that they would be willing to cooperate in view of their caustic criticisms of the Interneship Program.

I emphasize the placement in the larger congregations because I have watched the men over the years as they have served as student-rabbis in small and recently organized communities. I know that there is little that the men can learn in these smaller communities that would be of value to them as internes. The programs are too limited and too loosely organized to be of service. I am also convinced that it is not fair for these men to secure their experience at the expense of the smaller congregations and the communities to which they might be assigned.

One activity that certainly could be entrusted to the interneships under supervision of the rabbi is the conduct of auxiliary or supplementary services during the High Holydays.

III

SEMINARS

In addition to the service in the congregations to which the graduates will be assigned, the men should be required to attend seminars that will be of value to them in widening their knowledge and in developing their training and in deepening their experience. Each seminar should last for three or four months, and two or three seminars could run concurrently either in the afternoon or in the evening. An expert should be in charge of each seminar, that is, a man who is specializing in the problems with which the seminar deals. It should be his function to organize the seminar, to prepare the syllabus, to invite speakers, and to guide the discussion. Among the seminars I would suggest the following:

1. *Seminar on Synagogue Problems.* This seminar should include the following topics: 1) Architecture; 2) Construction and Equipment; 3) Organization and Administration; 4) Programs of Worship; 5) Programs of Education; 6) Programs of Social Service; 7) Programs of Men's Clubs; 8) Programs of Women's Organizations; 9) Programs of Youth Groups.

This seminar should not be a theoretical or academic discussion of topics, but an actual study of programs in operation. In other words, the seminar should be on a casework basis, as seminars are in medical schools and in law schools. In the congregations that I have listed in the East new and progressive programs are being developed and interesting experiments are being conducted. And one thing that the seminar can do is to study the achievements of the congregations and to evaluate the programs. Much material has been gathered by different divisions of the Union of American Hebrew Congregations. In 1930 I recommended at a meeting of the Central Conference of American Rabbis that a Bureau of Synagogue Research be organized and some sections of such a Bureau have been developed and the material is now available.

2. *Seminar on Jewish Religious Movements.* The internes should be allowed time to visit the different types of synagogues and to sit down in seminar fashion with the leaders of the Orthodox, the Conservative, the Reconstructionist, and the Reform groups. This seminar would include meetings with the New York Board of Rabbis, the leaders of the Union of Orthodox Jewish Congregations, the leaders of the Union of Orthodox Rabbis, the leaders of the United Synagogue, the leaders of the Rabbinical Assembly, and the leaders of the Union of American Hebrew Congregations. The purpose of this seminar would be to make the men acquainted not only with the leaders of Jewish religious movements, but with the philosophies of the movements themselves. It is most important that the internes during their period of interne-

ship become directly acquainted with Jewish groups other than their own. They should also find it possible to study the sections of the community to which these movements minister. There is no community in which there is so wide a variety of Jewish movements. And through this seminar it should be possible to develop a more comprehensive understanding of the people of Israel. Rabbis in this way would learn that they are the rabbis of the community and not merely of the congregation.

3. *Seminar on Marriage and Family Counseling.* Some of the best work being done in the field of marriage and family counseling is centered in New York City, Philadelphia, and Boston. In these cities are some of the ablest men and women developing programs in this new field. The internes should have an opportunity to attend a seminar in which they would meet with the experts, and especially with those who are leaders in the American Association of Marriage Counselors and other agencies. Among the leaders are: Dr. Abraham Stone, Dr. Janet Fowler Nelson, Dr. Lena Levine, Dr. David Mace, Dr. Emily Mudd, and Dr. Ernest G. Osborne. The internes should not only know the leaders but should learn something about the programs that are being developed in the different cities, the lectures, the conferences, and the Film Forums. This seminar would take the form of a workshop. We have in the Social Science Alcove one of the best collections in the city on marriage and family problems, including books, pamphlets, magazines, and bibliographies. This seminar would be an extension of the course given in the Jewish Institute of Religion and would be on a graduate level. The rabbis can be of service to their congregation only to the extent that they train themselves in marriage and family counseling procedures and techniques as well as in the objectives.

4. *Seminar on Human Behavior.* It is now recognized that the study of human behavior must precede the study of human relations. Foundations in different parts of the country are stressing this new and important discipline. Some of the best work in human behavior is now being done in New York, New Haven, Princeton, and other nearby centers and social laboratories. The internes certainly should have an opportunity to meet with the leaders in this field, and especially with such men and women as Dr. Lawrence K.

Frank, Dr. Margaret Mead, Dr. Anna Wolf, and Dr. Thomas Hora. This seminar would help the men to understand better the factors that we are now studied in the field of human behavior: 1) the somatic; 2) the psychical; 3) the social; 4) the ethical; 5) the origin of defects, hereditary, congenital, and acquired; and how these defects should be corrected. This is one of the most important fields in which the internes should spend adequate time. We assume that in the ministry men are dealing with human behavior and human relations. But we do little to make it possible for them to become well-grounded in the knowledge of the causes that condition human conduct, and clinical material that is now available. This is one of the developing programs that should unquestionably be included in the year of interneship.

5. *Seminar on Jewish Organizations.* New York City is the center in which the larger Jewish organizations are located. This seminar should bring the internes into direct contact with the lay and professional leaders, and the programs that these organizations are developing on the local, state, and national levels. For example, the men should meet with the lay and professional leaders of: 1) The American Jewish Committee; 2) The American Jewish Congress; 3) The Jewish Labor Committee; 4) The B'nai B'rith and Anti-Defamation League; 5) The Zionist Organization of America; 6) Hadassah; 7) Federation of Jewish Philanthropies. Instead of merely reading and studying the reports of these organizations the internes should meet with the men who are developing the programs and the community organizations in the cities and states and in the nation.

6. *Seminar on Non-Jewish Organizations.* The internes should have an opportunity to meet with the leaders in non-Jewish organizations and to become personally acquainted with the programs that are being developed in the different fields of social activity. For example: 1) The Amalgamated Clothing Workers of America and Jacob S. Potofsky; 2) The International Ladies Garment Workers and David Dubinsky; 3) The American Civil Liberties Union and Roger Baldwin and Patrick Murphy Malin; 4) The Association for Democratic Action; 5) The Council of Churches; 6) and especially the leaders in the different divisions of the United Na-

tions. It is incredible that men in the ministry should be in New York and not meet with the leaders of the United Nations to discuss with them in seminar fashion the programs they are formulating. For example: 1) UNESCO; 2) The Declaration of Human Rights; 3) the Genocide Pact; 4) The World Health Organizations. Some men in the ministry I find have not even read the Charter of the United Nations.

IV

FIELD WORK

It would be helpful to the men preparing for the rabbinate if they could be allowed to do field work in two or three areas of service. This field work, however, would have to be carefully supervised by someone who is assigned to this particular type of work. Without supervision the field work would prove desultory and unprofitable. Among the areas in which field work could be developed are the following:

1. The men could be allowed time in which to serve as assistant chaplains or members of the Social Service Department in: 1) Hospitals; 2) Penal Institutions; 3) Child Care Agencies; 4) Children's Courts and Family Courts. This field work would aid them to understand better the ways in which we are now serving the sick, the delinquent, and the distressed. I do not advise too much time in the psychiatric wards or institutions for the care of mental cases. The best statistics we have show that only about 10% of the population suffer from mental conditions that are in need of psychiatric care, and only one out of 18 or 19 of the population ever would be in need of commitment to institutions. This means that 90% of the population with whom the rabbis deal are within the range of "normal." The 10% that constitute what we call mental hygiene cases should not be treated by rabbis or amateur psychiatrists, but should be referred to experts in the field of psychiatry or psychotherapy or psychoanalysis. In spite of all that is being written and said I am convinced after forty years in mental hygiene work that it is hazardous for men and women who are not thoroughly

trained and widely experienced to undertake even what appears to be simple mental hygiene work. The rabbi has sufficient to do to take care of the 90% classified as "normal."

2. The new trend is away from institutions and toward community programs. In the field of social welfare the leaders now recognize that we have been too institution-minded and that we must learn to think in terms of: 1) Community Needs; 2) Community Problems; 3) Community Programs. Within the next twenty-five years it is very probable that synagogues will come to take a deeper interest in the community of which they are a part; and I, therefore, believe that it would be helpful to these men if they could become at least acquainted with community needs in the following fields: 1) Health; 2) Education; 3) Recreation; 4) Housing. Juvenile delinquency is one of the urgent problems in every community across the country and is increasing in seriousness from year to year. It is impossible for anyone to understand juvenile delinquency who does not know the community. The Synagogue certainly should be interested in this problem, as it is one of the safeguards of the moral life of the community.

3. In addition to field work in institutions and in the community it would be helpful if the men could become acquainted with legislative bodies and governmental procedures. If the rabbi is to have any part in ending incompetence and corruption and crime on the local or state or national level he must become acquainted with social legislation and the leaders of social reform. In New York City the men could visit the City Council and meet its leaders. In Albany they could visit the Legislature and see how it functions, and also meet the Governor and have conferences with the heads of the State departments. It would also be most helpful if the men could visit Washington in order to see Congress in action and to learn something of the way in which the federal legislators operate. Very few men even know how to come into contact with the most helpful leaders in Washington.

4. Large and important conferences are constantly being held in New York City in many fields in which the rabbi should be interested and active. Attendance at these conferences and even participation in the discussions and workshops could be made a part of the field work for internes.

III

THE SYNAGOGUE AND THE COMMUNITY

STEPHEN WISE FREE SYNAGOGUE

THE SYNAGOGUE AND THE COMMUNITY

The projects described in this section together constitute the social service program of the Free Synagogue. Each project was undertaken as an experiment in order to meet an unmet need in the community or a need inadequately covered. The significant outcome to us is that so many of these experiments eventually expanded into community agencies and became part of the network of welfare organizations. This we regard as our most important contribution. We realize fully, however, how much more is still to be done; and we are keenly aware of the many children and the men and women and families that suffer for want of a more complete social program.

INTRODUCTION

What is the relationship of the synagogue to the community? I have been in some communities in the United States in which the synagogue is an utterly isolated institution. It is closed all week except for the few hours of worship or classes. The relationship to the community is so tenuous and so vague that the synagogue could disappear overnight and no one would remember it had ever existed. I have been in other communities, especially in the smaller towns, in which the synagogue is the one important institution of the Jewish people. The only relationship, however, it maintains with the community is through its membership and affiliated organizations, such as the Sisterhood or Brotherhood. In these instances the synagogue is not related in any vital way to community life or community problems. Even in the larger cities I have studied the synagogues have little or no relationship to the communities in which they are situated. They are open for worship at stated hours during the week, and for classes and for meetings of organizations associated with the congregation. But they develop no programs that relate them actively to the community out of which they spring. At best they are little more than architectural monuments; at worst they are ornate mausoleums. Even when they are located on the Avenue they appear like spectators watching the procession of life pass by.

1. COMMUNITY NEEDS

In 1930, at a meeting of the Central Conference of American Rabbis in Providence, Rhode Island, I presented a paper entitled, "Outline Organization of Bureau of Synagogue Research." Therein I advocated establishment of a bureau that would undertake to do for the synagogue what the "Bureau of Jewish Social Research" has done for social institutions in the Jewish field and what the "Institute of Social and Religious Research" has done for the Protestant churches in America. Some of the suggestions in this paper have been developed into activities by departments of the Union of American Hebrew Congregations. But the full program outlined is still to be translated into a much needed agency. The need for and the purpose of a Bureau of Synagogue Research I stated in the following paragraphs:

"The rapid growth of synagogues in America during the last quarter century and the tremendous sums of money being invested in construction and maintenance seem to indicate that the synagogue is in the midst of one of its most flourishing periods of development. It is well known, however, to those acquainted with the field and the facts, that many synagogues in both the smaller and larger communities are not functioning as effectively as they should, and that large sections of the people do not look upon it as an institution rendering the maximum service we have a right to expect. In some communities congregations have involved themselves in debts that make it impossible for them to progress. The result is that so much time and strength is spent in meeting payment on mortgages and in building up the organization that no time is left for the program for which the synagogue itself was created. Instead of being an instrument of service, it becomes an end in itself to maintain and perpetuate.

"Here lies the heart of the problem. Conditions in American social life are changing rapidly and new needs are developing in both the Jewish and non-Jewish community. But we have not addressed ourselves to the urgent and central question: What is to be the function of the synagogue in the social order that is now taking shape? Unless we find it possible to answer this question correctly as a result of careful study and research the social order will outgrow the synagogue, and the synagogue will cease to exercise any influence whatever in the life of men and women and communities. The Synagogue in the course of its history has served as a House of Prayer, a Place of Instruction, and a Religious Center for Community Service. In these age-old functions we may find some suggestion for its further development. Twenty-five years ago we began to stress the thought that we must socialize our religion and the synagogue. Today the great need seems to be not to socialize the synagogue and religion, but to religionize social life and all our social enterprises. If the synagogue is to serve this purpose it must reorganize itself and envisage a new and nobler objective. If it is to aid in the establishment of the Kingdom of God it must reconstruct itself into a finer instrument of service and set for itself a larger vision of achievement.

"Before we can proceed to develop a program that will relate the synagogue and the congregation to the community we must first answer these four questions: What are the needs of the community? How are the needs being met at the present time? How can the social needs of the community be coped with more adequately? What is the relation of the synagogue to the social needs of the community and how can it serve in meeting the needs more adequately?

For example, one of the acute problems almost everywhere in the United States today is that of juvenile delinquency. The need is for a program of care that will curb and control the

rising rate of crime in our juvenile group. In many places programs have been developed through such agencies as Children's Aid Societies, Child Guidance Clinics, Children's
Courts, and cultural institutions. But in no communities thus
far have we formulated a program that adequately meets this
acute social need.

"The Synagogue, like the Church, certainly cannot be indifferent, for both are concerned with the moral welfare of our
young people and are counted among the guardians of the
moral life. I do not find, however, that many synagogues are
aware of the facts of juvenile delinquency in their own baili-
wicks. They do not know even the bare statistics from year to
year. Nor do I find that the synagogue in many communities,
including even the rabbi, is acquainted with the group of
agencies the community has created in this field. Nor has the
synagogue considered in what way the community can more
adequately meet the need. And certainly only in exceptional
instances is it endeavoring to do anything whatever, individ-
ually or in cooperation with other agencies, to save our youth
from the breakdowns that now express themselves in juvenile
delinquency.

"The social programs of the Sisterhoods in New York,
described in an earlier chapter, were an endeavor on the part
of the synagogues to relate themselves to the community. But
these programs of social service have unfortunately disappeared. The synagogue center is another way in which the
synagogues have sought to relate themselves to community
life. One of the first to be established, if not the first, was the
one Rabbi Leonard Levy organized in Pittsburgh in the early
years of this century. Next came the great Sinai Center that
Dr. Emil G. Hirsch established in Chicago in 1912. Both
these, like other centers in large synagogues, have, however,
limited themselves almost exclusively to educational, recreational, and cultural programs. In the new Sinai Temple in
Chicago, under the leadership of Dr. Louis Mann, and Dr.
Richard Hertz (now of Detroit), a new program has been developed in association with the Jewish Community Centers of

Chicago. In a recent address before the National Jewish Welfare Board, Dr. Hertz spoke as follows: 'Sinai has therefore become accustomed to think in terms of a broader concept of synagogue function than the more conventional type. It has been more than just a house of prayer and a house of study: as a house of assembly for the whole community, its social aims and objectives have developed concepts underlining the importance of well-adjusted, happy lives; developing strong Jewish loyalties among youth; fulfilling social needs through a sense of belongingness; and providing wholesome auspices for worthwhile activities.'

"Happily, these aims and objectives are second nature to the Jewish Center movement. This is one reason why I have always believed that synagogues and Jewish centers share much more in common with each other than either has been willing to admit. They are really partners and not competitors.

"The rabbis of the United States, I find, are becoming increasingly concerned with the social needs of the community. More and more they realize that the synagogue falls short of fulfillment unless it becomes a religious center for community service as well as a house of worship and a seat of education. In the Report of the Commission on Justice and Peace of the Central Conference of American Rabbis for the year 1951 I find this statement: 'Your Commission on Justice and Peace acknowledges with humility that its greatest failure to date has been in the area of implementing the social idealism of our people within our own congregations. With exceptions as notable as they are rare, we have limited ourselves to lofty pronouncements, but have not devised ways and means of teaching the practical application of these pronouncements to our people or of activating them in the search for a more decent society.'

"The practical work we do in our communities, and even more the non-partisan political activity to which we can stimulate our congregations as an expression of their Jewish prophetic zeal, will be both a manifest of our sincerity and a determinant of our effectiveness. We have always properly insisted

that Judaism is a way of life. This must be as true in the areas
represented by this Commission as with respect to ritual
observance and to ethical conduct generally. We would urge
most strongly, therefore, that a larger program in next year's
conference schedule be devoted to the reporting in detail of
successful committees on public affairs already in operation
within our congregations, and specific practical proposals for
the extension of such activity among the groups which the
members of this conference have the high privilege of serving"
(Yearbook, p. 106).

2. SOCIAL CARE OF THE SICK

Now I wish to describe the way in which we have related the Free
Synagogue to the community. Many people have asked me why we
began with care of the sick. The reasons are clear. Service to the
sick is one of the oldest commandments in Jewish life and can be
traced back at least two thousand years. All through the centuries
we find the Jewish people organizing programs to assist the ailing
so far as their knowledge and skill would allow. In the United
States one of the first institutions to be established was the hospital.
When we founded the Social Service Department of the Free Synagogue in 1907 the hospitals and dispensaries, however, limited their
service to medical, surgical, and nursing care. There was no systematic and scientific social care of the Jewish sick in any institution
in New York.

When I became assistant superintendent of Mt. Sinai Hospital
in New York in 1905 it was part of my duty to interview patients
upon admission, to visit them in the wards, and to officially discharge them when they left the institution. I soon discovered that
Mt. Sinai had an excellent medical service, a splendid nursing service, and a most efficient administrative program under the direction of Dr. S. S. Goldwater. But I realized early in the work that
the social needs of the patients were almost completely disregarded and forgotten. I then began a study of the patients admitted
to the hospital wards. This was in the same year that Dr. Richard
Cabot of Boston began a similar study of patients admitted to the

Massachusetts General Dispensary. By 1906 I had accumulated sufficient material to write an article entitled "The Social Function of the Hospital." This was the first statement of the problem, and the first outline of the new program of social care of the sick. The article was published in what was then known as "Charities and the Commons," predecessor of "The Survey." In this article occurs the following:

"What becomes of the family of the patient who enters the hospital? This inquiry may sound entirely gratuitous, and the most ready reply may be the counter-question: What has the hospital to do with the patient's family? Nothing, it is at once granted, if the scope of the institution is to be fixed by tradition and its function limited to the bare treatment of disease. But why should the hospital thus contract its vision and work? Is there no more to a sick man than his sickness? May he not have a wife and children; may he not be the one support of others, dependent and helpless? These suppositions, however, are ignored. While the patient lies upon a sickbed, the hospital gives no thought to the way in which time passes with the mother or little ones, or the manner in which rent, food, and clothing are provided for them. The children may weep bitterly with hunger, the mother may rub away her strength in profitless toil, and the hospital may continue to stand stern and composed in the thought that need will direct them to the proper place. The important fact is overlooked that inexperience and pardonable human pride may postpone or even permanently bar the way to suitable and adequate relief. An appeal is occasionally made to the office for aid and advice, but no effort is made by the hospital to seek out those who never gather together sufficient courage to venture this approach. This misfortune strikes hardest in that class which in normal circumstances is able to earn a living wage, but is wholly unprepared to meet the abnormal conditions that follow from an attack of sickness."

It was this presentation of the problem that moved Paul Warburg, then a member of the Board of Directors, to give the first $2000 to serve as foundation of what has become the Social Service Department of Mt. Sinai Hospital. I recall clearly the Sunday morning he stopped at the office to chat for a few moments, as he often did, after the meeting of the Board. He asked me, "How is the work progressing and how are you enjoying your experience as assistant superintendent?" I replied. "Mr. Warburg, I am enjoying this experience greatly and I am learning many things that every minister ought to know. We have a great medical staff and a devoted corps of nurses and a most efficient administrator. But there is one need that I think we are overlooking." Said he, "What is that?" I answered, "The social needs of the patients who are admitted to the wards." He looked puzzled. "What do you mean by that?" I then told him of some of my experiences in the admitting room, the wards, and the discharge office. I pointed out the fact that men and women were being admitted to the wards and that nothing whatever was being done about the families they had left at home; that mothers were admitted as emergency cases, but that nothing whatever was arranged for care of the children in the home, that patients were often discharged greatly in need of convalescent care and of surgical appliances, with nothing being done by the hospital to provide them with what they needed. He became deeply interested and asked, "What would it cost to make a study of these needs of which you speak?" I was young and inexperienced, and replied, "I think that if we had $2000, Mr. Warburg, we could at least make a survey." He startled me by at once making out a check for that sum—"Let me know when the survey is completed." We completed the survey, and Mr. Warburg, with other members of the Board and the Women's Auxiliary, aided me in establishing the Social Service Department before I left the hospital.

It was natural, therefore, for us to make social care of the Jewish sick one of our projects when we founded the Free Synagogue in 1907. We realized fully, as a result of my survey and experience, that this was one of the unmet needs of the community. We might have begun our work at Mt. Sinai Hospital, which would have welcomed our cooperation. But after studying the field carefully we concluded that we would find the group most in need of service in a city institution called Bellevue Hospital. It was to Bellevue that other institutions transferred the cases they could not treat, and it was to Bellevue that Jewish patients went who could not be admitted to any other institution. At that time it had a Jewish admission of about six thousand men, women, and children every year. These patients came from the lowest income groups, and everyone, therefore, that entered was in need of social as well as medical and nursing care. We therefore asked for the privilege of serving the Jewish sick in this institution. We were heartily welcomed by the Social Service Department, then being organized by Miss Mary Wadleigh. It was our function to meet the social needs of the Jewish patients as we discovered them upon admission, during their stay in the wards, and at the time of discharge. We developed a system which brought to our desk in the Social Service Department of Bellevue Hospital within twenty-four hours a notice of every Jewish admission and every Jewish discharge. We accepted full responsibility for meeting the needs of the Jewish patients.

In the course of the years we succeeded in covering all the wards in Bellevue, medical, surgical, maternity, tuberculosis, and the minor services. We organized a staff that included trained, experienced, salaried medical social workers, and a corps of volunteers from the membership of the Free Synagogue. The medical social workers, then drawn largely from the nursing staff, were in daily and immediate contact with all the Jewish patients admitted to the wards. The volunteers came to the hospital three times a week, Monday, Wednesday, and Friday afternoons. We had our own office, to which came the Jewish patients upon discharge, those, that is, who were in need of care. This service was one of the most beneficent projects in our program. The volunteers, a group that included Mrs. Henrietta Fischlowitz, Mrs. Benjamin Schloss, Mrs. May V. Fisher (who later became chairman of our Bellevue Hospital Committee), Mr. Frederick L. Guggenheimer (later chairman of the Social Service Department and president of the Free Synagogue), Mr. Edward Bukofzer, and many others, not only visited the patients in the wards; they went to the homes of the patients and arranged for covering their social needs and their convalescent care. From week to week we reviewed each case, and in Case Committee meetings succeeded in developing the early techniques of medical social service, or what we prefer to call the social care of the sick.

No one who has not been a patient in a hospital ward can quite realize how lonely it is during the day and how oppressive during the night, and how much it means for someone to come in and say *"Shalom alechem,"* and to assure the patient that the children at home will be cared for, and that provision will be made for convalescence when he is discharged. Those to whom we brought relief and comfort, we learned, were always more concerned about the family at home than about themselves.

It is difficult and perhaps unnecessary to list all the needs we discovered. The most important thing was that there is something more to a sick man than his sickness, and that this is frequently of more importance than the illness itself. A man who enters the hospital with a gastric ulcer is always worried about his family, and this worry may retard his recovery. A woman who enters, as a rule suddenly, to undergo an operation, is constantly thinking of her husband and home and children. This undoubtedly hinders her convalescence also.

None of us will forget the tragedy that taught us the necessity for home visits and adequate provision for the children. This was the case of a woman admitted for an emergency operation. Her husband was a machine operator, who had to leave early in the morning. Not knowing what to do with the children, he locked them in the room when he left. On the second day the little boy found a box of matches and began to play with them. Before anyone could open the apartment both children had been burned to death. After this tragedy our first question of every woman was, "Who is taking care of your children?"

We also learned that the patients in a large city institution felt themselves in an alien environment. The doctors were not Jewish, nor were the nurses or attendants. They had no understanding of the background and customs and needs of the Jewish patients. It therefore became our duty not only to interpret the hospital to the patient but also to interpret the patient to the hospital. The difference in race, religion, language, and background between the patient and those who served him easily led to misunderstanding and retardation of recovery.

I remember clearly entering one of the wards of Bellevue and noticing a commotion. I walked to the place of the trouble, and discovered three orderlies trying to hold a little Jew in bed. He was doing his utmost to get out, talking loudly in Yiddish, of which the orderlies had no knowledge whatever. I asked one orderly what was the cause of the trouble, and he said, "We don't know; he only wants to get out of the hospital." I asked for the privilege of speaking to him. In a few moments he quieted down and told me that the doctors wanted to operate on him, and that he was frightened and was determined to escape. I told this to the orderlies. They replied, "It is not so; the doctors have no intention of operating on this man." That puzzled me, and I began an inquiry. The facts were simple enough; during morning rounds the surgeon and his associates had examined the patients, and while at the foot of the bed of the little Jew had discussed the operation they planned to perform on a patient three beds away. All the little man understood was the word "operation," and he assumed, since they were standing at his bed, that they planned to operate on him. I explained the situation to him. He agreed to remain in bed, to be discharged some days later completely cured and happy. This was a simple case of interpretation, but only one illustration of what occurred again and again, and the need for workers who understood the patients, their language, and their background. We must also remember that doctors and nurses are often too overworked to explain what the patients need to know in order to remain contented.

From Bellevue Hospital we extended the program to Lebanon Hospital in the Bronx, which at that time had no Social Service Department whatever. In this institution we covered both the wards and the clinics. It was in the dispensary that we organized some of our most interesting projects. One was the first Infant Hygiene Clinic in this section of the city. It came about in this way. In 1909 I attended the conference on "Infant Mortality and Morbidity" at Yale University. Here we learned that in the United States 16 out of every 100 babies born alive died before their first birthday. I returned with this startling information and at once urged the Social Service Board to develop a program to curb this evil and reduce the suffering of babies and their parents.

We succeeded in interesting a group of pediatricians, among whom Dr. Sidney Haas was the most eminent, and they became the staff of the "Infant Hygiene Clinic." We soon learned that the chief cause of high mortality was the ignorance of parents, and that the second was contaminated food. The mothers of the neighborhood therefore were invited to come to the clinic with their babies, and to be instructed in the care of their children. This was the beginning of the program that has grown in importance in many hospitals and in many parts of New York City and the United States. The Department of Health of the City of New York has taken a leading part in establishing the program, and has encouraged institutions to cooperate in its endeavor to save babies and to reduce infant illness.

The most advanced programs in this field now go far beyond our early attempt merely to reduce the number of infant deaths. Today the woman is invited to enroll in the pre-natal clinic as soon as she knows she is to be blessed with motherhood. She is then kept under observation until time for the birth. Then she is admitted to the hospital for the delivery. While there she is given instruction and is directed to go to the post-natal clinic immediately after discharge. Here both she and the baby are kept under observation until the child reaches the age of four or five. The result is that the death rate of infants has been reduced from 16 out of every 100 in 1909, to between 2 and 3 out of 100 in the well-organized sections of the city—today, 1954. Human life has become too precious to permit babies to die because of the ignorance of their parents.

We did not content ourselves, however, with instruction of the mother in baby care and prevention of disease. One of the things we learned was that women were suffering from too frequent pregnancies and too many children. We therefore began, even in these early days, a program that would encourage families to space their children more wisely. This was the beginning of our birth control program, which amounted to nothing more than transferring to the low income families the knowledge possessed by those better circumstanced, who could consult obstetricians and gynecologists

and learn the modern methods of contraception. We had no difficulty whatever in developing this program. In fact the women welcomed it and the doctors cooperated with us in both interest and
earnestness.

We must not forget the part that purified food has played in this
vital health program. The story is told that a woman once went to
Dr. Osler of Johns Hopkins University and said, "Dr. Osler, I am
sorry to tell you that the Lord has seen fit to take my baby." Dr.
Osler looked at the woman and replied, "Madam, it was not the
Lord that took your baby; it was the contaminated milk of Balti-
more." In the early part of this century there is no doubt whatever
that infants and children died of contaminated food. The milk
served to infants and children today comes from cows that are
regularly inspected; and the milk is pasteurized, which means that
it is purified. Too much credit cannot be given to Mr. and Mrs.
Nathan Straus, who furthered this movement and established the
first centers for the distribution of pasteurized milk in the poorer
sections of our city.

The Board of Health, of course, has undertaken to advance this
program, in saving children not only from contaminated food but
from the diseases that used to sweep youngsters into early graves.
Smallpox, diphtheria, scarlet fever, measles, and other diseases of
childhood are now disappearing, and more children are surviving
the hazards of babyhood and of childhood. The members of the
Social Service Department can reasonably find comfort in knowing that we have had some part in this service, and that we learned
early in our work that it is far more important to educate parents
and to save babies and children through prevention than to establish clinics for treatment of the sick. We have never lost our interest in this service, and have constantly emphasized the need for
education and proper food in the program of community health.

We did not stop, however, with establishment of medical social
service or the social care of the sick in Bellevue and in Lebanon
Hospital and Dispensary. We cooperated with other hospitals, dispensaries, and social agencies in development of what has become
the fourth department of every large and well-equipped institution,

that is, the Department of Hospital or Medical Social Service. We visited other communities, city after city, and in lectures and conferences and written articles and experimental programs undertook to aid others to understand that it is not sufficient to provide medical, nursing, and administrative care, but also social care. One great physician, Dr. Richard Cabot of Boston, once said that in every case of sickness there are two factors. One is the disease and the other is the patient's attitude toward the disease. The attitude is sometimes more important than the disease itself; and the attitude of the patient is often dependent to a large extent upon the degree to which his social and spiritual needs are met.

Social care of the sick is now an accepted program of service. But we are convinced that this program is still in its incipient stage. Even today we have not begun to meet the social and spiritual needs of all the patients in all the hospitals and dispensaries either in this or other cities, nor have we begun to cover the social and spiritual needs outside the hospital and dispensary. I am inclined to believe that as group medicine grows in this and in other communities the group organization will employ not only nurses but medical social workers who will undertake to study and to meet the social needs of the afflicted. There are few families that would not benefit through the counsel and guidance of well-trained, experienced medical social workers.

If any synagogues in America are seeking a social program to develop, I would urgently recommend that they study the care of the sick in their communities. They will find, as we have, that the ill are in need of four kinds of care: medical, nursing, social, and spiritual; and they will discover that the need for social and spiritual care is just as great as for medical and nursing care. In the higher income brackets families are able to provide themselves with all four forms. But below these levels the sick suffer for want of adequate service. Not all the sick in any community receive adequate medical care. Not all are provided with adequate nursing care. A large portion even today receive no social and no spiritual care. This is a great unmet human need that the synagogue, if properly organized for community service, can undertake in every community.

3. TUBERCULOSIS PROGRAM

Out of our service at Bellevue Hospital grew two significant experiments and programs. The first was in the field of tuberculosis, and the second in mental hygiene. In that first two or three years of our work in the wards for the tuberculous we found ourselves unable to achieve any lasting results with our Jewish patients. Men and women and their families were as a rule subsidized, we learned, by what was then called the United Hebrew Charities. We were unable to accomplish anything permanent with these families because the allowance granted by the United Hebrew Charities, though as much as this organization could afford, was pitifully insufficient. The tuberculous were being maintained in their poverty and continued in their tuberculosis; they were not being aided to outgrow one or to recover from the other.

In 1910 we recommended that a "Joint Tuberculosis Committee" be formed by the United Hebrew Charities and the Free Synagogue, and together we agreed to conduct an experiment with a group of tuberculous families in the hope of achieving something definite and lasting, with adequate allowances and social supervision. The Charities agreed to grant their customary allowance, and the Free Synagogue agreed to add necessary supplementary aid. This experiment, with about 50 cases, continued for three years and cost a total of $50,593. Of this amount the United Hebrew Charities contributed $28,660, and the Free Synagogue $21,927. The results, with adequate allowance and social supervision, were most gratifying and promising, so much so that we decided to enlarge the experiment and to invite the Montefiore Home, which conducted a Sanatorium for the Jewish Tuberculous at Bedford Hills, Westchester County, to join with us in an appeal to the community for funds with which to continue the work on a more extensive scale.

Mr. Jacob H. Schiff, then president of the Montefiore Home and Bedford Sanatorium, had vetoed a somewhat similar plan prepared by Dr. Lee K. Frankel in 1905, on the ground that a new organization for the Jewish tuberculous would *distract* funds from the Montefiore Home. In 1912 Mr. Schiff and his Board were still of the same opinion. They believed that their institution was adequately covering the problem of the Jewish tuberculous in New York City. I recall asking Mr. Schiff and his Board one question: "Do you know what becomes of the patients after they are discharged from the Montefiore Home and Bedford Sanatorium?" They confessed they did not know, and we succeeded in persuading them to join with us in investigating their discharged patients. This investigation included only the patients discharged in 1909, 1910, and 1911—459 in all. It was most thorough and complete, and scientifically tested at every point on both medical and social bases. Every case we discovered was followed up medically and socially by an expert. I quote from a Report by the Chairman of the Joint Committee, Mr. Fred Stein, then a member of the Montefiore Hospital Board:

"Of the 109 cases discharged in 1909, we located 26, or 24%. Five were worse, 16 were stationary, and five were better. Of the 191 cases discharged in 1910, we located 53, or 30%. Twenty-four were worse, 24 were stationary, and five were better. Of the 159 discharged in 1911, we located 70 or 48%. Thirty-six were worse, 31 were stationary, and three were better. From these figures it was clear that of the cases that could be located 52% had grown worse at the time of the investigation, which was from six months to a year after discharge from the institution. It would seem to suggest, therefore, that the sanatoria as they are now administered turn patients out into the world partially restored to health, and do not take any further interest in their welfare or disease-spreading potentialities. The question therefore arises whether there is not some practical method for supplementing the institutional treatment, which represents an investment of millions of dollars, in such manner as to make it more efficient both economically and socially."

This careful and critical investigation of patients discharged from a tuberculosis sanatorium, the first on record, proved not only that 52% of the work done in Bedford Sanatorium was of little value, but that $52 out of every $100 spent in treating the patients in this institution was wasted in less than a year's time. We came to the conclusion that the relapses and the waste were due altogether to two factors: First, the home conditions to which the patients returned; and second, the industrial conditions into which the patient was forced. I remember well a man writing us that he had just returned from Bedford Sanatorium and that he and his family were in great need. I visited the family and found that they lived on Allen Street, second floor front, in two rooms. One room had two windows, and one had none. The elevated railroad shut out the light and poured in the noise. To this home the man had returned to convalesce, in company with his wife and two children. He was planning to return as quickly as possible to the factory in which he had worked and in which he had developed tuberculosis. The factory was a sweatshop. Nothing could emphasize better the folly of keeping a man in a sanatorium while his family festered in the tenement, and the absurdity of sending him back to the social and industrial conditions out of which his illness had developed.

That much could be done to save the patients and the members of the family if the home conditions alone were adequately improved was proved by the constructive experiment conducted by the United Hebrew Charities and the Free Synagogue. Of the 41 cases in the arrested stage when taken under care, 85% had suffered no relapse. One was in a doubtful state at the end of the investigation, and five had relapsed through reinfection and were brought back to the arrested condition. With the accomplishments of this experiment and the results of the critical investigation of discharged cases, no one could escape the conclusion that something ought to be done. The eventual outcome, the results of many conferences, was creation of the "Joint Tuberculosis Committee" of New York, with a guaranteed income of from $60,000 to $70,000 a year with which to conduct a three-year experiment with 200 cases. To this fund the Free Synagogue alone contributed $10,000 a year. This larger experiment, we were convinced, would point the way to adequate care of the tuberculous. In this new program we planned to do something to stop the supply at its source. The Jewish tuberculous were in need not only of medical, nursing, and social care, but of something else, industrial care, or what we termed industrial convalescence. This was an entirely new concept in the care of the tuberculous. But to us it was an inevitable part of any constructive program.

The important question we faced was this: How should we meet this need of industrial convalescence? We considered first an agricultural colony, and I recall that our Committee spent much time in exploring areas in the Hudson Valley. We then considered an industrial colony and examined sites that seemed suitable. But neither would have proved successful in the case of the patients with whom we were working. We learned that they objected to remaining far away from the city and in almost every case the family refused to move to the country. They were restless and dissatisfied until they returned. Furthermore, we were convinced that the agricultural colony and the industrial colony would provide for but a small percentage of the patients discharged from Bedford Sanatorium.

We therefore concluded that the only thing was to organize an industrial regime that would accommodate itself to the needs of the post-sanatorium cases. We proceeded to organize a factory in which we could adjust the work to the patient. This, the most constructive part of the program for care of the Jewish tuberculous, led to establishment of what is now called the Altro Workshop. We were somewhat in doubt as to the type of work to develop. Some members of the Committee believed we would be compelled to arrange only light employment. But other members and the doctors aiding us were of the opinion that if the work were properly regulated the men and women would be able to engage in the same kinds of work they had been accustomed to in the textile field. The outcome of this experiment has more than justified our early expectations and convictions.

The Altro Workshop, situated in the Bronx, at present employs 150 men and women. These all receive medical, nursing, and social care, and are carried through the period of industrial convalescence. They are allowed to work only as many hours a day as the doctors believe their condition permits. They begin with two hours as a rule, and their employment is graduated over the weeks and months until they are prepared for normal employment. The Altro Workshop manufactures garments for hospitals and sanatoria, under supervision of the Department of Health. The annual output is about $750,000. But this large production is not so important as the wage that is paid the worker. Each is paid at the prevailing rate in the garment industry. The total paid out in 1952 amounted to $240,000.

The Altro Workshop program, however, provides the patients with something more than industrial convalescence. It gives him the encouraging feeling that he is able to work at least part-time and is helping to maintain himself. This is a direct contribution to recovery. Moreover, the patient feels that he is preserving his self-respect and developing self-reliance. A visit to the Workshop will convince anyone of the constructive character and wisdom of this program. A talk with anyone of the workers will convince the most skeptical that it is achieving unexpected medical results and paying unanticipated human dividends.

It has always been our hope that this program for rehabilitation of the Jewish tuberculous would not be limited to the number that can be comfortably and safely employed in the Altro Workshop. From year to year we have urged that it be extended to all patients eligible for industrial convalescence. The hospitals and clinics recognize the importance of this work; the city, and even the Federal Government, do so as well. But for some reason difficult to determine the program has not been adopted by other agencies, local, state, or national. It may be that other institutions, the City Department of Hospitals, and the National Government are more concerned with treatment of active tuberculosis than in rehabilitation of those brought to the arrested stage. The emphasis has been upon treatment of the sick rather than upon prevention of the disease and the industrial rehabilitation of the recovered. There has been, of course, in the United States as a whole and in New York City, a reduction both in the infection rate and the death rate of tuberculosis. This has been due, however, to improvement of living conditions more than to any other cause. Elimination of the sweatshop, the end of the "lung blocks" in the slum areas, and the rise in the standard of living have all contributed. Periodic examination of children and X-raying of groups in the community have also aided in detection of danger spots and prevention of trouble. We know and have known for a long time that tuberculosis is largely a disease of low resistance, and that the best way to prevent it is to raise the resistance rate through raising the standard of living.

I must also add that it has always been my hope that the Altro Workshop not limit itself to the industrial convalescence of the tuberculous; but enlarge its program to include other groups of the handicapped, physical and mental. Very early in our work we recommended that the Altro Workshop experiment with a group of cardiacs, men and women afflicted with heart trouble. During the last few years it has been discovered that men and women with heart conditions can also learn to work, and that they will improve if given adequate medical, nursing, social, and industrial care.

We also recommended a program of industrial convalescence with a mental hygiene group, but thus far this has not been done. This would require a different type of program. We are inclined to believe that the work program for the mental hygiene group should not be limited to a workshop. There really is no reason why the Altro Workshop with its trained and experienced staff should not become in time a rehabilitation center for all the handicapped of the Jewish community. Such a center is desperately needed, and it would be wise social planning for the Workshop to undertake this program in cooperation with the Federation Employment Service, which undertakes to test men and women for aptitudes and different types of employment.

In the development of this program I cannot speak too enthusiastically of the services rendered by the director of the work, Edward Hochhauser, his assistant, Miss Celia Hentel, and the staff they have trained and supervised. Both Mr. Hochhauser and Miss Hentel enrolled in one of the first classes for volunteers in the Free Synagogue when very young. Through their services as volunteers they became seriously interested in social work, and gradually equipped themselves for what has become a new profession. Today among the best executives in the tuberculosis field, they are constantly consulted by local and national experts. Had the Free Synagogue done nothing more than to initiate and aid in establishing this tuberculosis program and had we done nothing more than to give to the community two of its most efficient and socially-minded executives, we should have been justified in our conviction that we had made a definite and constructive contribution to social planning.

Synagogues in other parts of the country do not face the same problems in the tuberculosis field that we do in New York with its 2,000,000 Jews. I realize this fully. But there are few communities and there is no state in which the tuberculosis problem is fully covered. Any synagogue in search of a program of service will find the industrial convalescence or rehabilitation efforts among the tuberculous a current and acute need. The rehabilitation program developed by the Altro Workshop may readily serve as a pattern.

4. MENTAL HYGIENE PROGRAMS

The second experiment and program developing out of our experience at Bellevue Hospital has been in the mental hygiene field. We have conducted three projects, which together constitute one of our most important contributions to community service and social welfare.

The first began in 1912. In studying admissions to the psychiatric wards at Bellevue we discovered that 67% of the patients were under thirty-five. This tragedy of mental breakdown during early manhood and womanhood focused our attention upon an unmet need, and for a number of years we conducted a series of clinics at the Synagogue House in the hope of discovering the wisest way to take care of Jewish mental hygiene cases in New York. This first project lasted three years, costing a total of $21,618, to which the New York Foundation contributed $7,500 and the Free Synagogue $14,118. As a result of this project we presented to the New York Foundation a Report that I quote in full for its historical value and its social outlook.

PLAN FOR MENTAL HYGIENE WORK AMONG THE JEWS

In order that the Mental Hygiene Work conducted by the Mental Hygiene Committee of the Social Service Department of the Free Synagogue with the cooperation of the New York Foundation during the last three years may be enlarged and maintained in such manner as adequately to meet the needs in our community we recommend:

1. That a Committee be created to be known as the Committee on Mental Hygiene among the Jews. This Committee, we believe, ought to serve as a clearing house and coordinating agency for all Jewish mental hygiene cases as does the Committee for the Care of the Jewish Tuberculous recently organized in accordance with the plan suggested by Dr. Frankel and now operating in the field of tuberculosis among the Jews. This Committee, we believe, ought to be representative in character and composed of members delegated by different organizations interested in Mental Hygiene in this city, especially the United Hebrew Charities, the Free Synagogue, the Mental Hygiene Committee of the State Charities Aid Association, and the National Committee on Mental Hygiene.

2. That the Committee so to be created conduct a campaign of education and enlightenment in Mental Hygiene among the Jewish people. This campaign could be worked out in cooperation with the Jewish Press and the Committee on Mental Hygiene, both of which have already arranged exhibits and published literature which could be modified and used in translation among the Jewish people.

3. That the Committee so to be created establish and maintain Clinics for the care of Jewish mental hygiene cases in Greater New York similar to the two clinics that have been conducted during the past three years. The Committee and Clinics would concern themselves with the following groups of cases:

A. *Cases Discharged from Insane Asylums and in Need of Home Supervision and Convalescent Care.* During the summer of 1915, in the course of an investigation which we conducted, we found that there were in the four State Insane Asylums covering the Metropolitan district the following number of Jewish patients:

Manhattan State Hospital.... men..... 481		
women .. 619	1100
Central Islip State Hospital... men..... 463		
women .. 323	786
Kings Park State Hospital.... men..... 199		
women .. 258	457
Long Island State Hospital.... men..... 39		
women .. 45	84
Total......	2427

We also found that during the year the following number of Jewish patients were discharged:

Manhattan State Hospital..............	246
Central Islip State Hospital	300
Kings Park State Hospital..............	86
Long Island State Hospital.............	40
Total......	672

Almost every patient discharged is in need of after-care, as is recommended by the State Hospital Commission in its last Annual Report. This after-care would save many from relapsing, would facilitate the recovery of every case, and could be given through the Clinics that this Committee would conduct.

B. *Cases of Mild Mental Disturbance.* These patients are discharged from the psychopathic wards of Manhattan and Brooklyn as not sufficiently advanced to require institutional treatment, but they are in constant danger of growing worse. Our experience teaches us that in a very large percentage of cases the patients can be saved from the Insane Asylum by change of occupation, readjustment in the home, and careful training and discipline on the part of Medical Social Workers who have specialized in Mental Hygiene Care.

C. *Families of Patients in the Insane Asylum.* In these cases the father or mother is sent to the Insane Asylum and the rest of the family are left in sad need of assistance and supervision. Both these needs, including examination and adequate relief, could be met if the Committee on Mental Hygiene Among the Jews and the United Hebrew Charities could effect such cooperation with each other as now obtains between the United Hebrew Charities and the Committee for the Care of the Jewish Tuberculous.

D. *The Alien Insane.* This class consists of a large number of men and women that are in danger of deportation under the Federal Immigration Laws. In many instances that have come to our attention we find deportation not justifiable, and these cases the Committee could continue to consider and save from the tragedy of being torn from their families and incarcerated in institutions in Russia, a procedure that utterly robs recoverable cases of any hope of restoration to health and sanity.

4. That the Committee so to be created be aided to secure a fund of $21,000 for the first year. Four Clinics we believe are necessary in order to cover the work in Greater New York. The annual budget for each Clinic we calculate to be as follows:

Rental	$ 200
Clinic Psychiatrist	300
Medical Social Worker	1200
Assistant Social Worker	900
Total	$2600

Four Clinics at $2600 each; total $10,400.

In addition the Committee would require the services of a Director and Secretary. The salary of the Director would be about $2000; of the secretary $720. To this ought to be added about $400 for stationery, postage, and incidental expenses. This is exclusive of such financial assistance as may be necessary and such supplementary aid as may be required in addition to that now allowed by the United Hebrew Charities. On

the basis of our experience during the last three years we estimate that relief for the number of cases that would come
under care in four Clinics would be about $8000. In other
words, the Committee would require the following sum:

For Four Clinics	$10,400
For Director	2,000
For Secretary	720
For stationery, postage, and incidental expenses	400
For Relief	8,000
Total	$21,520

Of this amount the Free Synagogue is ready to contribute the
sum of $5000 for the first year and earnestly trusts that the
New York Foundation will find it possible to make a similar
grant. This would leave $11,000 or $12,000 for the Committee
to secure, which we believe the community at large would be
willing to contribute toward this new and very urgent work
among our people.

This Committee, the creation of which we recommend, would
also be able to give a close and comprehensive study to the
whole problem of Mental Hygiene among the Jews and would
in time take such steps as may be necessary to create and establish institutions and agencies that are desperately needed in
order to do the most effective work, such as:

a. *A Convalescent Home for Mental Hygiene Cases.* At
the present time no Convalescent Home in the vicinity
of New York will accept mental cases, and it is necessary
to place the patients in Sanatoria for the Insane or in
private families, both of which methods are most inad-
visable.

b. *A Workshop for Mental Hygiene Cases.* The great
need in the majority of cases is suitable occupation.
Proper occupation is in Mental Hygiene Work a therapeutic agent and is employed as such in the more pro-

gressive institutions for the care of the insane. For convalescence and reestablishment it is absolutely essential.

c. *A Psychiatric Institute.*   At the present time all patients with symptoms of mental disturbance are committed to Psychopathic Wards of Bellevue Hospital or Kings County Hospital. Admission to these Wards at once classes the patient as a public charge and in the minds of their friends and relatives places them under suspicion of insanity. What is needed is a Mental Hygiene Institute in which these patients can be observed and in which many would clear up and be saved from the Insane Asylum.

This larger work, however, would require sums of money of which we do not think at present. But the funds, we believe, the Committee might be able to secure from men and women to whom the seriousness and urgency of this whole problem would appeal. Mental Hygiene, the community more and more will come to realize, is one of the fundamental and most difficult problems which we have to face.

The second Mental Hygiene project was conducted in the psychiatric wards of Bellevue Hospital, upon which we concentrated all our efforts after relinquishing to the city the care of the Jewish patients in the general medical and surgical wards. In the psychiatric wards of Bellevue Hospital we developed a program of service to meet the needs of the Jewish patients and their families, because the psychiatric wards are not treatment wards but diagnostic and distributing centers in which the patients are kept for only a limited time and then committed to a State Hospital or discharged to the community. The nature of this service was necessarily temporary and emergent in character. We soon discovered that this program and service for both patients and families was desperately needed, for there is no group that is so shaken and shattered by the onset of disease as the group of patients admitted to the psychiatric wards and their families. Men and women can understand a case of pneumonia or appendicitis. But it is difficult for them to comprehend a case of mental derangement or emotional disturbance.

About 3000 Jewish patients are admitted to the psychiatric wards of Bellevue Hospital every year, and this group probably constitutes the largest Jewish group of psychiatric cases to be found anywhere. The work with the patients, of course, was limited because of the short time patients were housed in the wards. But many needs developed in the families we were able to meet. The most important fact we discovered, however, was that an increasingly large number of Jewish patients were being discharged to relatives and friends either "on contract" or "in custody." Nothing was being done to follow up these cases or to aid them in making the necessary adjustments in the community.

As a result of this experiment in the wards, we presented to Federation a plan contained in the following:

RECOMMENDATIONS

On the basis of our study and experience in the mental hygiene field, not only during the period of this current experiment but over a period of thirty-five years of service, we are convinced that the time has arrived for the Free Synagogue Social Service Department and Federation to establish a new agency in the community. This agency, to be known perhaps as "The Jewish Mental Hygiene Committee," or by some other title, would undertake to serve in the mental hygiene field like other centralized agencies in the fields of tuberculosis, child care, delinquency, and care of the aged. The program of the Jewish Mental Hygiene Committee, however, would differ in many ways from the programs of other centralized agencies, and should undertake to develop, we believe, the following sections:

I

An Information and Consultation Center to which men and women could go for authoritative information and guidance and where they could whenever necessary have a preliminary interview in order to determine their needs and the best way in which the needs could be met. This Information and Consultation Center would require a staff composed of a psychiatrist (part time), a psychiatric social worker, a director, and a secretary. In the course of the years, the Free Synagogue Social Service Department has accumulated a vast amount of information concerning state hospitals, private sanatoria, available psychiatrists, and other matters in the field of mental hygiene, and during the last two years has actually served as an Information and Consultation Center in embryonic form. This material and service could now be made available to the general public.

II

A staff of psychiatric social workers who would be stationed in the psychiatric wards of Bellevue Hospital and Kings County Hospital to meet the immediate and emergency needs of the Jewish patients. We are convinced that the Jewish group admitted to the psychiatric wards requires psychiatric social workers who have a thorough understanding of the background, the customs, the language, and the problems peculiar to the Jewish people. One psychiatric social worker is needed for every 50 patients admitted, and a headworker or supervisor is also required for every five workers. Whether the paid social workers should be paid by the city or maintained by the Jewish community is one of the problems that must be carefully considered. It is probable that the Free Synagogue and Federation could gradually withdraw their staff as the city increases its allowance for psychiatric social workers.

III

A staff of psychiatric social workers is required to cover the extra-mural or follow-up program that is needed in both the families of patients committed to state institutions and in the care of patients discharged to the custody of relatives and physicians and friends. This group is uncovered by any existing agency, and from our study of community agencies and facilities we are convinced that the follow-up program cannot be undertaken by any existing agency in the community. The program as we envisage it requires an agency with a staff especially trained for this type of service and with resources sufficient to meet the needs of this group of patients and their families. How many psychiatric social workers would be required it is difficult to determine in advance, but we urge that this section of the work begin with five psychiatric social workers, a supervisor, and two secretaries.

IV

An educational program that would through lectures and literature aid the members of the Jewish group to a better understanding of the meaning of mental hygiene and mental hygiene care is greatly needed. This is an urgent need in the community at the present time and would do much to save the members of the Jewish community from the dangers of misinformation and misdirection in the field of mental hygiene. This program could be developed through such agencies in synagogues, community centers, fraternal organizations, and other groups that reach the people directly.

V

A Division of Research that would study the needs of the mental hygiene group in the Jewish community as a whole, and that would determine the facilities that are required in order that the needs of the Jewish mental hygiene group may be adequately met, is recommended. The staff of the Research Division would not limit itself, as we understand it, to the groups of patients in the psychiatric wards in city hospitals, but would also study the needs of groups outside both city hospitals and state institutions. Only small segments of the large mental hygiene problems of the Jewish community have been studied thus far and there is urgent need of a study that would be comprehensive and authoritative.

VI

In order that this new agency may be established without delay and the different sections or divisions developed ade-.

quately, we urge that the Mental Hygiene Committee of the Social Service Department of the Free Synagogue be enlarged to include representatives of other agencies in the community interested and active in the field of mental hygiene. And we urge that this enlarged committee be entrusted with the task of developing the program as far and as fast as available funds and resources will permit.

This report was presented to the Federation of Jewish Philanthropies with a budget that called for an expenditure of $102,900 a year. The officers of Federation studied the program carefully. But the Distribution Committee found it impossible to appropriate the funds with which to create and maintain the agency to be known as the Jewish Mental Hygiene Committee. They therefore suggested that the Social Service Department of the Synagogue limit itself to the extra-mural program, that is, to the patients discharged from the psychiatric wards of Bellevue Hospital to relatives and friends. We agreed to undertake this program and to maintain it in cooperation with Federation for a period of three years.

This program has become our third mental hygiene experiment and our latest project. As far as we are able to learn this is the first program of study and service to be made of a group of patients discharged from the psychiatric wards to the community. We believe that the conclusions we have reached and the recommendations we are prepared to make will be of interest and assistance not only to the Jewish but to the general community as well.

CONCLUSIONS AND RECOMMENDATIONS

Introduction

The latest project that we have conducted in the mental hygiene field began October 1, 1948. This project has concerned itself with the Jewish patients discharged from the psychiatric wards of Bellevue Hospital to relatives and friends in the community. The purpose of this experiment has been three-fold: 1) to study the needs of this group of patients and their families; 2) to develop a program of service to meet the needs of this group; 3) to indicate the needs that could not be met because of inadequate resources or the absence of community facilities. As far as we are able to learn, this is the first program of study and service to be made of a group of patients discharged from the psychiatric wards to the community. We believe that the conclusions we have reached and the recommendations we are prepared to make will be of interest and assistance not only to the Jewish community but to the general community as well.

I

Our first conclusion is that the patients discharged from the psychiatric wards of Bellevue Hospital to the community together with their families constitute a group desperately in need of service, but heretofore unserved adequately by any social agency. This group is growing in numbers as the years pass. A decade ago not more than 20% of the Jewish patients discharged from the

psychiatric wards of Bellevue Hospital were discharged to relatives and friends in the community. The rest, about 80%, were
committed to state hospitals. At the present time, the percentage
of Jewish patients discharged to the community has risen to 47%.
This increase has been due in part to the fact that state hospitals are
overcrowded and understaffed; and also in part to the fact that
psychiatrists in charge of the wards are now of the opinion that a
larger percentage of patients can be maintained in the community
if they have adequate care and service.

II

Our second conclusion is that between 70% and 75% of the
Jewish patients discharged from the psychiatric wards of Bellevue
Hospital and taken under care can be maintained upon a reasonable level of efficiency if they are given adequate casework, psychiatric, and other forms of social care. A most important point in
this program of service lies in the approach of our agency to
patients and their families. Many social agencies believe that
they should wait until people apply to them for care. We find,
however, that with this group in the mental hygiene field the
wisest plan is to offer service and to do this at the earliest possible
moment.

The reasons for offering service and for encouraging the patients
and their families to come to us are clear and convincing. In the
first place, in many cases the patients and their families are not
aware of their own needs and do not recognize their need for help
in achieving improvement and recovery. In the second place, many
patients and their families either disguise or deliberately misrepresent their needs. They require patient assistance and skillful
interpretation in order to recognize their real needs and to accept
the service they require. In the third place, many patients and
families for different reasons, personal or social, conceal their needs.
This is a difficult group with which to work, for it takes much time
and long experience and expert skill to uncover the needs and to
aid and encourage patients and families to face their problems
frankly and without fear.

The results of offering service to the patients and their families have been encouraging. In the first six months of our service only 52% of the patients to whom we offered service responded. In the second year of our service 68% responded to our letters and offer of service. An intensive follow-up for a period of six months brought the total up to 71%. Another point to emphasize is that these patients and families, when they respond, need guidance and supervision in establishing contact with the agency in the community best able to serve them. Like most people in the community they know little of the agencies operating in the mental hygiene field and without counsel and guidance they waste much precious time and money. Only an agency specializing in the mental hygiene field is acquainted with all the community resources and is able to give these men and women the direction and assistance they require in the hour of need.

III

Our third conclusion is that these patients and their families require in most instances not a short-term but a long-term period of casework and psychiatric and social care. When we began this experiment, we thought it would be possible to close cases within a short period, that is, within a period of three months. This we have been able to do with some cases. But the great majority have been in need of sustained and continued service. In other words, we find that cases in the mental hygiene field are seldom completely cured. In most cases the condition can only be improved and the patient must be carried forward from month to month under adequate casework, psychiatric and social care, and supervision and encouragement. In this field of service we must expect lapses and recurrent episodes, and it is most important that in every case the patient should feel that there is someone and some agency to which he can turn when a recurrent crisis develops. This in itself gives the patient a sense of assurance and support.

IV

Our fourth conclusion is that if the program of care we have developed is given this group of patients and their families, the community can be saved a tremendous cost in both expenditure and in human suffering. Without this care patients lapse to a lower level of efficiency or relapse into conditions that require commitment to institutions. The average cost of care of the service we have developed is about $100 per patient per year. In the state hospital the cost of care at present is about $75 per month. If the patient is kept for a year the cost of care is $900. We also find that in addition to the cost of care of the patient in an institution, the community is frequently compelled to cover the cost of care of the family of the patient. If the patient has been a wage-earner or a mother in the household, the community is under the necessity of taking the children under care as well.

V

Our fifth conclusion is that there are a number of needs in this group that we have not been able to meet and that cannot be met at the present time because of the limitation of facilities in the community. These needs are chiefly: 1) convalescent care; 2) a work program; 3) a program of care for children who are discharged from the psychiatric wards of the hospital; 4) a program of care for the adolescent group; 5) a program of care for the aged and senile.

1. *CONVALESCENT CARE.* It is very difficult to persuade existing convalescent homes to accept mental hygiene patients. Only in rare cases and through constant persuasion are we able to secure convalescent care for members of this group. We therefore urge that one of the existing convalescent homes be encouraged to equip itself for the convalescent care of mental hygiene cases. This would mean a staff with special training and experience in mental hygiene, and it would also mean special facilities, including occupational therapy. These patients now suffer exclusion without good reason. They are just as much in need of convalescent care as patients who are recovering from medical or surgical conditions, and they are no more dangerous.

2. *WORK PROGRAM.* It is very difficult, if not impossible, to place the majority of these patients in customary occupations. Most of them are in need of simple routine forms of work that will not overtax their mental and emotional capacity. The only way in

which to provide employment for these patients is through a specially developed work program that would include vocational guidance, vocational training, and vocational placement. Our suggestion is that the Altro Workshops, which have had thirty years of experience in the tuberculosis field and recently in the cardiac field, be established as the rehabilitation center for the Jewish community. As a rehabilitation center this agency could develop a work program for mental hygiene cases as well as for the tuberculous and the cardiacs.

3. *CHILDREN DISCHARGED FROM PSYCHIATRIC WARDS.* These children constitute a special problem in the community that no agency is undertaking to solve at the present time. In most cases these children are diagnosed as childhood schizophrenia. They require a special type of service which includes not only casework and psychiatric care but also a special educational and social program. The public school system is not equipped to accept these children. In order to meet their needs it would be necessary to organize a new and enlarged program of service. Perhaps this could be undertaken by the Jewish Board of Guardians, that is now developing a more intensive program of care for disturbed children.

4. *THE ADOLESCENT GROUP.* There is no agency in the community at the present time that is equipped to serve adequately the adolescent boy or girl who is mentally and emotionally disturbed. This is one of the most urgent needs in community life. We are now convinced, as a result of our experience and findings, that this group of adolescents is in need of intensive, individualized service that includes counseling, psychiatric casework, and vocational service. We have found that when such services are made available to the adolescent, he or she can be aided to make a reasonable adjustment in social life, and that the community can be saved the cost of care through other agencies and in city and state institutions.

5. *THE SENILE GROUP.* There is a large group of senile cases that cannot be admitted to existing homes for the aged and infirm; and that on the other hand are not ill enough to require commitment to state institutions. In fact, they do not need the kind of care that is provided in an institution for the insane. A program of

care is needed for this group that lies just between the home for the aged and infirm and the program of the state institution. Until the state is prepared to set aside a pavilion in one of the state hospitals for this group, we urge that one of the homes for the aged and infirm in the Jewish community undertake to develop a program of service for senile cases. This would not be difficult, for some of the homes for the aged and infirm are now taking care of the senile cases that develop in their own institutional population.

The total cost of the third experiment for three years of study and service amounted to $150,000. Of this amount Federation contributed $90,000 and the Social Service Department of the Free Synagogue $60,000. In order that this large sum of money expended in the development of the experiment, and the three years of study and service invested in the project, not be a loss, we recommended to Federation that it consider with the Free Synagogue the four possibilities to ensure continuation and advancement of this program and adequate care of the large group of patients discharged from the psychiatric wards of Bellevue Hospital to the community.

The first course of action we recommended was that the city be asked to take over the program and develop it as the after-care division of the psychiatric service in Bellevue Hospital and Kings County Hospital. We realized, however, that the city was not prepared to do this and would probably not consider it for many years to come. It is our hope, however, that eventually the city and state will recognize the importance of this service and accept the program.

The second course of action we recommended was that with the help of Federation a Jewish Mental Hygiene Committee be organized to take over the staff and program and patients. This course of action we have recommended a number of times, and we still consider it the most advisable. So we stated in our letter to Federation, dated January 22, 1951:

"We have carefully considered what recommendation to make upon the basis of the conclusions we are reaching and our recommendation is this: that a new agency be organized to take over and to develop the project that we have carried to the point of demonstration. It is now clear to us that this group of patients and their families heretofore un-cared for are desperately in need of the program of social casework and psychiatric service that we have built up since the beginning of the ex-periment. We believe that Federation will agree that an experiment that has taken three years to develop and that has involved the expenditure of $150,000 should not be allowed to lapse. The need is too evident and urgent and the program too clear and conclusive. We shall, of course, be prepared to continue this program until another agency is ready to take it over, providing Federation will continue its support."

In the Jewish field we need a Jewish Mental Hygiene Committee to develop a mental hygiene program, as the Committee for the Care of the Jewish Tuberculous has developed the tuberculosis program.

A third course of action would be to transfer the program to some other existing agency that is interested especially in mental hygiene and mental hygiene problems. Our first choice was Hill-side Hospital, which could develop this program as an extra-mural division of their work. Hillside with its background and staff would be the logical agency in the field.

The fourth course is expressed in the following recommendation to Federation:

"If, however, it is impossible to create a new agency, the Jewish Mental Hygiene Committee, or to transfer this work to Hillside, we see no other course of action open to us but to continue to develop the program and as we stated in our letter to Federation on April 25, 1951." We quote the following paragraph:

"This program of service however is too urgent and too desperately needed to lapse at this point. We are therefore willing to continue to develop the program with such funds as are available from the Syna-gogue and Federation in the hope that in time the Jewish community will accept our recommendation to establish a Jewish Mental Hygiene agency that will correspond with the Committee for the Care of the Jewish Tuberculous in the health field, and the Child Adoption Com-mittee in the child care field. Just as soon as we have assembled our ma-terial and prepared our report on our three years experiment, we shall submit the full report and our conclusions to Federation and also to the Commissioner of Hospitals and the State Mental Hygiene Department, in the conviction that both the city and the state as well as the Jewish community will recognize the value and the validity of this program of care for this group of patients who heretofore have been unserved."

Hillside Hospital, however, declined to accept the program as part of its larger work, on the ground that Federation was not prepared to allow sufficient funds to develop it adequately. The program, therefore, was submitted to the psychiatric division of Mt. Sinai Hospital, which agreed to continue it for a year and to do everything possible to serve the discharged patients with the amount of money Federation was prepared to allow, that is, a sum of $25,000.

A full and complete report of this third project has been carefully prepared and published. Entitled "What Becomes Of Them?" it contains a detailed study divided into the following sections: Introduction, Description of Group, Methods of Work, Needs Discovered, Cost and Continuation of Third Experiment, Conclusions and Recommendations. This report has been distributed widely to mental hygiene agencies, has awakened interest in every part of the country, and has received many interesting and encouraging comments and criticisms. The following comment is by Dr. E. R. Schlesinger, Associate Director, Division of Medical Services, State of New York Department of Health:

"I found this report of great interest, especially the so-called 'third experiment' on services to patients discharged to the community from the Bellevue Hospital Psychiatric Division. It represents an important contribution to the study of community facilities needed for adequate care of patients with psychiatric conditions outside of mental hospitals, especially from the viewpoint of reducing the need for subsequent mental hospitalization and for maximum rehabilitation of the patient to make him at least partially self-supporting. The objectives of the 'third experiment' are quite similar to those of studies carried out or proposed by this Department in other health fields, i.e., to study the needs of patients and their families, to develop a program of service to meet these needs, and to indicate unmet needs requiring further action. Praiseworthy also is the desire to study the problem scientifically and to appraise and evaluate the results properly.

"The report suggests very strongly that if the services provided in this 'third experiment' are continued, 'the community can be saved a tremendous cost in both expenditure and in human suffering.' It points out the high cost in care of the patient in the event institutionalization becomes necessary, and it also points to the cost to the community when the latter is under the necessity of taking the children under care if the patient has been a wage earner or a mother in the household. Unfortunately, this conclusion is not documented by any detailed analysis of the end results in the group of patients given services under the study. These data are presumably available, and it seems to me that they should be included as completely as possible in the report. The detailed statistical analysis of the types of patients seen in the Bellevue Hospital Psychiatric Division is of interest, but this information does not have as much bearing on types of community services needed as would an analysis of the end results of those actually given care."

We urge synagogues in other communities to study these conclusions and recommendations carefully. The mental hygiene group constitutes one of our largest problems in every community. It has been estimated that one out of every ten in the population will at some time during life be in need of psychiatric care; and that one out of every 18 or 19 in the population will be in need of institutional care. These patients come from every strata of society. The question we must ask ourselves is this: What can our synagogue do in cooperation with other agencies, local and state, to assure these stricken men and women and children the different forms of care that they so desperately need? There is much that every congregation can accomplish in every community to aid in the development of an adequate program of mental hygiene care.

5. CHILD ADOPTION PROGRAM

From the inception of the Social Service Department we have been interested and active in the care of babies, children, and adolescents. Some of our earliest projects were concerned with these groups and their needs. But it was not until 1916 that the Child Adoption Program of the Free Synagogue was organized, in a very simple way. A relative of Mrs. Stephen S. Wise, always interested in babies and children, asked if she could not obtain a child for adoption. Mrs. Wise, visiting the orphan asylums in New York, found a lovely little baby for this childless couple. Other couples heard of this experience, within and without the Synagogue, and in the course of a few months Mrs. Wise was searching for babies and placing them in homes both within and without New York City.

Out of this small beginning the Child Adoption Committee of the Free Synagogue has developed, and become one of the most important agencies in the community, one of the most progressive child adoption organizations in the country. The babies have come from unmarried mothers. In the early years these were of the immigrant group, young women who had come to America from countries in Eastern Europe, without proper guidance or guardianship. They readily became victims of unscrupulous men, who deserted them as soon as they became pregnant. Within recent years the babies have come from another group, high school and college women who have fallen victim to a new group of men, with the breakdown of moral standards in our communities. No baby is accepted until the Committee is convinced that this is the wise course from the point of view of both baby and mother. In fact, one of the earliest developments was establishment of a special "Committee for Unmarried Mothers."

Few realize the problems that arise in transfer of a child from an unmarried mother to a committee for adoption. It is true that some young women are only too anxious to be relieved of the burden of an unwanted child and gladly agree to the transfer as soon as the baby is born. But in almost every case the surrender of a child is a severe shock to the mother, and she must be carried through this period of stress even more carefully than through the months of pregnancy. Only those who have been in direct and immediate contact with this field can realize the seriousness of the problems involved, and what care must be exercised in not only arranging for transfer of the child but in aftercare of the mother. For, once the child is transferred, the mother knows that as a rule she will not be able to see the child again; and in many cases this results in a trauma or physical shock that may prove serious, and usually does.

Only recently a woman of forty spoke to me after the service and asked for an appointment. I found her nervous and depressed, filled with a sense of guilt. She finally confessed that twenty years before, while still unmarried, she had given birth to a baby girl. At first she tried to keep the child with her, but finally found this too difficult for her resources. She placed the infant for adoption but never forgave herself for surrendering her baby. I was able to trace the child, who had grown into a splendid young woman, had married a physician, and had a baby of her own. I succeeded in re-establishing the relationship between this woman and her own offspring, and she took the train for a Western city. There, living with her daughter and grandchild, she writes that she has completely recovered from her nervousness and depression and lost all sense of blame. Nothing could illustrate better the need for the aftercare of unmarried mothers and the guilt they suffer through surrender of their children.

The placement of children for adoption means more than is implied in the motto: "A homeless child in a childless home." Every baby accepted for placement is now sent to a shelter maintained by the Committee. Here it is examined by a pediatrician and a psychologist for at least a period of six months. When the child is declared normal and ready for adoption, the Committee endeavors to place it with an eligible couple on the waiting list. The list is always long, as in every child adoption agency, and each couple is carefully studied before being accepted. The Committee has established criteria in determining whether the couple applying for a baby is suitable. This includes their age, economic circumstances, cultural development, religious affiliation, and the health of both the man and the woman.

The number of babies placed by the Committee, however, is limited, and at the present time it is not able to place more than 100 to 125 a year. This is the result of the "black market" or traffic in babies that has developed in different parts of the country. Little groups of physicians and lawyers and nurses organize themselves into a self-constituted agency, and in some manner make contact with unmarried mothers and with couples who want babies. There is no investigation made of either the background of the baby or the qualifications of the couple, and many tragedies result from this unauthorized, and in some states illegal, form of placement. It is difficult and disappointing for people who want to adopt children to wait their turn, sometimes for months and years, but this is the only way in which to assure proper placement of the child, whose welfare is the Committee's prime concern. The only solution is a law making placement of children for adoption illegal except through an authorized agency. The State is, after all, the guardian of its children and the children are wards of the State.

Every child given for adoption is saved, it is clear, from the hampering influence of institutionalism during its most plastic and formative period. No matter how well-equipped the institution, or scientific the care, no science and no institution can take the place of a home and the love of foster parents. This fact has finally been accepted by the community.

It is not too much to say that the child adoption procedure has changed the whole program of child care in the Jewish field in New York. Fifty years ago every child that became a charge upon the community was placed in an orphan asylum. A little later we began rather hesitatingly to board out children, first in foster homes and then with their widowed mothers. But we came to the conclusion that, where the child is without parents or relatives willing and competent to rear them, the best plan is adoption. Fifty years ago we thought of the institution first and adoption last. Now we think of adoption first and the institution last. The result is that only those children are now placed in institutions who are physically or psychically handicapped and who require institutional treatment or custodial care.

The Child Adoption Committee of the Free Synagogue, especially under the chairmanship of Justine Wise Polier, daughter of Dr. and Mrs. Wise and a judge in the Children's Court, has also encouraged legislation that outlaws unauthorized adoption procedures and makes adoption more scientific. Only those who have suffered through the initial stages of this work can appreciate the difficulties we faced in opposing both unauthorized placement and institutional care. It is interesting to note that fifty years ago what was known as the Home for Hebrew Infants, today does not contain one child. In fact, it has become an institution for the care of the aged and the infirm. Both the Jewish and the general community have been saved the cost of care for every child placed for adoption. The total sum is unbelievably large.

Child Care

One of the first projects we organized was the program for care of boys and girls in destitute families and substandard neighborhoods. These children were in constant danger of physical, mental, or moral breakdown. The program began with a simple service of sending children to camps during the summer. But we soon discovered that the camp program took care of only a small part of the problem and that it must be supplemented with a program of service for the rest of the year. This we developed for a group of boys and girls, out of funds especially contributed and set aside for the purpose. They were organized into groups and classes that met in settlements and neighborhood houses, and were supervised by select and trained leaders. Some of the leaders were paid and others volunteers. This program, however, we have recently terminated, both because of limitation of funds and because other agencies have risen in the course of the years, able to serve these boys and girls through neighborhood centers. The Educational Alliance, for example, has taken over the group and the program we developed in cooperation with this agency during an experimental period of two years. The Men's Club of the Free Synagogue continues to send boys to camp and also arranges for little parties and entertainments. At the Father and Son Dinner of the Men's Club, a group of boys is invited as guests of men who have no sons of their own.

At the present time our work with children is largely limited to care of a group of boys and girls referred to us by the New York City Youth Board, and to others referred from the public schools and the Bureau of Child Guidance. The New York Youth Board is an agency created by the State in 1945 to search out and serve children in congested and underprivileged sections of the city, in the hope of saving them from delinquency. The New York City Youth Board works in cooperation with the public schools, studies the children referred to them by teachers and principals and other members of the staff, and then arranges with private agencies for the care of those in need of service.

As a rule these children come from homes in which there are serious problems. Sometimes there is an estrangement between mother and father; or the mother or father is separated from the family; or one parent has disappeared altogether or is dead. The youngsters are all from dismal and dangerous neighborhoods, bleak and barren homes, and families broken through desertion, separation, divorce, or death. This means that not only the child must be taken under care but the family also. For not the child but the family is the unit of suffering, and therefore must be the unit of care. The children are seriously disturbed and in need of expert study and skillful treatment. In many cases we have found it possible to re-educate the members of the family to a better understanding of the children, and in virtually every case we have been able to help the child through our program of care. To what degree the New York City Youth Board through its affiliated agencies will be able to save boys and girls from delinquency is now being demonstrated.

In order to serve the children adequately it has been necessary for us to build up a personnel of doctors and psychiatrists and a staff of trained and experienced social workers. For in many cases referred to us we have found it necessary to arrange for either medical or psychiatric care or both, and in addition social work with the child and the family. Some of the children have been found in distress because of a physical weakness or defect. One would be suffering with a glandular condition and another with rheumatism. Almost every child was emotionally disturbed and in need of psychotherapy, and frequently the source of the trouble lay in the family situation.

One little girl of twelve was referred to us by the public school, with a statement from the teacher that she fell asleep every day during the morning sessions. A visit to the home and a talk with the mother disclosed the reasons. The little girl's father had deserted the family. The mother was serving as janitress in the apartment house, and every morning woke the girl up at five o'clock to help her gather the garbage cans and the ashes. The child was utterly exhausted before she left home. In a later chapter I shall deal more in detail with the causes of misbehavior and maladjustment we have discovered.

6. PROGRAM FOR ADOLESCENTS

One of the urgent needs in both the Jewish and general community at present is adequate care of adolescents, both boys and girls. The agencies for the care of children carry them through the age of sixteen, but little is done to aid the adolescent group after that age. At a recent meeting of the heads of the child care agencies in the community the chairmen were startled to learn that they graduated children at the age of sixteen, and knew very little of what happened to them during their adolescent period.

We are convinced as a result of our studies and experiments that this group requires a well-developed and comprehensive program that includes different forms of care. Even the normal adolescent is in need of treatment that we are only beginning to understand and to develop. It is a common thing to hear the adolescent say that his parents and others do not understand him; the truth of the matter is that he is right. We do not understand all the physical forces that awaken and develop during the pubescent and adolescent period; and we certainly do not understand all the psychological forces that emerge and assert themselves during this difficult period. If we had an instrument that could X-ray the psychical life of the adolescent from year to year, we should probably discover that there are few who pass through that stage into adulthood without conflict and maladjustment. The adolescent is reborn into an entirely new world, both within and without, and it is as difficult for him to adjust himself as it is for the baby to adjust itself to the world into which it is born.

If this is true, and I believe it is, of the so-called normal adolescent it is doubly true of the disturbed adolescent, that is, of the one who suffers from physical, psychical, or social weaknesses or defects. This group of disturbed adolescents constitutes a grave problem in our community and in every community. They are at the present time inadequately served, as no one will doubt who is acquainted with the field. But we have found that when an adequate service is made available to the disturbed adolescent he can be helped to make a reasonable adjustment to social life and that the community can be saved the cost of care through agencies and institutions. These adolescent boys and girls have been referred to us by the high schools and colleges and social agencies of the city, and it is interesting to note that when we wrote to the schools to inform them of the service we were developing we were amazed to discover the urgency of the need and how welcome the service would be.

There is no social wisdom in assuming that the adolescent group in the community can be cared for without a full and comprehensive program. Every mother and father who has reared children through that period knows how difficult the adolescent can become, and indeed does, even in a normal, well-regulated home. Only the ignorant or the indifferent are unaware of what happens to children at that stage. If even intelligent parents are in search of counsel and guidance, how much more are they needed in the case of the adolescent coming from a home in which there is ignorance or estrangement, or one destitute of the insight and the understanding that only a well-developed parent can give. I do not want an outside agency to substitute for mother and father. But we must recognize that mothers and fathers are in many cases unable to cope with the problems their adolescent children present.

The synagogues of the country are developing, as are the churches, what are called "Youth Groups." But there are few that have on their staff men and women especially trained to understand and to aid the adolescent. The youth programs I have studied are in charge of young men and women themselves little more than adolescents, lacking the training and experience to permit them to counsel the adolescent wisely and guide him through these turbulent years. In fact the programs in operation include little more than social gatherings. These are necessary at this stage of development as at other periods. But they can form only one part of a suitable program. I cannot help but feel that in most synagogues and churches the most precious thing youth possesses is disregarded, that is, the spirit of idealism. Little if anything is done to cultivate the spirit in youth. It is no wonder that young men and women become cynical. We do so little to save them. A great teacher, Hugo Muensterberg, once said that people respond at the level at which we strike. At Harvard he found, as we have, that young men and women respond at the elevation of the highest ideals when the ideals are presented by one who is himself an idealist.

The need for an adequate program for children and adolescents is evident to every person now engaged in the field of service. We are all distressed over conditions. During the last fifty years we have created a multitude of agencies for the care of children; and on every level, local, state, and national, in studying and in serving children. In fact, the twentieth has been known as "The Century of the Child." The series of White House Conferences on Children that began in 1909 and the establishment of the Children's Bureau in Washington are proof of our concern and eagerness to save children from the hazards of childhood.

But in spite of everything we have done there is a nation-wide increase in what is called "juvenile delinquency." The reports from Washington and from sources across the country not only tell us that there has been an increase in the number of juvenile delinquents; the age of juvenile delinquency has dropped steadily during the last quarter century and, worse than this, the offenses committed grow more serious from day to day. Today children are arrested and brought to court for commission of acts we formerly believed only adult criminals capable of—burglary, holdups, arson, and murder. These facts, that during the past fifty years we have made children the center of attention, and that in spite of this there is a serious and distressing increase in the problem of delinquency, are sufficient to give us grave concern. Certainly the synagogues and churches, which are among the guardians of the moral life of the community, cannot remain either indifferent or inactive; otherwise they convict themselves of their own indifference and delinquency.

Scholarship Program

One of the most interesting and beneficent activities of the Social Service Department of the Free Synagogue is the Elizabeth Engel Hoffman Scholarship Fund. This was established by Mr. and Mrs.

Charles Hoffman, charter members of the Free Synagogue, who suffered the tragic loss of a lovely young daughter. In her memory they established a Fund which yields about $1000 a year, for scholarships to young women who wish to prepare themselves for vocations and professions. The committee in charge studies every application, and allows scholarships that range from a small amount each month to larger sums that cover tuition and living expenses. Not only does the committee allot the scholarships, but a member takes a scholar under personal care and gives her the guidance and supervision she requires.

Girls have been aided to prepare themselves for various vocations. Some have become secretaries, some nurses, teachers, laboratory technicians, social workers. In a number of instances the girls have repaid the Fund, and in this way aided us to aid others. The letters we receive from these young women prove how helpful the committee has been and how grateful they are for our equipping them for a suitable occupation. It is not necessary to add that an aptitude test is given in order to guide the committee in assisting the girl. The care exercised in this work is evident from the results achieved and the number of scholarship alumni who keep in constant touch with the committee. In many, in fact in most cases, the girls are also in need of medical and psychiatric care as well as social study.

The case of one young woman will illustrate the matter. This girl is now living in one of the Homes for Girls because conditions in her family make it impossible for her to remain in her own home. The discord due to estrangement of father and mother is so great and so chronic that it has seriously affected her. She has two conditions that require treatment: one physical, that manifests itself in eruptions on the arms and face, and a psychical condition that is a form of neurosis. As a result of the medical and psychiatric care we have provided, the social care in the Home for Girls, and the spiritual guidance by the member of the Committee in charge, the girl's condition has greatly improved; she has been graduated from Hunter College and is preparing herself for a vocation as technician. As a result of these improvements she is now finding it possible to associate with groups and is for the first time in her life beginning to enjoy social relationships. It would have been utterly useless merely to offer a small scholarship in a case with so many needs.

Synagogues in other communities will undoubtedly find many suggestions in these programs of service for children and adolescents, for there is no community in which these problems are adequately covered; and there is much that synagogues can do alone and in cooperation with other agencies to safeguard children and to guide the adolescents through this difficult period of development.

7. MARRIAGE AND FAMILY COUNSELING

Our program on marriage and family counseling I regard as one of our most important projects. This program, dating back to the first years of our work, grew directly out of our service to the families we took under care both within the congregation and in the community at large. As a result of our experiences and out of the deep interest in the development of marriage and family life which Mrs. Goldstein and I shared, we began to develop the objectives and techniques of both pre-marital and post-marital service.

Our experience taught us that many families were in distress because of discord and dissension in the family circle, due not to one but to a number of causes. Our first step was to organize a series of Conferences on Marriage and The Family, addressed by the ablest experts we could secure—men and women in law, medicine, psychiatry, and home economics, who were also interested and active in marriage and family development. These brought together groups of men and women from the community as well as from the congregation, and to our surprise filled the auditorium of the Synagogue House from year to year. After each address we arranged for a question and answer period in which the speakers discussed the problems that were perplexing the audience as well as ourselves. These questions from the audience were a revelation to us, and gave us as nothing else could some insight into the difficulties that were disturbing families in the community. We came to understand the sources of distress, and learned to formulate the foundations on which marriage and the family must be built if marriage is to be protected and the family conserved. We learned that there were legal, economic, biological, psychological, and ethical foundations. And we also learned that maladjustment on any or all of these levels leads to discord and eventually to disruption. Surprised at the large response in the community, we came to the conclusion that a larger community program should be undertaken and developed.

The next step was organization of a course on marriage and family counseling in 1922, which I gave to the students in the just founded Jewish Institute of Religion. This was the first attempt on the part of any Jewish seminary to discuss with the men preparing themselves for the rabbinate the problems they would face in their ministry to couples and to families. The course was given through a full year, and my purpose was to offer the men at least an introduction to the new programs on marriage and family counseling beginning to emerge.

I discussed the problems in pre-marital conferences, and especially the responsibility resting upon ministers in performing marriages. They were surprised to learn that the marriage license was not mandatory but only an authorization issued by the state, and that the license in itself was not sufficient to assure the minister that conditions were such as to warrant sanctification of a marriage ceremony. In truth the marriage law, which is the law of the state, is at least fifty years behind our present knowledge. Even today some ministers are unaware that marriage is a legal contract and that this contract presupposes certain conditions in order to be valid. The state does nothing, however, to determine whether or not all the validating conditions are present. In addition, the contract confers certain rights upon the parties and also responsibilities upon both husband and wife. It does nothing to make the couple acquainted with either its rights or its responsibilities. It therefore becomes necessary for the minister to assume this task.

In addition to a discussion of pre-marital problems, the course also included discussion of the problems of marriage and family life as they develop during the years. There is no congregation and no community of which I know in which these problems are not found, and it is therefore necessary for the minister to understand the ways in which to meet them. This means training in the methods of social diagnosis and principles of social treatment, and also an acquaintance with agencies in the community that can be called into cooperation. In order to be serviceable in the field of marriage and family counseling, it is necessary for the counselor to know the attitudes to be developed in approaching the people and the problems. He must know how to assemble the evidence; how to determine the causes of distress; how to plan out a course of treatment; and also, and this is most important, the scope and purpose of counseling; and he must learn his own limitations.

One of the difficulties we face is that men and women come to us so late. They have not learned in most cases that this service is available in the community. If instead of coming at the end of five or ten or fifteen years they would consult us in the incipient stage, we could do much more to aid them. But only a few seminaries seem to be aware of the training and equipment ministers need in order to be effective in this field. Too much time is given to the life and the literature of the past, and too little time to the present. It is important to know the past; but the past can be condensed. How unwise it would be to ask medical students to spend their time in the literature of alchemy when they should be working in the chemistry laboratories. And yet this is exactly what we are doing in the rabbinate.

The next step developed out of our experience was organization of the Committee on Marriage, the Family, and the Home, of the Central Conference of American Rabbis. In 1934, when I became chairman of the Commission on Social Justice, I included in our Annual Report the following paragraph and recommendation:

"The subject of marriage and the family is rapidly coming into the foreground of social thought and concern. This is due to the large number of divorces, separations, and estrangements in both the Jewish and non-Jewish groups. These estrangements, separations, and divorces may be due in large part to the tremendous changes that are taking place in the foundation, structure, organization, and function of the family today. Whatever the cause or causes, these conditions constitute a challenge to every man in the ministry. The minister is in a strategic position in regard to marriage and the family, but he frequently is unable to be of service because of lack of training, experience, and a program of work. Upon the rabbi, even more than upon the minister of other groups, rests a special obligation. In Israel the family has always been regarded not merely as a biological product, nor as a social institution, nor as a legal entity, but as a sacred circle and a sanctuary of our people. It is our duty to protect the family against disintegration and defilement and to safeguard the home as a source of spiritual enrichment and creative power in Israel. We recommend that the Central Conference of American Rabbis devote one or more of its sessions next year to a discussion of the problems of marriage and the family and the development of a program of service through the rabbi and the synagogue."

This recommendation was not acted upon in 1934, and I repeated the paragraph in 1935. It was then referred to the Executive Committee of the Conference. But the Executive Committee failed to take action. In 1936 the recommendation was submitted to the Conference as a whole and approved by the members present. We therefore in 1937 organized the new Committee on Marriage, the Family, and the Home, and I accepted the chairmanship in order to develop the program. I served as chairman for four years.

Then followed the organization of the New York State Conference on Marriage and the Family in 1936, and the National Council on Family Relations in 1938, in cooperation with national leaders. The origin of these organizations is interesting as a matter of record. In 1935 I was invited to deliver the Memorial Lecture at Columbia University in commemoration of Anna Garlin Spencer, who had given courses on marriage and family problems at Teachers College. Mrs. Spencer was a Unitarian minister deeply interested in the subject, and the author of one of the best books in the field, that still remains a classic, "The Family and Its Members."

In the course of my address, at which both students and faculty members were present, I ventured to present the thesis that marriage and the family were the concern of the state as well as the school and church and synagogue; and recommended that the state establish Marriage and Family Consultation Centers as it had already set up Child Guidance Centers and other centers of education and counseling.

This recommendation awakened widespread interest and an intense response, especially among members of the faculty. We decided to organize a committee to call upon the Governor to discuss the recommendation. The committee included Dr. William F. Snow, of the American Social Hygiene Association; Dr. Maurice A. Bigelow, of Teachers College; Professor Joseph Kirk Folsom, of Vassar College; and Mrs. Sidonie Gruenberg, of the Child Study Association of America. Governor Herbert H. Lehman received us graciously and listened to our presentation with great interest. He then requested us to submit a brief, to include the outline of a program. This brief we prepared very carefully and forwarded to the Governor.

Upon our second visit Governor Lehman said, "When you first came to see me I was of the opinion that the matter of marriage and family life should be left in the hands of the church and the synagogue and the school; but after studying your brief I have come to the conclusion that the State has a responsibility in this matter that we must all recognize. The State authorizes and sanctions marriage, but at the present time does little more than issue a license. How can I help you?" We told him that we were planning to establish the New York State Conference on Marriage and the Family, and suggested that it would be of great assistance if he would agree to address the opening meeting and give the movement the prestige of his presence. This he generously agreed to do.

In the fall of 1936 we held our first meeting at the Roosevelt Hotel. The New York State Conference on Marriage and the Family continued for a period of ten years, during which time I served as chairman. From year to year we held Conferences; and we were fortunate enough to secure distinguished speakers from the fields of education, law, health, and social work. This list included Dr. Frank Kingdon, president of the University of Newark; Dr. Henry Noble MacCracken, president of Vassar College; Katherine F. Lenroot, Chief of the Children's Bureau of Washington; and Pearl Buck, Nobel prize winner in literature. Those associated with the movement will never forget their stimulating and impressive addresses. We endeavored to bring together leaders from various areas and agencies interested in marriage and the family, and to coordinate their efforts. The New York State Conference on Marriage and the Family has now been succeeded by the Tri-State Conference on Marriage and the Family, which includes representatives from New York, New Jersey, and Connecticut.

The National Council on Family Relations, organized in 1938, held its first meeting in New York City in the winter of '38 and '39. This organization was largely the work of Professor Ernest W. Burgess of the University of Chicago. I met Professor Burgess in the spring of 1938 on a visit to Chicago. I discussed the possibility of developing a program in other sections similar to the one we had established in New York State and in the East. His distinction as a student of marriage and the family, his prestige as a teacher and author in the field of sociology, made it possible for us to bring together in the National Council men and women from all over the country and from law, education, economics, medicine, and psychiatry. Through the Council we endeavored to organize state and regional conferences on marriage and the family, succeeding in awakening interest in every section of the country.

But perhaps the greatest service we rendered was to bring together men and women engaged in these studies and to make available to all our findings. Our aim was to make the National Council a center of information and influence throughout the United States and to focus upon the family the activities emerging in different areas of thought and of action. It met annually, one year in the East and the next in the Middle West, and it is perhaps not too much to say that through it a widespread, scientific interest developed in marriage and family life in community after community. We then came to realize that we were limiting ourselves too greatly to experts and doing too little to serve men and women and families in need of the information being gathered in the social laboratory. Our objective then became to make available to increasing circles of men and women the information possessed by a few, to democratize our knowledge.

As a result of our long and intensive experience in this field, I had assembled a large amount of material on the subject of marriage and the family, and together with Mrs. Goldstein and our daughters, Eleanore and Beatrice, I decided to write two books, one for the layman and one for the experts. This was in 1936. The book for laymen was entitled, "The Meaning of Marriage and the Foundations of the Family," issued by the Bloch Publishing Company in 1942. Mr. Charles E. Bloch, a lifelong friend, believed as I did that a book on this theme giving the Jewish interpretation of marriage and family life would be welcomed by the rabbis, as a means of acquainting their people with the latest findings in the social field, as well as Jewish tradition. We therefore agreed to sell the book at cost. In this little volume I discussed the principle problems arising in pre-marital and post-marital counseling, and especially the structure, organization, function, and foundations of marriage and family life as we have now come to understand them.

When I began my studies fifty years ago, we were concerned chiefly with the problem of divorce. The divorce rate in America was increasing rapidly, and we were searching for ways to curb and control the evil. I became convinced that we had started at the wrong end, and that instead of studying the ills of divorce we should begin to study the foundations on which marriage and family life must rest if these institutions are to survive the stress of current social tensions. We put the whole problem in the form of an epigram: the chief cause of divorce is marriage—that is, the wrong kind of marriage. Therefore let us try to discover what marriage ought to be and must be if marriage and family life are to develop in accordance with the highest social standards and social ideals.

The book for experts, entitled "Marriage and Family Counseling," was published by the McGraw-Hill Book Company in 1945. This was the first systematic and scientific attempt to formulate a program on these matters. In preparing the material I drew upon the disciplines which I had found it necessary to learn—law, economics, medicine, psychology, psychiatry, ethics, and religion. To make the volume serviceable I decided to include not only the principles we had formulated and the conclusions reached, but case material to serve as illustrations of the problems. I have found that the problems arise chiefly in five areas or upon five levels—the legal, economic, biological, psychological, and ethical.

In the literature on marriage and the family I have discovered that some books deal with the history of marriage, some with the legal aspects, a few with economic problems, many with biological relationships, some recent books with the psychological factors, and only a few with ethical ideals; therefore I decided not to write from the point of view of any one specialist, but to present a balanced picture; not a book that would emphasize any one aspect of marriage, but that would present a conspectus of the major problems and the major causes of discord and dissension and disruption in marriage and family life.

This book has been widely used as collateral reading and has served as a reference book for lawyers, doctors, social workers, and others interested. If I were to revise it I should include material assembled in the social laboratories across the country, and perhaps enlarge the section dealing with the psychological level of marriage and family relationships. More and more we are coming to see that marriage in our time is becoming a comradeship, and this must rest upon psychological factors rather than other foundations. I should also, I am certain, place more emphasis upon the ethical ideals of marriage and family life. In almost every case that comes to me I find weaknesses and defects which make the marriage relationship difficult, if not impossible. The most important need is to cultivate the ideals of marriage on the ethical level.

It has been my hope that not only rabbis but ministers of other religions become more deeply interested in this program. To aid them with an introduction and a program, I prepared a paper on "The Rabbi and Marriage and Family Counseling," which I delivered before The Rabbinical Assembly of America, the organization of Conservative rabbis, in 1947. I have re-read this paper carefully, and believe that if it is studied by ministers it will serve as outline of a program that should be organized in every synagogue and church. I therefore reprint it here.

The most important development in this field was the White House Conference on the Family held in Washington in 1948. I

have served on the organizing committee of three such Conferences: The White House Conference on Children in a Democracy
in 1940, The White House Conference on The Family in 1948,
The White House Conference on The Aging in 1950. But to me
the most significant and comprehensive and scientific of all was
that on the family. Many of us in the field had been dreaming of
such a Conference for a number of years and had discussed it with
the leaders in Washington. As a result of our activities the National
Planning Association became interested in helping to organize this
Conference. The experts in Washington and in other communities, having assembled a vast amount of material bearing upon marriage and family life in America, presented the conclusions in a
series of meetings that were carefully planned and well developed.
The conclusions have been published, and there is no doubt that
the White House Conference on the Family did much to stimulate
an interest in marriage and family life across the country; more
than this, it rendered a great service in making available to larger
and larger circles in social life the information that had been in
possession of only a few. It democratized our knowledge of marriage and family life up to 1948.

THE RABBI

AND

MARRIAGE AND FAMILY COUNSEL

INTRODUCTION

You have graciously invited me to share in this program, I assume, because you are as gravely concerned over conditions developing today as are other students of marriage and family life. A
few months ago the Bureau of Vital Statistics in Washington issued
a pamphlet which contained a series of statistics that were startling
even to social scientists. One table disclosed the fact that in 1937
a total of 249,000 divorces had been granted in the United States;

and an estimated 502,000 in 1945. A report received two days ago from Washington states that in 1946 approximately 620,000 divorces were granted in the United States. Another table reveals the almost incredible fact that in 1937, one divorce was granted in the United States to every five or six marriages performed; and that in 1945 the ratio had risen to one divorce to every three marriages performed, in the country as a whole. In some sections of the United States, on the Pacific coast for example, the ratio was practically one divorce to every marriage performed. These statistics recite a disturbing story.

We must remember, however, that the number of divorces, tragic though it be, constitutes only a part of the picture. To the number of divorces we must add the number of separations, legal or voluntary, for which we have no statistics; to the number of separations we must add the number of desertions, intermittent or permanent, of which we have no record but that have undoubtedly increased during the post-war period; and to the number of desertions we must add the number of estrangements, temporary or chronic, that are so widely prevalent and that still need to be studied. In addition to the estrangements, desertions, separations and divorces, we know that there are many families in which tensions and antagonisms develop that are due to deep-seated causes of hostility and conflict. The picture, when complete, presents a dismal and distressing commentary upon marriage and family life in America.

Causes of Disorganization

The disruption in marriage and the disorganization in the family that we witness today are due not to one but to a number of causes. They are due, in the first place, to the changes that are taking place within the framework of the family itself. Changes are taking place in the structure, in the form of organization, in our concept of the function of the family, and even in the very foundations upon which the family rests. The traditional foundations are crumbling and new foundations are being laid out of the material derived from new fields of knowledge and experience. In the second place, disruption and disorganization are due to the fact that century-old social constraints are relaxing and age-old social pressures are dissolving and disappearing. For generations the institution of the family was surrounded and sustained by a network of customs, conventions, standards, and laws. This social network is now rent at many points as the result of the emergence of new social attitudes and new philosophies of life. The family, however, has not as yet developed that inward strength that is necessary to maintain it when outward controls are relaxed and removed. The simple patterns of the past have been shattered and the family is utterly confounded in the presence of a social order that itself is in a state of confusion. It is not a matter of wonder that many families stumble in their bewilderment and disintegrate.

We must note in the third place that the family is suffering from the impact and shock of social crises, social convulsions, and social cataclysms. The housing crisis is undoubtedly one hazard and cause of family disintegration. A woman who is deeply concerned with family life and also a student of housing conditions, closed her report with these words: "We as mothers ought to know that it is impossible to rear the right kind of family in the wrong kind of home." The economic collapse that began in 1929 unquestionably contributed largely to the breakdown of the family. Unemployment, low income, destitution, all breed suffering and despair, and lead inevitably to the demoralization of the family. War programs always speed up certain social processes and always speed down others. All the productive capacities of a people are speeded up during a war period; but the post-war period is always one of increasing disruption in marriage and disorganization in the family. The larger the percentage of the population engaged in the war effort, the wider the social effects and the greater the social damage and deterioration.

The gravest cause of disruption and disorganization, however, is not found in the changes which are taking place within the family nor in the dissolution of social constraints, nor even in local, national, and international economic and political disturbances. It is found in the disintegration of moral codes and in the collapse of ethical ideals. We, as representatives of religion and as teachers in Israel, believe in the supremacy of the moral law and that ethics

constitutes the organic law of a social life. In our work from day to
day, however, in the field of marriage and family counseling, we
cannot help but realize that men and women do not recognize that
the moral law is supreme in family relationships as well as in other
areas, and that ethical ideals do not inspire and hallow their attitudes and conduct. The corrosion that has taken place in the
wider circles of our social life and the corruption that character-
izes ethical ideals today account in large measure for the failure of
men and women to achieve stability and security and happiness in
marriage and family life.

Responsibility of Religion

These are the major causes of the breakdown now occurring:
the changes taking place within the framework of the family, the
dissolution of old constraints, the impact of social crises, and the
disintegration of the moral code. But we as representatives of
religion must frankly recognize the fact that we ourselves are not
without blame. The churches and the synagogues, the seminaries
and the ministers of America, have done little within the last generation to anticipate and to prevent the tragedies that we now face
in marriage and family life. Not long ago I read a report on the subject of marriage and divorce to be presented at a conference of
religious leaders, lay and clerical. This report was prepared by a
group of men and women whose names stand high in the field of
social science and social movements. One statement in this report
I shall not forget. It read as follows: "The ministers of our church
spend a whole year in preparing our children for the sacrament of
confirmation. But they spend no time whatever in preparing our
young people for the far more important sacrament of marriage."

This statement applies in some measure, perhaps in large measure, to every religious group at the present time. It certainly applies to the rabbis of America, whether they be Orthodox, Conservative, or Reform. If we are honest with ourselves we shall admit
that we spend little time in preparing our young people for the
career of marriage and even less time in serving and counseling
families that are in distress. Few of us have introduced into the curriculum of our schools courses on marriage and family life. Few of

us insist upon pre-marital conferences as this program is now
understood. Few of us assure ourselves that the marriages we perform will rest upon foundations that will insure a reasonable degree of permanency and the maximum of human happiness. Too
many of us assume that the marriage license issued by the State is
sufficient warrant for the ceremony we perform. We make this assumption in spite of our knowledge that the marriage laws in the
United States are weak and that the marriage law of not one state
in the union requires what we now know to be the conditions necessary for security and stability in family organization.

Courses in Seminaries

What program, we must ask ourselves, should we formulate in
order to meet the current crisis in marriage and family life and to
fulfill our own responsibility as representatives of religion? One
thing we should do is to urge the seminaries to introduce into the
curriculum courses that will properly prepare candidates for the
rabbinate for service in the field of marriage and family counseling. The rabbi in America today serves in a fourfold capacity and
has a fourfold function. He serves as a preacher, and as a preacher
it is his function to interpret the problems of our time in terms of
Jewish experience, Jewish teachings, and Jewish ideals. He serves
as an educator, and as an educator must be trained to organize and
supervise the department of education in his synagogue and in the
community. He serves as a leader in community life and in the advancement of social movements, for we realize that the synagogue
is not only a house of worship and a seat of education; it is also a
religious center for community service and social action. In addition to serving as preacher, educator, and leader in social movements, the rabbi must also serve as pastor, or to use the current and
better term, as a counselor. He cannot, however, serve as counselor
in the field of marriage and family relationships without adequate
preparation, without the necessary training and experience and
personality. The seminaries of America, I regret to say, do not
seem to appreciate the importance of this course in the curriculum
and in the program of the rabbi in America.

Even in the Jewish Institute of Religion, where I have been giving a course on Marriage and the Family for twenty-five years, I am allowed only one hour a week for one academic year. One hour a week for one year means thirty hours during the four years of study. In other words, the course on Marriage and the Family occupies only a little more than 1% in the space of the curriculum as a whole. This allotment of time seems to me to lack not only proper proportion but proper perspective on the part of the committee on the curriculum. It is important to study and to understand the precious heritage of our people, our history, our literature, our religion, our culture; and it is important to learn how to integrate the heritage of Israel into the life of the Jew today. But it is also important to recognize that we are serving as rabbis in the twentieth century and that we should be in possession of the knowledge gathered by social scientists in social laboratories and that we should be equipped with the techniques that have been developed in the art of marriage and family counseling. Without this new knowledge and new techniques we shall be unable to serve our people in time of trouble and to aid them in the solution of the problems that inevitably develop in marriage and in family relationships.

Role of the Rabbi

Another thing that we can do, those of us who are in the active ministry, is to train ourselves adequately to serve as counselors. There is no reason why, in our graduate years, we should not take courses that are offered by experts in the field of marriage and family education and counseling. In all the larger universities courses in this field are now being given, especially during the summer session, by men and women whose knowledge and experience qualify them to guide us in our own preparation. There is no reason why we should not study the literature that is now being issued by social scientists and that is based upon research conducted in the social science laboratories of the country. Magazine articles, pamphlets, and books are now appearing from month to month that will give us authoritative information and that will provide us with new material for our program. There is no reason why we should not sit down in seminar fashion with those men and

women who through training and experience and research have
acquired an understanding of the content of the pre-marital conference and who have mastered the technique of family counseling.
In all the larger cities there are now marriage and family consultation centers with a staff of men and women who are thoroughly
competent to conduct the seminars and to discuss with us the major
topics that come within the scope of this new form of service and
this emerging profession. There is no reason, certainly, why a commission on marriage and the family and the home should not be
formed in every rabbinical organization. There is every reason,
indeed, that urges the formation of this commission that could
make available to us the courses, the literature, the seminars that
we need. These commissions, the members of the rabbinical organization must understand, cannot function effectively unless
they have voted the power and the funds with which to develop the
programs that are needed.

In preparing ourselves, however, for this newly developed and
highly specialized type of service we must not make the mistake of
over-emphasizing any one aspect of the program. In order to become a counselor in the field of marriage and family life it is
necessary to know something about the laws, but it is not necessary
to become a lawyer; it is necessary to know something about home
economics, but it is not necessary to become a home economist; it
is necessary to know something about medicine, but it is not necessary to become a physician; it is necessary to know something about
psychology and psychiatry and psychoanalysis, but it is not necessary to become a psychologist or a psychiatrist or a psychoanalyst.
I emphasize this last point because there is some danger in this stage
of mental hygiene interest and progress that we may make the mistake of over-emphasizing the psychological and psychiatric factors
and interpretation, that we may even go so far as to substitute psychiatry for religion. What we need is a balanced program and a
program that includes the ethical and the spiritual as well as the
legal, the economic, the medical, and the psychological elements.
The longer I am at work in this field and the wider my experience,
the more I am convinced that the ethical and spiritual factor enters
into almost every case of discord and in many cases is the major

cause of disruption and disorganization. It takes time and patience and skill and insight, we must admit, to discover this fact and to convince the men and women who come to us of the ethical implications of their problem and the need for moral re-education and spiritual reconstruction.

We may differ as to the full content of the pre-marital conference but we cannot help but agree upon two points. The first is that the young people who come to us to be married are as a rule meagerly equipped for marriage and family life. They have been, it is true, members of a family, but have probably lived a large part of their time outside of the home and have taken only a small part in the development of family life and the solution of family problems. They had read and studied little on the subject of marriage and the family. In truth, it is amazing to discover how unacquainted they are with the literature and how vague is their conception of marriage and family life. They know not even the elements of Jewish tradition and Jewish teachings and Jewish ideals as they relate themselves to marriage and the family. It is certainly our duty in the pre-marital conference to discuss with them the Jewish interpretation of marriage and the Jewish concept of the structure and organization and function of the family. If these concepts and these interpretations are cultivated and incorporated into their married life there will be less danger of discord and disruption.

The second thing upon which we can agree is that our major concern is to assist the young people we marry to build their marriage and family life upon foundations that will insure them the permanency and the happiness that is humanly possible. They must understand the legal implications of marriage, that marriage is a contract that assumes certain conditions, that confers certain rights, and that imposes certain responsibilities. They must understand the economic basis, that marriage is a joint economic enterprise in which both the husband and the wife share, that home economics is a program for the development of which both are responsible. They must also understand the biological foundation: the meaning of heredity and health, and the necessity of a full and complete examination by a competent physician both before mar-

riage and periodically after marriage takes place. They must also
understand the psychological factors that play so large a part in
marriage, the compatibility of temperament, community of interests and the comradeship that marriage means in our time. But
most of all they must understand the ethical teachings and the
spiritual ideals of marriage. Unless they learn to live together in a
spirit of sincerity and trust, unless they are prepared to be patient
and forbearing with each other, unless they are willing to surrender themselves, not to each other but to the ideals of marriage
as we understand it, they cannot hope to achieve the joy and the
victory of a high and noble marriage relationship. They must
understand that these are the foundations and that their marriage
will grow strong and flourish only to the degree that they dedicate
themselves to the new career of husbandhood and wifehood and
parenthood. There is no satisfaction in merely reciting a formula,
but there is a profound happiness in aiding young people to establish their marriage on the highest level and under the dispensation
of the ideal of holiness.

We may also differ in regard to the procedure and the purpose
of family counseling; but we must all agree that in developing ourselves as counselors it is necessary to train ourselves scientifically
and to master the new techniques that are now well established in
this field. The first step is to learn how to gather the evidence that
is necessary in every case. This may seem simple; but in every case
that comes to us it proves difficult. For men and women naturally
and inevitably are special pleaders and present only that evidence
which will convince us of the rightness of their position. It is my
experience that the more carefully planned and the more plausible
the presentation the more it is under suspicion. The case that the
man presents includes the picture of his wife, but the picture of
his wife that he gives may not correspond at all with the picture
that we get when we see the woman herself. It is sometimes necessary to gather evidence from a number of sources and it is always
necessary to test the evidence carefully and to select what is relevant
and true. The second step is to make a diagnosis on the basis of the
evidence gathered. This also may seem simple; but it is always a

complex and sometimes a discouraging task, for in order to discover the cause or causes of distress it is necessary to explore all the circles of life and experience in which the cause or causes may be found. They may be found in the individual man or woman, or in the family itself, or in the home in which the family dwells, or in the neighborhood in which the family is located, or in the occupational area, or even in the larger social environment. We may discover, to our surprise, that we shall be compelled to change the diagnosis as we continue to gather new evidence and to explore the circles in which the major and the minor causes may be found.

The third step is to plan out a program of treatment and to translate this program into counseling practice. This procedure is even more difficult than gathering evidence and discovering the cause of distress. No one program of treatment can serve all cases. There are no panaceas in family counseling. We know that the purpose of treatment is to relieve distress, to rebuild those who have broken down, and to remove the cause of the trouble. But in carrying out the program of treatment we find it necessary always to be guided by principles of social therapeutics. These principles, such as the unit of treatment, differentiation, the hygiene method, and cooperation, require not only to be understood but to be employed in our practice. Those who come to us expect sympathy, of course; they also expect an intelligent understanding of their case; most of all they expect expertness and authority. Otherwise they will be disappointed and we ourselves and our profession will suffer discredit. It is also important to learn our own limitations in the process of gathering evidence and of making a diagnosis and in treatment. No one person is so well trained, so thoroughly experienced, so comprehensive in his capacities and qualities, that he is able to treat every case of family distress. It is necessary therefore to know when to call upon others, upon specialists in other fields, such as law, home economics, medicine, and psychiatry. Above all, we must avoid the danger that is always present in every profession. Family counseling is too grave a procedure to tolerate the amateur or the dilettante or the charlatan. It is our duty to encourage only those who by virtue of their training and experience and personal powers can speak and act with authority.

Synagogue Program

The third thing that we can do is to formulate a program for the synagogue and for the community to whom we minister. We can, in the first place, arrange lecture courses, as some of us have done, lecture courses that will make available to larger and larger circles of men and women, the knowledge that is not limited to a few. In fact, one of the aims of the synagogue program in education for marriage and family life should be to translate into language that will be intelligible to lay groups of men and women what the social scientists have discovered through their research; and what sociologists are teaching their classes in college and university. In other words, our aim must be to democratize our knowledge of marriage and family life through the democratic method of community education. It seems unnecessary to add that the lecturers should themselves be experts in their own field and that the lectures should be not sensational but scientific. In the second place, we can organize round tables or discussion groups or seminars for men and women, both unmarried and married, who wish to discuss thoroughly the topics treated in the lecture series. These discussion groups or seminars have proved exceedingly helpful wherever they have been organized. It is advisable to allow the members of the group to select the topics they wish to study carefully. If an expert is engaged to lead the group, as should be done, he or she would be able to not only prepare a syllabus but to assign readings in standard works on the subject of marriage and the family. One word of caution it is important to add. The expert who is to serve as leader should have a Jewish background and should be competent to answer questions and to discuss topics from the point of view of Jewish tradition and Jewish teachings. It is not enough to be an expert in law or home economics or medicine or psychiatry.

In the third place, we can build up a library. In every synagogue there should be a library that contains standard books and pamphlets and magazines on the subject of marriage and the family. The books could be loaned to the members and especially to those who attend the lecture courses and who enroll in the discussion groups. Magazines could be reserved for reading in the library by all those who wish to keep themselves posted upon the latest developments in the field from month to month. The pamphlets could be purchased in quantities, which would make it possible for members to secure them at a very reasonable rate. In the appendix to the volume, "The Meaning of Marriage and the Foundation to the Family" (Bloch Publishing Company), I have given a a list of books both Jewish and general and also a list of magazines that could serve as a basis for the synagogue library. In the volume, "Marriage and Family Counseling" (McGraw-Hill Publishing Company), I have included a list of the larger and more important organizations and agencies that issue pamphlet literature and that will be glad to send samples to those who apply. These pamphlets as a rule cost no more than five or ten cents apiece and are all written by men and women who are experts in their respective fields. Selected literature, including books, magazines, and pamphlets, can always be on display and can be placed upon the literature table whenever a public lecture is given. Through the library we can render a great service to the members of the congregation and the community. They will be surprised to learn how much material is being issued today and they will feel encouraged when they see the titles and the authors, to secure the pamphlets or the magazines or the books that would be of service to them. Notices can and should be posted from time to time announcing the acquisition of new and important volumes.

In the fourth place, and most important of all, we can establish as a part of the synagogue program a consultation center to which men and women can come for information and guidance and counsel. I do not use the term marriage clinic because the word clinic implies disease, and I do not think of marriage and family life as a disease even in their present state. Consultation centers are, in fact, being established in different parts of the country, in different states and in different cities. In some instances consultation centers grow out of family welfare agencies; in some cases they grow out of maternity centers; in some cases they grow out of churches and synagogues; and in some cases they are established as independent institutions. If our synagogue is large enough, if our synagogue has the resources in funds and personnel to make this venture possible, there is no reason why a consultation center should not be included within the scope of the synagogue program. On the contrary, there is every reason why this should be made a department of synagogue and congregation activities as truly as are worship, education, youth work, and social service. It should, in my judgment, be included within the budget of the synagogue and subsidized and maintained, as our other departments, in accordance with the needs of the congregation and the community. In some of the larger synagogues and churches the rabbi or minister serves in the consultation center as a consultant. His very position as a rabbi or minister gives him an advantage, an advantage, however, that can become effective only to the degree that he himself learns to speak with expertness and authority. As a consultant he will, of course, associate with himself a panel of men and women whom he can call into cooperation for discussion and treatment of special problems.

But if our synagogue is not large enough to permit the development of a consultation center as a part of its program, then we should, I firmly believe, cooperate with other synagogues and with churches and other organizations in the community, in the establishment of a community marriage and family consultation center. In some communities this has been achieved and the consultation centers are functioning not only effectively but superbly. Churches and synagogues, family welfare agencies, health organizations, educational institutions, and community centers have all joined together to establish a consultation center. In the course of time the state will recognize its responsibility in this field and will establish consultation centers as it is now establishing child guidance centers and other agencies in the field of human relations. But mainly it is important that the churches and synagogues in America do their utmost to extend to the congregation and to the community the services so desperately needed for education in family life and in marriage and family counseling. This gives the synagogue or the church immediate contact with society and a realism in its program that is now often absent. Unless the synagogue and the church do undertake to establish consultation centers other agencies will do so, and the synagogue and the church and the religion they represent will lose an important function and a precious opportunity to retrieve leadership in community life and community service. The form of organization, the problems of administration, the qualifications of the staff, and the program of work of a consultation center are fully discussed in Part 3 of "Marriage and Family Counseling." This presentation of counseling in practice is based upon a careful study of consultation centers now operated in the United States.

Conclusion

There is a valid and vital reason for this program in the synagogue. The family as a social institution is advancing rapidly into the foreground of social study and social concern. During the whole of the 19th century our stress was upon the individual and the emancipation and protection of the individual man and woman. During the 20th century, for the last fifty years, our emphasis has been upon society and social maladjustment and social organization. In our eagerness to emancipate the individual and in our anxiety to reconstruct the social system we have failed to give proper value to two facts; one, that the individual is, first of all, a member of the family; and two, that the family is basic to social life. If the family is insecure, the social order itself is in danger. We realize now, as a result of research in anthropology and sociology, that in the course of social evolution the family has served and has developed many functions. It has a biological function; it has served to perpetuate and to preserve the race. It has an economic function; it has served as a means to protect and to meet the needs of its members. It has a social function; it has served to give social status to men and women. It has a psychological function; it has served to educate and cultivate the human personality of those who constitute the family. No other institution can act as a substitute for the family. It has its own laws of development and its own function to fulfill.

All of this is true in regard to the family in general. But the Jewish family has in addition a special function. The Jewish people owe their survival in large part to three institutions: to the synagogue, to the school, and most of all, to the family. The family in Israel is not only a refuge and a defense in time of trial and persecution. It is a sanctuary and source of courage and inspiration and joy in every period of Jewish life. It is through the family that the heritage of our people is transmitted from one generation to the next; and it is through the family that the century-old treasury of social experience and spiritual wealth is enlarged and enriched. The highest function the family can perform is to educate and train and discipline the young men and women who themselves in time will constitute the new social order for which we pray. It will be the task of these young men and women, through their own talents and acquired skills, to increase the material resources; to advance the intellectual horizons; to deepen the spiritual reservoirs upon which society must draw for nourishment and progress. In the changing dream of parenthood we have come to see that children are entrusted to our care not in order that they may serve us or worship at our graves, but in order that they may translate into reality the ideals through which we, their elders, can only grope through a blinding mist of agony and tears. It is out of the family of today that the world of tomorrow must inevitably come. In its highest sense, the family is a covenant with posterity.

*   *   *

OTHER PROJECTS

In addition to these major programs, social care of the sick, industrial care of the tuberculous, mental hygiene experiments, care of children and adolescents, and marriage and family counseling, we have from time to time developed other projects in the Social Service Department. These projects have all been interesting to us and may prove helpful as suggestions to other congregations.

Emergency Relief

Throughout the years we have maintained a service of emergency relief to aid men and women temporarily in need. Such often find it difficult, for varied reasons, to secure funds from the Department of Public Welfare or from other agencies in the community. In a city like New York there is a great need for this service, for emergencies constantly arise in the life of men and women and in families. We have always believed that emergency relief should be immediate and adequate and expert. This means that the program must be in charge of someone with training and experience and the proper personality.

Storeroom

Almost from the beginning of our work we have maintained a storeroom at the Synagogue House. To this members of the congregation and friends in the community have sent clothing they could afford to discard. This clothing has been carefully sorted out and distributed to men and women who have applied to us. From the storeroom we have also sent many cartons to the land of Israel, to be given to communities in which the need was greatest. The storeroom has all through the years served a most useful and necessary purpose.

Infantile Paralysis Program

When the great epidemic broke out in 1916 we arranged at once for a program of after-care of the children admitted to the infantile paralysis wards in Bellevue Hospital. The hospital could do no more than accept and isolate these patients, who were brought to the little red building sometimes in the arms of their parents, or in wheelchairs and on stretchers. After leaving the hospital they needed weeks and months of care. This we endeavored to provide through the program we developed with the help of a group of doctors, who generously aided us in counsel and in treatment.

Workshop for the Unemployed

During the depression of the Thirties the entire social hall of the Synagogue House was converted into a workshop for the unemployed. Men and women were employed at current wages throughout the period. We also established, in connection with the workshop, a Loan Fund out of which loans were made to men and women who could not find work and who were in a state of destitution. This project proved one of the most serviceable of our activities in those days.

War Work

During both the First and the Second World Wars we organized programs to aid men and women who were in need because of the breakup of families as a result of war service. Few realize how serious the draft of fathers may become. In every war families find themselves in distress, and through our program we did as much as our resources would permit to relieve the suffering that came as a result. The existing agencies, like the Red Cross, are not always able to cover the cases that need counsel and guidance and relief.

Work for Refugees

One of the most important projects we developed in the Social Service Department was the program of care for victims of the Hitler regime. This was in charge of one of our ablest volunteers, Mrs. Harriet L. Loewenstein, assisted by Mrs. Ben Bloch and Mrs. Malcolm Steiner and a corps of volunteers, including a group of lawyers. These volunteers served hundreds of men and women and children during the tragic years of the Hitler period. The committee secured affidavits from members, and through these arranged for the admission of refugees to America. The refugees were housed in temporary quarters when they arrived, and then placed in various occupations and communities where they could become self-supporting. A large part of the congregation was involved in this program of care and placement. On the basis of our experience we learned that it was possible to persuade communities in the interior to accept one or two or three families. So far as our records reveal in time these families became self-supporting and a part of community life. This was not surprising, for the men and women who came to us from stricken Germany were all products of a generation of culture, and all were highly trained and skilled. This group has made a distinctive contribution to community life wherever they have settled and they have become loyal and industrious citizens of America.

8. CAUSES OF CONDUCT

In reviewing our experiences with children, adolescents, and adults, and in evaluating our experiments with different groups, I have come to realize that we must now develop a program of study and service larger than anything we have heretofore undertaken. We hear much at the present time of "human relations," that is, the relations of human beings to each other. But human relations, whether in the family or in the community or in larger circles, rest primarily upon human behavior, that is, upon the conduct of the individual as a human being. Human behavior itself, even in the simplest human being, is the outcome and expression of human personality. Human personality, we realize now, is a highly complex entity; and it is therefore necessary for us to analyze it, its content, its character, and its consequences. The children, adolescents, and adults who come to us present examples of conduct that may be described as deviations in human behavior, that is, deviations from what we have come to regard as the normal. These may be due to one or more factors, generally the latter. Perhaps up to this time we have made the mistake of emphasizing one or another factor and have disregarded the rest. We certainly have made the mistake of not seeing and serving the individual as a whole. Too often we have allowed ourselves to deal with aspects and fragments. We forget that the individual, even when not completely integrated, is a whole personality. In the program we are now developing we are therefore including a study of the following factors: somatic, psychological, social, ethical, and "X" or the unknown. These factors and their characteristic expressions may be in origin hereditary, congenital, or acquired.

The Somatic Factor

In many of our cases it is perfectly clear that the deviation in conduct is due to some defect in the physical organism. Changes in the structure or functioning of the human body, in the anatomical or psychological balance within the organism, may readily lead to variations in the pattern of behavior. A clubfoot or a pronounced lateral curvature of the spine may be a cause of changes. This is readily apparent, but it is not so evident that a change in the internal organism of the human body will be reflected in behavior. For example, the lassitude that results from the lowered oxygen carrying power of the blood in anemia, the restlessness and uneasiness that come from an increased metabolic rate due to an overactive thyroid, or the inactivity that is due to extreme obesity, are not uncommon. It is evident also that a gastric ulcer or an intestinal disturbance due to chemical changes may directly affect behavior.

In fact, we are only beginning to understand the chemistry of the human body and the degree to which human conduct is the result of chemical mal-functioning and the extent to which the human body responds to purely chemical changes. That human behavior and therefore human relations are determined in part by somatic defects, that is, defects in the human organism, we have known for a long time; but today we know much more about the way in which behavior is affected by abnormalities in both the structure and the functioning of the physical organism. It is therefore necessary to have a thorough and complete examination by a physician in order to determine the nature and the degree of the defect. We must remember that psychosomatic medicine emphasizes the somatic factor as well as the psychic.

The Psychological Factor

The development of psychology, psychiatry, and psychoanalysis during the last fifty years has given us a clearer understanding of the relationship of human behavior to the psychical constitution, its structure, its functionings, and its pathology. It is therefore advisable in almost every case to arrange for a psychological examination. It may be that there is some defect in one of the senses. Over-development or under-development of any one of them will affect behavior. A hypersensitive sense of sight or hardness of hearing may be a real cause of distress and deviation. Psychologists differ as to the meaning of instincts, but it is perfectly clear that the instincts of hunger and sex greatly motivate human behavior. Any defect in the instinctive life of the individual will lead to pathological forms of conduct. It is now generally understood that behavior is in large part an expression of emotional states, and that the relationship between conduct and emotion is more direct and immediate than we were accustomed to believe. Any defect in the realm of the emotions, such as simple temporary disturbances or emotional instability, may account for much of what we call misbehavior.

We are now beginning to understand more accurately the part that emotion plays and how deep emotional forces run. We are also aware of the fact that defects in the intellectual faculty may account for many deviations. These defects may run from simple cases of subnormal mentality to complex pathological states that we call insanity. The intelligence quotient is only one indication of the stage of development of the intellect. Many of the children, adolescents, and adults who come to us are just as immature mentally, as they are emotionally and physically immature. Here, of course, we must not forget what is now so well known, that many of the psychological defects lie in the subconscious life. This area of our psychical constitution we are now learning how to explore and to understand.

The Social Factor

The social sciences, now in full development, have helped us understand how profoundly individual behavior is influenced and determined by the factors of environment and the social complex. Some students go so far as to insist that all behavior is the outgrowth of the culture in which the individual lives. In our study of the individual and his deviations we find that conditions in the family are of major importance. The individual is born into a family and spends the first years of his life within the family circle. The atmosphere and the environment condition the behavior of child, adolescent, and adult. Maladjustments between husband and wife, father and mother, parents and children, what is now termed interpersonal relations, affect the conduct of each individual. The home also we cannot afford to ignore. Recent studies prove beyond all question that conditions there play a larger part in determining conduct than we formerly believed. An overcrowded or congested home, one without adequate conveniences or furnishings, that is barren and bleak, that breaks down the barriers of privacy, seriously affects the behavior of all those within it.

The neighborhood is most important. Social studies of urban as well as rural districts all prove the degree to which children and adolescents and adults are influenced in their behavior by the neighborhood in which they live. The presence of gangs, the absence of recreational facilities and of health agencies and educational institutions, directly and indirectly influence conduct within the area. The occupation of the individual is often a source of distress that may seriously affect his conduct. Overwork, seasonal unemployment, industrial accidents, occupational diseases, even uncongeniality of activity, may account for attitudes that cannot otherwise be explained.

The Ethical Factor

It is now evident that the somatic, psychological, and social factors separately and together do not completely account for human behavior. We must include the study of the moral sense and the ethical factor. The word ethics comes from the Greek word "ethos," and the word moral comes from the Latin "mores." Both originally meant virtually the same thing; but at the present time there seems to be a distinction. The moral seems to refer to the innate sense of right and wrong, and the term ethical to the cultivated sense of what is right and what is not. In this area few tests have been developed, but it is possible to study some aspects of the problem. We know more about the moral sense today than we did fifty years ago. A more careful study of human personality reveals the fact that the moral sense is as much a part of our psychical constitution as the mathematical or musical sense. Defects in the moral sense influence conduct to a greater degree than we have allowed ourselves to believe in our over-emphasis upon the somatic, the psychological, and the social. We also realize at present that every group has developed what are called codes of conduct. In every culture men and women have formulated codes that are enforced through various institutions, including those of government and religion. Codes, however, often lag behind the moral sense and the ethical development of the individual; and the result is conflict that seriously affects conduct. We also include within this area standards of value. These change with time and place. Values that are valid at one time and in one place seem to have no validity in other times and other places. But there is no question that the standard of values accepted in a group influences and shapes the behavior of the individuals who compose the group.

The Unknown Factor

A close study of human nature and human behavior, an analysis of the conduct and characteristics of the human personality, impel us to the conclusion that there are manifestations of human behavior that cannot be explained by any of the factors with which we are now acquainted, that is, the somatic, psychological, social, or ethical. This becomes clear especially in the study of the men and women who have developed into the great creative geniuses of earth. As far as we know at present there is nothing in the somatic, psychological, social, or ethical factors to account for the genius of Michael Angelo, of Beethoven, of Lincoln, or of Einstein. The appearance of the genius in art or music or science or statesmanship or religion is one of the mysteries of life. Even when we add together all that we know of the background environment and personality of these men and women there remains a surplus for which nothing seems to account.

Evidently there is an "X" or unknown factor in human personality that thus far has eluded all study and understanding. It is possible that to some degree this is present in every normal personality. We must therefore be cautious in our present stage of knowledge of human behavior. We do know that somatic conditions are accountable for some forms of human behavior, for when we modify these factors, behavior is modified. We also know that psychological states determine human behavior, for when we modify the psychological states, behavior changes. We certainly know that social factors account for many deviations, for when we change the social factor, conduct changes; and we are now beginning to see more clearly that defects in the moral sense or the ethical faculty are accountable for much misconduct; for when we correct the defects, conduct itself is corrected. But all these together do not account for some conduct or human behavior.

The Origin

It is important here as in all fields of study to discover if possible the origin of these factors, that is, how they arise and out of what conditions. We do know that some somatic, psychological, and ethical factors may be properly described as hereditary, that is, they are due to characteristics inherited from parents or grandparents. This is especially true of such extreme cases as haemophilia and manic-depressive insanity. We also know that in some instances the origin is not hereditary but congenital. Some accident of birth accounts for many somatic, psychological, and ethical characteristics. The accident may occur *in utero* or at time of birth. This is one of the difficult things to determine unless the defect is obvious, as in the case of malformation of the body. We also have learned that personality may be the result not of hereditary influences or congenital accidents, but of human experience, that is, the characteristics may be acquired from the environment and culture in which the individual lives. It is not always easy to determine the origin of personality characteristics. It is easy to recognize similar traits in parents and children, but we must remember that individuals are imitative and that what seems at first hereditary, may be only imitative. Some individuals are more impressionable than others, and emulate those around them more readily. But it is always helpful to know whether the characteristics with which we are dealing are congenital or acquired. This determines our program of care.

The Present Emphasis

During fifty years in the field of social work and social welfare, we have learned much about the somatic or physical factor, much about the psychological and social factor. And more and more we are learning how to correct defects in physical, psychical, and social conditions. But we are only now beginning to study intensively the moral sense or the ethical faculty. Until we have succeeded in developing tests that reveal moral and ethical defects, and until we have learned how to develop techniques to correct them, we shall not make much progress in curbing some of our evils, such as delinquency. For it must be evident that much delinquency is due to defects not in the somatic, psychological, or social, but in the moral, makeup of the individual. In cases that have come under our care and that we have had an opportunity to study, we have learned something of such defects. In some instances the moral sense seems to be absent altogether. In many cases the individual, child, adolescent, or adult, is morally immature, just as he may be physically, mentally, or emotionally immature. In other cases he is morally disturbed and confused. This occurs especially during adolescence and in times of social conflict. Persons have grown up without proper training or guidance or control. In still other instances we find that the moral sense is distorted, even diseased, and in extreme cases I have found the individual in a state of complete moral disintegration. These are some of the defects that have become clear to us. Now we are endeavoring to discover ways in which to correct them so far as this is possible.

Definition

The first step in study of the ethical factor is to be clear as to definition. We must learn to distinguish between: 1) habit; 2) the sense of right and wrong; 3) what we believe to be right and what we believe to be wrong. Habit is a mode of conduct that may be and usually is the outgrowth of a repetition of acts, or it may be the result of group custom and group pressure. Habit does not as a rule involve morals except by implication. It is simply an expression of human behavior without moral content or ethical tone. The sense of right and wrong, that is, the moral sense, is an integral part of the normal human personality, as much so as any other sense or faculty. It awakens and develops as do other senses or faculties in the course of our growth. This is part of the teachings of what is called the Intuitional School, which finds its fullest expression in the "categorical imperative." There are, of course, cases in which the individual is without a sense of right and wrong. These must be described as abnormal. In the normal individual the moral sense is "like a jewel that shines with its own light." What is right and what is wrong, what the individual believes to be right and what the individual believes to be wrong, depend in part upon what he believes to be good or bad for himself and for others. It also depends upon the code of the particular group of which he is a part, and upon the culture in which he lives.

Development

When the moral sense awakens and the ethical faculty begins to function in the average or normal individual is still a matter of doubt. Infants and little children do not seem to reveal any moral sense. Their conduct is largely if not altogether the result of do's and don'ts—thou shalt and thou shalt not—within the restricted area of habit. There is no moral motive or ethical goal. Is it possible with our present knowledge to determine when and at what age level the moral sense or ethical faculty begins to function? When does the individual begin to do things not out of habit but because he believes that some things are right and others wrong? Through what stages does the moral sense or the ethical faculty evolve and develop? There is evidence to support the statement that changes take place in their content. They contain new elements at different stages of development. The moral sense grows from the simple to the complex, as do other faculties.

This is clear when we compare the moral sense of a child with that of a mature and ethically well-developed individual. In the beginning the moral sense properly limits itself to what is right or wrong, or to what is good or bad for the individual; later it expands to what is right or wrong or good or bad for the family; and then it expands to larger and larger circles until it includes the community, the nation, and humankind. The range of expansion measures its growth. If it is possible to determine at what level the changes take place, it will be possible to rate the individual morally or ethically as we now rate him emotionally, intellectually, and physically.

For example, at what stage does the individual not only distinguish between what belongs to him and what to others, but reveals the feeling or moral tone that is involved in mine or thine? When does he not only distinguish between fact and fancy, but recognizes the difference between telling the truth and telling a falsehood, that is, that one is right and that the other wrong? At what stage does he recognize what he owes to others, developing a sense of responsibility? We can go through the entire list of moral attributes and ethical characteristics. It is important to know the stages of development in order to know what to expect of individuals at different ages. For example, we do not expect little children to be patient and to give patience a moral meaning. But we do expect mature men and women to exercise patience with each other and to appreciate the moral implications. It is perfectly clear that some individuals develop morally and ethically faster and further than others. Some children, for example, even in early adolescence reveal appreciation of tolerance and justice and mercy. It is often surprising to discover how early the moral sense does develop and how clearly some children recognize what is right and what wrong. On the other hand, it is often disappointing to discover how retarded some men and women are ethically, and how immature morally. Some never seem to develop a full sense of responsibility, never realize the degree to which they are responsible for the welfare even of those who are nearest to them. Their own personal pleasures seem of more importance than maintenance and protection of their children. The degree to which children are neglected because of lack of parental responsibility is even now not fully recognized.

Tests

What tests can we devise or what studies can we make to determine when different moral aspects normally appear in the child, the adolescent, and the adult? One way in which to awaken a response to the moral sense is through verbal presentation of an incident involving a moral element. For example, telling the story of Cain and Abel, or of David and Bathsheba. If the hearer simply listens or responds with nothing more than interest, this is not sufficient. The story may be told or the incident presented in such a way as to be utterly devoid of moral meaning. But no one can read the story of Cain and Abel or of David and Bathsheba, as presented in the Bible, without realizing their moral meaning and their ethical message.

It is also possible to appeal to the moral sense or the ethical faculty through written or printed material. This can be selected from any literature or from current publications, including the daily press. It can be handed to the individual either in private or in group work, and the response noted. It is interesting to watch the responses of people reading the newspaper in the subway. Their facial expressions or other evidences tell the story.

A third way is through presentation of pictures, either original or reproduced. Many pictures of the great artists contain moral themes. It is important, however, to distinguish between response to the presentation of the picture as a piece of art, and as illustrating a moral situation. A visit to an art gallery with a group of children is always illuminating.

A fourth medium is the motion picture, which appeals vividly to individuals and awakens immediate response. But one must distinguish between the emotional response that is purely a matter of entertainment, and a response that is a matter of ethics. That motion pictures directly involve the moral sense is evident in any audience.

But the most effective method of testing is through actual experiences and situations. These bring the individual into direct and immediate contact with the whole complex episode. For example, seeing a man beating a dog or maltreating a horse is a much more immediate way of awakening the moral sense and of arousing protest than verbal or written presentations, or a painting or motion picture. It is altogether possible that we have failed to appreciate the degree to which this process takes place throughout our lives from day to day, even from hour to hour. We have learned how to study the physical reactions of individuals, infants, children, adolescents, and adults, to actual situations. And we have also learned how to study their emotional reactions to situations, as they present themselves in daily experience. We have even learned how to watch and measure the mental reactions of men and women, as well as adolescents and children, to changing environment and to simple and complex problems of experience. But we have not carefully studied the response or reaction of the moral sense or the ethical faculty. Individuals do respond morally and ethically in words, in writing, through their whole personalities;

and we must now devise tests that will determine the nature and the degree of response. Is it weak, is it intermittent, is it strong, is it steady and intense? Even when there is no response whatever, the test is of value.

Defects

In its full and mature development the moral sense or ethical faculty expresses itself positively through approval and negatively through disapproval. A study of these modes of expression will aid us to understand the defects that develop in the moral sense or the ethical faculty. Among others we may list the following:

1. Mine—Thine
2. Good—Bad
3. Patience—Impatience
4. Tolerance—Intolerance
5. Mercy—Cruelty
6. Generosity—Miserliness
7. Truth—Falsehood
8. Responsibility—Irresponsibility
9. Justice—Injustice
10. Kindness—Unkindness
11. Unselfishness—Selfishness
12. Respect—Disrespect
13. Honor—Dishonor
14. Chastity—Unchastity
15. Fidelity—Infidelity
16. Holiness—Desecration
17. Innocence—Guilt
18. Reverence—Irreverence

Correction of Defects

This is the area in which little has thus far been done and in which the whole program of moral therapy needs to be developed. Diagnosis in the area is difficult, but the treatment program is even more so. At our present stage, however, we may indicate three procedures. 1) Education. It is possible to help individuals to understand the meaning of social codes and standards of value. And one can aid them to understand their own moral defects or the points at which they fail to act as normal ethical individuals. This program of education of the moral sense or the ethical faculty is still in an early stage of development. 2) Training. Not only men and women, but adolescents and children, can train themselves or be trained to correct defects in their moral constitutions. This means the building up of new ways of thought, and the development of new feelings, attitudes, and modes of expression. The training process is always a long and difficult one, for it involves not only the growing out of defects but growing into new ways of life. Those who have tried to train themselves in even simple changes of personality will appreciate how difficult the retraining process actually is. 3) Discipline. The word discipline for some time was banished from the vocabulary of human behavior, but it is now being reinstated. We have come to see that we discipline our muscles from babyhood up and that only thereby can we achieve expertness. We have come to see that we discipline our mental faculties through the procedure of education and that it is only thus that we are able to cope with problems. We are learning that we must discipline our emotions if we are to develop a rounded and harmonious personality. There is no reason to believe that we can not train moral sense and ethical faculty.

Cultivation of the Moral Sense

This is the large area in which least has been done. In fact, for a long time educators and others interested in human behavior seemed to assume that the moral sense either could not be cultivated or would grow naturally of its own accord. Only rarely have courses been introduced designed to cultivate that sense or to develop the ethical faculty. Courses in school and college as a rule content themselves with discussions *about* morals and *about* ethics. They do not attempt to touch the moral life itself. This has been one of the tragic failures in education, especially in religious education. Here and there evidence is appearing that we are coming to recognize the possibility of cultivating a sense of values, which means it is possible to cultivate the moral sense and the ethical faculty. There is no doubt that atmosphere and environment, custom and culture, command and the authority of the code, all are influential in training these faculties. The most potent influence, perhaps, is the moral personality of the teacher or leader. The man or woman himself a profound and active moral individual will inevitably awaken and strengthen the moral sense and the ethical faculty of those who come within their range. Those who have met men and women of this type, who are not echoes but active expressions of what may be called a moral being, realize that morals and ethics are actually contagious. One comment I shall never forget: "It is impossible to be in this person's presence and to even think of anything unworthy." As this experiment proceeds, it is hoped that we shall learn a little more than we now know of the ways in which to cultivate the moral sense and to develop the ethical faculty.

Ethics and Judaism

From the very beginning and throughout the centuries, the emphasis in Judaism has been upon the moral sense or the ethical faculty. Even a brief review of the development of Judaism reveals the fact that this element is part of every aspect of religion.

1) Creed. The concept of God is essentially ethical. God is a God of justice, of mercy, of holiness. The great teachers emphasize the uniqueness rather than the unity of the concept. They are more concerned with moral content and ethical attributes than with mathematics or metaphysics.

2) Ceremonies. Many of the holidays in the Hebrew calendar are invested with a moral meaning. The Sabbath, in the Deuteronomical version, is a moral institution. New Year's Day, the Day of Atonement, and Passover have deep moral implications and ethical meanings.

3) Codes. The codes include civil, ceremonial, and criminal laws, but the emphasis is always upon the moral. From the Laws of Noah and the Ten Commandments to the more complete and complicated codes in the Bible, the Talmud, and modern times, the stress is upon the moral element. The prime purpose of the Commandments is to develop a moral sense and an ethical personality.

4) Communion. The covenant between God and Israel and Israel and God, is not a military alliance; it is not an economic treaty; it is not a political constitution. It is an ethical document and implies an ethical relationship.

IV

THE SYNAGOGUE AND SOCIAL ACTION

THE SYNAGOGUE AND SOCIAL ACTION

In the Free Synagogue we have not only undertaken to meet needs of groups in the community; we have also been interested in advancing larger social programs and in furthering social movements. In this section on Social Action I have indicated some of the areas in which we have been active. We believe that it is the function of the synagogue not merely to develop a social service program, but to do its utmost to promote improvement in cultural relations, in economic justice, and in political democracy. Other congregations will find in these chapters suggestions for similar ventures in the field of social reform and social reorganization.

1. PROGRAM OF SOCIAL ACTION

In the section on the Synagogue and the Community, I have described the ways in which the Free Synagogue has proved of service to men, women, and children; and to groups in the community. In this section I want to indicate in what way it has been effective in advancement of social movements and the furtherance of social causes.

The plan for a Program of Social Action in the Synagogue is not new. As far back as 1934, when I was serving as chairman of the Commission on Social Justice of the Central Conference of American Rabbis, I included the following recommendations in the report adopted by the members of the Conference:

"We recommend a Committee on Social Justice in every congregation, as there is a Committee on Worship and Education. This committee should be composed of representatives of the synagogue, the sisterhood, and the brotherhood. Through this committee the members of the Social Justice Commission will be able to address the members of the congregation and affiliated organizations as well as the rabbi. In order that the Social Justice Committee in the congregation may organize and function effectively, the Commission will prepare material for guidance and forms of service and will cooperate with the congregations in developing the program. The chief purpose of this plan is to build up in the congregation itself an understanding of the program of social justice and sentiment and support for social causes. In this manner we trust the congregation will be organized for action in advancing social measures in the community and social movements in larger circles of life. The congregations as well as the rabbis should become active agents for the promotion of social justice."

While this recommendation was adopted by the members of the Central Conference of American Rabbis, the congregations of the Union of American Hebrew Congregations did not attempt, except in rare instances, to translate it into social action. It was our hope that the more important synagogue would endeavor to organize programs of social action, and would cooperate with the local, national, and international organizations in furthering community welfare and in advancing the larger movements for human betterment. But this hope has not been fulfilled. In the report of the Commission on Justice and Peace for the year 1951 is found the following paragraph:

"Your Commission on Justice and Peace acknowledges with humility that its greatest failure to date has been in the area of implementing the social idealism of our people within our own congregations. With exceptions as notable as they are rare, we have limited ourselves to lofty pronouncements, but have not devised ways and means of teaching the practical application of these pronouncements to our people or of activating them in the search for a more decent society.

"The practical work we do in our communities, and even more the non-partisan political activity to which we can stimulate our congregants as an expression of their Jewish prophetic zeal, will be both a manifest of our sincerity and a determinant of our effectiveness. We have always properly insisted that Judaism is a way of life. This must be as true in the areas represented by this Commission as with respect to ritual observance and to ethical conduct generally.

"We would urge most strongly, therefore, that a major program in next year's conference schedule be devoted to the reporting in detail of successful committees on public affairs already in operation within our congregations, and specific practical proposals for the extension of such activity among the groups which the members of this Conference have the high privilege of serving."

There is every reason why the Synagogue should engage in social action. One of the oldest prayers in our liturgy is a prayer for establishment of a new social order or for the Kingdom of God. In *Alenu,* which is over two thousand years old, we pray not only for the ending of social evils but for a social order that will embody the social ideals of Israel. The paraphrase of this prayer in the Union Prayer Book expresses this aspiration in moving terms:

"May the time not be distant, O God, when Thy name shall be worshiped in all the earth, when unbelief shall disappear and error be no more. We fervently pray that the day may come when all men shall invoke Thy name, when corruption and evil shall give way to purity and goodness, when superstition shall no longer enslave the mind, nor idolatry blind the eye, when all inhabitants of the earth shall know that to Thee alone every knee must bend and every tongue give homage. O may all, created in Thine image, recognize that they are brethren, so that, one in spirit and one in fellowship, they may be for ever united before Thee. Then shall Thy kingdom be established on earth and the word of Thine ancient seer be fulfilled: The Lord will reign for ever and ever."

According to Jewish teaching the Kingdom of God, or the Golden Age, does not lie in the past, nor is it in the heavens above, nor is it in the isles beyond the sea. Dr. Solomon Schechter, in a scholarly essay, has proved beyond all question that the Kingdom lies within us and is of this world. It is not imposed upon us from above nor from below; it is our own creation and our own handiwork. We are the architects and the artisans of the social order in the midst of which we dwell. We are, of course, limited to some extent by the land in which we live, by its character and by its resources. But it is for us to determine whether the community of which we are a part is to be filled with incompetence, corruption, and crime; or to be governed and maintained on the high level of efficiency and honesty and morality. It is for us to decide whether our country shall exalt evil and injustice, or justice and truth. Shall the world be rife with suspicion and hate, or will we establish it in accordance with the high ethical principles of the Kingdom of God?

Every synagogue in every community is under the religious obligation to engage in social action, and to do all possible to improve and to perfect the community, the country, and the world order. In our program in the Free Synagogue we have concerned ourselves with the basic social enterprises of health, education, recreation, and housing. And we have also considered the evils that arise in our cultural organization, our economic system, and our political order. In reviewing our activities I find that we have endeavored to function on different levels: First the community, then the state, then the country, and finally the international organization. On all these levels we have been concerned with conditions that needed correction, and with evils we were convinced should be overcome and ended. We have developed programs to further movements and to advance causes that would mean social betterment and establishment of the social order for which we pray. In the following chapters I shall describe our action in a number of different areas in the hope that these will serve as a stimulus to other congregations. In our methods we have availed ourselves of the techniques now employed in furtherance of social programs, that is, education, legislation, and mass protest wherever we have been able to develop interest and activity. At no time have we felt able to be silent in the presence of social injustice and evil. This is to us the meaning of the prophetic element in Judaism, social action for the establishment of an ethical social order.

The Union of American Hebrew Congregations and the Central Conference of American Rabbis have now established a Joint Commission on Social Action. This is in charge of Rabbi Eugene Lipman as director, and Albert Vorspan as executive secretary, with an Advisory Committee composed of both rabbis and laymen. The ma-

terial the Commission is now issuing and the program it is planning encourage us to believe that social action will now be incorporated into the program of every congregation of the Union, and
that the congregations will be stimulated and guided in their growing desire to translate into social practice the principles and ideals
of Judaism.

2. HEALTH

The health movement is one of the fundamental social enterprises in which the Synagogue can become interested and should
be active. We have a long tradition of interest and activity in the
matter of health. In the Bible there are many laws of health, and
in later codes there are not only laws but some unexpectedly progressive programs. The Jewish people have been so concerned with
health that the entire code of dietary laws have been interpreted as
health measures. It is not surprising, therefore, that we should become interested in the health movement that has become one of
the most important in this century.

When we study the movement we discover that it has passed
through three stages. The first is treatment of the sick; the second,
prevention of disease; and the third, promotion of health. These
stages are clearly evident in the movement for physical health, and
they are becoming especially clear and definite now in the movement for mental health. The question that synagogues should ask
themselves is this: What are we doing to improve the treatment of
the sick; what are we doing to aid in the prevention of disease;
what are we doing to assist in the promotion of health?

One of the fundamental principles of Judaism is the sacredness
of human life. And yet I have been in some communities in which
the rabbis and the congregations are so little interested in the
movement to preserve human life, to protect men and women and
children from disease, and to promote health, that they do not
know the death rate of infants and children and adults in their
own district, their own community, or the nation. They know
nothing at all of the agencies that have been created to safeguard
the life of the people.

In order to awaken interest and activity in this field, we organized the Committee on Social Action, appointing as members representatives of the congregation and affiliated organizations. We then attempted to organize a series of subcommittees, some of which have functioned effectively. One is the Subcommittee on Health, which ventured recently to study the health needs of the section of the city in which the Free Synagogue is situated.

The chairman of the subcommittee, Professor Beatrice Konheim, a member of the Department of Physiology and Hygiene at Hunter College, is active in a number of health organizations. Under her chairmanship the subcommittee some years ago discovered that the district on the Middle West Side of New York was adequately covered through existing health agencies, especially those clustered around 59th Street and Amsterdam Avenue. But when the great Medical Center was built in Washington Heights, all these agencies except the Roosevelt Hospital, moved to Washington Heights. The neighborhood lost the College of Physicians and Surgeons, the Children's Hospital, the Sloane Maternity Hospital, and others. The result is that the district is now most inadequately served, though it has a larger population that it had twenty-five or thirty years ago. The subcommittee has been endeavoring to persuade the city authorities to establish a Health Center on the Middle West Side, as in a number of other districts in Greater New York. The plans for this Center have been drawn, but the authorities have moved slowly. Here is an illustration of the way in which the Synagogue can become effective in the field of social action and in the social enterprise of health.

Treatment of the Sick

But synagogues should not stop with a survey. If we are serious in our health program we should acquaint ourselves with the facts of sickness in the community. We learn that from 3% to 5% of the population is ill enough at all times to be in need of medical care. This means that of the eight million men, women, and children in Greater New York, about 5% or 400,000 are always in need of medical attention. To what degree are the needs of this group being met by the dispensaries, hospitals, sanatoria, convalescent homes, Health Insurance Plans, Blue Shield organizations, and the medical men in our community? We must not forget that the sick are in need not only of medical and surgical care, but also nursing, social, and spiritual care. Only those of us who have had the advantage of expert service realize how much skill is required even to make a diagnosis and how large an apparatus is necessary to assure adequate treatment. It is only when we accept the best being done by the ablest men as a standard of measurement, that we realize how far short we fall in meeting the needs of the sick through existing agencies. No one has been able to calculate the number of the population receiving adequate treatment in the matter of sickness. But everyone in the Health Movement realizes how much is still to be done.

In his recent message to Congress, President Eisenhower stated his belief that health should be accessible to every member of the community in America. But he also declared disbelief in "Socialized Medicine." This term, now become an epithet, recalls a debate in which I participated with Dr. Richard Cabot, then Professor of Internal Medicine at Harvard Medical School. Dr. Cabot approved what is now called "Socialized Medicine," and I was unwise enough to oppose him—a distinguished physician and teacher and one of the most original thinkers I have known. After we had presented our views, came the period of rebuttal.

Thus spoke Dr. Cabot: "I would like to ask Dr. Goldstein two questions. The first is this: Do you believe in universal compulsory public education?" I answered: "Of course I do. Universal compulsory public education is one of the traditional enterprises in America." Then Dr. Cabot said, "My second question is this: Do you believe that education is any more fundamental than health?" I answered, "Certainly; health is even more basic than education." The debate, of course, was over.

The all-important problem that is still unsolved is simply this: How can we make the care of the sick available and accessible to every member of the community? There is not one community in the country, as the President has correctly stated, that is adequately equipped, and that assures to every member the kind of treatment we know is necessary if the sick are to be treated in accordance with current medical standards at their highest. We have not sufficient clinics and hospitals and sanatoria and physicians. In fact, there are only a limited number of physicians today with the training and experience and office equipment to offer the sick the highest type of medical care. It is also true that in no community with which I am acquainted is nursing care available for all. Private nursing and the Visiting Nursing Service, organized in many communities, cover only a limited number. The third form, social care, which includes the new program of rehabilitation, is available to only a small number of patients. And the fourth kind, spiritual care, is hardly recognized as a community need. In my judgment, and on the basis of our long experience with the sick, I am convinced that the synagogues should be interested in programs that would provide the ailing with the various forms of care, and especially with the spiritual help they require. The only spiritual care the synagogues provide is through pastoral visits of the rabbis, who are not always trained and competent even in this field.

Prevention of Disease

It is not necessary to be a student of the history of medicine to know that within the last hundred years we have succeeded in reducing the death rate and incidence of many diseases, and that we have learned to control the great plagues that formerly decimated the peoples of the earth. The prevention of disease is one of the most heartening achievements of the health movement. Smallpox has been virtually eliminated through vaccination. Typhoid fever has been all but ended through purification of the water supply. Diphtheria and scarlet fever, that formerly ended innumerable young lives and caused infinite suffering, no longer terrify mothers and fathers. Even pneumonia, a few years ago the despair of doctors, is now under control. But there is still much to be done.

What are we doing in the Synagogue to aid the crusade against cancer, heart disease, tuberculosis, infantile paralysis, and venereal disease? A few years ago, when I invited the director of the division on venereal disease of the Department of Health to speak in the Synagogue in a course of lectures, he brought with him members of the staff and motion pictures to illustrate the progress being made. The auditorium was packed with people, but some members of the congregation and the Executive Council wondered what role we had to play in the prevention of venereal disease. It did not take long to convince them that we could not be silent in the presence of an evil so widespread, and so destructive to both the health and the morals of the people. Since then no one has ever questioned our action in the prevention of disease.

The Synagogue, of course, cannot be expected to develop a program of prevention. This is the function of the Department of Health and of related agencies. But there are a number of ways in which it can cooperate with the Department and the other agencies. For one thing it can engage in a program of education through lecture courses and conferences and the distribution of literature. More and more leaders in the health field are coming to realize that one of the things that must be done to prevent disease is to educate the members of the community. It is amazing to discover how little men and women know of anatomy, physiology, and pathology, and the ways in which to save themselves from maladies or conditions that lead to them. And it is most encouraging to discover how eager they are to save themselves even at the cost of a complete change in their regime of life.

Two members of the staff of the Department of Physiology and Health of Hunter College, Dr. Beatrice Konheim and Mrs. Dorothy Naiman, have published a study of the results of an intensive educational campaign conducted with the families represented by their students. This, in a recent issue of "Public Health," reveals not only the success of the venture but their eagerness to acquire knowledge that will save them from disease. In truth the community is more interested in preventing disease than in acquiring health. I recall that some years ago we arranged a series of lectures in the Free Synagogue covering this topic, each to be given by an expert. We entitled the series, "Achievement of Health." When Dr. Dwight Chapin, one of our consultants, reviewed the material, he said, "The subjects are good, and the speakers are excellent, but the title must be changed. People are not interested in health nearly as much as they are in preventing disease." This is the psychological factor that must be kept in mind in formulating a program of education in cooperation with the Department of Health or other organizations. People are interested in saving themselves from heart trouble and cancer and diabetes, and they will respond to these crusades of prevention much more rapidly than they will to a program of "Health."

Promotion of Health

The promotion of health is the latest stage of the health movement. It includes a large and well-developed program that runs from the simple matter of nutrition to the complicated item of the optimum population. To a large extent, promotion of health depends upon advancement of the standard of living. Within the last one hundred years we have added at least twenty years to the average life of man, and within the last fifty the percentage of the population over sixty-five has increased from 4½% to about 9%. The population group of that age and over in 1900 was not more than 4,500,000. Today it exceeds 10,000,000. These achievements in the increase in the average span and of the older group are obviously in part the result of better treatment of the sick and the more effective prevention of disease; but they are more largely due to the raising of the standard of living.

This program, now world-wide, is one of the most significant and successful ventures of the United Nations and the United States Government. The food supply is being increased on every continent and in every country. More food is being grown and processed and consumed all over the world. Largely as a result of scientific agriculture and animal breeding, the old Malthusian doctrine has become obsolete. Not only are we learning how to lift the health index through better nutrition, but we are gradually learning to share our surpluses with countries in which there is a food deficit. The transfer of wheat to India and the more recent wheat shipments to Pakistan to relieve the hunger of the subcontinent of Asia is an indication of growth in social interest and social sympathies, and also social conscience. Certainly synagogues that represent religion at its best must be profoundly interested and active in this worldwide program.

As the Synagogue cannot be expected to develop a program of

prevention of disease so it cannot be expected to formulate a program for the promotion of health. But there are a number of things it can do to promote the health of the community. It can work with other organizations for an improvement in the standard of living, that is, in nutrition, in housing, and in income. For, as has been said, upon the standard of living depends in large part the promotion of health.

Another thing the Synagogue can do is to work with other organizations for the elimination of unsanitary conditions that impede the achievement of health. For example, it is important that it help save the community from impure water, polluted milk, and contaminated food.

At this stage there is no excuse for unsanitary conditions that endanger the community. All too often these exist for utterly incredible and unwarranted reasons. During the time I was in Cincinnati I developed an attack of typhoid fever. When I reached my home in Chicago our family physician wrote down as the cause of this reportable case, "The Ohio River." He was altogether correct. I learned later that it took twenty years to build a plant to purify the water of Cincinnati. It could have been built within two years. But the politicians and the Cox machine delayed its completion for corrupt and mercenary reasons. During the entire eight years I spent in Cincinnati I did not hear one protest from one pulpit against this intolerable program of political corruption that menaced the life of the community. I doubt very much whether this could occur today. The men in the ministry are much more alive to the dangers. But there are still many areas in which the synagogues can be effective in protest against conditions that make the achievement of health and the advancement of health programs impossible.

Treatment of the Mentally Ill

The mental hygiene movement, it is generally conceded, began with the tragic, epoch-making experience of Clifford Beers; but even before Beers opened his crusade in 1909 we were becoming interested in the treatment of the mentally ill in our state hospitals. This is a program on the state level, and a number of rabbis and ministers of other religions have become vitally interested. State hospitals are still overcrowded, understaffed, and inadequately maintained, but we have at least come to realize that the mentally afflicted are to be treated as sick individuals; and much is now being done in both state and private institutions to improve their treatment.

The truth of the matter is, however, we are only beginning to realize how vast this problem is. The ablest experts agree that one out of ten in the population will at some time be in need of mental hygiene care, and that one out of every eighteen or nineteen will require custodial care. This means that 10% of the population, or 16,000,000, will at some time require psychotherapy, and that 9,000,000 to 10,000,000 will at some time need institutional treatment. The Synagogue must strive to the utmost to provide this vast group with the care they need. No one can visit the psychiatric wards of a hospital or those in a state institution and not feel moved to do everything possible to provide these patients with such attention as is now available. At present every student of the mental hygiene movement will admit that only a small percentage in our state hospitals have the advantage of modern care, and that a still smaller percentage outside the state hospitals is served in accordance with our present knowledge. The mental hygiene experiments conducted by the Free Synagogue described in the previous section constitute a concrete evidence of not only our interest but our activity in this field.

A number of rabbis within the last twenty-five years have become seriously interested in the problem, and have succeeded in enlisting their congregations in developing serviceable programs of improvement. Among these men was the late Benedict B. Glazer of Detroit, who did much to awaken his community and the people of the state to the needs of mental hygiene cases. He learned what is true to a greater or lesser degree in every state, that the institutions for care of mental hygiene cases of the State of Michigan were overcrowded and understaffed. This is true even of New York, one of the most progressive in the development of mental hygiene facilities.

The result of overcrowding and understaffed institutions and in-adequately equipped hospitals is that only a limited number of pa-tients receive full and proper treatment. The largest percentage are given nothing more than custodial care. It is true, of course, that in America we have not sufficient men and women trained to treat mental hygiene cases, not more, I understand, than 5000. One thing, therefore, that the synagogues and churches in every state can undertake is to work persistently for an increase in the per-sonnel of state institutions, in psychiatrists, psychiatric nurses, and psychiatric social workers, and chaplains especially qualified to serve the mentally ill and to meet their spiritual needs.

The State of New York, under the leadership of Governor Dewey, is now appropriating an additional $300,000 to advance the institutional care of mental hygiene cases. At a recent meeting of the Governors of the States of the Union, the care of such cases was made the principle order of business. There is no doubt that as a result of growing interest and action there will be improvement in the care of institutional patients. But to me it is significant that the synagogues and the churches have not been fully enlisted in this program, nor have they volunteered to take an active part in its advancement. Surely there is no field in which religious leaders and congregations should be more deeply interested. It seems as though we were still living in the shadow of the Middle Ages and recent centuries. We are not only treating the mentally ill as if they were sinners instead of being sick, but are still engaged in a program of concealment and a conspiracy of silence. This is an indictment, I know; but I also know that it is true.

Prevention of Mental Disease

Only those acquainted with the mental hygiene program realize how short a distance we have traveled in the prevention of mental cases. It is true that some types of mental disease are declining. Paresis, which is due to syphilitic infection, is actually disappearing as a result of our control of venereal disease. Delirium tremens is also declining as a result of our better understanding of alcoholism and its consequences. But we still know little or nothing of ways in which to prevent manic-depressive insanity or schizophrenia. Fifty years from now we shall probably comprehend more about these conditions and how to anticipate and forestall breakdowns. But even in our present stage of knowledge or ignorance we do know that many cases of neurosis and probably some psychosis can be prevented.

Men and women, young and middle aged and old, suffer trauma or shocks that lead to neurotic and psychotic conditions. If we are to prevent the development of these conditions, we must learn how to safeguard people from shock. Crises are an inevitable part of life, but this does not mean that this must result in shock and collapse. In surgery, medical men know how to deal with this contingency, and surgical shock, which formerly was not infrequent, is today rare. In time the same thing will be true in the mental hygiene field. Perhaps one of the most promising programs in prevention is the intelligent training and sympathetic protection of children. We know that many cases of mental disturbance have their origin in the threatening and traumatic experiences of infancy and childhood. I have seen many cases in which a neurosis can be traced back to the period of pregnancy. The child was rejected even before it was born.

We do not know enough about mental hygiene cases, that is, about nervous and mental disease, to develop a program of prevention as we now prevent smallpox, yellow fever, and typhoid. But we do know enough about neurosis and psychosis to save many men and women from commitment to state hospitals. In the experiments conducted by the Social Service Department of the Free Synagogue we have learned that a large percentage of patients now committed, perhaps 50%, can be maintained upon a reasonable level of efficiency if they have the advantage of proper care and supervision. This includes psychiatric and social care and especially a program of work, or occupational care, adjusted to working capacity. During the three years' experiment with patients discharged to the community from the psychiatric wards of Bellevue Hospital we did succeed in aiding more than half to maintain themselves in the community through psychiatric, social, and occupational care. Surely to save persons from commitment to state hospitals and to aid them to maintain themselves on a reasonable level in the community is a form of prevention.

I have a letter from Los Angeles in which Mr. Louis Ziskind, executive director of the Committee for Personal Service, describes a new agency established by his organization, entitled "Gate Ways." This agency has a three-fold program: 1) after-care; 2) treatment; 3) and, most important, guidance and supervision of patients who can be saved from commitment. This is probably the next important step in the field, one that we recommended some years ago, establishment of a Mental Hygiene Center to which members of the community may go for authoritative information, for interviews, for consultation, for guidance and supervision in the solution of their problems, for assistance in their endeavor to save themselves from commitment. In reading over the list of those interested in the establishment of "Gate Ways" I miss the name of any rabbi. I cannot but feel that Los Angeles with its large number of synagogues and its congregational wealth should be actively engaged in promoting this new program, not indirectly through membership in Federation, but directly in organizing and maintaining and developing a program that is so desperately needed in this large Jewish community.

Promotion of Mental Health

We know little about the treatment of the mentally ill; we know less about the prevention of mental disease; and we know least of all how to promote mental health. But some things we do know, and here religion can play an important role. We are aware that tension and friction and antagonism in the family circle and in the home not only disturb the relationship of individuals to each other but lead to mental and emotional states that in turn bring on mental and emotional illnesses. One thing synagogues certainly can do is to develop a program of family relationships that will end tensions, estrangements, and alienations.

Not a day passes in the work I am doing that I do not have to deal with this problem. It is amazing to discover how persistently men and women, husbands and wives, mothers and fathers, will not only poison themselves with bitterness and hatred but also the lives of their children. The fact that so many survive such parents is evidence of the unexpected resources and resiliency that children possess.

Another thing the synagogue can do is to help parents understand the stages through which their children must pass and that they themselves must undergo. One of the most effective programs we have developed in the Free Synagogue is the Film Forum, designed through lectures and motion pictures and discussion to make parents acquainted with the problems of adolescents and how these can be intelligently understood and solved. If we are to promote mental health, we must realize more fully the degree to which mental health depends upon the atmosphere and the environment not only of the home but of the community and of society. It is not surprising to find children living in a state of fear and terror, with nightmares and tantrums, when the world around us is surcharged with the frightful images of misunderstanding and mistrust and hostility.

Another way in which we can aid people to reduce the conditions that sometimes cause and always aggravate psychical disturbances is to teach them how to avoid frustrations. Frustration is the result of the inability of an individual to cope with problems that arise in life. It is therefore necessary for men to limit themselves in accordance with their own capacities. This sounds simple, but it is always difficult. It means first that we must learn to recognize our own limitations, and few of us are aware of our limits. It means next that we must learn not only to recognize our limitations but that we must learn to accept them. This is always a difficult process even for the ablest of us, for acceptance is frequently fraught with not only a new attitude but a new interpretation of life. And in the third place we must learn to work out a program of activity in accordance with our limitations and those that we learn to accept.

But this is not all. The rabbi and the congregation as representatives of religion can develop the positive program necessary for the promotion of mental health. This requires building up the interests of men and women, confidence in their own powers, and the courage they need to face life and to cope with life's problems. This positive program may and probably must begin with individuals.

But it can readily be developed into a group activity, or what is now termed group therapy. There is no reason why synagogues and churches should not organize groups in need of this form of mental hygiene care. In truth, it should be one of the functions of religion to cultivate in men and women a spirit of confidence and courage and faith in their own inner and latent resources. Long ago William James taught us that we all have great reservoirs of reserve strength upon which we must learn to draw in order to develop our capacities to the full.

There is one more thing I believe teachers of religion can do to promote health, and that is, aid people to recognize the tension arising out of conflicts in their moral or ethical life. In the course of my work I have been impressed more and more with the fact that much tension is due to our failure to resolve the conflicts on this level. One illustration is that of a young woman twenty-two years of age. Some months before she came to me she developed gastric intestinal symptoms that compelled her to consult a physician. After treating her for some weeks the physician came to the conclusion that there was no organic basis for her symptoms and urged her to see a psychiatrist.

The psychiatrist worked with her for a number of weeks but made no progress. He knew something of the work we were doing and asked the young woman to see me. Towards the close of the first interview she said to me, "What do you think is the trouble? I have seen a physician and also a psychiatrist. What is your opinion?" I replied, "On the basis of what you have told me I am inclined to think that the source of your trouble lies on the moral level. Are you engaged in a program of deception?" The young woman looked startled and said, "How do you know?" Then she confessed that she was engaged in an affair and was in a constant state of conflict between her conduct and her conscience. When we succeeded in resolving this ethical conflict, the psychical symptoms subsided and the physical symptoms disappeared.

I could cite case after case in which the same type of conflict, with variations of course, is the source of the trouble. In some cases the moral problem is simple and in some it is complex. It may be of recent origin, or date back many years. One thing we must remember is that men and women do not want to recognize that they are doing something wrong. In some instances they are not aware of the true cause of their trouble. In others they disguise the source of the trouble in different ways. And in still other cases they deliberately misrepresent or conceal the conduct accountable for the conflict. On occasion I have found that men and women would prefer to believe they were suffering with a complex when the real trouble was that they were disregarding or violating their consciences.

3. EDUCATION

Another basic social enterprise is education. Here too we have a long Jewish tradition. For centuries, for at least two thousand years, we have been interested in education and in educational programs, little children to adolescents, to adults and the aged. Here, however, we must distinguish between Jewish and general educational programs. The Jewish people have taken seriously the command: "Thou shalt teach them to thy children." We therefore find them in every age and every country establishing a system of education. At times this system is simple and primitive; at others it is well-developed and rich in content. The main objective of Jewish education is to transmit from one generation to another the heritage of the people of Israel and to cultivate a full appreciation of what it means to be a Jew. At the present time Jewish educational programs are being stressed and expanded. In some synagogues the program is limited to a Sunday morning school from nine to twelve. Others in addition conduct an afternoon program three or four times a week, and in some there are full daily programs that constitute a parochial school. In many communities these programs are independent of the synagogue and are conducted by unrelated organizations.

In the field of social action, however, we are not concerned primarily with the programs of Jewish education nor with the arguments for or against Jewish parochial schools. Our concern here is with the field of general education and the relation of the synagogue to the general educational systems of the community. However, synagogues have done little to improve general education in their localities. In most communities congregations and synagogues, controlled by the principle of the separation of church and state, fear to invade the field of education, which in America is a state function.

Some rabbis, however, believe they and their congregations can be active in the educational systems without violating the principle of separation of church and state. They have therefore begun to study the needs of the community in the field, the ways in which these are now being covered, and the degree to which they are inadequately met or not met at all. They are interested as citizens, for example, in the composition of the Board of Education, and in the methods whereby members of the Board are appointed. They are members of parent-teacher and public education associations, and cooperate with these organizations for community needs. If the synagogues are, as we believe, religious centers for community service and social action, we cannot ignore the needs of education any more than we can ignore them in the field of health. We are not apart from the community, mere spectators; we are in every sense a part thereof, directly and immediately affected by what takes place in the schools of our city. Our children attend these schools. It is our duty as parents and American citizens to know what kind they are, the competency of the teaching staff and of the curriculum, and the programs they are developing as educational centers for community service. Some rabbis and congregations become active and perturbed only when they discover that there is danger of prejudice, group friction, and antagonism developing through the schools. It is important to safeguard the children in our community from the poison of prejudice and group hostility. But our program of social action must not be limited to what we now call "defense." It must go far beyond this narrow and group limitation.

The Plant

A committee of men and women in the Free Synagogue, after a somewhat restricted study of the educational facilities in our district, came back with a report that startled us. Some schools were over a hundred years old, and so obsolete in construction and inadequate in equipment that they could not serve their purpose any longer. They should be destroyed and other schools of modern construction and equipment erected in their place. Some were so antiquated that they did not contain the conveniences we would expect even in a tenement house. They belonged to the slum era.

The committee also found that there was no high school on the Middle West Side and that the children in the local apartment houses had to travel across Central Park or up to Washington Heights or the Bronx in order to secure a high school education. This small study confirmed the findings of larger committees and organizations which operate in the district, and some members of the Synagogue have become active in furthering a movement for better schools and for more adequate facilities on the elementary and high school levels. The other boroughs of New York and outlying districts have grown so rapidly and the demands for educational facilities have been so insistent that the whole of Manhattan and especially the Middle West Side have been neglected.

In one of the meetings with the president of the Board of Education we were told that the trouble with the West Side was that the people there were not sufficiently vocal and did not make their voices heard when the budget for the Department of Education was considered by the Board of Estimate. There is no doubt that other boroughs and adjacent communities have better educational facilities than our district. There certainly can be no violation of the principle of the separation of church and state in pleading for better schools for our children.

A comparison of the schools built fifty and seventy-five years ago with those now being constructed in the outlying and suburban sections of New York emphasizes the changes that have taken place in our conception of the educational program. Not only are the new schools better constructed, with larger windows admitting more sunlight and ventilation. They are better equipped, and they illustrate new concepts of the school plant, meeting the new responsibilities with which we are charging the school system. The color scheme is better designed, and the seating is now so arranged that there is interplay among members of the class. We have been graduated from the military regime in the educational system. But this is not all.

Special rooms and equipment are being added not only to accommodate the new departments of arts and crafts, but to adequately accommodate and serve children physically, mentally, and emotionally handicapped. These groups that heretofore have been shut out of the school system and served, if at all, by private agencies, are being brought within the school program. I refer particularly to the mentally retarded, the emotionally disturbed, and the physically handicapped, such as cerebral palsy cases. We are now beginning to see that every child in the community is entitled to whatever form of education his condition requires. Some will always be members of the "shut-in" classes, such as those afflicted with rheumatic fever, but the vast majority of the handicapped do not need bed care, and in fact do much better when encouraged to enroll in school classes and to participate, so far as their limitations permit, in the normal life of growing children. To segregate or to isolate them as we have done up to this time is to emphasize their handicaps. We are just beginning to learn the meaning of the term rehabilitation, as it applies not only to the crippled and adults, but to the handicapped of all types and age groups. As we learn more about the methods of rehabilitation, physical, mental, and emotional, we also learn how to serve all children in the community more efficiently and also more humanely. In order that these special groups may be adequately served and that the play-program for the normal children properly developed, we must make provision for more adequate equipment and for increased accommodations.

Curriculum

I have been in communities in which the rabbi and officers of the synagogue know nothing whatever of the curriculum in their Department of Education. I know that this is a subject that requires highly trained and expert educators. In our congregations, however, we have men and women who are highly trained, who can speak with authority, and whose conclusions and judgments would be helpful to the authorities in charge of our schools. They do serve in parent-teacher associations, and often are of great value. There is, however, no reason why a committee of the synagogue should not be interested in improving the curriculum. I would not limit these committees to minor items, such as reading "The Merchant of Venice." Obviously, the curriculum should be free of any item in the classroom or the assembly that would develop group misunderstanding or friction.

But there is a more positive program to urge upon the schools. One of the most important of these was tried in Philadelphia. There Rachel Dubois worked out a series of assemblies in which the several racial and religious groups each undertook to present the contributions of their group to the development of community life. For the first time boys and girls became acquainted with the cultural contributions of the diverse people who make up America, and the result was an immediate diminution of prejudice and a decline in group antagonism. The elementary and high schools and colleges are not pots in which boys and girls are to be melted into the same mold. One of our finest tasks is to cultivate in our children appreciation of self and group, and the contribution of other groups to the wealth of democracy. One function of education is to develop human personality. This we can do only through a curriculum designed to strengthen our feelings of self-respect, self-regard, and self-reliance.

There is one element in the curriculum in which synagogues and churches cannot fail to take active interest—morals or ethics, or what the educators now call "character development." I do not mean sectarian teachings or religious indoctrination, but cultivation of the moral sense and development of the ethical faculty. At the present time especially do we need to stress this element. Every day brings added evidence that the codes of conduct embodying the simplest moral teachings and ethical principles are in a state of collapse. It is not surprising that there is a constant increase in juvenile delinquency all over the country. How can we expect anything else when the environment of every community is poisoned with corruption? The children can no more escape this poison than the polluted atmosphere of our urban civilization.

In our family life we are doing little, if anything, to build up in our children moral standards of conduct. And in our houses of worship we are more concerned with theological and cultural conceptions than with education of the moral sense and training in ethics. In the chapter on Human Behavior I have endeavored to outline the conclusions we have reached on the basis of our experience through the years. I know that some forms of misbehavior are due to physical or somatic defects, such as glandular disturbances. I also know that some forms are due to psychical defects, mental or emotional deviations or disturbances. And I also am aware that some arise out of social factors in the family, home, neighborhood, or community. But I am convinced that neither physical nor psychological nor social weaknesses will account for much misbehavior; and that we have failed to curb the increase in delinquency because we have relied too greatly upon programs that limit themselves to the physical or social or psychological factors. I seriously question whether the emphasis upon methods of therapy in these fields will do much to solve our problems. I do not mean that we should disregard psychology, psychiatry, or psychoanalysis in the education of children or treatment of the delinquent. But we cannot hope for a moral generation and an ethical form of conduct until we help children understand the meaning of truth and justice and unselfishness and integrity. We discipline our muscles and our minds, and we are learning to discipline our emotions. We must learn to regulate our impulses and to cultivate the moral sense. The full meaning of integrity with all its implications must be our guide in this element of the curriculum.

Personnel

The teaching staff in New York City is generally well-trained and competent, and the salaries are higher than the average in elementary schools, high schools, and colleges. They must pass severe examinations and maintain high standards of teaching. But there are many schools in which there are weak teachers, and others too old to continue to teach. This is a difficult problem, a delicate situation to correct, but our first concern must be with the children. Some provision should be made to safeguard them and assure the ablest instruction and the wisest guidance.

One of the difficulties is the matter of tenure, especially on the college level. I have known members of a college staff who were not only incompetent but a menace to their classes. They were originally appointed inadvisedly and those in charge have found it extremely difficult to remove them, especially because of the protection they have enjoyed from groups in the community. But this is not all. It not infrequently happens that principals and assistant superintendents are appointed not on the basis of merit but as a result of social or political pressure. The Board of Education, and the Board of Higher Education that supervises the colleges in New York, include among their members men and women appointed by the politicians temporarily in office. I do not regard it as a violation of the principles of democracy for the rabbi and the congregation to do their utmost to secure appointment of the ablest men and women in the community to supervise the Department of Education on the different levels. In fact, as a result of our experience in New York, I am convinced that religious organizations themselves do not always insist upon appointment of the ablest men and women.

It is certainly not the function of the Synagogue to pass upon the mastery of material or of method possessed by the teacher. This belongs to the Examining Board. But it is the concern of religious groups to interest themselves in at least three other qualifications. First, it must be seen that our children are taught by teachers who are free of all prejudice. I have known schools in which some teachers have been so thoroughly prejudiced in favor of their own faith or against the faiths of others that this attitude has influenced and poisoned their teaching. We have a right to insist that the teachers in our elementary schools, high schools, and public colleges be so free of intolerance that their language and their conduct will not taint their instruction. This is a matter that comes to the surface every now and then, especially during religious holiday seasons and when topics are introduced into the curriculum that inevitably appeal to prejudice.

The second matter upon which we have a right to insist is that every teacher be sufficiently trained in human behavior to recognize the symptoms of various sorts of defects. He should be able to determine when the conduct of a child or an adolescent is due to some physical, psychological, social, or ethical weakness. The truth of the matter is that many teachers concentrate so intensely upon the material they are expected to present and the methods to be employed that they fail altogether to detect the causes of disturbed conditions in their students. Unless each has sufficient training in human behavior and human relations to recognize the sources of trouble it will be impossible to aid the student, even to consult a counselor. Giving the youngster a demerit, sending him out of the room, or dismissing him from class or school, is too often only a confession of the teacher's own limitations.

The third concern is the teacher's own integrity. We seem to assume that all teachers are morally mature and ethically well-developed. I know that this is a delicate matter. But how can we expect our children to attain high moral standards unless the teachers with whom they spend so much time are themselves examples in word and in deed of the character or integrity we want them to possess. When John Ruskin was asked how he became a great art critic, he answered simply but emphatically, "My father never allowed me to stand before a poor picture." What sort of pictures do we allow our children to stand before from day to day? Character is contagious. If we want our children to have it we must insist upon character in the teachers as well as in ourselves.

Academic Freedom

At the present time rabbis and congregations cannot disregard one of the most important problems in the community, that of academic freedom. I do not believe we should engage or maintain in office any teacher in elementary or high school or college who teaches doctrines that defeat democracy. This seems self-evident. But on the other hand I believe firmly that teachers must be free to expound the truth in every department of knowledge. This means that each one must be free to discuss the pros and cons of every controversial question. I do not know how it is possible to reach the truth except through freedom of discussion, freedom of information, and freedom of spirit.

I am convinced that the current attacks upon the schools and colleges are conducted by men and women who are concerned not with education but with a social orthodoxy evidencing their fear of progress and liberalism. I am also convinced that the present investigations by committees of Congress have as their purpose not the safeguarding of democracy but an increase in political prestige and power. I am acquainted with some of the so-called agents and investigators of these committees, having met them in my work with national and international organizations, and I have no hesitation whatever in stating that in my judgment they are utterly untrustworthy.

At the present time the climate in our educational life is not conducive to academic freedom. On the contrary, there is a distinct atmosphere of fear that is gravely affecting our whole educational system. This fear is the result of the activity of pressure groups who cannot distinguish between disloyalty and dissent. These groups are essentially totalitarian in spirit, and insist upon teachers conforming to systems fundamentally undemocratic. Dissent is of the essence of democracy. Beginning with the justices of the Supreme Court, we not only have the right but the duty to think our own thoughts and express our own opinions. The history of democracy proves that the minority opinion frequently becomes that of the majority.

There is less danger of dissent, of course, in the natural sciences and literature than in the social sciences. Men may differ in their understanding and interpretation of the laws of physics, chemistry, and biology, as well as of literary criticism. But there is serious danger when they differ from the majority in formulation and application of what are termed the laws of economics and political science and history. In these areas the fear of pressure groups has become so great that teachers in our elementary and high schools and colleges are fearful even to be known as liberal; and certainly they are so intimidated that they are afraid to become involved in controversial questions.

I am in close touch with teachers active on the different levels— the elementary school, the high school, and the college—and I have come to believe that the great majority on every level are so infected with fear that they have ceased to have any opinions of their own. Worse than this, they have become the most intense defenders of social orthodoxy. I am inclined to believe that the teaching group in our communities have become so conservative socially that they impede social progress. Academic freedom means the freedom to differ, to be a nonconformist, to become what at one time was called a social liberal. We no longer persecute men and women for their religious heresies, and we certainly do not in a democracy persecute them for scientific or artistic heresies. But we do condemn those who dare to differ in the matter of the social system. We seem to forget that freedom in the social sciences, especially in economics and political science, is the price we must pay for progress.

Community Programs

In some communities committees have been of great service in persuading the school authorities to introduce activities that have aided us to a better relationship between the school and the community and between groups in the community itself. There are principals in our city fully aware of the larger service schools can render through extracurricular activities, not included in the official curriculum of the Board of Education. But there is still much to be done. One thing we should like to see is expansion of the service of the elementary school and the high school. There is no reason why these modern buildings should not be open both during the day and evening all the year round. In some sections of the city there is a desperate need for afternoon activities for children, and evening activities for adults. This program we have begun to develop through the play-school in the afternoon and during the summer or vacation period.

The synagogues of the city could be of great service in discovering the social needs of the community and of still greater service in aiding the schools to meet them. I cannot but feel that one of the most important needs in every community is for higher ethical standards in the conduct of children and adolescents and adults. Up to this time we have made only tentative attempts to deal with this problem. I have before me a pamphlet issued by the National Education Association in Washington, D.C. entitled, "Human Values in the Grammar School." It is not enough for us to train the intellect and to increase the fund of knowledge. We must advance beyond this and undertake serious development of the moral sense of children and the ethical standards of the community.

The school is not only one of a group of social agencies. It is more than this; it is central to community life. We may not recognize this fact at the present time; but we shall come to realize that upon the school rests a responsibility for leadership in community organization and the development of community programs. This means more than arranging for meetings of groups within the school buildings, though even in this elementary activity not all schools are as generous as they should be. Many a community committee or agency in search of a place for weekly or monthly meetings and conferences finds it difficult to discover accommodations.

I am, however, thinking of a much larger program. I should like to see in every school a Division or Department of Social Studies, to do more than discuss social topics with the students. Some colleges, like the City College of New York, have gone far beyond this. They have organized departments that gather together authoritative social material of the district or the community in which they are situated. If such a department were organized in every school, as I should like it to be, it would do more than assemble the social material we need for clear understanding of the district or the community. It would also determine the social needs of the district, not only in education but in such fields as health and housing and recreation. But the department under proper leadership would go further than this. It would undertake to organize the social agencies of the district for social action. The school, the high school, and the college are in a strategic position. More than any other agency they represent the community. The school is an instrument of democracy.

One thing we lack at the present time is leadership, which means that we lack men and women in our school system who have large social interests and vision, and most of all social passion. In studying social agencies, organizations, and institutions in the community I feel that too many schools are too limited and that many of them are actually isolated. They are limited to an educational program in the narrow sense of the term, and they are isolated in the sense that they are out of contact with the community of which they are an essential part. If Parent-Teachers' Associations are seeking for a progressive program to develop herein lies their opportunity. Here and there they have come to realize they have a larger task than to meet once a month for discussion of their children's activities.

Social Service in the School

Another thing we should like to see is establishment in every school in underprivileged areas of a social service department similar to those in every well-organized hospital. At present a meager amount of work is being done in the field through visiting teachers and Bureaus of Child Guidance. But the visiting teachers are few in number and the Bureaus of Child Guidance are inadequately staffed and equipped. If the school in an underprivileged district were provided with a social service department properly organized, its problems could be studied and understood and met without delay and without loss. This department, of course, would work in cooperation with existing agencies in the community.

I recall urging a program of this kind in an address before a teachers' association in Boston in 1914. The response was immediate and enthusiastic, and in time I venture to say we shall discover ways in which to meet this need. This will require additional funds, but the investment will result in greatly improved community life. I know that teachers and principals now refer acute cases of social distress to existing agencies, but there are a number of disadvantages in this plan. First, the teacher is not aware of the social factors that influence the conduct of their children, nor are they at present sensitive to social conditions that need to be corrected. A social service department would develop a new sense of social awareness in the teaching staff and aid the teachers in discovering at the earliest possible moment the needs of the children and their families. Second, a break in continuity would be avoided if the school had its own department and would refer to other agencies only those cases in need of special treatment and financial assistance.

I do not mean that the social service department of the school should become a substitute for the welfare agency of the community.

But it should develop a program that would make the school and its department of social service useful to the members of the community who are in need because of social problems. For one thing the department could build up what we call a "resource file," available to teachers, parents, and other members of the community. It could also serve as a guide to the social facilities in the community. At the present time parents and others waste precious time and energy in trying to discover the best way to meet their social needs. Men and women are constantly looking for authoritative information and advice. In other words, the social service department in the school would become a consultation center to which members of the community could go for expert counsel and guidance.

This may sound academic or visionary. But the truth of the matter is that even today many teachers, principals, and deans do serve as consultants. They are constantly dealing with social problems in the life of the children or the students. But knowing the field somewhat, as I do, I am convinced that they are unable to be of fullest service because of their limitations. In the social service department I visualize there would be a staff composed of men and women who through training, experience, and personality would prove competent to serve in solution of social problems. I should even advocate that the department in the school be granted a fund out of which to meet emergency needs. As a result of long experience I know that such needs do arise and that they should be met immediately and adequately and of course expertly.

Every social agency has rules and procedures that make it difficult for those in need to secure assistance without delay. Another function of the staff would be to make direct contact with the proper agency, that is, with the agency which can best solve the problem. Only those who have training and experience and who know the resources of the community are able to select the proper agency to take charge of the man or woman or child involved. The program may sound radical, but its beginning has already been established through what is called the visiting teacher. However, the visiting teacher is today expected to cover too large an area and is not always equipped to serve effectively. There was a time when the social

workers in the hospital were all drawn from the nursing staff. Today
the hospital finds it advisable to engage social workers who are
trained for social service. The same thing, I am inclined to think,
will happen with the schools. At the present time only teachers are
employed as members of the staff. The day will come when we shall
admit socially trained men and women and place them in charge
of the social service department in the school.

4. RECREATION

The recreational movement in America is only of recent development. We are just beginning to realize that play or recreation is one
of the legitimate activities of life, especially for children, and that
the growing period of leisure time makes recreation and recreational programs a serious social need. Anyone who has walked or
rode through the streets of New York realizes how limited the recreational facilities are for every age group in the community. Many
playgrounds have been opened within the last twenty-five years, and
many facilities have been established in Central and other parks and
on Riverside Drive, but in neighborhood after neighborhood children are discovered on the street, in constant danger from traffic.
Some streets are shut off as play streets after school hours, but these
offer little opportunity for the kind of recreation our children need.
It is true that every school in the city should have what some already
have, that is, recreational programs both within and without the
school building.

Some principals realize this and have undertaken to develop recreational programs that not only save the child from danger but that
aid them in their social development; and they have also begun to
establish recreational programs to meet the needs of the adolescent
groups as well as groups of adults. Only a beginning has been made,
however. In one junior high school of which I know the Parent-
Teachers' Association has undertaken to develop recreational facilities, including concerts and dances, for boys and girls. It is natural
for children to want to play, and they should learn to do so in
ways that will develop them physically, mentally, and socially. If

children are not encouraged to play in the right way they will learn the wrong way. Every student of social life realizes that the gang is a perverted expression of a natural play instinct.

Our recreational facilities are not limited to playgrounds and parks. We must include motion pictures and theaters, museums and art galleries, and also radio and television. The interest of the synagogue in these facilities and activities cannot be restricted altogether to their absence or presence in the community. We are concerned with the kind of recreation that is provided through these media. It is a strange fact, but a fact nevertheless, that the poorer the neighborhood the lower the standard of recreational activities. Theaters and motion pictures that would not be tolerated in the better sections of the city are free to operate in the poorer. There is no reason why this should be permitted.

Among recreational facilities we must also include neighborhood houses and settlements and community centers. There is no reason, however, why centers with large social programs should be located only in underprivileged areas. Community centers if properly constructed and equipped can meet social needs in the recreational field. They can provide parlors in which men and women of the community may gather. They can equip game-rooms to which different age groups may be assigned, and they can also offer other recreational activities, such as halls and music for social gatherings and dances.

The great need for community centers in all sections of the city must be perfectly obvious to anyone acquainted with those living in apartment-hotels, rooming-houses, and overcrowded homes. Where else can people who live in apartment-hotels go except to their own rooms or to the lobby? Where can men and women go who work in offices and shops and factories and live in rooming-houses that line every side-street in New York? I often wonder how these men and women, young people especially, survive the drab existence to which they are condemned. Even worse are the homes that today are so overcrowded with members of the family or families that there is no place there for recreational opportunities. What a social blessing it would be if we could develop in every district of the city community centers that would study and meet the needs of the people of the district. These are just as necessary for a full community life as the school.

For Young People

Recreation and juvenile delinquency are closely related, for we now recognize that many children get into trouble during after-school hours and during the summer. When we consider that there are nearly 30,000,000 children in America of school age, and when we study the facilities available to them after school and during the summer, we realize how far short we have fallen in solution of this problem. Here is work for the Synagogue and the Church. They are both concerned with the moral welfare of the community, and juvenile delinquency strikes at the very heart of communal moral-ity. The tragic fact is that juvenile delinquency has increased during the last fifty years not only relatively but absolutely. There are more juvenile delinquents to every 1,000 children in the population than there were fifty years ago, and the total number in the country has now reached startling figures. The reports from the Children's Courts alone show that about 350,000 children become court cases. Not only has the number increased but something else has happened that is most disturbing. The age level has dropped from decade to decade. I recall that when I took my first course in criminology in the Sociology Department of the University of Chicago fifty-odd years ago, we were concerned with the group of twenty-five years of age and over. This was in the days of Lombroso and his school. Since that time the level has descended from twenty-five to twenty, from twenty to fifteen, and now even children under fifteen are classed as delinquents. In truth, the juvenile courts are limited by law to children under sixteen. No one can tell at what age level delin-quents will begin five years from now. But even more disturbing than their number and age level is the seriousness of the acts with which they are charged.

Children under sixteen are arrested now for such grave crimes as unlawful entry, burglary, arson, assault, holdups, rape, and murder. At one time these were crimes charged only to adults. We never thought children could be guilty of such misconduct. This problem of juvenile delinquency has developed in spite of the fact that during the past fifty years we have organized more agencies and institutions for the care of children than at any other time in our history. In fact the twentieth century has been known as the Century of the Child. In every large community there are agencies concerned with child welfare, endeavoring to protect children and to guard them against the dangers of breakdown. During the last forty years we have had a series of White House Conferences on Children that led to establishment of the Children's Bureau in Washington. Out of these have come programs for the correction of conditions that endanger the welfare of children, and others designed to protect the child already imperiled. A number of research organizations have devoted themselves to the study of juvenile delinquency, such as the Baker Foundation in Boston and the Juvenile Research Association in Chicago. One of the most illuminating studies has been made by Sheldon and Eleanor Glueck of Harvard University. They have recently completed and interpreted a ten year study of the problem, entitled, "Unraveling Juvenile Delinquency." The conclusions of this monumental piece of research and the interpretation of the material still leave us in doubt as to the causes. But the study has given us a more accurate and comprehensive picture than we previously possessed.

The Gluecks took 1000 boys from approximately the same social level, 500 of whom had come into conflict with the law and were therefore classified as juvenile delinquents; and 500 of whom were not charged with unlawful conduct and therefore were not classified as juvenile delinquents. These groups, one serving as the control, were studied thoroughly by doctors, psychiatrists, anthropologists, and social workers, in the hope of discovering the factors that lead to the delinquency of some boys rather than others. Differences in physical and psychical constitution are not sufficiently great to warrant us in saying that 500 of the 1,000 boys got into trouble because of somatic or psychological factors. But it is clear from the facts assembled and analyzed that family conditions and character structure played an important part in the conduct or misconduct of these groups. Family conditions and character structure are closely related. The conduct of the boys reflects the standards in family life. But more important is the fact that the character of these boys, their sense of values and their ethical concepts expressed in conduct, are closely related to the social complex and the social atmosphere. The Gluecks do not draw this conclusion, but it is perfectly clear from the study that the ways in which these boys spend their time out of school influence and determine their character and their conduct. It is difficult to escape the conclusion that if adequate recreational facilities had been available in the communities from which these boys came that many who fell into conflict with the law would have been saved. The community had done little if anything to correct the conditions in the boys' families, and still less to safeguard the delinquents against the weaknesses of character structure that led to misbehavior.

It is clear from these studies that a program of recreation alone will not solve the problem. For juvenile delinquency is sometimes due to physical defects in the child or adolescent; to social maladjustments; or to moral weaknesses and wrong ethical standards. But a well-developed program of recreation will do much to modify physical, psychological, and social defects, and to remedy weaknesses and standards. Especially is this true if the program of recreation for children and young people includes games and sports. I feel that much of the distortions and corruption in the sport world today, on the high school and college level as well as professional, are due to wrong standards and moral defects that develop and go uncorrected during childhood and adolescence. In games and sports and other forms of recreation it is quite possible for the instructor or supervisor to cultivate proper standards of conduct, association, and competition.

It is distressing to realize that young men allow themselves to be bribed and corrupted through sports. Those who have been following exposures during the last few years realize that the root of the trouble is in the moral life of these young men and women. A fully developed and progressive recreational program, however, would not limit itself to the children and young people who enroll and seek companions. Experiments have already been conducted that prove that even leaders and members of gangs can be converted if we go out to seek them and to win their confidence and cooperation. The program of the cellar club and the district gang is evidence of our failure to approach this problem in the proper spirit. Children and young people are not naturally vicious and malicious except in perverted and pathological cases. The vandals and the hoodlums in our city simply mean that we have begun too late and have begun in the wrong way. The trouble lies less in the children and the adolescents than in the delinquencies of society itself.

For Adults

A recreational program for adults would necessarily include two groups, the unmarried and the married. The unmarried group in the community is seldom considered or even studied. They constitute, however, an important section that has special problems and requires a carefully developed program. It is not generally known how large this group is. The latest information I have from population experts is that the unmarried males in the population from fifteen years upward constitute about 31%, and that the unmarried females from fifteen years are about 26%. This means that 27% or 28% of the population in these years are unmarried. On the basis of the census of 1950 this would comprise about thirty million males and females.

If these figures hold for the country they mean that a large section of the population in every community is uncared for by current recreational facilities. Our personal experience in the field of the rabbinate and marriage and family counseling confirms this statement. Not a week passes that the problem is not brought to our attention. In its simplest form it may be phrased in this way: Where can unmarried people gather and meet each other and feel safe? The Red Book of the Telephone Company lists a number of agencies registered as "Centers of Social Contact." Thus the needs of the unmarried for social contacts and recreational programs are being exploited by commercialized agencies. In this community as in others there are thousands of unmarried adults who have no recreational life, and who live from day to day, from year to year, without opportunity for meeting one another. Anyone acquainted with the field appreciates this social need and the loneliness that the unmarried feel. The consequences of our failure to make proper provision for the recreational needs of the unmarried are sometimes serious, expressing themselves in physical and psychical disturbances.

Not all of us realize the degree to which even married adults are limited in their recreation. Men and women who are married often speak of this. The women are busy day and night in taking care of the home and the children, and the men, occupied in office, shop, or factory, find little opportunity for recreation after they reach home.

Dr. Richard Cabot, in his book "What Men Live By," discusses four programs that to him are most important: Work, Worship, Love, Play. Dr. Cabot is correct. Play or recreation is a legitimate and necessary part of the program of life. I am thinking particularly of the working classes and the middle income group. In the housing projects we are now setting apart space for playgrounds and related activities. I believe that the time is near when we shall recognize that in every housing project space should be allocated for such purposes. There should be rooms and halls in each project to which men and women, as well as young people and children, can go, and where they can express themselves through games and other forms of play. To house them in closed-up apartments as we do at the present time is to neglect one of the most necessary activities in the life of these people.

If the working classes and the middle income groups were adequately accommodated and provision made for their recreational needs, they would live under less tension and develop less irritation with one another. Play releases and drains off irritations and impatience that lead to conflicts in family and neighborhood life. Many a person has complained to us, "We have no relief from the strain and drabness and weariness of our daily life. We never go out together, we seldom meet other people, we have no social contacts." Even the middle and upper income groups are endeavoring to seek relief through baby-sitting, a new development. Sooner or later we shall realize in every community the great need for recreational facilities for both the married and the unmarried, and accept the responsibility for meeting this need.

For the Aging

Recreation for children is of course only one need in the community. If the Synagogue and Church are to meet other needs, they must make provision for recreational activities for adolescents, adults, and also the aging. That the first groups are in want of recreational activities in the various city districts is perfectly clear. But there is only a growing awareness of the fact that the aging too require facilities to permit them to spend their leisure hours in a wholesome manner. Perhaps there is no group more acutely in need of study. We seem to forget that the aging have the greatest amount of unemployed time and that this time becomes not only a source of boredom but of distress. These men and women have lost their children through death or marriage or neglect, and they have found few inward resources on which to draw. They have no means of employing the skills they have developed and that they still possess to a diminishing degree. What they really need is not merely filling up the empty hours, but ways in which to employ the strength and powers now wasted. A recreational program for the aging would not limit itself to games, such as card playing, but would aid them in work programs, to make them feel that they are still of some value and can offer some contribution to the welfare of the community. Every student of this problem, as is evident from the White House Conference on the Aging, realizes the social waste we suffer through our failure to make adequate provision for the employment of the leisure time available in this group.

A program for the aging as I see it requires three steps. The first is appointment of a committee to study the problem, to be composed in large part of men and women sixty-five years old and over, and therefore directly interested. This committee would review the material thus far gathered and study the available literature. Accent is now on the aging. Many articles and books are appearing based upon experiments already conducted.

The second step would be organization of discussion groups of not more than twenty-five men and women. These would meet weekly to discuss the common interests, needs, and problems of the aging, in health, education, recreation, housing, and employment.

There is, as we know, a therapeutic value in group discussion, espe-cially if it is led by an expert in his own field. The group would in-vite from month to month specialists in the various aspects of geriatrics and gerontology.

The third step would naturally grow out of the group discussions, a program of service to members of the group and to others who seek counsel and guidance. This would include answers to these ques-tions: 1) What are the physical and psychical disturbances or diseases of the aging, and how can those in the different income brackets meet the cost of medical care? 2) What are the intellectual interests of the aging and how can these best be met? It is a great mistake, we know now, to assume that we stop growing intellectually at any age, if we are alive and alert. 3) What are the best forms of recreation for the aging and where can recreational facilities be established? Hobbies come within the scope of recreation, but recreation by no means limits itself to this item. There are activities in which the aging can engage that range from the simplest social gathering to classical and artistic expression. 4) What really are the greatest needs of the aging? Experiments are being developed that are sur-prisingly successful, but of which not many are able to avail them-selves. How can we make this information available to all?

The most troublesome and urgent questions are, of course: 5) in-come, and 6) employment. There are many sources of income, but not all can be made available to the aging. Some few are able to draw upon savings, pensions, and annuities. But the great majority must depend in part upon the Social Security program of the Federal Government and such additional funds as they may be able to earn. It is becoming increasingly clear that retirement at sixty-five years of age or at any age may be a source of decline and deteriora-tion for the individual, and also result in great social waste. If the White House Conference on Aging and other studies prove any-thing, it is that men and women for their own sakes and that of society, should be encouraged to continue functioning in accord-ance with their capacities.

We know that physical incapacity limits, or makes impossible, physical labor; and that intellectual and emotional disturbances unfit men and women for certain occupations, such as teaching. But we also know that many continue to function at various degrees of efficiency throughout their years. We discovered during the war and the subsequent period of prosperity the service the aging can render if properly encouraged. Now what has all this to do with recreation? Just this: That the program for the aging is essentially one that employs what would otherwise be leisure or wasted time. It can, and should, be made a recreational activity in the highest sense of the term. Recreation may also mean a change in the tempo of life and in occupation. Through a well-conceived program of recreation men are recreated. Nothing restores the aging to activity more surely than the feeling that they are engaged in a useful and enjoyable occupation. It is an error to think that the years of the aging are years of pessimism. They may be and often are filled with optimism and serenity.

Recreation and the Synagogue

Perhaps if we were wise and venturesome in this matter of recreation we should insist that synagogues and churches become active in providing recreational facilities. I am impatient as I walk through neighborhoods in this community and see houses of worship closed except for a few hours a week during the season, and sealed up altogether during the summer, when needs are greatest. This seems a tragic and inexcusable waste of building space and equipment. But some have built social centers that have become important community agencies in both education and recreation. I feel that every church and synagogue with rooms and halls and equipment that could be employed for recreational purposes, should organize programs for children, adolescents, adults, and the aged. It these were free, as they should be, of all proselytizing taint and addressed themselves solely to the recreational needs of the children, the institutions would render a greatly needed service to the community. Any committee of social action that studied the recreational problem in our city or district would be compelled to return to the synagogue and recommend a program of recreation that would profitably employ the accommodations in every building. Why well-equipped floors and rooms in a synagogue or church should be reserved for

only a few hours on Sunday morning or during the week, is difficult
for any socially minded person to understand. In too many the only
activity that interests the board of trustees or those in charge is one
that yields an income. We cannot allow ourselves to think in commercial terms. We are not in business for profit. We are organized
for service.

Some synagogues are successfully developing recreational programs. One item is the film, which should not be limited to film
forums. To me it would be a legitimate expenditure to invest funds
in the rental of films, that is, good pictures that entertain as well
as instruct. Another item is the social gathering and the dance.
It is much better for the community to gather to dance in the social
hall of the synagogue than in some of the places to which men and
women now go. Another means of recreation developing in synagogues is the "little theater," which not only encourages members
of the congregation to engage in theatricals, but to present plays and
musicals that entertain the congregation and their friends.

Plainly the synagogue is becoming a social center, and is meeting
the recreational and social needs of its members and the community.
But there is still much to be done. There is no reason why game-
rooms should not be equipped for the use of different age groups
in the congregation. It is not necessary to encourage or permit
gambling. I know that there are some who fear that a program of
this kind would secularize the synagogue. But if it is properly developed and supervised it will lift the level of recreational life and
establish proper standards even in this field.

We must not forget to include in the recreational activities the
Oneg Shabbat held in so many synagogues after the Friday evening
service. The cup of tea or coffee and the cake or cookies served at
the after-service gathering give men and women an opportunity
to meet socially and serves a definite purpose. I have heard some
officials comment upon the number of strangers who come to the
social gathering after worship. If they remembered that these men
and women have no other place to go, they would realize that the
Oneg Shabbat gathering meets a real need in the life of the community.

5. HOUSING

Housing is another basic social enterprise in which every syna-gogue and church must be interested. For it is as important as food and clothing, and as much a matter of social concern as health or education or recreation. The community recognizes this. For over a hundred years New York has been treating housing as a serious problem and as a social evil. In the course of these years many or-ganizations have attempted to reduce congestion and to eliminate slums, and many agencies have presented plans for improvement. Study after study has revealed anew that overcrowding and inade-quate facilities are dangers to human welfare. The slums, in the first place, breed disease. The records of the Health Department prove that there is a higher rate of disease and a higher death rate in slum areas than in other parts of the city. Some have been so utterly unsanitary and so deeply infected that they have become known as "lung blocks."

Secondly, we know through studies of neighborhoods by the Sociology Departments of the University of Chicago, New York University, and other colleges that slums also breed delinquency and vice and crime. It has been determined that social groups de-teriorate when they move into slum areas. These congested and di-lapidated sections of the city constitute a cesspool of evil. Inevitably the poison spreads to other sections. No community can regard itself as healthy and wholesome as long as the unsanitary areas exist. In self-protection, if for no other reason, the community as a whole must rid itself of these festering social sores. There is no city in which there is not a housing problem, and in which the problem has not become acute within the last decade. But not every com-munity is fully aware of the extent and depth of the evil.

Not only does the slum breed disease and delinquency and vice and crime. It does more. One aspect was expressed by a psychiatrist when he said to me, "No one will ever be able to calculate the amount of discord and distress and the number of emotional and mental breakdowns that are due to overcrowding and poor hous-ing." When people are herded together into congested and unsani-tary rooms they not only irritate each other; they develop conflicts that make mental health impossible. In order to grow normally in our mental and emotional life men and women, adolescents and children, must have space and some degree of quiet. Some slums are so destitute of every facility, so barren and so bleak, that every member of the family wants to escape from the home as quickly as possible.

There is another aspect that we must not overlook. Overcrowding and congestion break down the barriers of privacy and make impossible development of family life on a reasonably normal level. Mrs. Goldstein, who was deeply interested in both the housing problem and family development, closed one of her reports with these words: "We as mothers ought to know that it is impossible to rear the right kind of family in the wrong kind of home." This one sentence sums up the evil of compressing too many people into too small a place with improper provision for meeting family needs. We must realize that it is utterly inhuman to condemn families and masses of men and women and children to uninhabitable hovels that destroy human life and violate every standard of human value and welfare. The slum is an indictment of society and an index of the social conscience of the community. The fact that communities are now organizing committees and commissions to reduce this evil is an evidence of the awakened conscience of citizens all over America.

We must realize, however, that the housing evil is not limited to the city. We find it in towns and even in rural districts all over the country. In the years that I traveled about the United States to many communities I was always taken on rides through the residential parts of the city and shown the lovely homes of the wealthier people. In every case I surprised my host when I asked to be taken to the poorer sections and to see where the working-class lived. I never failed to find a slum district. In southern mill districts the evil was particularly evident and distressing. In town after town I found families living in wooden shacks owned by the mill corporations and rented out to the workers, usually at exorbitant rates. These shacks were utterly without conveniences or facilities, and some so poorly constructed that they made anything like normal living utterly impossible.

I have read a report of a housing study made in the city of Washington. In the capital of the United States with all its beautiful buildings there were still in 1954 blighted areas so dilapidated that they constituted nothing less than a disgrace to America. This study covers 75 acres of Washington's South-West section. Here 57% of the houses have outside toilets, 60% have no baths, 82% have no wash or laundry basins, 29% have no electricity, and 83% have no central heating. This district lies within five minutes from the Capitol. In 1945 Congress passed the Redevelopment Act. But the real estate interests in Washington contended that Congress had no power to authorize condemnation of real estate for slum clearance. The matter is now before the Supreme Court. In New York and other states this issue has already been decided. The state has the power through housing authorities to condemn slums and to replace them with housing projects. Without this power we should be utterly helpless.

In New York City some progress has been made during the last twenty years. The chairman of the City Housing Authority reports that 780 acres of the city's worst slums have been rebuilt and that 60,301 slum dwelling units have been destroyed. In their place 103,753 new dwelling units have been constructed. But this is less than one-tenth of the 900,000 acres it is estimated need to be cleared and rebuilt. In spite of the housing projects constructed along the East River Drive, in Harlem, the Bronx, and Brooklyn, and in spite of the fact that one billion dollars have been invested in housing since 1936, one out of five in the population is still a slum dweller.

One of the most disturbing factors in New York is the deterioration, and development of new slum areas, in sections of the city once middle income residential districts. This is especially true of side streets on the Middle West Side, and of large sections in Harlem and the Bronx. West of Central Park street after street is filling up with low income groups crowded into what were formerly brownstone houses. A recent study of an eight block area in this section, conducted by the Citizens Housing and Planning Council, revealed the fact that the population had increased from 13,900 in 1950 to 19,000 in 1953. Many single rooms in these blocks were occupied by whole families of from three to five persons. 71% of the furnished units shared baths and toilets with one to six other families or single tenants. Only 38% of the buildings were in good repair. The facilities were primitive and utterly inadequate. This new trend, called "creeping slums," is the result largely of the migration of Puerto Ricans. We have done nothing to anticipate the needs of this group, and are doing virtually nothing to correct the evil.

The synagogues and the churches have not been altogether uninterested or inactive. Some years ago Bishop Manning of the Episcopal Church built a model tenement flat in the nave of the Cathedral of St. John the Divine. He did this in order to awaken his congregation and to arouse the community. He patterned this model tenement after a flat in the San Juan section on the middle West Side, one of the worst slum areas in the city. It was so infested with evil that at night two policemen patrolled together. I recall when we brought Mayor LaGuardia to see this section. After making the tour he said, "This must be ended!" The houses were boarded up and destroyed. The ground is now occupied by the Amsterdam Housing Project, which provides proper housing facilities for people formerly condemned to uninhabitable slum conditions. But the churches and synagogues have not been nearly so interested and active as they should have been. The truth is that they have done little more than second the efforts of community organizations which for years have been endeavoring to end the evil and establish an adequate housing program.

The religious institutions have not had a program nor have they assumed leadership in this movement. The ministers and rabbis have not engaged in the crusade for better housing. They are so busy with other programs within and without their organizations that they have not been able to do more than give intermittent support to a movement that requires constant and intensive activity. The clergymen, to be sure, are not experts in this field. But I feel strongly that they should be something more than amateur social reformers. What they seem to lack is the passion for social reform that flamed in the hearts of the last generation of religious leaders.

I recall vividly my first experience in this field in New York. This was in 1904, when I was asked to make a study of conditions on the

East Side. After the tour was completed there was a meeting at the home of the chairman of the committee, on Fifth Avenue.

Said the chairman to me, "Now you have seen our slums and you have made the survey, what is your solution to the problem?"

I looked at him for a moment and replied, "Mr. Chairman, there is only one solution."

"What is that?"

"Dynamite!"

He was so startled that he nearly leaped from his chair. But what other solution has proved effective in past years? Fifty years ago tenement house reformers were cutting windows into railroad flats to let in a little light and a little air. In the course of this half century we have discussed and developed many plans. The study of the housing evil continues. One study has just been issued by the Housing Committee of the Community Service Society, active in housing reform for nearly a century. This repeats the same tragic story of overcrowding and of violation of every standard established in our community.

Of one thing we are certain, that the existing governmental agencies have proved utterly unable to curb spread of the slums. One reason is that there is no one agency responsible. The responsibility for correcting violations is divided among six different departments in New York City. In order to check on slums in one small area the present Mayor, Robert Wagner, has organized the representatives of these departments, housing, zoning, sanitation, health, and the others. But even these will not be able to correct the violations they discover. They will discover what we have always found, that it is easy to pass legislation, but exceedingly difficult to enforce laws, and even more difficult to punish those responsible for violations.

Another plan, the limited dividend corporations, has also failed to provide us with the housing needed for the low income groups. Even when the city does its utmost to encourage private builders, through tax exemption and other devices, it does not succeed in persuading groups and corporations to build housing projects. In fact private builders insist that they cannot possibly erect fireproof and adequately equipped housing projects for the rental that low income groups can afford. What the low income groups can afford is always a matter of debate. At present there seems to be general agreement that apartments and housing projects should rent at not less than $9 a room and that the rental should increase in accordance with accommodations from $15 to $20 a room. We must assume the conclusion many of us came to a half century ago, that housing is as much a public enterprise as the public school and the public hospital, and that the housing program, at least for low income groups, should be taken out of the hands of private builders and placed entirely in control of the Government.

This is what is happening in many communities. The Housing Authority is authorized to proceed with condemnation of such buildings as are judged uninhabitable and to construct housing projects with funds contributed by the city, the state, and the Federal Government. The bond issues based upon these funds are liquidated through rentals. The Housing Authority is also authorized to maintain and to administer the housing projects. In other words, the Authority is the landlord. But it has no power to control the most important items that enter into construction of housing projects, that is, the cost of land, material, and labor. Until we go beyond our present program and grant the Housing Authority powers greater than it now possesses, it will be impossible to build as rapidly and as cheaply as the problem requires.

The housing program is not a simple one; it must be considered at different levels of income of the various groups. We are not here concerned with those who can afford to pay $50 per room a month. Their needs can be met through private builders. Nor are we concerned with those who can pay from $30 to $50. The needs of this group likewise can be met by private builders. For the latter agree that they can construct fireproof accommodations with adequate equipment at these rates and still make a profit. But we are concerned with the middle income group that cannot afford to pay more than $30 and most of whom are able to pay nearer $20. In order to meet their needs it is necessary for builders to be granted assistance in the form of tax exemption or other subsidies. This is the group that at present find it difficult to secure accommodations. But those most in need of our concern are the low income group, that cannot afford more than $10 per room a month. Their annual income renders higher rents impossible. How serious this problem is at this level we realize when we learn that 75% of the families in America have incomes less than necessary to maintain them upon a decent and self-respecting level of life. This sounds incredible. But we must remember that the income of the United States is not divided equitably among the families of the country. Only 25% have incomes sufficiently high to permit them to live reasonably well at the present cost of living.

It is therefore necessary for us to reconcile ourselves to public housing, that is, to constructing homes for great groups of people with a clear understanding that these houses are to be built by the Government, and controlled and managed by the Government without profit. I say reconcile, because it has taken a long time for men and women in this country to realize that there are some social enterprises that must be socialized and that must be taken out of the area of private ownership, control, and profit. When I say Government I mean the Municipal, the State, and the Federal Governments. All have housing programs much too limited. The Federal Government especially has a program utterly inadequate to meet the needs of income groups least able to take care of themselves. We are still living in the shadow of private enterprise, that is, private ownership, private control, and private profit. Twenty years ago the Central Conference of American Rabbis stated in their Social Justice program that they favored public ownership in housing. We know of course that there is much opposition. At a rent hearing in New York on plans for a housing project in the Bronx the real estate interests were vehemently opposed, and no doubt expressed the sentiment of their group. We must also remember that many members of our congregations are owners of real estate, from which they derive not only a profit but a large part of their income. Therefore, when the rabbis advocate public housing, even for the lowest income groups, they find themselves in conflict with their own congregations. But the fact that many of our members own real estate and derive a part of their income from such ventures must not determine our program of action. If the low income groups can be served only through public housing, then public housing we must support.

Another point to be emphasized is that a great change has come in the pattern of housing construction, even for low income groups, during the last fifty years. Fifty years ago these families were housed in flats without heat or electricity or any of the conveniences and facilities we now believe necessary. The housing projects today must provide heat, electricity, toilet and bath facilities, and safe cooking conveniences. We know it is utterly impossible for private builders to construct such houses and to rent the rooms at what the income groups can afford, that is, not more than and probably less than $10 per room per month. There is no profit in such ventures, meaning no private profit. But there is a great social advantage in housing families in these groups in homes that are comfortable and adequate and that mean a higher standard of living. Another point we must keep in mind is that public housing must not be restricted, limited to any one group. There must be no limitations that will exclude people of any race or religion or nationality. Segregation in housing is just as intolerable as in education or employment. The housing projects we are constructing must be open and accessible to every group. This is also a dangerous doctrine, but one that will in time be sustained even by the courts. We should not, however, wait until the courts act. Congregations should take the lead in developing a social program in accordance with our social principles and ideals. How else can we hope to improve the life of all groups in the community except through practicing our own principles?

One interesting venture in the housing field is the action of some larger and stronger unions. Some few years ago the Amalgamated Clothing Workers of America erected a cooperative apartment project in the Bronx that has worked out very well. There is every reason to hope that the unions that are now expanding will invest their welfare funds in housing projects for their own members. This they can do in accordance with the law and with great advantage to themselves, since the projects would not be profit making enterprises. Another trend, it is interesting to note, is that we are now including within large housing projects not alone apartments and family accommodations, but recreational and health facilities. In one of the projects on the upper East Side Mt. Sinai Hospital will maintain a clinic staffed with its own men. This has been opposed by some medical men and societies, but unsuccessfully.

In another housing project planned for the upper West Side is a District Health Center that will probably be maintained by the Department of Health. This will serve not only families living in the project but the entire health district. A committee is now planning its program, which will include not only the activities of other Health Centers in the community, but also new activities to give the program more complete scope and the people in the housing project and health district better protection against disease.

In some housing projects we are also including day nurseries and kindergartens, mainly to accommodate children of working mothers. There is no reason why these mothers should travel great distances in order to place their children in nurseries maintained by outside organizations. It is difficult enough for them to work during the day and to take care of their homes. Plainly, we are considering the needs of the people and trying to meet them as adequately as we can.

There is one more suggestion I have thought about for a long time. In addition to the other activities I have mentioned I believe that in every large housing project there should be a social service office or what might be called a consultation center to which people could go for counsel and guidance when in difficulties. But it would do more than this. My hope is that the staff would study the individuals and families in the housing project, build up a friendly relation with each family, and endeavor to meet their needs as early as possible and as far as community facilities permit.

Of one thing I am sure, as a result of my experience in the field of social welfare, that we begin to aid people too late in the development of their troubles. Many agencies wait until people apply. But the new trend is for us not to tarry until people are so acutely in distress that they must seek us; it is our duty to seek them and an early solution of their problems. I have no fear of invading privacy nor of pauperization. If the staff of the Social Service Department within the housing project is properly trained and experienced, they will be able not only to establish right relations with the families living there, but to forestall many a disaster.

To sum up: Legislation has failed to prevent people from moving into unsuitable houses and has also failed to safeguard them against violation of the codes covering tenements. The limited dividend corporation has not succeeded in providing us with the homes we need for the working classes. Private enterprise certainly has failed to meet housing needs and is not interested in programs that yield no profit. The only solution is public housing with funds advanced by the city, the state, and especially by the Federal Government. This is the program that synagogues and churches should advocate and support.

6. GROUP RELATIONSHIPS

Another problem with which the Synagogue must be concerned, especially in our urban areas, is that of group relationships. Our urban population is composed of various groups and in some communities there are many varieties—racial, religious, national, and social. These differ in background, conventions, and customs, as well as in attitudes and outlooks on life. The members often live a segregated life, hence often do not know one another. It is not surprising, therefore, that in our communities we find misunderstanding, suspicion, friction, and group antagonism, developing under stress. Professor Giddings, of Columbia University, used to speak constantly of the two social principles he believed were operative in group relationships. One was "consciousness of kind," and the other was "dislike of the unlike." The first means that it is natural for men and women to associate with those who are of like mind and manner; to cultivate a form of life that is congenial, using this term in its original sense. This is a sociological formulation of the proverb, "Birds of a feather flock together."

We recognize that this type of organization is natural. But we must also recognize that it has its limitations and its dangers. It restricts us to the group into which we are born and in which we live and move and have our being. The danger is that we come to think of our own group not only in exclusive terms but in terms of superiority. Once we have reached this point we are in danger again of believing that our way of life is not only superior but that it is the only true way, and that only those who think and live and act as we do are worthy of association and salvation. "Consciousness of kind" may, unless corrected, lead to chauvinism and the doctrine of divine election.

The other principle, "dislike of the unlike," does not seem altogether valid, and requires more extended study and exploration. It is not always true that we dislike the unlike. On the contrary, we may be very curious about the unlike and in many cases greatly attracted to them. This is a fact with which everyone is acquainted who studies social relationships. The question therefore arises, when do we begin to dislike the unlike? Or to put this thought in another way, when do we develop our prejudices? One thing seems certain. Prejudice is not an inherited characteristic. Children do not inherit bias against other children or groups or against the unlike. I have seen little children in hospital wards and in institutions playing with no regard for race, religion, nationality, or social background; and I have seen, as others have, older children play games with no evidence whatever of dislike of the unlike. Prejudice seems to be an attribute we acquire in the course of our experience, either in home or school, in synagogue or church or community.

If we were to analyze prejudice we should probably find it based upon nothing more than ignorance of others. John Finley was correct when he reminded us that the word prejudice is composed of two words, *pre* and *judice,* to prejudge. It is also possible that in analyzing prejudice we may find that we begin to dislike the unlike only when the unlike for some reason becomes offensive or a burden or danger to our group. The customs and manners of another group may in our judgment be coarse and uncouth. Or the responsibility of caring for another group may tax our resources and become a burden. Or the invasion or presence of another group may serve as a threat, or be interpreted as a threat, to our own status, and therefore becomes a danger.

We have only begun to explore the area of xenophobia. Even the most liberal of us are not altogether free of fear of a stranger who has for some reason turned offensive to us or a danger to our welfare. The origin of these attitudes seems imbedded in the very environment in which we grow up and in the institutions of which we become a part, that is, the family, the school, the Church, the Synagogue, the fraternal organization, and in fact every social complex with which we are associated. Not all of us take the time to study our own prejudices and to trace their origin, and then to try to eliminate the poison from our system.

On one occasion, a group of ministers of which I was a part agreed to arrange an "experience meeting" in which we would frankly and openly discuss our prejudices. Perhaps the most telling and startling testimony came from one of the most liberal men I have ever known, John Haynes Holmes. Dr. Holmes confessed that for a long time he had been troubled because of a lingering prejudice toward the Catholic group. He said, "I have never had any prejudice whatever against the Negro or the Jew. We were accustomed in our home to see the Negro come and go and to sit at our table, but even when I was a student at Harvard, I found myself harboring a prejudice against the Catholics. Upon studying my own prejudice I discovered that I had grown up during my childhood and adolescence in a New England community in which the A.P.A. movement was rampant. The American Protective Association was the New England version of the Klu Klux Klan. The virulence of this poison spread throughout the community and I breathed it in as did others, and it undoubtedly affected my whole outlook upon group life. Now that I know the origin of this prejudice, I am able to purge myself of this poison and to meet the Catholic as well as the Jew and the Negro in a spirit of fellowship."

In order to eliminate the consequences of group conflict and antagonism and hostility we have developed several programs. One program rests upon education. We have tried to end misunderstanding between groups by educating them to understand one another. To a degree we have succeeded. Rachel DuBois in Philadelphia employed the educational method in the schools of the city. She gave the children tests in order to determine their attitudes toward groups other than the one to which they belonged. She then arranged for a series of assemblies designed to make them acquainted with the life of the other groups. Then, in another series of tests, she discovered that the assemblies had not only made the groups acquainted but had helped them to understand one another and had reduced misunderstanding and prejudice. This method can be extended, and is being employed in many synagogues and churches at the present time.

In the Stephen Wise Free Synagogue the children of the Religious School have invited other groups to share with them in various services, such as the *seder,* and they have visited other groups in their own churches and on their own holidays. These have included the Negroes, Chinese, Japanese, Puerto Ricans, and representatives of Protestant denominations. The result of this program has been not only an acquaintance among the groups, but the development of common interests and a spirit of cooperation. Every exchange of the pulpit has achieved the same result in the congregation. From year to year we invite distinguished representatives of other races, religions, and nationalities. It is illuminating to watch the congregation at these services, which are most instructive, and to hear the comments afterward. In many a service of this kind the members of the congregation pass through a new spiritual experience. Not only is their horizon enlarged, but their latent or active prejudices are eliminated. Surely this method could be further developed and greater results achieved with patience and perseverance.

I have had a number of experiences which confirm the feeling that these exchanges of ministers and union services are helpful. I remember receiving an invitation from the minister of Christ Church in Bethlehem, Pennsylvania. He wrote, "I am arranging a course of Sunday evening services on the general theme 'Peculiar Peoples,' and we should very much like to have you come and speak for us." I accepted the invitation partly to discover who the other "peculiar peoples" were. The church was packed that Sunday evening and I could feel the interest and excitement as we marched down the aisle in back of the choir to the altar.

When time for the sermon came the minister addressed us in this manner, "This course on 'Peculiar Peoples' is gradually reaching a climax. Two weeks ago we had a Chinese in the pulpit. Last week we had a Negro, and tonight we have Dr. Goldstein." The congregation waited, it seemed to me, somewhat breathlessly for me to arise and to speak. I shall never forget their surprise and sigh of relief when I began in the English tongue. This, I think, was their first contact with a rabbi, and certainly the first exposition they had heard of the principles of Judaism.

I also recall speaking at a religious service in Utica, New York. It was announced as a "Union Service." I looked about the congregation and asked the chairman, "Are there any Catholics and Jews attending?" He answered, "I think there are some Jews who heard of your coming. But we have invited only the Protestants." It seemed to them that to bring even Protestants sects together in Utica was a great community achievement. When I ended, I was convinced that they realized they should have included Catholics and Jews as well as Protestants. Why they should have asked a rabbi to address a "Union Service" of Protestants only I never was able to learn.

Another method of correcting group relationships and ending prejudice is legislation. In cities and states and the Federal Government we have passed laws designed to eliminate segregation and discrimination; and in some cities and states we have created committees or governmental agencies designed to enforce these laws. I was a member of the Executive Committee of the New York State Committee on Discrimination in Employment from 1941 to 1944, and I know how reluctant the members were to enforce legislation and to appeal to the courts. This Committee, like counterparts in other states, has endeavored to use education and persuasion to end discrimination in employment, and on the whole they have achieved much. There is no doubt that as a result of the city and state committees there is less discrimination today than twenty-five years ago, in employment, education, and housing.

The most important piece of legislation is the 14th Amendment and its interpretation. And The Supreme Court has determined that the 14th Amendment outlaws segregation in the different states of the Union, and does not mean merely equal facilities. This decision was epoch-making.

There were many problems involved. But even were the judgment of the Court adverse, the churches and the synagogues would still have had to insist upon an interpretation that all men are created equal and that all must be accorded equal opportunities for advancement, education, and development, otherwise we would have failed in our own faith.

In addition to education and legislation we have endeavored to end discrimination and to eliminate group friction through a number of organizations. The American Jewish Committee, the American Jewish Congress, and the Anti-Defamation League are all concerned with this problem. These, however, have to a great extent become "defense organizations." They have found it necessary to limit themselves largely to defending the Jewish group against misrepresentation and discrimination in the different areas in which this may occur. Their studies of the fields of entertainment, education, and employment, and the action taken through education and legislation, have undoubtedly removed some of the sources of misunderstanding, misrepresentation, and hostility.

A more positive approach has been developed by other groups, such as the National Conference of Christians and Jews. This organization, that has advanced from local to state, national, and international programs, has endeavored to end prejudice and develop better group relations through tours and conferences, in which the representatives of the different groups, Catholic, Protestant, and Jewish, have participated. Perhaps it is now possible to recognize the stages through which these and similar agencies have passed. In the beginning we thought we could accomplish our objective by arranging for luncheons and dinners at which the representatives of the various racial and religious groups would come together. We found that they came not only to dine but to compliment each other and to congratulate themselves upon achieving better community relationships. The luncheons, dinners, and tours helped to make people better acquainted and did remove some misunderstanding. Those of us, however, who were active in this first stage of the movement were sometimes doubtful of the results achieved. We felt we had done little more than touch the surface, and that the problem of prejudice itself remained unsolved.

The second stage was certainly an advance. Instead of coming together for compliments and congratulations, representatives of the groups agreed to meet and present their respective contributions to common community welfare in America. Those of us who passed through this stage remember the surprise the groups experienced when they learned what other groups had added to the culture of the community and the country. There was no attempt by the representatives at conversion; but there was a genuine endeavor on the part of each to acquaint the others with what his own had contributed to the treasury of human experience. This was not difficult, because every one had made important contributions, especially to the life of America.

The Catholic group, the Protestant, the Jewish, the Negro, and the Indian—all these and others have brought contributions without which we should be much poorer than we are. Each has enriched life in some way—culturally, economically, and politically. For every one has not only a history but a literature and art and science. For each group to learn to appreciate the contributions of others is a long step toward solution of the problem of prejudice and in easing group antagonism and hostility. The truth is that many groups do not themselves realize the contributions they have made. The one thing we must guard against at this stage is the concept of the "Melting Pot." We do not want people to be melted down into the same mold. On the contrary, what we seek is to encourage each group to make its own distinctive contribution and to develop its own peculiar genius. The picture of a symphony orchestra composed of different instruments all creating a harmony is far more accurate than that of the "Melting Pot."

In the next and third stage, we made even greater progress. Instead of coming together for compliments or to present the contributions of our respective groups, we gathered in this stage to discuss group grievances. This was going much more deeply into the problem. At one of the meetings held at Columbia University the Protestant, Catholic, and Jewish groups all agreed to draw up bills of particulars, to state frankly the faulty conditions or rather attitudes we suffered on the part of others. I remember that when the Jewish representative presented his bill of grievances and listed the misunderstandings and injustices from which his group suffered, both Protestants and Catholics nodded their heads in agreement. We all recognized that the Jews were victims of unfounded and unwarranted attitudes.

Then when the representative of the Catholics presented his bill of grievances, both the Jewish and Protestant groups seemed a little surprised. Yet we were compelled to recognize that in some parts of America Catholics are victims of prejudice. This is especially true in the South; and no one who remembers the presidential campaign of Al Smith will ever doubt it. It is not generally known, however, that it is difficult for a Catholic young woman to secure a place as a teacher in the South. But when the representative of the Protestant group presented his list of grievances, both Catholics and Jews were not only surprised; they were astonished. They had not believed that there was any part of the country in which Protestants, who constitute the majority, suffered prejudice, and yet we now know this to be true. We learned, for example, that in the state of Massachusetts, of all states, it is difficult for a Protestant young woman to secure a position as teacher in the public school system. This is only one example. The meeting as a whole was frank and open and most revealing to all of us.

We must recognize that there are differences between groups as there are differences between individuals. But the ways in which we differ are not as fundamental as those in which we are alike. We have much more in common, all of us—individuals and groups—than we have differences. I have read in the literature of anthropology, especially in the late Professor Dixon's book on the "Racial History of Mankind," that the human race may be divided into three groups: one has long heads, one round, and one broad. This is especially true of Europe. When I finished reading I was amazed at the amount of scientific material the anthropologists had gathered together in order to prove their theory of the "cephalic index."

But after thinking the matter over carefully I came to this conclusion. It is important to know that some groups have long heads, some round heads, and others broad heads. But it is far more important to remember that all groups have heads, and that all have hearts, and that all have hands. They have heads so that they can think about one another; they have hearts so that they may feel for each other; and they have hands so that they may work together for their common welfare. There is an ancient Jewish legend that when God decided to create man He did not make him out of the dust of Palestine. He gathered together dust from the four corners of the earth, and into this He breathed the spirit of life. We are only beginning to recognize the degree to which we are alike, both physically and mentally; and that what we all have in common is far more important and fundamental than the ways in which we differ.

Anthropologists and ethnologists are coming to see, from historical and comparative studies, that cultures even in widely separated areas of the world have more in common than they have in diversity. Men and women of different cultures speak different tongues, but there is a common element of language. They have varied modes of expression, but all have the common element of literature. They portray different forms of art, but all have the common element of artistic expression. They worship in a variety of religions, but maintain the common element of religious experience. There are different types of social organization, but the common element of government.

A trip through the Metropolitan Museum of Art and the Museum of Natural History in New York confirms these statements. It is surprising to discover how much we all have in common on every level of civilization. At times one is tempted to believe that the differences are due in large part to variations in time and stage of development. It may be that all the groups derive their culture from one original source; or that in the course of the centuries they have borrowed from one another, in an interchange of cultures; or that the groups have developed independently, but in accordance with fundamental human needs common to humankind. At the present time groups in Asia are achieving in a generation what it took those in Europe hundreds of years to accomplish; and groups in Africa within the next generation will develop culturally at even a more rapid pace. They have the advantage of interchange both of ideas and experiences. It is amazing to discover how rapidly Asiatic and African groups are adopting the cultures and costumes of Europeans and Americans.

A number of years ago a distinguished Protestant preacher, Dr. Crapsey, then on trial for heresy, delivered the sermon in the Free Synagogue. He divided his talk into three parts. In the first he discussed creed, saying, "When I compare our creeds with each other, yours and mine, I find that we are rather far apart, though they all are concerned with the same fundamental problems in religion." Then, discussing ceremonies, he remarked, "When I compare our ceremonies and festivals and rituals with each other I find that many of your ceremonies are very similar to ours and that many of them embody the same fundamental religious concepts." In the third part of his sermon he discussed social ideals: "When I compare your social ideals with ours I find that we have everything in common and that we have a common program of action to develop."

Perhaps in this conclusion Dr. Crapsey expressed the conviction to which many of us have come, that the best way to purge ourselves, our homes, our communities, and our institutions of prejudice is to work together for the advancement of the social ideals we hold in common. We may think differently in the matter of theology; we may observe ceremonies that are only similar to each other; but we can unite in a common effort to advance our common welfare. To work together is one of the best ways in which to develop good group relationships. This we shall do when we learn to take our religion seriously at its highest. When Jesus was asked to name the first great Commandment, he answered, "Thou shalt love the Lord thy God." When asked to name the second, he answered, "Thou shalt love thy neighbor as thyself." Both come from the Old Testament. But had Jesus been asked to name the third great Commandment he undoubtedly would have said, "Thou shalt love the stranger as thyself." This is also quoted from the Old Testament. It is the answer to xenophobia.

7. CIVIC REFORM

One area of social action to which the Synagogue and the Church cannot possibly be indifferent is civic reform. There is always a certain amount of incompetence and corruption and crime in the community, and periodically these evils come to the point where it becomes absolutely necessary for citizens to act. At the present time we are passing through, or are in the midst of, another wave of investigation, local, state, and national. There is, of course, a group in every congregation that insists that religion must not enter politics. This is composed in part of men and women who sincerely believe that the Church and the Synagogue should concern themselves only with religious matters, by which they mean theological doctrines and ceremonial observances. But the group also contains some so obsessed by the principle of the separation of church and state that they vehemently oppose any action which seems to involve the church and synagogue in matters of government. But I am inclined to believe that these are in large part of men and women who for various reasons, chiefly political, do not want Church or Synagogue to interfere with the existing regime. I have found that those who protest most vigorously usually are members of the party in power. Again and again in my experience I have found members of the congregation and Board of Trustees who resent any interest or activity on the part of religious leaders in the field of civic reform. But we must remember that incompetence, corruption, and crime are social evils and that the Church and the Synagogue cannot be silent in the presence of evil without betraying their own function and mission as moral guardians of the community.

Before describing our experience I think it is important to indicate a little more clearly what we mean by civic reform. In most cases the term is limited to conditions in municipal government. But there are like evils in state government, to which we cannot close our eyes. Not infrequently conditions in the state are just as evil as in the city. Beyond this, we must also concern ourselves with what is happening in the capital of our country and in the federal service. Within the past fifty years we have gone through periods in which we were compelled to admit with shame that even in the Federal Government there are incompetence, corruption, and crime. Another point we must emphasize is that civic reform does not and certainly should not concern itself only with correction of evils. This is but the first step. After correcting evils it is important to establish a positive program. A positive program in civic reform on the local, state, or national level may prove to be even more difficult to develop than the ending of the evils; for every right-minded man and woman will agree that social evils must be obviated. But not all agree upon the same social philosophy. For example, every thoughtful and earnest citizen agrees that we should not tolerate in government men who are incompetent, corrupt, or guilty of crime. But not all will assent that the city or state or nation own and control the basic social enterprises. We are still living in an area of private ownership, private management, and private property. It is therefore difficult to develop a positive program of civic reform in conflict with the social current philosophy of private enterprise.

Early in my career as a rabbi I learned this lesson. In 1907 I served a congregation in one of the suburbs of Brooklyn to supplement my income from the Free Synagogue, which in the early years had a very small budget. There I once preached against the political corruption that was then the shame of our city. Immediately after the sermon the president of the congregation protested, and so did a number of his friends. I discovered, however, what I did not know when I accepted the post—that the president was involved in questionable practices in the community, so unethical that they seemed to me to disqualify him to serve as president. I went to him, told him what I had discovered, and asked that he resign. To my disappointment and chagrin he refused, demanding, "Why don't you resign?" To strengthen his position he called a meeting of the Board of Trustees, but before the meeting appointed an additional number of trustees from among his friends, which was contrary to the Religious Corporation Law of the state. A number of members sympathized with my position, and when the meeting of the Board was called a brilliant young lawyer arose and said, "This meeting is called in violation of the Religious Corporation Law of the State of New York and is therefore invalid." The president looked at him in anger. "To what law do you refer?" The lawyer then read from the law, which clearly stated that the Board of Trustees could consist of only a limited number and that the president therefore had exceeded his powers. The president, becoming more irate, stated with all the vehemence of which he was capable, "I declare that law out of order!" A good part of the congregation resented his action and seceded. We then formed a new congregation, dedicated to a new religious and ethical program in the community.

I never felt that I could be patient with evil in government any more than I could be patient with wrongdoing in any other area of life. All through my career I have felt under the necessity of establishing a government in the city, state, and nation that would express the spirit of democracy and democratize our cultural order and economic system as well as our political organization. I have preached constantly that the whole social order must be democratized from the center to the circumference, which means that we must establish not only a political democracy but also an economic and a cultural democracy.

I recall very clearly that this social philosophy began to take form during my adolescence and in the years I lived in Chicago. It certainly was my belief while I was in Cincinnati. For in 1904 I supported Eugene V. Debs for President, not only because he was a protester against social evils but because of the positive social philosophy he presented. When I came to New York I continued to preach this social philosophy and to work with those committed to the same program. In 1929 I accepted the chairmanship of the Citizens' Committee for the election of Norman Thomas, because I saw in Thomas not only a protest against the incompetence, corruption, and crime in the city government of New York, but also because I believed in the validity of the social program he advocated. Some members of the congregation did not like this action on my part. They gave all the customary reasons for disapproval. But I discovered the real truth that they were all members of the Democratic Party, allied with Tammany Hall. The vote for Norman Thomas in 1929, to the surprise of all of us, totaled 250,000 and more. We looked upon this as a protest vote, and those of us who had been active in the campaign decided it would be an act of betrayal on our part against 250,000 citizens if we did nothing but protest. We met in the home of Norman Thomas shortly after the election, to organize what we called the City Affairs Committee and to adopt a program of action.

This was the simple beginning of what became one of the most active, energetic, and successful civic reform movements in the history of New York. With but few resources, we decided to arrange for a public meeting to test out the people who had voted with us. John Haynes Holmes was kind enough to offer us his Parish House in the rear of the church, then on 34th Street and Park Avenue. We gladly accepted, for we had no funds with which to rent a hall. Our committee arranged to have supper together before the meeting, which was set for a Sunday afternoon. When we arrived within sight of the church we found a great crowd massed around the Parish House and the church. Dr. Holmes threw up his hands and said, "It looks as if we have another fire!"

He opened the church, and within a few moments it was packed, with thousands assembled on the outside clamoring to get in. I had the privilege of presiding, and no one present will forget the tremendous enthusiasm of the people both inside and outside. This meeting gave us courage to organize officially, and to plan a series of public gatherings in Carnegie Hall and other places, everyone of which overflowed the auditorium. The original City Affairs Committee included Norman Thomas, John Haynes Holmes, Stephen S. Wise, John Howard Melish, John Howland Lathrop, and myself. All were in our maturity and all had had training and experience in the fields of civic work and civic reform. Dr. Melish had been a reform leader in Cincinnati; Dr. Wise had already delivered his "Night of Shame" address; and Norman Thomas and John Howland Lathrop had been engaged in that work for years. I speak of this because I am convinced that civic crusades cannot hope to succeed if they are led by immature amateurs and by men who lack the passion for civic righteousness.

Even though we were not amateurs ourselves, we realized that in order to proceed effectively and aggressively it would be necessary to have the cooperation of experts and the counsel of the ablest men we could find. We engaged Paul Blanchard as Executive Secretary, and succeeded in enlisting the active cooperation of such men as Joseph D. McGoldrick, an expert in municipal government, and Samuel Seabury, a distinguished lawyer and civic-minded citizen. Norman Thomas, John Haynes Holmes, and Stephen S. Wise became our ablest spokesmen. We met from week to week to discuss our problems, to outline our program, and to advance what we believed would be a movement for civic betterment. We realized at once that incompetence, corruption, and crime were abstract terms, and that these evils would not exist if there were not men with these disabilities in the city government. This was a most important point for us, for it convinced the people of New York that we were concerned with concrete and specific problems and that we were not politicians with abstractions in the realm of homiletics. It was not too difficult to gather the evidence we needed to expose Tammany Hall and to indict the political leaders of that time. The politicians had become so bold and so reckless that it was not too difficult to uncover their practices. In every department we found evidence of incompetent management and mal-administration, corruption, bribery, and dishonesty; but worst of all, we discovered that the politicians were working in collusion with gangsters and criminals. The citizens of New York had every reason to suspect what was taking place, but they did not become thoroughly aroused until we openly focused their wrath upon the leaders who had betrayed the city.

There were a number of men who stood out prominently because of their evil conduct, and these were included in our crusade against the evil conditions that disgraced New York. But the outstanding figure of the time was James J. Walker, mayor of the city and leader of the Democratic Party. We knew we would have to do something vigorous and dramatic in order to dislodge him. I remember vividly the afternoon meeting when we agreed it would be a strategic move on our part to impeach James J. Walker. Some people smiled and some scoffed. How could we impeach the man who had become the darling of New York, and who was so deeply entrenched in the affection of the people in spite of, and perhaps because of, his weaknesses and night club antics? But we decided to study the Charter and found, not to our surprise, that James J. Walker had been guilty not only of malfeasance in office but also of other crimes. On the basis of our findings we proceeded to impeach him. It is not generally known, but the first impeachment papers of James J. Walker were drawn up in Dr. Stephen S. Wise's study in the Free Synagogue, with the full committee in attendance around the table. The case was presented to the Governor of the State of New York, Franklin Delano Roosevelt. The Governor hesitated to act. But when Samuel Seabury decided to prosecute the case he agreed to hold hearings. The evidence the City Affairs Committee presented through Seabury and his counsel was so cogent and conclusive that the outcome was inevitable. James J. Walker found it advisable to take a trip to Europe for his health, and the crusade for civic reform was won. This was a signal victory, for it put an end for the time being to control of the City of New York by the evil forces of Tammany Hall; and it introduced a decade of civic improvement and civic honesty through the election and administration of Mayor Fiorello H. LaGuardia.

In this program we did not have the cooperation, I regret to say, of all the churches and all the synagogues. There were many ministers in New York who still believed with their congregants that the church and the synagogue should not invade the province of politics. The action of the Catholic Church was especially disappointing to those of us endeavoring to rid the city of James J. Walker and Tammany Hall. The mayor invoked every power he possessed, to protect himself, going far beyond decency. For at the time that he was under indictment he decided to lead the St. Patrick's Day parade up Fifth Avenue. This was a bold and defiant bid for popular vindication. We were not surprised that the crowds gathered to see the parade and to applaud him; but we were astonished at what happened. When it reached St. Patrick's Cathedral on Fifth Avenue and Fiftieth Street the parade stopped. The doors of St. Patrick's Cathedral opened, and Cardinal Hayes in full regalia and followed by his whole retinue of associates and assistants marched down to the curb and shook hands with James J. Walker. So far as we knew this was the first time that anything like this had occurred. We could understand and condemn Walker's conduct; but we could not understand nor could we condone the action of the Catholic Church in this civic crisis. The Church could not exonerate itself on the ground that it did not believe in mixing religion and politics, for through this official action it gave its blessing and support to the man guilty not only of personal misconduct but of betraying the city into the hands of incompetent, corrupt, and criminal politicians. As far as the records show the Catholic Church has not cooperated with any reform movement in any crisis in the government of the City of New York. But in spite of this attitude on its part and of many other churches and synagogues the crusades for civic betterment have been triumphant.

In the state government we face a different and somewhat more difficult problem. First, the Governor in New York State and in most other states is usually an able and honest man. The heads of the state departments are generally able and trustworthy. But this does not mean that there are not incompetence and inefficiency in the government and Legislature, and that there is not dishonesty and corruption among the politicians, nor collusion between the politicians and the underworld. The recent exposures in relation to harness racing clearly prove these statements are not without foundation. More than this, the investigations conducted by the State Crime Commission reveal criminal associations of widespread extent. One difficulty in regard to the state government is that it is more remote from the people than the city government, and only those who have been in close touch with the capital of the state and the machinery of its government realize the defects and the dangers. Another difficulty is that the state government is distributed over so large an area that it is difficult for anyone not in close touch with the machinery to discover what is taking place at distant points. The ramifications are so many and widespread that not even the Governor, though able and honest, can be aware of what is taking place. The third difficulty is that responsibility for what takes place in the state government is not always centered in the Governor and his immediate commissioners and associates. The result is that incompetence, corruption, and crime develop at distances from the capitals, and the conditions do not become evident until they grow acute. It is therefore doubly difficult for the citizens to be cognizant of what is happening in the government of the state until exposure uncovers the evils.

During my many visits to Albany, and as the result of attending hearings before committees of the Legislature, I have often felt that there should be a state organization as active in protecting the people of the state as municipal organizations have been. The churches and the synagogues certainly could do more than they are at the present time. We have state organizations of churches and synagogues or affiliated groups, but thus far they have not concerned themselves with what takes place in the government of the state. Some church bodies, it is true, have legislative representatives at Albany and in other capitals. But these seem to limit themselves to legislation that may be contrary to the teachings and doctrines of a particular church, or that is designed to advance church policies. In all these years I have never heard of a representative of any religious group protest against evils in the state government. Individual ministers from time to time have arisen to speak; but they have spoken as individuals and not as representatives of religious bodies.

Here is an opportunity for a group of religious leaders to engage in a program of civic reform of statewide extent. But in order to be effective it would be necessary for these men and women to be trained in an understanding of state government and to be experienced in the ways of politicians. One thing they certainly can do: study the record and activities not alone of members of the Legislature, but of the leaders of political parties throughout the commonwealth. They would be amazed to discover how much they could learn and the extent to which they could serve as guardians of the welfare of the people. Members of the Legislature and the state government are free to be incompetent and corrupt because they know they are not under observation and that the citizens do not know the facts. This is a radical recommendation and will not be approved by the churches, synagogues, and officers of congregations. "We have enough to do," they say, "without entering politics."

In the Federal Government civic reform is at once a more complicated and more challenging problem. From a distance Washington presents one picture. But near at hand the picture changes. For over a decade I was closely associated with Benjamin Marsh, of the "People's Lobby," and from him and my many trips to Washington I learned something of the problems we face in the capital of our country. Marsh knew Washington thoroughly, and the members of Congress not only respected him for his disinterestedness but admired him for his command of material. He was always well posted on every problem he discussed with the members of the House and Senate, and he enjoyed the confidence of key men in the capital. In these hearings and conferences I learned there are some very able men in both houses, and some of great distinction.

But there are also men in the Senate, and particularly in the House of Representatives, who are of limited capacity and not able to cope with federal problems. On one occasion I expressed my surprise at this fact to one of the ablest members. He said, "You must remember that not all the members of Congress are trained in economics and political science and the art of government. Many have had only a meager education and only local experience. It takes time for them to grow to a national outlook." It is safe to say that not many men in Congress, who are in the executive department of the Government, are themselves corrupt. But it is fair to assert that they often condone practices in their associates and subordinates that are unethical and at times illegal. The Kefauver investigation revealed one fact, that the criminal groups across the country could not continue and prosper if not for the protection they expect and receive from politicians in the federal as well as in the state and municipal governments. Civic reform has not yet purged government on any level, of inefficiency and bribery and criminal collusion.

When we turn from the evils in government and endeavor to develop positive programs we meet new problems. Everyone who has tried to improve social conditions through legislation knows that he must expect criticism and opposition. I have faced this many times, but one experience will illustrate what happens. This was on the occasion when Father McGowan, of the National Catholic Welfare Conference, James Myers, of the National Council of Churches, and I were working together in Washington as representatives of our respective religious groups. As a result of our study of the social crisis during the thirties we came to the conclusion that one of the greatest evils of the time was mal-distribution of the national income. Even during the depression or economic collapse there was sufficient income in the country to maintain every family upon a decent and self-supporting level. The trouble was

that the national income was not equitably distributed. We therefore decided to present a program to correct this evil. In company
with a group of experts in the field of taxation we prepared a brief
in which we advocated taxation not only for revenue but for the
purpose of redistributing income. The center of our emphasis and
the cardinal point was the contention that the Federal Government
should not only approve a minimum wage but enforce a maximum
income. It was our belief that the wage of the wage-earner could
never be high enough to be just unless the maximum income was
low enough to make justice possible. When we presented this brief
to the Ways and Means Committee of the House of Representatives
the chairman asked us, "What do you propose as the maximum income?" We answered, "$25,000 a year." This was six years before
President Roosevelt advocated the same program and the same
recommendation. The Ways and Means Committee rejected our
recommendation.

But the news wires out of Washington carried our presentation
and recommendation to every section of the country. I had hardly
returned to New York before I received a number of messages of
criticism and protest. One telegram was from a prominent Jewish
leader in St. Louis, then president of an important congregation
and an influential member of the Union of American Hebrew Congregations. He protested violently against the presentation and
wanted to know on what authority I had spoken for the Jews. I wrote
him that as chairman of the Social Justice Commission of the Central
Conference of American Rabbis I had advocated only what the rabbis had agreed upon in their Annual Conference. He wrote back, "I
am horrified to learn that the members of the Central Conference
of American Rabbis are engaged in a conspiracy to re-elect Mr.
Roosevelt." It is needless to add that he did not sympathize with the
program of the New Deal. In my answer I assured him that the
rabbis were not primarily concerned with the re-election of Mr.
Roosevelt, but that they were very greatly concerned with the advancement of a program of social justice. The next week he sent me
a clipping from the St. Louis Post Despatch that contained a sermon by a Baptist minister insisting that ministers and churches
must not enter the field of politics. At the bottom of the clipping

this distinguished Jewish leader wrote, "Will the rabbis please take note." I wrote him at once as follows, "The members of the Central Conference of American Rabbis take their gospel from the prophets of Israel and not from the Baptist minister of St. Louis." His answer was what I expected it would be: "I resign." This experience illustrates very clearly what we must expect when we engage in positive programs of civic reform, whether upon the municipal, state, or national level. Most men are ardent in their endeavor to maintain the social system that maintains them.

8. CIVIL LIBERTIES

Civil liberties is one field of social action in which the synagogues and the churches have been not only interested but active. This is not surprising for two reasons. In the first place, religion in order to develop and progress must possess the fundamental freedoms; and second, the limitation or denial of civil liberties constitutes one of the most serious evils of our time. Civil liberties have a long history, dating back to the Magna Carta and the achievement of elementary political rights. As the centuries have passed we have gradually enlarged the area of civil liberties through the "Rights of Man" of the French Revolution and the "Bill of Rights" of the American Constitution, until today we are thinking not only of political rights but also of economic, educational, and social rights, or to use the most general term, human rights.

The "Universal Declaration of Human Rights" formulated by a Commission of the United Nations represents the advanced thought of our own time. We at last have come to see that freedom of speech, assembly, the press, and religion, can have little meaning unless we also have freedom of thought, of education, of inquiry and research, freedom to work, to earn a living, and to develop ourselves and our capacities and our personalities. It is important to emphasize this larger meaning of civil liberties not only because we have come to understand our own needs, but because in many sections of the earth men and women will not listen to a discussion of political rights if they are denied the right to maintain themselves and to develop in decency and self-respect. In other words, political rights have little meaning without economic and social rights. This is the new scope in the "Universal Decaration of Human Rights."

The limitation and violation of civil liberties become acute with every war. In wartime and during the aftermath of war, security becomes the chief concern of the Government; and in order to assure security it seems necessary in the judgment of some to limit our freedoms. The great danger, however, is that men both within and without the Government do not always distinguish between dissent and disloyalty, nor do they always recognize the difference between the right of revolution and treason. In disloyalty and treason there is always present an unethical motive. They mean the betrayal of one's country to an enemy. Benedict Arnold is a classic example. But dissent is certainly not unethical. The members of the Supreme Court of the United States dissent, and members of Congress dissent from one another and from the Administration. This is what democracy means. The right of revolution is also not necessarily unethical. The United States was born through exercising that right, and the right to revolt against tyranny is too precious to surrender even in times of turmoil. Without it some of the great religions would not have come into being. Prophetic Judaism is a revolt against the religion of the priesthood; Christianity is a revolt against the ritualism of the established order; Protestanism is a revolt against the Church of Rome. The grave danger is that men of the established order think in terms of conformity, and condemn as disloyal and treasonable those who do not conform, forgetting that conformity means to conform to what our own special group wishes to maintain and to preserve. To dissent from conformity and to revolt against tyranny is an ethical imperative. These rights religion cannot surrender without violating its own spirit of progress. We must be free in order to grow and to fulfill our own destiny.

During the First World War the violation of civil liberties became especially acute. State after state in the United States passed what were called, strangely enough, "Syndicalist Laws"; and cities enacted ordinances that attempted to limit liberties guaranteed by the Constitution of the United States. During the war we could do little to mitigate or end these evils. The rights of freedom of speech, freedom of assembly, and freedom of the press were not only limited but openly violated. The State of New Jersey served as example of what could and did happen in America. One minister was arrested for attempting to read the Constitution of the United States on the steps of the Court House in Paterson. The charge against him was that he had not secured a permit. In another city in New Jersey a little group of us were prevented from walking within three blocks of a factory in which a strike was being waged. To approach nearer, we were told, would violate a city ordinance. In Jersey City proper, controlled by the infamous Mayor Hague, we were prevented again and again from exercising the right of free speech, free assembly, and free press.

These are only a few examples of what occurred during the First World War and thereafter. In every section of the country the same story was repeated. Committees and groups of citizens who attempted to challenge the "Syndicalist Laws" were not only arrested but charged with treason. This was a period of grave reaction, doubly disappointing in view of the fact that the war had been fought in order to make the world safe for democracy and democratic principles. The argument was then as always that the country was in danger and must be protected, which meant that it must be protected against those venturing to dissent. Then as always dissent and non-comformity were interpreted as disloyalty and treason. Those who questioned the wisdom of the lawmakers were openly condemned as conspirators with the enemy.

Conditions became so grave and the danger to all our liberties so threatening that some action had to be taken. We invited a little group of ministers to meet at the Synagogue House for discussion and to outline a program of action. In this group were John Haynes Holmes, Harry Emerson Fosdick, Bishop Francis J. McConnell, and John Howland Lathrop, as well as Stephen S. Wise and myself. We were all deeply concerned not only about the violations of freedom of speech, assembly, and press, but also about others, such as freedom of worship and the freedom to unionize and to elect representatives of labor's own choosing. After reviewing the problem carefully with the Civil Liberties Union, especially with Roger Baldwin, we decided to go to Washington to ask for a conference with a group of liberal-minded senators. In Washington we arranged to meet with Senators William Borah, Edward Costigan, Fulton Cutting, and Robert La Follette, Jr. These men, we learned, were as much concerned over the violations of civil liberties as we, and they frankly asked, "What action would you recommend?" We had all had some experience in legislation, municipal, state, and federal, and we recommended an investigation of the violation of civil liberties in the states. The senators inquired, "Who do you think should undertake this task?" We suggested the Judiciary Committee of the Senate as the proper body. This was a bold recommendation. Senator Borah, always a defender of states' rights, said, "I do not see how a committee of the United States Senate can investigate the violations of civil liberties in the individual states. This would be an invasion of states' rights." Senator Costigan, at that time one of the wisest men in the Senate, turned to Senator Borah and remarked, "But, my dear senator, we are all citizens of the United States and our liberties are guaranteed by the Constitution of the United States."

The next step was to invite representatives of education and labor to meet with us. Among these were William Green, of The American Federation of Labor; John L. Lewis, of the United Mine Workers of America; Sidney Hillman, of The Amalgamated Clothing Workers; and John Dewey, of Columbia University. These and other men immediately came to our support. At a large dinner meeting at the Cosmos Club in Washington we presented our case to the liberal members of the Senate and of the House. It was a stirring meeting. Robert La Follette, Jr. agreed to introduce a bill calling for an investigation of the "Syndicalist Laws" and the violation of civil liberties in the states. This was the beginning of the great La Follette investigation, which continued for three years and exposed violations in state after state.

Hearings were held in Washington from week to week. It was the function of our committee to bring together men and women from all parts of the country and from different groups to testify. The educational and labor groups were especially active and effective. We also succeeded in awakening the religious groups, who marshaled representatives of the Federal Council of Churches, the

National Catholic Welfare Conference, and the Central Conference of American Rabbis. The proceedings were publicized across the country, and the La Follette Committee with its staff uncovered conditions that threatened our liberties in every area. Academic freedom was being violated as it is today, and political rights were being extinguished in every part of the United States. But the evidence assembled and presented by the witnesses proved that not only were rights being violated but that utterly un-American techniques were being employed.

One young Protestant minister was condemned as a traitor in Texas because in a Christian Endeavor Society meeting he advocated social equality of all races. More important than the charge, however, was the fact that the evidence of his "crime" was secured through a dictograph secretly planted in the hall by a Post of the American Legion. This is only one illustration, however, of what was happening all over the country. In the labor field particularly, conditions were uncovered by the La Follette Committee that shocked the citizens of America. Not only did the Committee discover that corporations were assembling arsenals in their buildings, but that they were employing a system of espionage that violated every standard of civil liberties. Private detectives and agencies were employed by the larger corporations concerned with only one thing, a defeat of unionism in America. "Labor spies" were introduced into the unions for the sole purpose of disrupting the meetings and destroying the organizations that were endeavoring to establish themselves in accordance with the rights of labor to organize and to bargain collectively through representatives of their own choosing. The Committee could not prevent the strikes, lockouts, and bloodshed that occurred during this period. But it did succeed in exposing evils and in arousing the working people of the country. Many of the "Syndicalist Laws" were repealed and we recovered to some degree freedom of speech, assembly, and the press. But much more important, the working classes in America recovered their courage and their determination to emancipate themselves from corporation controls that would have meant little more than industrial servitude if they had been allowed to develop. Too much credit cannot be given the La Follette Committee for the service it rendered in a period when civil liberties, especially in the industrial field, were not only threatened but deliberately denied.

Today we are passing through another period of danger. But this does not arise from laws of the states and ordinances of the cities that violate liberties guaranteed by the Constitution of the United States. Instead the perils are now due to the very men elected to protect and safeguard our liberties, members of the Senate and the House of Representatives. Incredible as it may sound, the gravest danger to the liberties in our democracy are now due to small groups of men in Congress who are members of so-called "Investigating Committees." No one questions the right of Congress to investigate through legitimate committees and to employ methods in accordance with democratic procedures. But we do question the right of committees to employ the techniques of insinuation and misrepresentation and half truths and whole falsehoods. These Committees base their operations upon the claim that the country is in grave danger of communist control. They insist that communists have infiltrated government, education, and industry, as well as the army and the ministry of religion. The leader of this movement is the junior senator from Wisconsin, Joseph M. McCarthy, and he has become master of the methods of McCarthyism. McCarthy, however, is not alone in his crusade to save America. He is seconded by two other "Investigating Committees," the Velde Committee and the Jenner Committee; and he is supported by members of both the Senate and the House of Representatives who share his views, who approve of his techniques, and who provide him with appropriations with which to conduct his probes. The members of Congress cannot relieve themselves of responsibility for the actions of their "Investigating Committees," and the consequences that inevitably follow.

We do not condone the activities of communists or communism in any area in America, in government, education, industry, the army, or religion. Again and again we have condemned it, as we have condemned fascism, as a danger to democracy. But we also condemn the methods of "investigation" that take the form of heresy trials and inquisitions. It is difficult to escape the feeling that the men conducting these "investigations" are more concerned with political prestige and political power than with the menace of communism. The consequences of their methods are evident in many important areas of our life. In the government services, both domestic and foreign, there has been a large number of resignations of important men and also a distinct lowering of morale. Members of both the domestic and foreign government services are disinclined to expose themselves to attacks of McCarthyism. They do not feel free to comment and to criticize and to report the facts as they discover them. Naturally they dread the charge of disloyalty, and this makes it impossible for them to work in the spirit of freedom.

In the field of education a number of distinguished educators have courageously opposed the "investigations" of colleges and faculties. But in many communities the teaching staff is haunted by fear, and they are especially fearful of this new "crime" of guilt by association. Freedom of speech and assembly and the press have all suffered. But more important, freedoms of thought and inquiry and research have suffered even more. The teaching profession in many communities is so thoroughly intimidated that freedom has become a shadow and has lost its substance. When this profession loses its sense of freedom it loses the most precious thing it possesses in a democracy.

In industry, in offices, and in shops and factories there is a growing epidemic of suspicion and mistrust. The "undercover" man or woman and the new system of espionage have frightened many workers and terrified their families. They do not know when they will be charged with disloyalty or treason and lose their means of livelihood. This is an extremely serious matter, for it means not only a threat to the freedoms enumerated in the "Bill of Rights," but also to the freedom to work and to earn a living for self and for family.

In religion the ministers have reacted vigorously and with courage to the charges that they are advocates of communism and agents of communist organizations. The leaders not only resent the charge of disloyalty, but insist upon the right to speak the truth as the truth is revealed to them. They have openly and without equivocation condemned both the men and the methods of the investigating committees. There are, of course, some men in the ministry who are timid, and so eager to conform that they are ready to acquiesce even when their liberties are limited and violated. There are also congregations in which the members are so conservative that they are fearful of the taint of liberalism. This is not surprising, for these congregations regard religion as a bulwark and buttress of the established social order. But fortunately this is not true of the leaders of religion and religious organizations. When the Velde Committee released the statement that Dr. Stephen S. Wise and Dr. Judah L. Magnus had been associated with communist organizations, and that Dr. John Haynes Holmes and Professor Harry Ward were the spokesmen of communism I wrote the chairman of the Committee the following letter:

September 16, 1953

Hon. Harold H. Velde
House of Representatives
Washington, D. C.

Dear Sir:

I was Dr. Stephen S. Wise's associate in the rabbinate of the Free Synagogue for over forty years, from 1907 until the day of his death, and I knew him intimately; I knew Dr. Judah L. Magnus from the time we were students at the Hebrew Union College in 1900; I have known Dr. John Haynes Holmes and Dr. Harry Ward as dear and cherished friends for nearly half a century. I do not write this letter to your Committee in defense of these men. They need no defense. Their lives of patriotic and heroic service to their country and to every humanitarian cause are sufficient answers to every slanderous statement issued to the press through your Committee.

But I do write, as an American citizen and as a minister of religion, to protest against the infamous misuse and abuse of power practiced by your Committee. The members of your Committee have flagrantly disregarded the elementary rule of evidence in American law, namely, that a man is presumed innocent until he is proved guilty; the members of your Commit-

tee have permitted utterly incredible and scandalous statements to be made in their presence without challenge; but
worse than this, the members of your Committee have publicized these unfounded and unverified charges. This conduct
on the part of your Committee has brought discredit and
shame upon Congress and upon America.

I do not know whether there is a law under which the members of your Committee can be impeached and removed from
office. But I do know that we elect members of Congress in the
conviction that they will recognize the responsibility and the
trust that their office imposes upon them. The members of
your Committee have betrayed this trust and have proved
themselves irresponsible. They have violated every rule of
decency and of honor. In view of the manner in which you
have dishonored yourselves and Congress and America, I trust
that the present Administration and the members of Congress
will find some way in which to relieve us of the disgrace and
humiliation that the American people have suffered at the
hands of your Committee.

Yours truly,

SIDNEY E. GOLDSTEIN
Associate Rabbi
Stephen Wise Free Synagogue

CC: President Dwight D. Eisenhower

I read this letter to the members of the congregation at a Friday
evening service and stated that if the "Investigating Committee"
subpoenaed me I would refuse to respond, and that I would follow
the counsel of Albert Einstein and go to prison rather than submit
myself to the inquisition of the Velde Committee. The response of
the congregation was immediate and most heartening. Hugo Muensterberg was correct: "The people respond upon the level at which
we strike." Too many of us strike at too low a level in presenting
the case of civil liberties to our congregations. A committee of the
National Council of Churches has issued a statement (March 18,
1954) which expresses the protest of the Protestant Churches in the

matter of "investigations" and McCarthyism. This statement is so well conceived and so well formulated that I quote it here in full.

*   *   *

Deeply concerned by certain trends in American public life the National Council of Churches in March, 1953, created a "Committee on the Maintenance of American Freedom" and instructed it to "watch developments that threaten the freedom of any of our people or their institutions, whether through denying the basic right of freedom of thought, through Communist infiltration, or wrong methods of meeting that infiltration."

I.

One such threat has come from procedural abuses by Congressional committees. Remedial measures are now being proposed, and we commend the President, the leaders of both major parties, and the members of Congress who have spoken out and demanded reforms. If these reforms are to be adequate they should provide protection from at least the following:

1. The stigmatizing of individuals and organizations on the basis of unsupported accusations and casual associations.

2. The forcing of citizens, under pretext of investigation of subversive activities, to testify concerning their personal economic and political beliefs.

3. The functioning of Congressional committees as legislative courts to determine the guilt or innocence of individuals.

4. The denying to "witnesses" opportunity to bring out material favorable to their side of the case through questions by witnesses' own counsel and opportunity to test the validity of accusations through cross-examination of accusers.

5. The permitting to a committee member or counsel the reading into the record against a "witness" defamatory material and charges without requiring the accuser personally to confront the accused.

6. The usurping by Congressional committees of powers not granted to Congress by the Constitution and their failing to

concentrate on the primary task of collecting information for purposes of new legislation.

7. The scheduling of hearings, subpoenaing of witnesses, and evaluating of their testimony by chairmen of committees without the concurrence of, or consultation with, their fellow committee members.

8. The releasing from the files of a Congressional committee of so-called "information" consisting of unverified and un-evaluated data in such a way that the committee can be used to help spread and give credence to malicious gossip.

II.

Another threat has come from competition among rival Congressional committees, creating the impression that they seek publicity, personal aggrandizement, and political advantage rather than basic facts. In order to concentrate energy on the legitimate and essential tasks of resisting the Communist threat, and in order to avoid wastage and duplication of effort and to minimize the risk of the exploitation of public interest and fear, we urge the establishment of a single joint Congressional committee for the investigation of subversive activity.

III.

A more basic threat has been a growing tendency on the part of our people and their representatives in government to suppose that it is within the competence of the state to determine what is and what is not American. The American way is to preserve freedom by encouraging diversity within the unity of the nation and by trusting truth to prevail over error in open discussion. The American way is to rely upon individuals to develop and express individual opinions. The American way is to depend upon the educational institutions to seek the truth and teach it without fear. The American way is to look to the churches in the richness of their diversity to bring to the nation light and discipline from God to maintain a responsible freedom.

IV.

Aggravating these threats to American freedom is the prevailing mood of restlessness and tension. This arises in part from the real menace of communism, which our nation is resisting by strength. It arises in part from the lack of a sense of security within our people which no physical strength can produce. Spiritual security can be achieved only by strengthening the nation's faith in God. The responsibility for deepening this faith rests with the churches.

In this period of danger to our civil liberties the churches and the synagogues can be of great service. In order to educate their members in understanding the meaning of civil liberties and to strengthen their faith in freedom we can do at least the following:

1) Distribute copies of "The Universal Declaration of Human Rights" to all members of the congregation. Copies can be secured from the Information Office of the United Nations.
2) Organize discussion groups to study "The Universal Declaration of Human Rights" with the expositions and commentaries that have been issued. These can be secured from the office of UNESCO and the Association of the United Nations.
3) Cooperate with organizations like the American Civil Liberties Union in advancing the cause of civil liberties.
4) Train themselves to distinguish between the methods of McCarthyism and the procedures of democracy, that is, to distinguish between the methods of misrepresentation and the methods of truth.

9. CENSORSHIP

The problem of censorship is complicated and difficult, but one in which the church and the synagogue cannot fail to be interested and active. Essentially, censorship is a legal matter and ultimately one for the courts to decide. But we must recognize that in a number of cities, like Boston and Chicago, there is official municipal censorship. We must also recognize that in a number of states, like

New York and Pennsylvania, there is official censorship, usually under the control of the Department of Education. And we must know that from time to time bills are introduced into Congress designed to establish censorship in the Federal Government. Censorship is always a danger that threatens freedom of speech, freedom of assembly, and freedom of the press.

On the other hand, we must recognize that in every community conditions develop that are a danger to the moral life of the community. From time to time these conditions are found in magazines and books. Sometimes they are in the theatre, and especially in burlesque houses. And sometimes they exist in motion pictures. In addition to these areas conditions may develop in dance halls and night clubs that are also a danger to the moral life of the community. The Church and the Synagogue as guardians of the moral life of the people cannot ignore these conditions any more than the Department of Health can ignore a cesspool of infection that threatens the general health. The problem is to determine what is a danger to the moral life of the community, and also so to act that we shall safeguard freedom of speech, assembly, press, and worship.

It was because I was opposed to censorship by the government, local, state, or federal, that I cooperated with the Protestant and Catholic groups in an effort to curb and to control two sources of danger to our moral life, the theatre and the motion picture. During the Thirties the burlesque theatres in New York were owned and managed by the Minsky Brothers; and these became a source of grave concern to all of us, Protestants and Catholics and Jews. The situation became so serious and the evil so flagrant that the Protestant and the Catholic groups urged immediate action, and in this I joined as a representative of the Central Conference of American Rabbis. We arranged for a meeting with the Commissioner of Licenses of the City of New York, who under the law had the power to revoke the licenses of the theatres if he had reason to believe they had become a source of danger to community morals. We urged him not to act as a censor but to insist that the case be tried in court. It was necessary to gather the evidence and to present it to the Grand Jury. This was not a pleasant thing to do. But the representatives of the religious groups did agree to attend the burlesque performances together with representatives of the Commissioner of Licenses; and then to present the evidence. The Grand Jury indicted owners, managers, and actors, all of whom we believed guilty of violating the law of decency. The District Attorney assigned one of his ablest assistants to conduct the case for the Commissioner of Licenses. The argument he presented was so clear and convincing that the jury had no difficulty in deciding that the theatres were guilty of indecent exhibitions. This decision closed the burlesque houses in New York, but did not end the evil of indecency in the city.

The second problem, motion pictures, had to be attacked in another way. There was no doubt that the industry was at that time producing films that violated the accepted standards of decency. The condition that caused me great concern was the fact that it was so largely controlled by Jewish corporations. In fact the danger of its becoming a source of anti-Semitism was exceedingly great. A committee of the Central Conference of American Rabbis, composed of Dr. Samuel Goldenson, Dr. William H. Fineshreiber, and myself asked for a conference with the leaders. We appealed to them to change the standards of production. But it was not until we introduced a pamphlet written by the Bishop of the Catholic Church of Los Angeles that we could secure action. In this pamphlet the bishop charged the motion picture industry with demoralizing life in America through the type of pictures being presented, and he openly charged that the Jews were responsible. As a result of this meeting messages were sent to Hollywood, and a change of production standards and production methods was effected. The industry agreed to establish a production code that would meet our standards. But in various parts of the country a demand developed for government censorship on the federal level. After studying the problem carefully I prepared a paper the conclusion of which I append to this chapter, as it contains recommendations I have found no reason to withdraw in the course of the years. The recent decisions of the Supreme Court in the case of "The Miracle," "La Ronde," and "Murder" prove beyond question of the difficulty of enacting laws to legalize censorship. The majority of the members of the court were of the opinion that the phrases employed were too vague. The court did not outlaw censorship but it did outlaw the decisions of the censors.

These decisions of the Supreme Court have done more; they have completely changed the basis on which laws concerning the motion picture must be built. Twenty years ago the motion picture was classified by the Supreme Court as a form of entertainment and therefore not within the range of "freedom of the press." Today as a result of this decision the motion picture is not so classified and is brought under the constitutional provision that protects freedom of the press. It is therefore necessary for those opposed to any picture to prove that it violates the constitutional provision of press freedom. The Legislature of the State of New York has rephrased the laws that refer to motion pictures and the Governor has signed the bills. They have attempted to re-define the terms obscenity, indecency, immorality, sacrilege, and incitement to crime; but whether the court will ultimately accept this rephrasing and these new definitions no one can foretell. We must recognize that standards change from time to time and from culture to culture. What is regarded as obscene and indecent and immoral in one generation is not thought of in the same way in another. What one religious group considers sacrilegious another would construe otherwise. What one organization describes as an incitement to crime the judges may altogether reject. In view of these facts it is perfectly evident that we cannot entrust censorship, local, state, or federal, to an individual, whether he be a Commissioner of Licenses, a member of the State Department of Education, or an officer of the Federal Government. Such authority should not be placed in the hands of any one man or any one group.

This does not mean, however, that churches and synagogues can or should absolve themselves of the moral responsibility to safeguard the community. Through their Committees on Social Action or some other committee, they should be concerned with the dangers that threaten the moral life of the people, especially adolescents and children. It is not our function to act as censors; but it is our duty to protest against publications and pictures and exhibitions that are a menace to our moral life. It is our duty to protest against dance halls and night clubs and every other evil that menaces our people. The laws as they stand are adequate; but their interpretation and enforcement must rest not with us but with the courts of the land. This may be a slow process, but it is the process of democracy.

THE MOTION PICTURE AND SOCIAL CONTROL

CONCLUSION

The conclusion to which we come, after surveying the different solutions offered us, is that unlimited license, Government censorship, and self-regulation on the part of the industry have all proved ineffective and are doomed to fail. They cannot protect the public against the dangers of evil pictures; nor are they able to lift the motion picture to the level of clean entertainment, progressive education, and inspiring art. The point at which to begin a program of reconstruction, it is now clear, is not exhibition or distribution, but production; and production must be brought under social control, under control, that is, of a group of men and women who will supervise the production of pictures solely in the interest of community welfare and social progress. The motion picture corporations, we are well aware, are not at present in the mood to accept this solution of the problem; they still insist upon the right of self-regulation through the Hays organization. They do not seem to understand that through their repeated failure and offenses during the last twenty years they have forfeited the right to regulate an industry and to fashion the policy that is to govern a great public enterprise. The time is very near at hand when they will be compelled to face the choice of social control on the one hand or Government censorship on the other. In order to escape Government censorship we trust that they will choose social control. If they do not make the choice themselves it is not unlikely that the choice will be made for them.

The present protest against the motion picture, men must understand, is unlike other protests in the past. It is not a sporadic and
isolated outburst of public sentiment against a single evil; it is
nothing less than one phase of a great wave of moral wrath that is
sweeping wide and deep through every segment of life. Everywhere
people are protesting against incompetency and corruption in our
political system; they are protesting against oppression, exploitation, and injustice in our economic organization; and they are also
protesting against debasement and degradation in our cultural
agencies and institutions. These protests are not surface symptoms;
they presage a new awakening and resurgence in our ethical life
and a veritable renaissance of the spirit. The people are determined to assume control of their political, economic, and cultural
life; they are determined to socialize all the instruments and
processes of society as they have already socialized education; and
most of all they mean to employ these instrumentalities in the maintenance of democratic programs and in the advancement of democracy. The motion picture together with the radio and the press,
under social control, will be transformed into servants of the new
social order that is emerging out of the confusion into which the
old and outgrown system has finally collapsed.

10. BIRTH CONTROL

The movement of birth control, now known as planned parenthood, dates back to the last part of the 18th century. In 1798
Malthus, then a minister of the Church of England, published an
essay in which he maintained that the population of the world
was increasing faster than the food supply; and he urged that families limit the number of children. In the middle of the 19th
century Dryesdale in England openly advocated the "Small Family
System." In the latter part of the 19th century Holland officially
established the first birth control clinics under Dr. Jacob. In
America birth control developed into a movement during the first
decade of the 20th century. It grew rapidly from a local movement
in New York City to a state-wide movement centering in the Legislature in Albany, and later into a national movement with legis-

lation introduced into Congress. It has now spread to India and Japan and has become an important international program.

I first became active in the movement when Margaret Sanger was arrested in 1914 for distributing birth control literature and for engaging in birth control education in the City of New York. Like many other students of social welfare I had become interested in this matter as a solution of a number of social problems; and when Mrs. Sanger was taken to court I felt, as did many others, that the least I could do would be to offer her my services. This was the beginning of a long and close comradeship with a woman I had come to regard as one of the really great women of our time. From the outset of this program in America Margaret Sanger revealed all the qualities of courage and fortitude and social vision that have characterized her distinguished career through half a century. I had no doubt then and I have no doubt now that Margaret Sanger will be recognized in time as the leader and spokesman of an international humanitarian movement.

In the incipient stage we suffered many setbacks and much opposition on the part of groups whose support we should have enjoyed. We were even denied the right of freedom of speech, assembly, and press, and we were prevented from holding meetings in public. We tried to arrange for a meeting in Town Hall. We were granted the privilege of gathering in the Hall; but when we attempted to open the assembly we were informed by the police that the meeting could not be held, and when Margaret Sanger insisted upon the right to speak she was arrested and taken to court. A few of the men associated with her not only accompanied her to the station house, but asked for the privilege of serving as a substitute and also of being arrested. But the New York police with their accustomed chivalry insisted upon "ladies first," and the men were even excluded from the house and left standing outside.

We immediately answered this conduct on the part of the New York police by charging them with violation of the rights of freedom of assembly and freedom of speech. The case came to court, and when the judge asked the police captain when he had stopped the meeting, he answered with true Irish wit, "Surely, your honor, I stopped it before it began." The judge then asked him on whose authority he had prevented our group from holding a public meeting in a public hall, and his only answer was, "My superior officer ordered me to do this." We learned later that protest had been lodged against our attempt by representatives of the Catholic Church. It was also upon protest by the Church that the police were instructed to break into the birth control clinic and take possession of the records. Fortunately these records were classified as "medical and confidential." They were returned; and this was the last time we were prevented from holding a public meeting in the City of New York, in the State of New York, or in Washington.

The birth control movement by this time had grown to the point where we believed we ought to move forward to amend the law of the State of New York, which at that time outlawed birth control except as a medical procedure to save a woman's life. Our first step was to persuade a member of the Legislature to introduce a bill which would permit physicians to instruct young married people in the methods of control legally, as they were then doing illegally. The bill was reported to the Judiciary Committee and a group of us went to Albany to plead with the Committee to submit it to the Assembly for debate and action. We were sitting outside the meeting-room when a member came out. I asked him whether the bill was being considered. He said, "Yes, it is being considered, but it will not reach the Assembly." We asked him why not, and he replied, "Well, there are thirteen members on the Judiciary Committee. Eleven are in favor of reporting the bill out to the Assembly and two are opposed to it. But the representative of the Catholic Church has just informed us that the Church is opposed to the Bill. It therefore will not be reported out." This was an excellent illustration of democratic action and taught us the importance of building up public pressure.

A year or two later we succeeded in persuading the Legislative Committee to arrange for a public hearing in the Assembly. The Assembly Hall in which the hearing was held was crowded with representatives from all over the state, for and against. When my turn came to speak the chairman of the committee said, "Dr. Goldstein, you and your group have been trying to amend the state law for a number of years. What progress have you made?" I answered,

"Mr. Chairman, thanks to the action of your Committee, we have not made much progress in amending the law; but we have made a great deal of progress in violating the law."

Finally came the climax of all our efforts in New York State. In order to persuade the legislature that we had public support for the bill we arranged for a great public meeting in Carnegie Hall. This was in December 1935. The hall was crowded with people who by this time had come to understand the meaning of the movement. In the course of my address, I made a simple request. I stated that the birth control legislation that we had introduced was a piece of permissive legislation, and did not compel anyone to practice control who was opposed to the program. I then asked publicly that the Catholic Church withdraw its opposition to the bill and allow the majority of the people in the State of New York to legally secure the information to which they were entitled.

"During the last twenty-five years we have cooperated with the Catholic Church in the crusade against indecency and in advancing the cause of social justice. In the name of human welfare and social progress we now appeal to the Catholic Church to withdraw its opposition to the establishment of birth control clinics and to the amendment of the laws, state and federal, that no longer reflect the belief or practice of the great mass of people. We appeal on the ground that the program we advocate is not mandatory but permissive, and would not compel any person to act contrary to his conscience or his Church. We appeal on the ground that birth control would reduce the death rate of children, preserve mothers from premature death, and relieve distress and unemployment. We appeal on the ground that it is socially unethical to condemn men and women to ignorance and exploitation when scientific information and instruction would make them free."

The next Sunday morning, Cardinal Hayes did something he had never done before. In the presence of a congregation of 3000 in St. Patrick's Cathedral, he preached a sermon against birth control, and described those of us associated with the movement as "prophets of decadence." No sooner had the sermon been delivered than the papers began to call for a reply. We waited for the printed version which appeared late Sunday night and in the Monday morning edition of the papers in New York and across the country. This gave us the opportunity for which we were waiting, to answer the Cardinal and the Catholic Church in a public statement. I immediately drew up the following declaration, which was signed by the clergymen whose names appear at the bottom:

"The sermon delivered by Cardinal Hayes in St. Patrick's Cathedral Sunday morning, December 8th, on the subject of birth control was clearly meant to be more than a pronouncement of the Roman Catholic authorities to the members of the Church. The circumstances surrounding the delivery of the message, the fact that it was inspired by the mass meeting on birth control held in Carnegie Hall December 2, and the statement of the Cardinal that he spoke as an American citizen, as well as a shepherd of his flock, make the sermon a challenge to every right-thinking and morally-minded man and woman in America.

"No one questions that it is the duty of the Cardinal to remind the communicants of the Roman Catholic Church of its teachings on the subject of the limitation of the family and to urge Catholic men and women to live in accordance with the principles of their faith. We must, however, in the same measured, deliberate, and emphatic terms employed by the Cardinal, protest against any word or act of the dignitaries of the Church that would in effect impose upon other Americans the beliefs and practices of Roman Catholicism. The program advocated by the American Birth Control League and the National Committee on Federal Legislation for Birth Control is not mandatory, but permissive. It does not compel any man or woman to act contrary to his conscience or his Church. It leaves each one free to practice the principles that he believes to be wise and right. This is what is meant by democracy. For any one religious group to attempt to exercise authority over other groups, whether that authority be legal, social, or ethical, is undemocratic and out of place in America.

"The Cardinal, we regret to state, permits himself in this sermon to repeat arguments against birth control that have been disproved a number of times. Birth control, he insists, leads to race suicide. There is no evidence to support this assertion. A study of the vital statistics of the leading countries in the world prove that while the birth rate has dropped markedly during the last fifty years, the death rate has declined with equal rapidity. On the other hand, a high birth rate in backward countries is always accompanied by an equally high death rate. The population, in other words, is not composed of those who are born, but of those who survive. In the United States the difference between the birth rate and the death rate at present is so great as to add more than a million and a half to the population every year. This fact does not seem to prove that America is 'already a dying nation.'

"The Cardinal allows himself to reiterate the often-answered argument that birth control is followed by decadence. The social studies that have been made of families in which birth control is an acknowledged procedure do not reveal a lower standard of morality than is found in families that do not limit the number of children. The very opposite is the case. In the large family there is a higher rate of neglect and desertion, of waywardness and delinquency, than in the small family. The sanctity of the family does not depend upon conception or contraception, but upon the spirit of consecration with which men and women come together in a spirit of comradeship. The same conclusions are true concerning nations. The ethical standards in Holland, England, France, and the United States are certainly just as high as the standards of life in countries in which birth control is outlawed by both custom and statute. The security of the State does not depend upon laws that lead to unlimited procreation but upon the principles of social justice and the maintenance of civil rights and governmental integrity.

"We agree wholeheartedly with the Cardinal that the present social system is unjust and that it is our duty to reorganize the social order in such a way as to achieve a more equitable distribution of opportunity and income. The Cardinal, however, seems unaware of the fact known to every social worker and social scientist, namely, that an excessive number of children not only undermines the health of the mother but makes it utterly impossible for the large families to lift themselves out of destitution and despair. The families and the groups that have advanced themselves in the economic scale are the very ones that have endeavored to limit the number of children.

"The longest argument in the Cardinal's sermon and the one upon which he ultimately bases his case is found in the statement that birth control is contrary to the commandment of the Deity. This is true if by the Deity we mean the God that is found in ancient myth and legend. This is not true however if by the Deity we mean the God Who is revealed in the endless sweep of evolution and Whose majestic message is being slowly translated by science into the accents of the human tongue. The lower down we go in the scale of evolution the less limitation we find imposed upon the spawning process. The higher we rise the more restriction and restraint is placed, we discover, upon the powers of reproduction. In other words, instead of violating the law of nature and nature's God through birth control, we are merely giving sight and intelligence to what in nature is a blind and groping impulse. If the Cardinal chooses to accept the literal interpretation of Old Testament statements as infallible doctrine, we register no complaint; nor should he complain if we choose instead to base our faith upon the evidence, the knowledge, and the experience available in our own time.

"When we appeal to the Roman Catholic Church, as we do most solemnly, to withdraw its opposition to the establishment of birth control clinics and to the amendments to the law that would make possible a wider program of birth control service, we do not presume to offer to the members of the Roman Catholic communion any counsel that we believe should govern their conduct, nor do we ask the Roman Catholic Church to endorse or adopt our program. We only insist, as we believe we have a right to do in a democracy, upon the privilege of developing a system of social procedure that we believe to be socially wise and ethically correct; and that we are convinced will reduce the mortality of children, preserve mothers from invalidism and premature death, lighten the heavy burden of social distress and unemployment, and solve the urgent and acute problem of overpopulation that always leads to famine and plague, as in India and China, and that is often advanced as an excuse if not a cause for war, as in Germany, Japan, and Italy today.

"Signers of this Statement:

Dr. Edmund B. Chaffee, director, Labor Temple Presbyterian Church

Dr. Horace W. B. Donegan, St. James Protestant Episcopal Church

Prof. Harrison S. Elliott, Dept. of Religious Education, Union Theological Seminary

Dr. Harry Emerson Fosdick, The Riverside Church

Dr. Sidney E. Goldstein, Chairman, Commission on Social Justice, Central Conference of American Rabbis

Dr. John Haynes Holmes, The Community Church

The Very Reverend Arthur B. Kinsolving, II, Dean of the Cathedral of the Incarnation, Garden City, Long Island

Dr. John Howland Lathrop, Saviour-Unitarian Church, Brooklyn

Bishop Francis J. McConnell, Methodist Episcopal Church

Dr. John Howard Melish, Holy Trinity Protestant Episcopal Church

Rev. Canon H. Adye Prichard, Cathedral of St. John the Divine

Dr. Minot Simons, All Souls Unitarian Church

Rabbi Milton Steinberg, Chairman, Committee on Social Justice, Rabbinical Assembly of America."

Friends both within and without the Synagogue cautioned me against issuing this statement. Dr. Wise himself was much concerned about it. He felt as did others that if I attacked the Cardinal through this statement, I would alienate the Catholic Church, and, said these friends, we need the support of the Church in these days when we are facing Hitler and trying to establish the State of Israel. In spite of these cautions we issued the statement and we did succeed in alienating the Catholic Church. In every conference and in every movement since then I have suffered the open opposition of the Catholic hierarchy. Representatives of the Catholic organizations threatened to resign from the Welfare Council of the City of New York if the Planned Parenthood Association were admitted as a constituent member.

But in spite of the opposition of the Church the birth control movement has spread rapidly not only across the country but across the continents. Margaret Sanger and Abraham Stone and other representatives of the movement have at last been welcomed in India and in Japan. Birth control clinics are now being established in both these overpopulated countries. This problem of overpopulation can be solved only through application of birth control programs. Gandhi disapproved of birth control, believing that the population problem could be solved through self-control or abstinence. His disciple Nehru, however, realizes that abstinence is not the solution for India, and he is encouraging the movement in his own country through governmental action and support. The same thing is true in Japan; and what happens in India and Japan will take place in other countries of Asia and eventually spread to Africa. Europe has practiced birth control in most countries for a long time, and the movement has now conquered North America and many parts of South America. The Catholic Church will not be able to impede this movement now sweeping across the earth.

"The arguments in favor of birth control are also easily summarized. In the first place, limiting the number of children reduces infant and child mortality. It has been definitely established that the death rate of children in large families is twice that of children in small families. In the second place, birth control undoubtedly conserves the health of mothers. Too many and too frequent confinements undermine the health of women and lead to invalidism and premature death. Women know this and resort even to abortion in order to prevent birth of an unwanted child. Mothers have a right to grow up with their children; and in order to protect their health they intelligently space and limit the number of children in the family. In the third place, birth control undoubtedly often saves families from unnecessary social decline and the increase of suffering. Social workers will testify to the fact that family after family is in distress solely as a result of too many children, that is, the number exceeds the earning capacity of the father to adequately provide them with what children need. Over 250,000 children are born every year into families now living in a state of destitution. This is not fair to the child nor to the family nor to society. In the fourth place, it is important to remember the relationship of birth control to unemployment. 140 years ago Malthus called our attention to the pressure of population upon the food supply. To-day it is important to consider the pressure of the working population upon the job supply. Invention, mass-production, scientific management, are throwing millions of men out of employment. There is no social wisdom in bringing 150 potential workers into the world when there are only 100 jobs in prospect. The final argument is that birth control removes one of the excuses, if not one of the causes, of famine, plague, and war, namely, overpopulation. Overpopulation is an evil that can be ended only through the program of birth control" ("The Meaning of Marriage and the Foundations of the Family," pages 126–127).

Among the Jewish people there is some misunderstanding in regard to Jewish law and birth control. It is true that the ancient Jewish law was, "Be fruitful and multiply." This command is found in the first chapter of the Bible and is repeated at the end of the story of the Flood. But it is not generally known that it was modified and the principle re-interpreted. Professor Jacob Z. Lauterbach, one of our highest authorities on Jewish law, has studied the subject carefully and written a paper published in the Year Book of the Central Conference of American Rabbis for 1927. This paper is so important that I quote in full the conclusions of Dr. Lauterbach on the basis of his studies of Jewish codes and practices:

"In summing up the results of our discussion, I would say that while there may be some differences of opinion about one detail or another or about the exact meaning of one talmudic passage or another, we can formulate the following principles in regard to the question of birth control as based upon a correct understanding of the halakic teachings of the Talmud as accepted by the medieval rabbinic authorities, and especially upon the sound interpretation given by R. Solomon Lurya to some of these talmudic passages:

"1. The Talmudic-Rabbinic law does not consider the use of contraceptives as such immoral or against the law. It does not forbid birth control but it forbids birth suppression.

"2. The Talmudic-Rabbinic law requires that every Jew have at least two children in fulfillment of the biblical command to propagate the race which is incumbent upon every man.

"3. There are, however, conditions under which a man may be exempt from this prime duty: (a) when a man is engaged in religious work like the study of the Torah, and fears that he may be hindered in his work by taking on the responsibilities of a family; (b) when a man because of love or other considerations marries a woman who is incapable of having children, as an old or sterile woman; (c) when a man is married to a woman whose health is in such a condition as to make it dangerous for her to bear children. For, consideration for the saving of human life, Pekuach Nephesh, or even Sepak Pekuach Nephesh, set aside the obligation to fulfill a religious duty. In this case, then, the woman is allowed to use any contraceptives or even to permanently sterilize herself in order to escape the dangers that would threaten her at childbirth.

"4. In case a man has fulfilled the duty of propagation of the race, as when he has already two children, he is no longer obliged to beget children and the law does not forbid him to have intercourse with his wife even in a manner which would not result in conception. In such a case the woman certainly is allowed to use any kind of contraceptive or preventive. Of course, in any case, the use of contraceptives or of any device to prevent conception is allowed only when both parties, i.e., husband and wife, consent."

In 1930 the Central Conference of American Rabbis, after careful consideration of the personal, family, and social implications of birth control, passed the following resolution:

"We recognize the need of exercising great caution in dealing with the delicate problem of birth regulation in view of the widespread disregard of the old sanctions affecting the institution of marriage and of the family. We earnestly desire to guard against playing into the hands of those who would undermine the sanctity of these time-honored institutions through reckless notions and practices. We are especially mindful of the noble tradition obtaining among the Jewish people with respect to the holiness of domestic relations. But, at the same time, we are keenly aware of the many serious evils caused by a lack of birth regulation among those who by reason of lack of health or of a reasonable measure of economic resources or of intelligence or all of these, are prevented from giving to their children that worthy heritage to which all children are entitled. We therefore urge the recognition of the importance of intelligent birth regulation as one of the methods of coping with social problems."

The Rabbinical Assembly, composed of conservative rabbis in America, adopted the following resolution in July, 1934:

"As rabbis, we are deeply concerned with the preservation and extension of the human values inherent in the institution of the monogamous family. Careful study and observation have convinced us that birth control is a valuable method for overcoming some of the obstacles that prevent the proper functioning of the family under present conditions.

"Jewish tradition explicitly recognizes the desirability of the use of contraceptives when the health of the mother or the children is involved. It is obvious that there is an ultimate connection between the economic status of the family and the physical and psychic health of its members. We therefore regard it as legitimate, and completely in consonance with the spirit of Jewish tradition, to permit the use of contraceptives, on economic grounds as well, where the earning capacity of the family makes the postponement of childbearing or the limitation of the number of children socially wise and necessary.

"Hence we urge the passage of legislation by the Congress of the United States and the State Legislatures to permit the dissemination of contraceptive information by responsible medical agencies. We maintain that proper education in contraception and birth control will not destroy, but rather enhance, the spiritual values inherent in the family, and will make for the advancement of human happiness and welfare."

There are a number of ways in which congregations can be active in advancing this movement of birth control or planned parenthood. First, the congregation through the Committee on Social Action can cooperate with other agencies in the community in arranging for public meetings and forums that will correctly interpret the movement to men and women. A correct interpretation is necessary because of the many mis-statements constantly made. Second, the congregation through its Social Action Committee can cooperate with other agencies in establishment and maintenance of birth control clinics directed and developed in accordance with the program of the Planned Parenthood Organization. There are few communities in which a clinic of this kind is not necessary. Whether it be established independently or as part of the health program of the community or the state, local and state conditions must determine. Third, the congregation through its Social Action Committee can be of great service in enactment of social legislation that will make it possible for licensed and competent physicians to instruct married couples and couples about to be married in scientific methods of contraception. Proper social legislation will prevent much misery that now occurs as a result of misinformation and illegal practices.

11. UNEMPLOYMENT

In 1929 a crisis in our economic life suddenly descended, followed by a decade of increasing and serious unemployment. In its early stages we thought that the crisis was merely a depression similar to what we had suffered in other years. As the condition grew worse we believed we were passing through a period of dislocation in the machinery of our economic life, industry, commerce, and finance. As the crisis developed, however, and the suffering of the people deepened we were compelled to recognize that we were witnessing the breakdown of our whole social system. Every symptom we could study indicated that we were at the end of one of the great epochs in history as truly as the world was at the decline and fall of the Roman Empire or the collapse and disintegration of the feudal system. The old order, some of us were convinced, was doomed, and it was the conviction of many that it could not be restored, certainly not through the recitation of creeds, whether religious, political, or economic.

Unemployment increased not only from month to month but

from week to week, and entire communities found themselves in a state of idleness. But there was no way then as there is none even now to determine the exact number of men and women out of work. We had no machinery then and have none today, to do more than give us a rough estimate of the number able and willing to work but unable to find employment. At the peak of the period of unemployment it was generally estimated that 15 million men and women were unemployed and that fully 25 million people in America were living in a state of destitution. The President of the United States probably under-estimated the crisis when he said that one-third of the nation was ill-housed, ill-fed, and ill-clothed. No one who lived through this period will forget the misery and wretchedness we faced in every community.

In the early stage of this crisis the Federal Council of Churches called a Conference on Unemployment to meet in Washington. This was during the last year of the Hoover administration. The Council invited not only representatives of religious groups, but also of labor, and many of us looked forward to the Conference in the belief that some constructive action would be taken. But when we arrived in Washington we were informed by the officers in charge that we would not be permitted to pass resolutions either in protest or in the nature of a program. We had been called only to discuss the crisis and to focus the attention of the people upon the problem of unemployment.

A number of us, including myself, were of the opinion that no conference was needed to focus the attention of the country upon the problem. It was not only obvious, but in an acute stage. The utmost we could accomplish, however, was to persuade the officers to send a delegation to the White House to confer with the President. When the delegation returned from the White House we asked them for a report upon their conference. They told us they had informed the President that the churches and religious forces of the country were deeply concerned over the issue of unemployment. We then asked, "What did the President say?" They replied, "The President told us that he was glad to hear it."

I recall this report vividly, because it seemed at that time as it does even now, an evidence of the futility as well as the heartlessness of a Conference on Unemployment called solely for the purpose of discussion. A number of us left Washington utterly discouraged, and determined to organize another Conference to formulate a program as well as to protest against the inaction of the Administration in the midst of what we knew to be not only country-wide unemployment but suffering and near starvation.

With the aid of Benjamin Marsh, Executive Secretary of the People's Lobby in Washington, and Mrs. Ethel Clyde, who placed her resources at our service, we organized what we called the Joint Committee on Unemployment. This committee was composed of representatives of seventeen national organizations, including labor, farmers, education, religion, and others willing to cooperate with us. In addition to the central committee functioning in Washington we established smaller committees in most of the states, in order to build up sentiment and support for our program throughout the country. Our committee in Washington could interview members of Congress and try to persuade them to act; but we needed support from the various sections of the country to impress the members of Congress, both in Senate and House, with the urgency for action and for passage of legislation we favored.

These state committees really proved effective, especially when we employed our new technique. I recall that on one occasion the senator from a mid-western state attempted to block our program. We arranged for two members of the state committee to call at his home office on Monday morning to inquire how he meant to vote. This subcommittee was informed that the senator would undoubtedly vote right. On Tuesday morning another subcommittee of two or three called at the senator's home office. This subcommittee was informed that a letter would be sent him to inform him of the sentiment of the subcommittee. On Wednesday morning a third subcommittee called at the home office, and then the home secretary really began to get worried. He wired the senator that the people in the state were concerned about the legislation he was blocking. On Thursday morning another subcommittee called at the home office. The secretary then telephoned the senator. On Friday morning another subcommittee called at the home office and again on Saturday. The result was that on Monday morning the senator voted in favor of our recommendation for legislation.

The Executive Committee of the National Committee on Unemployment, of which I served as chairman for four years, met in Washington regularly almost every week, and these meetings together with the program we developed required me to spend much time in Washington. It was during these years that I became intimately acquainted with the men in Congress and the procedures of Congressional legislation. We arranged constantly for broadcasts over the radio, distribution of releases through the press, and conferences and hearings at which we presented the items of our program and our recommendations. In addition we organized and engineered marches of the unemployed upon Washington, and the fact that our committee did not hesitate to participate in these marches and demonstrations did impress the members of Congress.

None of us, however, deluded ourselves with the belief that we were solving the problem of unemployment. We knew only too well that the utmost we could do would be to ameliorate the suffering of the unemployed. We understood that the problem of unemployment itself could be solved only through a crisis in reverse. This came in 1939 with the beginning of the Second World War. Nothing short of this would have ended the economic collapse that had shaken the American economy to its foundations. Franklin D. Roosevelt is often credited with solution of the problem of unemployment; but those of us who were in Washington at the time and in the midst of the problem, realized that the utmost President Roosevelt accomplished would have failed utterly to end unemployment had it not been for the war orders that came to America from across the ocean. More and more America became the arsenal of democracy. It is a tragic fact that war alone solved the problem of unemployment.

But the most important thing our committee did was to formulate and present to Congress and to the country a program we believed would aid the unemployed, and would mitigate the misery hosts of innocent men and women were suffering. The items of this program it is worth discussing now, not only because of their progressive and liberal character in the thirties; but also because they have a bearing upon current unemployment that in spite of the present administration has engulfed entire communities.

The first item in the program was relief. We pleaded with Congress and the President to appropriate adequate sums of money in order immediately to relieve the distress of the unemployed; but we faced opposition in both Congress and the White House. President Hoover at the beginning said very frankly that he did not approve of governmental relief, federal or state or municipal, on the ground that it would dry up the springs of "private charity." It soon became evident, however, that "private charity" could not meet the emergency and that the Government would be compelled to assume the burden. Congress began with an appropriation of $500,000, but this quickly grew into millions. States and cities were also compelled to share in the program. This was the beginning of the great change that has taken place in the field of social welfare during the last twenty-five years. Family welfare agencies have surrendered their relief programs to the Government and are now devoting themselves to other forms of service. Even today relief continues to be necessary, as is evident from the fact that the rolls increase with the increase of unemployment. The statistics from such cities as Detroit as well as New York confirm this fact.

Another related item in the program of the Thirties was work relief. Through work relief men and women were assigned to what was called "made-work." This never achieved its purpose, that is, it never made the men and women feel that they were earning what they were being paid. On the contrary, those of us who vividly recall the projects realized then as now that work relief is often empty and humiliating, and sometimes degrading. A multitude of projects followed in every field for the unskilled, the semi-skilled, and the skilled; but the men and women engaged in these projects always felt they were being subsidized by the Government.

This was the period in which large camps were established to which young men were sent to perform various forms of work. Those assigned to camps also had the feeling that they were being subsidized, and many became thoroughly demoralized. The truth is that what men and women wanted then and now is not relief and not work relief; what they seek is work and wages. It is not improbable that the young men and women of the Thirties never altogether recovered from the deprivation and degradation to which they were subjected through the relief and work relief programs. These young men and women are now twenty years older, in middle life, and those who are sensitive to social attitudes and outlooks realize fully that the scars inflicted by the social trauma of the economic collapse are obvious and active. We cannot expect people to escape unscathed either the psychological effects of war or the psychological effects of economic collapse.

A second item in our program was unemployment insurance. This has now become an accepted social program in most of the states; but we must recognize in view of our experience that it has a number of disadvantages. It does not begin until two or three weeks after employment ceases; it continues for only a limited time, a maximum of twenty-six weeks; and the allowance is never adequate to maintain the unemployed and the families of the unemployed. Even in the Thirties some of us advocated what is now being widely discussed, an annual wage. Civil servants in local, state, and federal government enjoy an annual wage. The teaching profession and auxiliary groups have an annual wage, and so have a number of other groups in America. In most corporations executive officers are engaged upon an annual basis and their salary continues in spite of fluctuations in our economic life.

There are many arguments against the annual wage advanced by employers; but there are also many in favor. The most important is that it seems unfair to burden the wage-earning class with periods of unemployment and loss of income, when the unemployment and loss of income are due to no condition over which they have control.

The adequate annual maintenance of the working-classes who are willing, able, and eager to work is a social responsibility which society must in time agree to meet. It seems unjust to throw wage-earners out of work whenever there is a change of models, as in the automobile industry; or whenever there is a seasonal lapse in orders. If an annual wage were established as a general practice in industry, it is likely that employers would find some way in which to end seasonal occupations and to employ the working force even during a time when new models were being designed and installed. We must understand that even a few weeks of idleness during a dull season means not only a loss of income but an increase in debts and a decline in skill. Men, like machinery, deteriorate faster during periods of idleness than during employment.

The third item in our program was limitation of the working force. This we believed could be accomplished first through the elimination of child labor. We supported, as did other organizations, the movement for a Federal Child Labor Amendment. This movement failed as a result of the opposition of a number of groups, some industrial and some religious; but child labor has been largely curtailed through state legislation and indirectly through federal legislation. The children have been taken out of the mines and mills and sweat-shops. A report of the National Child Labor Committee states that there are still about two million children employed in migratory work and in berry-picking and similar occupations. In time even these will be placed in school and allowed to develop as normal children should. The evil of child labor must end not only in this country but in other countries of the world.

Another way of limiting the working force we advocated was old age insurance and pensions. I am not sure now that this was the wisest program. There is no doubt that some men and women lose their capacity to work at all as the years advance; but we have learned through more careful studies of the aging that many men and women, perhaps most, should not be retired because they reach a chronological age. It is our opinion now that they should be continued in some form of occupation in accord with their capacity. To retire them simply because they attain a certain age is to deprive society of the training and experience they have acquired, and to condemn them to premature disintegration. In fact, the proper employment of the aging has now become one of the most important problems in our economy. The general principle that should guide us was formulated during the White House Conference on the Aging: Men and women for their sake and for our sake should be employed in accordance with their capacity to work. What the capacity is must be determined in a study of individual cases. Of one thing we are sure, the aging can do more than we have assumed.

A third way of limiting the working force was to take mothers out of industry and keep them in their homes with their families. Again and again we found that children and mothers were employed solely because they could be persuaded to accept work at a lower wage than men. This was one of the conditions that disturbed all of us. The war program, however, and the changes in our economic life have compelled us to recognize that employment of mothers cannot be altogether abolished. During war and preparation for war there are not sufficient men in the working force to meet the demand. It becomes necessary for the country to draft women, even mothers. This is one of the evils of the war program.

In the second place, we find that many mothers work in order to supplement the husband's and father's income, if not sufficient to maintain the family upon a self-sustaining level. Many mothers also feel that only through working themselves will they be able to meet emergencies and extraordinary expenditures in the care of their children. For example, many want their children to have special dental or orthodontal care; and others wish special training of their children in music or dancing or the other arts. There can be no objection to mothers working if they do not labor at the expense and sacrifice of their home and their family. In these days of nursery schools and kindergartens it is possible for mothers to arrange for care of their children during their hours of employment.

In the third place, we must realize that there are some women married and with families who are especially trained for certain fields of work. At the present time there is desperate need for teachers all over the country, and women who have training and experience in the field can render a greatly needed service. Many women are now trained in laboratory work, and their service is needed at the present time in Health Departments, hospitals, and other agencies. We have come to see that women have a larger part in the development of our various programs than we believed during the last generation.

The fourth item in our program was limitation of the hours of labor. The thirty-five or forty hour week and the five day week prevailing in many areas make us forget the long hard struggle to reduce the hours of labor in the early part of the century. In the steel industry ten or twelve hours a day and seven days a week were common practice. The officers of the United States Steel Trust insisted that the industry could not be maintained except upon a seven day basis. When the United Mine Workers of America studied their own problem and came to the conclusion that they could produce sufficient coal for America and for export in five days a week and thirty hours a week, Mr. Gary was asked to comment. His words were characteristic. "The miners seem to forget that the Bible tells us 'Six days shalt thou work and do all thy labor.' " He did not, however, quote the Bible during the time the steel industries were working their men seven days a week.

As a result of new machinery and scientific management we are now able to increase the productive capacity of workmen and to produce what we need in much less time than we did thirty or forty years ago. There is no reason why men and women should be employed longer than is necessary to produce what society needs. In fact there is every reason for the hours of labor to be limited and the hours of leisure increased. Overwork means not only strain and premature exhaustion; it means that men and women are deprived of an opportunity to develop their powers and their spiritual life. The five day week and the thirty-five or forty hour week to which we have now come also allows fathers and mothers to spend more time with their families. Only those who remember working conditions a half century ago will realize how little time parents could then spend with their children. Medical science is chiefly responsible for the increased length of life; but the limitation of the hours of labor has also played its part, and has made it possible not only for us to live longer but to live more wisely.

The fifth item we stressed more than the others—construction. In the Thirties even more than now we needed a great national program of construction not only in order to keep men and women employed; but in order to meet the needs of the communities. We needed schools, hospitals, and above all, homes. No one then and no one now believes we have built to the level of our needs. In addition to schools and hospitals and homes we also required, as today, improved transportation and the development of great national reclamation projects. At present a large part of the working force is employed in manufacture of armaments and in preparation for war. As men and women are released from the war program they should immediately be assigned to the great construction program that is now only in the thinking or blue-print stage. We must remember that the industry is not isolated and that for every man employed in the building of schools and hospitals and homes, three or four others are employed in the production of material needed for construction.

What we lacked in the Thirties was social planning, short-term and long-range, and while we have learned something within the last twenty years, we are still without the long-range planning program we desperately need. We know that machinery depreciates with the years and every far-sighted manufacturer makes provision for renewal; and we also know that buildings depreciate. We do not plan for their renewal as farsightedly as we should. In block after block in New York and in other communities there are houses that are deteriorated to the point where they have become uninhabitable. Eventually they turn to slums and have to be removed. In every community there are schools so old and dilapidated that they are both unsuited and unsafe. As long as these conditions exist there is no excuse for unemployment directly in the construction industry and indirectly in many other allied areas of production.

The final item in our program was perhaps the most important of all, our recommendation in regard to purchasing power. In the early Thirties the statement was constantly made that the economic collapse was due to over-production. It was our contention that the crisis developed not as a result of over-production, but of under-consumption. We were then, as we are now, in a mass-economy. Mass-production requires mass-consumption; and mass-consumption requires mass-purchasing power. Every layman as well as every economist realizes that unless workers possess purchasing power they cannot buy; and if the workers cannot buy merchants cannot sell; and if merchants cannot sell farmers and manufacturers cannot engage in production. The trouble in the Thirties was not that we lacked purchasing power and income; the total national income and purchasing power even in those days was large enough to maintain every individual and every family in the United States upon a decent and self-respecting level of life. The problem was that the amount was inequitably and unjustly distributed. A large percentage of our people had too little and a small percentage had too much.

One of the causes, perhaps the chief cause, of the economic catastrophe was that the purchasing power was drained out of the mass and stored up in reservoirs controlled by a few. The national income, we recognized, could not be re-distributed through an increase in credit power. Credit at the top does not filter down into purchasing power at the bottom. The national income of the country could not, we also saw, be distributed through an increase in prices. Prices always advance faster than wages; for increase in price means an increase in the cost of living and a consequent decrease in real wages and purchasing power. There is only one way in which the national income can be justly and equitably distributed, and that is through a limitation upon the amount each man may retain from year to year.

In other words, we advocated that a limitation upon income must be upward as well as downward. There is a point below which no wage should fall as a matter of decency and justice; and there is also a point above which no income should rise, also as a matter of social justice and human decency. We must agree not only upon a minimum wage, but also upon a maximum income. The minimum wage can never be high enough to be just unless the maximum income is low enough to make justice possible. Some men may call this method of redistribution of the national income confiscation; we called it conscription. In the two great wars declared by Congress the Government conscripted our bodies and our brains. In a great emergency like the economic collapse the Government has not only the right but the duty to conscript our income and our wealth. The one question we then faced in America and the one we face today is whether income and wealth are to be conscripted and redistributed in accordance with law and through a new and radical system of taxation; or whether it is to be seized and appropriated by other means.

No social legislation can save a social system that is fundamentally unjust; but a new program of taxation that would justly redistribute the income of the people will succeed in establishing a new and better social order. For a normal economic life we must have four or five elements. We must have material; we must have machines; we must have men; we must have markets; and we must have money. All these elements we possessed in the Thirties; and we possess all today. Material we have in abundance; machinery we have in excess, much rusting in idleness; men we have in the army of the unemployed; markets we have both at home and abroad; and money we also possess. But the money we need and without which all the other elements cannot operate is damned up in vaults and controlled by the temporary masters of our economic organization.

12. WAR RESISTANCE

As far back as I can remember I have been unalterably opposed to war. When the Spanish-American War broke out with the cry, "Remember the Maine!" I was still a youth; but I recall clearly the indignation and the horror that swept over me. The scandals that developed during this war were enough to arouse every right-thinking person. The "embalmed beef" and the epidemics that caused the death of so many young men did not compensate for military and naval "victories." On the contrary, the capture of Cuba and the Philippines only intensified our hatred of war and emphasized its futility as a means of settling international disputes. In the years between the Spanish-American War and the outbreak of the First World War in 1914, I associated myself with the peace organizations that were endeavoring to formulate a program to prevent war. During the First World War I found it impossible, as did many others, to support the war program. We had elected Woodrow Wilson in 1916 in part because he had kept us out of war with Mexico, and we were deeply disappointed and distressed when he led us into the conflict in 1917.

I was so much opposed to war in 1916 that I refused a commission to serve as chaplain. But I did do everything I could to relieve the suffering of those who were victims of war and of war hysteria. During the frightful influenza epidemic in 1918 and 1919 I took charge of the program of the Jewish Welfare Board for visiting sick troops in the hospitals. Day after day and night after night we saw men die within twenty-four hours, men who had never been on the battlefield and who were still in uniform. The position I took in opposition was not an easy one to maintain in view of the fact that Dr. Stephen S. Wise and the congregation wholeheartedly supported the war and the war program. I could not believe then, as now, that war would solve our problems or that the end of war would bring the beginning of peace.

When the Peace Treaty of Paris was issued I found it impossible to support it; and together with a small group of men and women I insisted that it was so filled with injustices and violations of international rights that it would inevitably lead to another war. The most flagrant illustration was the surrender of Shantung to the Japanese. This seemed a betrayal of China, that had been an ally. But this was only one of the evils of the Treaty. The four leaders in Paris, Woodrow Wilson, Lloyd George, George Clemenceau, and Vittorio Orlando, announced as their guiding principle self-determination, and they maintained that their objective was to make the world safe for democracy. The peoples of the earth, however, have not been allowed to determine their own destiny nor has democracy been made safe in the world. On the contrary, the interval between the First and Second World Wars was a period of aftermath and of preparation for the Second.

It was because I could not reconcile myself to war as a means of settling international disputes that in 1930 I accepted the chairmanship of the War Resisters League of America and continued to serve as such until 1940. It seemed at that time that the program we adopted was fundamental. Albert Einstein was also utterly opposed to war, and we arranged a conference with him just before he sailed for Europe. Those of us who were present will never forget the seriousness and the solemnity with which he addressed us. "The Governments of the world," he said, "either are unwilling or are unable to end war. The responsibility therefore shifts to the shoulders of the people. The people can end war, in only one way—by refusing to fight." In this statement Einstein gave us the solution that can come only from the simplicity of genius. War cannot be fought without men. As long as men are willing to fight governments will use them in prosecution of the war method. The only thing we can do to end war is to withdraw manpower from the service of government.

The instrumentalities in which we have placed our faith during the last generation have failed us one by one. The peace treaties, for example, have proved powerless. The Nine Power Treaty signed in 1922 in Washington was designed to protect the integrity of China; it failed utterly. The Locarno Agreement of 1925 was designed to guarantee the boundaries of Western European countries from violation and invasion. I recall clearly the enthusiasm with which the Locarno Treaty was greeted by the international statesmen of those days, historians as well as diplomats. They returned with the conviction that Europe would be forever safe; this treaty also failed. The Kellogg-Briand Pact signed in August, 1928, in Paris clearly stated in its two articles that nations would renounce war as an instrument of national policy and would agree to settle their disputes by pacific means.

International treaties, however, must be studied in the light of the reservations and interpretations and compromises made by the governments that ratify them. When we studied those made in the case of each treaty, including the Peace Pact of Paris, we discovered that while they outlawed war in principle they sanctioned and legalized it in practice. But worse than this, the governments signed peace treaties with one hand and organized military campaigns with the other; and each hand knew well what the other was doing.

I happened to be in Geneva at the time the Kellogg-Briand Pact was being signed. Even then we heard rumors of secret agreements between the larger signatory nations. But it was not until some weeks after it had been signed that we discovered that France had agreed to allow England to build the largest possible navy and that England had allowed France to build the largest possible army. They did not mean to honor their own signatures.

When we returned to the United States in the fall of 1928 we learned that the President and Congress were preparing what was then called the "Big Navy Program." A little group of us representing the more progressive peace organizations decided to go to Washington and protest against this policy. We asked for an audience first of all with Senator Robert Wagner, the senior senator from New York. He received us courteously in his office; and we discovered that he was a man with an open mind but with a closed mouth. All he would say was, "I shall carefully consider your protest when the time comes to vote upon the big navy bill." We then decided to visit the junior senator, Dr. Royal S. Copeland, who had been Health Commissioner of the City of New York, and who had been sent to the Senate by the Hearst forces. He received us in a grand manner with true senatorial grandiloquence. We found him, however, to be a man with an open mouth but closed mind. When we said, "Mr. Senator, how can you possibly vote for the big navy bill when the United States has just signed the Kellogg-Briand Pact that outlaws war?" He answered in these words, "I have decided to approve the bill because I do not want the United States to lose the art of building battleships." We realized then that our cause was lost and that we would have to proceed in other ways and through other avenues if we were to achieve any progress. As the months passed we discovered that the President and the members of Congress had accepted the Kellogg-Briand Pact in the same way in which England and France had done. There was much talk about outlawing war in principle; but there was little interest in translating this principle into international practice.

Our most tragic disappointment, however, came in the fall of 1931. During the summer the representatives of the Peace Organizations of America had met regularly in conference in preparation for the large program of the Disarmament Conference to be held in Geneva in the spring of 1932. Every peace organization in the country was represented, from the American Peace Society on the extreme right to the War Resisters League on the extreme left. While we were in session preparing a program Japan threw her armies into Manchuria, in September 1931. This was a most disturbing move on the part of one of the great powers in the East. Some of us attending the Conference pleaded for a resolution of

protest. We were told, however, by the representatives on the right
and center that we must try to understand Oriental psychology and
be patient with Japan. This, however, did not satisfy the representatives on the left. We appealed to Mr. Stimson, Secretary of
State, to stop Japan in her program of aggression. But Secretary
Stimson could not secure the cooperation and support of Great
Britain, and he was able to do nothing more than to announce that
America would not recognize any conquest in violation of any
treaty signed with the United States. This did not seem sufficient
to stop Japan, and we decided to appeal directly to the Japanese
Ambassador in Washington. We asked for an audience, which
he granted. He received us not in the executive office of the em-
bassy, but in the parlor of his home. He was gracious and courte-
ous; but also we discovered one of the most astute diplomats in
Washington. We asked him how it was possible for Japan to invade Manchuria after having signed the Kellogg-Briand Pact, in
which Japan had agreed to outlaw war as an instrument of national
policy and had also agreed to settle her disputes by pacific means.

In the course of this conference we learned a lesson in diplomacy
we have never forgotten. When we cited Kellogg-Briand the Ambassador said, "You do not seem to understand the Kellogg-Briand
Pact." All of us had not only read it but we had studied the Pact
in the three languages in which it had been issued. When we asked
what he meant by his statement he added, "Mr. Kellogg himself
has given us the correct interpretation of the Kellogg-Briand Pact.
He has also told us that the Pact cannot and does not deprive any
nation of the right of self-defense." We looked in astonishment, not
because of the interpretation which we knew to be correct, but
because of its application to Manchuria. I said, "Mr. Ambassador,
you mean to say that Japan has sent her armies into Manchuria
as a measure of self-defense?" Manchuria was a thousand miles from
Tokyo and was then inhabited by thirty million coolies. The Ambassador replied, "Yes, that is the reason for our action." I then
said, "Mr. Ambassador, may I quote you on this statement?" He
looked at me quizzically: "If you do, I shall deny it."

Many of us have always deeply regretted the failure of the United

States and Great Britain to stop Japan in 1931. If we had stopped her program of aggression, it is not probable that Mussolini would have boldly invaded Ethiopia; and it is also possible that Hitler would have hesitated to invade Poland in 1931. In other words, had we acted as promptly in 1931 in Manchuria as the United Nations acted in Korea in 1951 we might have saved ourselves from the Second World War. Even those of us who believe in war resistance have come to the conclusion that we must act in self-defense and that we must also act to end aggression wherever and whenever aggression takes place.

Another instrumentality in which we have placed too much confidence is the Disarmament Conference. We remember the great Conference held in Geneva in 1932. For over ten years the peoples of the world looked forward eagerly to this gathering, organized to reduce armaments and to relieve the peoples of the intolerable burden of maintaining huge armies and great navies and expanding air services. When the members came together in Geneva, however, they did little more than discuss the size of guns, the tonnage of ships, and the meaning of effectives in warfare. They seemed to assume the necessity of the war system. There could be only one result to such an assumption and discussion. The Conference ended in the frustration of all our hopes and in tragic defeat. Like every other conference on disarmament it ended with a resolution to reduce and to limit armaments, a resolution that in some miraculous manner became a decision to increase and to expand. War cannot be ended by a procedure of reduction; it must be ended altogether or it will not be ended at all.

The truth of the matter is that the delegates to the Disarmament Conference of 1932 seemed to speak almost exclusively in the interest of military groups both within and without the Government. There was too much consultation with those whose primary purpose it was to promote war; too much consultation with armament and munition makers who too long had controlled the policies of Government and had postponed the coming of peace. The Advisory Committee of the Disarmament Conference should consist not of armament experts and military technicians but of the peoples of every country, those who know the horrors of war and who suffer under the weight of governmental policies for which they are not responsible and over which they have no control.

This disappointing commentary upon the Disarmament Conference of the League of Nations has a direct meaning for us who are interested in the program of the Disarmament Commission of the United Nations. Thus far the Commission has made no progress whatever. The most important item in its program is control of atomic warfare and the atomic and hydrogen bombs; but there seems to be little reason for hope that the nations will agree upon any of the plans presented. The Baruch Plan for control of atomic warfare and the Eisenhower recommendation for establishment of an atomic pool for peace purposes awakened not only interest but enthusiasm in many hearts. But it would be most unrealistic for us to rest our faith upon interest and enthusiasm.

The truth is that all the nations are openly or secretly engaged in developing new methods of destruction and annihilation. In the laboratories the scientists are experimenting with new forms of biological and chemical warfare. They have discovered gasses far more devastating and destructive than anything known in the First and Second World Wars. We have not only advanced atomic warfare; but we have created hydrogen bombs that make even the horrors of Hiroshima and Nagasaki seem like elementary exercises in human annihilation. We are spending incredible sums in prosecution of these methods of continental destructiveness. The assumption seems to be that these methods will become so terrible that governments and nations will fear to embark upon war. But there is little reason to believe that they will restrain themselves because of the destructiveness of weapons that they or their enemies possess. As long as war is accepted as a method of settling international disputes they will employ in its prosecution all the weapons they create, no matter how deadly and destructive.

A third instrumentality in which many of us placed our faith was the League of Nations. The League was organized to establish international cooperation, to reduce armaments, to end war, and to ensure social justice to all groups of people. The lesser controversies that arose during the life of the League, the Council or

Assembly or both were able to adjust through diplomacy, negotiation, or arbitration. But in the larger and graver conflicts on
every continent, the Council and the Assembly together found
themselves impotent to curb the governments or to control the ag-
gressors. In spite of, almost in defiance of, the League, South
America was racked with revolt. Asia has been seething like a
cauldron, and Europe has been thundering like a volcano. No one
could know when this new Vesuvius would burst forth and cover
the continent with fire and lava.

Many explanations have been given for the failure of the League
of Nations. One of the reasons certainly is that the larger nations
continued to develop their nationalistic programs. They sub-
scribed to the principles of the League as expressed in the Preamble
and in the Articles of the Covenant; but in practice they did not
allow these principles to interfere with their programs of nationalism, national ambitions, and national aggrandizement. Woodrow
Wilson and Jan Smuts and Lord Cecil were undoubtedly sincere in
their belief that the League would serve as an instrument to outlaw
and to end war. They did not, however, correctly read the minds
and hearts of the statesmen and diplomats and politicians of their
time. They themselves were idealists, convinced that the mood of
idealism that gave birth to the League of Nations would convert
the governments as well as the peoples of the earth. The rejection
of the Covenant by the Congress of the United States was a tragic
revelation to the authors of the League.

Now has come the United Nations, which was also born of the
spirit of idealism that followed the Second World War. Those of
us who have studied the resolutions and decisions and actions of
the Security Council and of the Assembly realize that the United
Nations has made some progress in correcting the weaknesses of
the League of Nations. But we must not forget that we are living
in a new age. The age of imperialism and colonialism has ended.
England, France, Holland, and the United States have all come to
realize that the peoples they have enslaved politically, economically, and culturally must be liberated. In truth this is an age in
which exploited and enslaved peoples on every continent are emancipating themselves from the chains of centuries. This is true es-

pecially of Asia. The peoples of Asia insist that they must be free to determine their own destiny and to develop their own concepts of government. Even in Africa the great mass of people on the dark continent are rapidly coming to the same conclusion. The United Nations therefore is wrestling with new and vaster problems than the League itself faced.

Thus far the United Nations through the Security Council and the Assembly has been able in part to end the conflicts in Germany, Austria, Korea, and Indo-China; but it has been unable to solve the problems in the Middle East and in North Africa. Whether the United Nations will be able to resolve these vast and complicated situations and to end war depends not upon the few eminent idealists of our time, but upon the determination of statesmen and diplomats and politicians to carry out their nationalistic programs regardless of their pledge to support the program of the United Nations. We must recognize that there has appeared in the world a recrudescence of nationalism, and that nationalism has been the cause of war for centuries, whether this be racial, religious, political, or economic. As long as that spirit inflames the hearts of people there can be no peace.

We shall not end war until we recognize and accept the fact that war is not an end in itself; but that it is always a means. It is a means of settling international disputes or of exploitation, aggression, and conquest. A little more than a century ago society approved of the duel as a method of settling disputes between individuals. This was an age-old custom that few men questioned. We ended the duel not by discussing the kind of pistol to be used, the kind of powder, or the number of paces between combatants. We ended it once and for all by outlawing this method of resolving personal quarrels. We required the two individuals to present their case to an impartial court and compelled them to accept arbitration. In other words, we substituted law and justice for the pistol, the sword, or the javelin.

In the same manner we must now insist that nations no longer resort to the outmoded savage method of war in deciding who is right and who is wrong. Nations will always differ in many things and disagreements will inevitably arise. These differences will often develop into conflicts, and therefore remain embedded in the social structure, whether the causes be racial, religious, national, or economic. The important thing to understand is that the conflicts themselves can and should be settled not through force and might, but in accordance with law and justice. After centuries of experience and decades of exploitation we have established methods of negotiation, diplomacy, and arbitration we must invoke even after open conflict. It is perfectly evident from what has occurred that there can be today no victors in war. There are only the victims and the vanquished. Sooner or later nations exhaust themselves, and in the end must resort to the methods of negotiation and arbitration.

The United Nations is the agency through which diplomacy, negotiation, and arbitration can and should be achieved. Its most important instrument, however, is not the Assembly nor the Security Council, but the World Court. The Court unfortunately has been somewhat obscured since establishment of the United Nations. If there is one service we can render it is to bring it and its program into the foreground of international thinking and international action. The World Court incorporates within itself the system of international law we have slowly developed since the days of Grotius. There is no longer an excuse for violence between nations. The nation that refuses to take its case to court for adjudication only indicts itself and writes its own verdict of guilt in the eyes of the world.

There is not a single point of tension in the world today that could not be eased through an opinion of the World Court. There is not a single conflict, actual or impending, that could not be settled through its judgment. Kashmir could be submitted to it. Korea certainly could have been. Indo-China without doubt is a case that could have been settled through that instrumentality. The disagreement in Palestine between Israel and the Arab nations is an illustration of what could be a matter of law and of justice. The one question these peoples and nations must ask themselves is whether they believe in force or in international law and justice. War will end when men and women reject the concept of force and accept the concept of law. This is the meaning of the doctrine of war resistance. It means that we resist war because we realize that war is futile and can end only in devastation and death; and because we realize that the only method that determines who is right and who is wrong is through law and the established courts of the world.

V

THE SYNAGOGUE AND SOCIAL ETHICS

THE SYNAGOGUE AND SOCIAL ETHICS

Underlying the program of social service and social action of the synagogue lies the social ethics of Judaism, the source of our inspiration. The sacredness of human life; the sanctity of the family; the fellowship and brotherhood of man; the supremacy of the moral law; the passion for justice in all social relationships; the vision of the Kingdom of God and its sovereignty in the soul of men; the conviction that the laws of ethics constitute the organic laws of social life:—these are the Jewish teachings expounded in the concluding section of this volume.

1. SOCIAL IMPLICATIONS OF JUDAISM

The history of religion, the comparative study of religion, the psychology of religion, reveal many new, significant, and impressive facts in the evolution of the religious life of every group and every culture. One of the most important facts is that each religious system thus far studied, contains four major elements: one, articles of belief or a creed; two, symbols, ceremonies, prayers, or a ritual; three, codes of conduct that relate themselves to the life of the individual, the family, and social organizations and institutions; and four, the mystic experience of communion with a power higher than ourselves. In some systems, the greatest emphasis is placed upon creed; in others, upon ceremonies; in some, upon codes; and in some, upon communion. In every religion, however, the emphasis changes from period to period. In one period the articles of belief, the dogmas that constitute the creed, seem most important, and every member of the group is expected to accept every doctrine; in another, the symbols, the ceremonies, and the ritual seem all-important, and every member is required to observe the ceremonies and to maintain the ritual without deviation or modification; in a third, the codes of conduct formulated from century to century seem of the utmost value, and every member is commanded to live in accordance with the codes and to practice what they teach in all relationships of life; in a fourth period, communion, or the mystic element, possesses profoundest meaning, and many assume that only through communion of the individual with a higher power can they enter into the essence of the religious life.

In the majestic temple we call Judaism, we find, as we do in other religions, the hall of creed. On the walls of this chamber, we discover inscribed the articles of faith in which the people of Israel have believed through the ages. The content of the creed, it is necessary to note, changes from century to century. Not only is this true, that the people of Israel have accepted and discarded various articles of faith at different times; but it is also true that at no time have all Jews everywhere accepted the same creed.

No central or supreme ecclesiastical authority has ever existed in Israel, with power to impose theological dogmas upon the whole people. Even when Maimonides (1135–1204), greatest Jewish thinker of the Middle Ages and the most widely admired, formulated (in his Commentary on the Mishnah, Tractate Sanhedrin) what he conceived to be the Thirteen Articles of Belief, he was challenged both by his contemporaries and by later teachers and leaders in Jewish life. It is true that local assemblies and regional synods and rabbinical conferences have endeavored to define the doctrines of Judaism and to delimit the faith of Israel; and it is also true that individual rabbis and rabbinical groups have at times attempted to excommunicate those who did not accept what they believed were the dogmas of Judaism. But these individuals and groups never, at any time, acquired sufficient authority and control to permit them to speak for the people of Israel in every land. Certainly, they never possessed the power to compel all members of the House of Israel to think their thoughts, speak their speech, and recite their articles of belief.

Not only does the content of the creed change from period to period, but the interpretation of each article changes in the course of the centuries. One of the fundamental articles of faith in Judaism is expressed in the *Shema* (Deuteronomy VI:4). This statement or affirmation of faith, recited by Jews everywhere in the original Hebrew or in translation, is a universal doctrine and is usually translated as follows: *Hear O Israel, the Lord our God, the Lord is One.* The meaning or interpretation of this statement is not the same in every age. The emphasis today is upon the concept of unity or oneness in contrast with the trinitarian conception of the Deity. This contrast is due to the difference between Jewish and Christian doctrine and teaching. But this was not the interpretation of the statement before the rise and spread of Christianity. In the centuries before the Council of Nicea, 325 C.E., in the Roman, the Greek, and the Egyptian periods, the emphasis was upon monotheism in contrast to polytheism. This is due to the teaching that Israel believes in one God, and other peoples in many gods. But even this interpretation of the Shema is not the earliest. In the early life of Israel, the biblical teachers, even the earliest prophets, did not deny that there were other gods, that other nations had their own Baal, Dagan, Moloch, Istar; but they did insist that these gods were not the gods of Israel, that Israel could acknowledge only its own God, יהוה, Yahweh. The emphasis in this early stage, the period of henotheism, therefore was upon the contrast between the God of Israel and the gods of other peoples.

This interpretation of the Shema is clearly expressed in one of the most dramatic episodes in the Bible, correctly called the Contest on Mount Carmel (I Kings XVIII:20–40). In this impassioned passage, the prophet Elijah appeals to his people: "How long will ye halt between two opinions? If the Lord be God, follow him; but if Baal, follow him." He then challenges the priests of Baal to a religious contest. He is to prepare a bullock for sacrifice and they are to prepare one also, and each is to call upon his god to consume the bullock. From morning until noon, and from noon until evening, the priests of Baal dance and call upon their god; but he answers them not. Elijah mocks and taunts the priests: "Cry aloud; for he is a god; either he is musing, or he is gone aside, or he is on a journey, or peradventure he sleepeth, and must be awakened." Then at eventide Elijah prays unto the Lord: "Hear me, O Lord, hear me, that this people may know that Thou, Lord, art God, for Thou didst turn their heart backward." Then the fire of the Lord fell, and consumed the burnt-offering, and the wood and the stone and the dust, and licked up the water that was in the trench, and when all the people saw it, they fell on their faces and they exclaimed: "The Lord, He is God, the Lord, He is God!" This is the verse recited at the close of the Day of Atonement, most sacred service in the Hebrew calendar. The meaning is unmistakable. The Lord, the Eternal, is the only God Israel can worship. Ibn Ezra, with his keen critical insight, seems to sense this. In his Commentary on the Shema, he equates the Hebrew word *echad* "one," with the word *levado,* which means "only" or "alone." The Shema therefore, in accordance with its original meaning, is to be rendered: "Hear O Israel, the Eternal is our God, the Eternal alone."

Even the concept of the character of God changes as the centuries increase and as the knowledge of the people expands and their experience deepens. This is the meaning of the message that God gives to Moses: "I am the Lord; and I appeared unto Abraham, unto Isaac, and unto Jacob, as God Almighty, *El Shaddai,* but by My Name, Yahweh, I made me not known to them" (Exodus VI:2). To Moses, in other words, came a new conception of the Deity, very different from the one revealed to the patriarchs. The rabbis go even further. What is the significance, they ask, of the oft-repeated phrase, "The God of Abraham, the God of Isaac, and the God of Jacob"? Why is the abridged form not used, "The God of Abraham, Isaac, and Jacob"? The word "God," they tell us, is repeated with each patriarch in order to teach us that a new conception of God comes to each generation.

Another illustration of this change in conception of the Deity, and a most striking one, is found in one of the most instructive legends associated with Elijah. In a great crisis in his life and in the life of his people, Elijah flees southward to Mount Horeb. Here he hopes that God will speak to him as He spoke to Moses, in the storm, in the earthquake, and in the fire; but when he stands upon the Mount, the storm passes, and God is not in the storm; the earthquake passes, and God is not in the earthquake; the fire passes, and God is not in the fire. Then comes the still small voice; and in that voice the prophet hears the message of God. To Moses God revealed Himself in the cataclysms of nature; to Elijah, centuries later, in the still small voice of the spirit. This is a tremendous change in the concept of God and in the way in which God reveals Himself to man.

But even this change, great as it is, cannot compare with what takes place between the time of Elijah and the great prophet known as Deutero-Isaiah, whose messages are found in Chapters 40–55 of the Book of Isaiah. In these chapters the prophet conceives of God in the most exalted terms: "Who hath measured the waters in the hollow of his hand, And meted out heaven with the span, And comprehended the dust of the earth in a measure, And weighed the mountains in scales, And the hills in a balance? Who hath meted out the spirit of the Lord? Or who was His counsellor that he might instruct Him? With whom took He counsel, and who instructed Him, And taught Him in the path of right, And taught Him knowledge, And made Him to know the way of discernment? Behold, the nations are as a drop of a bucket, And are counted as the small dust of the balance; Behold, the isles are as a mote in weight. And Lebanon is not sufficient fuel, Nor the beasts thereof sufficient for burnt-offerings. All the nations are as nothing before Him; They are accounted by Him as things of nought, and vanity. To whom then will ye liken God? Or what likeness will ye compare unto Him?" In these matchless verses, this supreme religious genius conceives of God not as the Lord of one locality or one land, nor of one people or one nation, but as God of the universe. He is the Sovereign of the hosts of Heaven and transcends all human measurements and comprehension. Kings and kingdoms, together, are instruments in His hands through which He destroys the wicked and sustains the good and establishes the right in the midst of the peoples of the earth.

The social implications of the concept of God, however, appear more clearly in the writings of the great prophets of the ninth, eighth, and seventh centuries B.C.E. Amos, most stern and austere of all, speaks of God as a God of justice. In the great address that opens his book, he denounces the nations outside Palestine, as well as the people of Israel. In every denunciation he charges the nations, Damascus, Philistia, Tyre, Edom, Ammon, Moab, with crimes each one of which is a violation of justice and social ethics.

In one of his most daring visions, he pictures God as standing beside a wall with a plumbline in His hand: "Behold, I will set a plumbline in the midst of my people Israel; I will not again pardon them any more" (Amos VII:7–9).

Hosea, most tender and forgiving of the prophets, constantly speaks of a God of pity and compassion and loving-kindness. Israel is guilty of infidelity and worship at alien altars; but God, again and again, pleads with them to return and to repent: "I will heal their backsliding, I will love them freely; For Mine anger is turned away from him. I will be as the dew unto Israel; He shall blossom as the lily, And cast forth the roots as Lebanon" (Hosea XIV:5, 6).

Micah sums up the social teachings of all the prophets and emphasizes the social-ethical concept of God in the incomparable passage known as the Valley of Judgment. What does God require of man? Not burnt-offerings, not thousands of rams, not tens of thousands of rivers of oil, not even the firstborn, for the sin of man's soul. "It hath been told thee, O man, what is good, And what the Lord doth require of thee: Only to do justly, and to love mercy, and to walk humbly with thy God (Micah VI:1–8). No finer definition of religion is found in our literature, and no more sublime conception of God in the literature of any people.

In addition to the hall of creed in the Temple of Judaism, there is also the hall of ceremonies. Here are all the symbols and ceremonial objects, all the vestments and rituals, that the people of Israel have fashioned in the course of the centuries. These are associated not only with the Sabbath, festivals, and holy days, but also with synagogue and home and daily life. The content of the body of ceremonies, like the content of the creed, has changed from time to time. There are some ceremonies that remain constant throughout the generations, such as observance of the Sabbath in the Hebrew calendar; and there are a number of prayers found in modern prayerbooks that go back to the days of the first Temple. The three-fold benediction of the priests is only one illustration (Num. VI:22–27).

But there are other ceremonies and rituals in Israel that have ceased to be observed altogether, and other parts that have developed only within recent times. More than this, we discover that at no time have all Jews observed the same body of ceremonies, employed the same rituals, and accepted the same symbols. This is what one would expect in view of historical development. For the people of Israel have developed from a nomadic and pastoral stage to the agricultural, and from the agricultural stage to the urban and industrial form of social organization; and in the course of the last two thousand years they have migrated to every country and have dwelt within different forms of civilization. Unconsciously, Israel has been influenced by many environments, and from each has absorbed different elements. The result is that the ceremonial element in Judaism changes not only from age to age, but from land to land, even from province to province, and occasionally from group to group.

The change that takes place in the interpretation of ceremonies is no less important than the change in content. The festival of Pass over has been reinterpreted a number of times in the course of Israel's experience. There is no doubt that it was originally a nature festival celebrated at the time of the vernal equinox. This vernal or spring festival is found among many peoples, and marks and expresses the rebirth of nature. The egg is nature's most natural symbol of rebirth; hence the egg becomes one and perhaps the most ancient symbol on the seder dish, though this symbol has been given later interpretations. When Israel became a pastoral people they offered, as did other peoples, the first fruit of the flock, that is, a lamb; hence the lamb bone in the seder. Later, when the tribes of Israel settled in Palestine and became an agricultural people, they brought to the sanctuary, as was customary among agricultural groups, the first fruit of the early spring harvest, a cake made of grain; hence the matzah on the seder dish and during Passover. When Israel emerged into a nation and developed a national consciousness, the leaders and religious teachers interpreted Passover in national terms, and celebrated the festival as the rebirth of the people, the emancipation of the nation from serfdom, the escape of Israel from Egypt, the house of bondage. The idea of rebirth, in other words, runs through the festival in all stages of its development. Christianity interprets the festival as marking the rebirth of Jesus, the resurrection of an individual. Judaism, however, interprets it in social terms. It is not an individual, not even a Messiah, but a people, that is reborn and redeemed.

Another illustration of the changes in both content and character of ceremonies is found in that which introduces the youth into the rites and responsibilities of the group. Among all peoples, the initiatory rite at puberty marks the introduction of the young man into the state of manhood and membership in the group. In Israel this initiatory rite is succeeded by the bar mitzvah ceremony; and bar mitzvah has been succeeded in our time by the confirmation service, through which both young men and young women enter into the covenant Israel made with God at Sinai. More significant than this ceremony, however, is the twenty-second chapter of the Book of Genesis known as "The Binding of Isaac" and "The Testing of Abraham." This chapter, read on New Year's Day, possesses great literary beauty and has significant historical value, but its chief importance lies in its religious implications. Abraham is commanded by God to offer up his son as a sacrifice. The sacrifice of the firstborn son was a custom among many ancient peoples. But at the critical moment God commands Abraham to withhold the knife that would slay his son and to offer up instead a ram caught in the nearby bushes. This passage not only measures the transition from human sacrifice to animal sacrifice; it is also a protest against the sacrifice of children. The sacrifice of animals as a part of the ritual of religion continued in Israel until the destruction of the Second Temple. Then the cult itself came to an end, and the ritual of prayer and song, which had been a part of the Temple service, survived and continued in the synagogue as a substitute for sacrifice.

The social implications of the ceremonies in Israel are explicitly and emphatically expressed in the higher interpretations of the Sabbath and the Day of Atonement. The first story of Creation, a priestly document, reaches its climax in establishment of the Sabbath as a day on which God rested: "And God blessed the seventh day and hallowed it" (Genesis I:1–II:3). It is not surprising therefore that in the version of the Ten Commandments found in Exodus, also of priestly origin, the reason given for observance of the Sabbath is the statement that God rested on the seventh day (Exodus XX:8). But in the later version in Deuteronomy another reason

altogether is offered: "And thou shalt remember that thou wast a
servant in the land of Egypt, and the Lord thy God brought thee
out thence by a mighty hand and by an outstretched arm; therefore
the Lord thy God commanded thee to keep the Sabbath day" (Deuteronomy V: 12–15). Here the reason for observing the Sabbath is
not theological but humanitarian and social. In both versions of the
Commandments, however, it is interesting and important to note
that not only are the master and the members of his family commanded to rest, but also the manservant and maidservant and cattle,
and likewise the stranger or alien. The Sabbath, in Israel at least, is
a social institution; it rests upon social needs and rose out of a social
spirit. It is truly one of the oldest and at the same time most progressive pieces of social legislation. In spite of later deviations and distortions the laws that surround and sustain the Sabbath are enacted
in order to preserve this period of rest, which must be construed not
only as rest of body but as refreshment of mind and re-creation of
spiritual strength.

The Day of Atonement, many seem to think, is concerned only
with the individual and with reconciliation of the individual with
God. But to those who know the spirit of Judaism and the liturgy
of the Synagogue it is clear that the Day involves much more than
personal guilt and repentance. Many of the sins men and women
commit are more than personal; they are social, in the larger sense
in which this term is used today. The rabbis and sages who assigned
the portions of the Pentateuch and the Prophets to be read on the
Day of Atonement unquestionably understood this meaning and
emphasized its message. This is evident in the selection of the passage read as the Haftarah on the morning of Atonement. This is
from the writings of Deutero-Isaiah. The prophet is utterly impatient with those who think they can atone for their sins through
fasting and sackcloth and ashes: "Behold, in the day of your fast ye
pursue your business, And exact all your labours. Behold, ye fast for
strife and contention, And to smite with the fist of wickedness; Ye
fast not this day So as to make your voice to be heard on high. Is
such the fast that I have chosen? The day for a man to afflict his
soul? Is it to bow down his head as a bulrush, And to spread sackcloth and ashes under him? Wilt thou call this a fast, And an accept-

able day to the Lord? Is not this the fast that I have chosen? To loose the fetters of wickedness, To undo the bands of the yoke, And to let the oppressed go free, And that ye break every yoke? Is it not to deal thy bread to the hungry, And that thou bring the poor that are cast out to thy house? When thou seest the naked, that thou cover him, And that thou hide not thyself from thine own flesh?" (Isaiah LVIII:4–7). The rabbis spoke in the spirit of our faith when they insisted that man must be reconciled to his fellowmen against whom he has sinned before he can hope for reconciliation with God.

Within recent years a new movement has developed, designed to revive and to revitalize the element of ceremonies in Israel. This seems to have a two-fold purpose: one, to enrich the service of the Synagogue; and two, to strengthen and safeguard the integrity of the Jewish people. That symbols and ceremonies and rituals can give warmth and beauty and splendor to the service there can be no doubt, especially if the inspiration be drawn from the realms of the great arts—music, painting, sculpture, and architecture. But it must be remembered that no symbol or ceremony can possess an abiding appeal unless it embodies some living religious truth. Without spiritual content it becomes an empty form. The second purpose, that is, to maintain and protect the integrity of the Jewish people, is clearly social in intent and objective. The degree to which this purpose can be fulfilled depends entirely upon the relationship between the inner life of the people and the outward form of the symbol and ceremony. It is true that the content, the character, and the interpretation of symbols and ceremonies and rituals do distinguish one people from another, but the danger is that men and women may fail to understand that the ceremony is only an esthetic expression of religious experience, the splendid raiment in which the spirit of religion may clothe itself. Ceremonies cannot be resurrected and imposed upon religion as a painting is hung upon a wall. Nor is it possible to endow a dead ceremony with new life simply by giving it a novel and sometimes a fantastic interpretation. Only if there be a regeneration of the religious spirit will the spirit of religion seek new forms of beauty in which to invest itself and to express the inner life of the Jewish people.

The third great hall to which we come in the age-old Temple of Judaism is the hall of codes. Here we discover not only the codes that have developed in Israel, but also the agencies, the organizations, and the institutions that translated them into social practice. These classic codifications include not alone the civil and criminal and juridical laws of the time but also the ceremonial and moral laws. In the Pentateuch there are three important codifications: one, The Book of the Covenant (Exodus XXI–XXIII:19); two, the Holiness Code (Leviticus XVII–XXVI); three, the legal portions of the Book of Deuteronomy. Following the Bible comes the great code that comprises the Mishnah, collected by Jehudah Ha-Nasi about 200 C. E., and the commentaries on this code found in the Talmud, completed about 500. The teachers and sages of the talmudic period clearly understood and constantly emphasized the place of conduct in religion. In the section of the Mishnah known as "The Ethics of the Fathers," *Pirke Aboth,* Simon the Just, one of the last survivors of the Great Synagogue, is quoted as saying, "Upon three things the world is founded: upon Torah, upon worship, upon the practice of charity" (Pirke Aboth I:2). Education and learning are important; prayer and devotion are important; but no less so is social service. Rabban Simeon the son of Gamaliel is also quoted as expressing his conception of religion in these terms: "By three things is the world preserved—by truth, by judgment, by peace." To this same teacher is ascribed the profound statement: "Not learning but doing is the primary thing" (Pirke Aboth I:17, 18). Not theory but practice is primal in religious life.

After the talmudic period come codifications of the law by the geonim in the East, such as that of Saadia; and after these comes the outstanding code of the Middle Ages, arranged by Maimonides in the thirteenth century and called by him the Mishneh Torah or Second Edition of the Law. The last important codification is found in the Shulḥan 'Aruk, arranged by Joseph ben Ephraim Caro in the sixteenth century (1488–1575). The Shulḥan 'Aruk is a digest of Joseph Caro's larger work, "Beth Joseph," and in essence and form and purpose is a code of life based on rabbinical Judaism. In this digest, written for young students, he follows the four divisions into which Rabbi Jacob ben Asher (1280–1340) arranged his *Tur:* (1) *Orah Hayyim,* Way of Life, dealing with the ritual law the Jew must observe from the time he rises until he goes to sleep; (2) *Yoreh Deah,* Teacher of Knowledge, dealing with prohibited and permitted things, the dietary laws, and the laws of purity as they relate to women; (3) *Eben ha-Ezer,* Stone of Health, concerning family relations or domestic law; and (4) *Hoshen ha-Mishpat,* Breastplate of Judgment, on civil law. With the commentaries of Moses Isserles (1520–1572) and others the Shulḥan 'Aruk became the code of rabbinical or orthodox, and to a degree conservative, Judaism. It covers the whole area of Jewish life—civil, criminal, administrative, ceremonial, and ethical. For centuries it served as the controlling guide of conduct for the Jew from the time he arose in the morning to the time he retired at night and from the beginning of the year until the end thereof.

These successive codifications of the laws of Israel inevitably changed in content, interpretation, and application as the people developed through stages of civilization. As they passed from the nomadic to the pastoral and from the pastoral to the agricultural and from the agricultural to the urban stage of organization, they formulated new laws to govern their life with each advance. Even if we subtract from these master codifications the laws that relate to credal, ceremonial, and administrative elements of religion, we are able to note the changes in the codes that concern conduct and the social relationships of men and women. The simplest and primary code of conduct is found in the Ten Commandments. The fifth concerns the family; the sixth, seventh, eighth, and ninth refer to the larger social relations. The tenth, "Thou shalt not covet," in its original form seems to concern itself only with the individual; but it is evident from the phrases added in both versions that this Commandment also has social implications; for it reads as follows: "Thou shalt not covet thy neighbour's house; thou shalt not covet thy neighbour's wife, nor his man-servant, nor his maid-servant, nor his ox, nor his ass, nor any thing that is thy neighbour's" (Exodus XX:14). The rabbis, moreover, with their psychological insight and understanding, state that the tenth Commandment is the most important of all, for the man who covets is in danger of committing overt acts and of violating all the other commandments as well. To this simple code new laws are added from time to time as the social organization of Israel extends itself and becomes more complicated. These laws relate themselves to the different aspects and circles of social action and institutions, the family, the home, economic life, the community, the government. But a careful study of the codes and their application sustains the statement that no code of conduct is universal, that is, no body of laws is accepted as binding and valid by all the people of Israel in every land and in every clime.

An excellent illustration of the changes that take place in interpretation of the law is found in the development of the law of divorce. In the biblical codes a man is free to divorce and dismiss his wife on what seem to us unessential and arbitrary grounds. "When a man taketh a wife and marrieth her, then it cometh to pass if she find no favor in his eyes because he hath found some unseemly thing in her, that he writeth her a bill of divorcement and giveth it in her hand and sendeth her out of his house" (Deuteronomy XXIV:1–4). This means that the husband may divorce his wife without her consent and without appeal. In the talmudic period, however, the legislation of the rabbis places a number of restrictions upon the man through an interpretation of the phrase "unseemly thing." The School of Shammai, as a rule literal and rigid, interprets this phrase to signify immoral conduct, that is, infidelity or adultery. The School of Hillel, on the other hand, as a rule liberal and progressive, interprets it to mean any condition or form of conduct that would violate the sanctity of religion. It was not until the eleventh century, however, that Rabbi Gershon went so far as to issue a decree in which he ordained that a woman not be put away or divorced except by her own consent, unless proved guilty of serious violations of the law. Later legislation goes even further. The wife now is entitled according to Jewish law to enforce divorce from her husband on account of certain conditions, such as: a loathsome chronic disease contracted after marriage, a disgusting trade in which the husband engages after marriage, and repeated ill treatment, such as beating or turning his wife out of the home or prohibiting the wife from visiting her parents' home, or change of religion or notorious immoral conduct or commission of a crime or impotence or refusal of connubial rights.

The codes of conduct in Israel have not remained merely legal and literary formulations. They have been translated into social practice and incorporated into agencies and organizations and institutions. Even at the time when the people were in the agricultural stage, programs were developed to meet the needs of the groups in distress. "And when ye reap the harvest of your land, thou shalt not wholly reap the corner of thy field, neither shalt thou gather the gleaning of thy harvest. And thou shalt not glean thy vineyard, neither shalt thou gather the fallen fruit of thy vineyard; thou shalt leave them for the poor and for the stranger: I am the Lord your God" (Leviticus XIX:9–10). It is important to note that not only are the poor of Israel included within the program, but that strangers or aliens who sojourn in the midst of the people also are to share. In this stage of development the day workers are likewise protected against those who would withhold their wages and oppress and exploit them. Those who lose their land through debt are restored to their ancestral patrimony in the Jubilee Year. In the post-biblical period a larger system of care is organized to serve the impoverished, the sick, the aged, the delinquent, and the wronged. These programs may seem elementary in light of the more progressive programs of today; but they are the sources out of which come all the later, and current, agencies and institutions. In fact, these codifications of the law serve as sources and sanctions of many of the organizations—local, national, international—which the Jewish people have developed in the course of the centuries.

For example, we find in these codes the beginnings of the Free Burial Society, the Free Loan Association, the Relief Society, and the Family Welfare Organization; and also the early forms of agencies designed to serve transients, the infirm, the aged; likewise, institutions for the care of neglected and orphan children, the juvenile and adult delinquent, and the physically and mentally ill.

The ancient custom, *Bikkur Holim,* visiting the sick, has, in the course of the centuries, been expanded into the splendid program of today. That includes not only treatment of the sick, but prevention of disease and promotion of health.

The interest and activity of the Jewish people in the modern health movement grow out of a long tradition of social concern. Out of these codes emerge also the beginnings of the Community Councils, the Federations, and the Welfare Funds that now form part of local, national, and international social enterprises. In truth, the vast network of agencies now engaged in overseas service and in the rescue and restoration of the Jewish people in Europe arose out of one of the oldest and most insistent commands in the codes, that is, *Pidyon Shebuim,* redemption of captives. Through many centuries of trials and tragic experiences the Jewish people have become keenly conscious of the needs of all groups in distress; and out of this consciousness has grown not only a sense of social responsibility and obligation, but also programs of service, and agencies, organizations, and institutions to meet all needs. The amazing fact is that these programs are not only progressive in character but reveal unusual foresight and vision. There is in fact no group in Israel that is not served in accordance with the highest standards attained in social work and with the greatest skill developed through scientific research and experimental procedures.

The inmost sanctuary in the Temple of Judaism is the chamber of communion, the קדש קדשים, the Holy of Holies. In this sanctuary there are no creeds inscribed upon the walls, no display of symbols and ceremonies and rituals, no tablets of commandments or codes, no representations of agencies, organizations, institutions. Here is only a hushed silence and a vibrant and radiant light. For within this sanctuary man comes into communion with God; here the soul of the individual enters a mystic relationship with the soul of the universe. According to Jewish tradition, the High Priest entered the Holy of Holies only once a year, on the Day of Atonement. Most men are fortunate if they are privileged to enter the sanctuary once in a lifetime. James Martineau, the great English teacher of religion and moral philosophy, once stopped in the middle of a lecture, turned to his class, and asked the members this simple question, "Where do you think God is?" The class answered, as most men would, "God is universal and therefore must be everywhere." Dr. Martineau then paused for a moment and said, "You say that God is everywhere. Will you please point out one place in which you have met Him?"

Jacob of old awoke to discover that the spot of earth on which he had been sleeping was none other than the House of God and the Gateway to Heaven (Genesis XXVIII: 11–17). Perhaps the great majority of men and women fail to recognize the precincts of the sanctuary within which they dwell because they are still spiritually not awake. No one can tell when the moment of awakening will come. It cannot be conjured into being at our call. On the contrary, the mystic communion may come when one least expects it, but until it comes there is no authentic and essential religious experience.

Out of this authentic religious experience are derived all the other elements of religion. Creed is an endeavor to think through the experience of communion, to express in terms of reason the meaning of communion concerning God, the universe, and man. It is, in other words, an intellectual interpretation of religious experience. Ceremonies and symbols and rituals represent efforts to embody in concrete forms, in forms of beauty, the meaning of communion in relation to the external and outward life. They comprise an esthetic interpretation of religious experience. Codes of conduct formulate the meaning of communion in terms of action, whether this action refers to our personal life, our family life, or our social relationships. It is the pragmatic interpretation of religious experience.

The danger is that men and women may mistake the creed or ceremony or code for communion. They may come to think of these derivations as apart from and independent of the essential element from which they are derived. They may recite the creed or observe the ceremony or fulfill the commandment and think they are enjoying a religious experience. This they do, however, only when the creed, ceremony, and commandment are direct and immediate expressions of the religious spirit. Otherwise, what they experience is not a religious feeling that is their own, but merely an echo of what someone else has deeply felt. In the religious life there must be an intimate and immediate relationship between the intellectual, the esthetic, the pragmatic expression of religion and spiritual communion. Only those who have experienced the insight and exaltation that come with communion will recognize the difference between the echo and the essence.

There is no doubt that communion or the mystic element in Judaism has at different times expressed itself in extreme forms. In these modes the mystic has separated himself from other men and become a member of an eclectic sect or a hermit. But in the simpler modes of expression Jewish mysticism always makes the mystic a part of the community and community life. In Ḥasidism the ḥasid is not a hermit but a community figure. This Gershom G. Sholem states clearly in his great work, "Major Trends in Jewish Mysticism."

"The fact is that from the beginning the Baal Shem, the founder of Ḥasidism, and his followers were anxious to remain in touch with the life of the community; and to this contact they assigned an especial value. . . . The greatest saints of Ḥasidism, the Baal Shem himself, Levi Isaac of Berdiczew, Jacob Isaac, 'the Seer of Lublin,' Moshe Leib of Sassow, and others were also its most popular figures. They loved the Jews, and their mystical glorification of this love did not decrease but rather added to its socially effective influence" (pages 341–342).

It is only when mysticism becomes a pseudo-communion between the individual and God, an experience to be sought for itself and a form of emotional indulgence, that it fails to move men to social action. The legitimate, the necessary, the inevitable expression of the religious spirit in Judaism is the social passion, for truth and justice and peace, for establishment of the Kingdom of God. This passion in Judaism is a more direct, a more powerful expression of communion than is either creed or ceremony or the Commandments. It is certainly true in the lives of the patriarchs and prophets of Israel, greatest geniuses in the history of religion.

Abraham is not only the founder of our faith, he is also father of the people of Israel. When God commands him to leave his country and his kindred and his father's house, He says: "And I will make of thee a great nation, and I will bless thee, and make thy name great; and be thou a blessing" (Genesis XII:2). When God appears unto Moses in the burning bush, Moses realizes that he is standing in the presence of the Eternal and upon holy ground; but the message that comes to him is full of social meaning: "And the Lord said: 'I have surely seen the affliction of My people that are in Egypt, and have heard their cry by reason of their taskmasters; for I know their pains; and I am come down to deliver them out of the hand of the Egyptians, and to bring them up out of that land unto a good land and a large, unto a land flowing with milk and honey'" (Exodus III:7–2). In other words, Moses through communion with God becomes redeemer of the people of Israel from the house of bondage.

In all the legends of Elijah the prophet appears as the messenger of God against the social evils of the age. Nowhere is this expressed more forcefully than in the story of Naboth's vineyard. Ahab, king of Israel, coveted the vineyard that belonged to Naboth, but Naboth refused to surrender the inheritance of his fathers even to the king. Jezebel, wife of the king, plotted a false charge of blasphemy against Naboth and had him stoned to death. When the king took possession of the vineyard, however, Elijah met him with these words: "Thus saith the Lord: 'In the place where dogs licked the blood of Naboth shall dogs lick thy blood, even thine'" (I Kings XXI:19). Both the king and his house were doomed and destroyed because of the social sins they had committed.

The most convincing illustration in the Bible of the relation of religion to social organization and social ideals is found in the sixth chapter of Isaiah. This pictures the consecration of the prophet, and clearly and correctly describes the psychological stages of religious experience through which he passes. Isaiah, standing in the Holy of Holies, beholds God sitting upon a high and exalted throne. The seraphim fly to and fro and chant to one another in chorus: "Holy, holy, holy is the Lord of hosts; The whole earth is full of His glory." Isaiah is overawed by the vision and is overcome by a sense of his own unworthiness. "Woe is me! for I am undone; Because I am a man of unclean lips, And I dwell in the midst of a people of unclean lips." One of the seraphim then touches the lips of the prophet with a glowing coal from off the altar and purges him of his sin and his guilt. "Thine iniquity is taken away, And thy sin is expiated." The prophet, purged and purified, is now able to hear the message of God. If Isaiah had been of another faith he might have spent the years in metaphysical meditation or misspent his life in rejoicing over his own personal salvation. The message that comes to him, however, moves him to a different form of action: "Go, and tell this people: Hear ye indeed, but understand not; And see ye indeed, but perceive not." The prophet asks, "Lord, how long?" And the answer is, "Until cities be waste without inhabitants, and the land become utterly destitute." The effect of the vision of God upon the prophet in Israel is to arouse Isaiah to a realization of the social evils of his time and to make of the man a protest against social injustices and a prophet of the Lord of hosts. Communion with God is itself the source of the passion for social righteousness.

Judaism, the religion of the Jewish people, it is evident, contains all four elements: creed, ceremony, codes, and communion. The emphasis upon these various elements is not the same at all times nor is the content identical among all Jews living at the same time in any age. The change, the evolution, the development, in all the elements of Judaism is one of the most precious principles of the people of Israel. It means that religion and religious concepts, ceremonies and rituals, commandments and codes, and even communion with God cannot be regarded as static and immutable. Revelation is a continuing, widening, deepening religious process. Not only is each generation free to express its own religious life; each is under the moral necessity of restating and reinterpreting its religious spirit in terms of its own expanding knowledge and maturing experience.

To attempt to fix any element of religion into a final mold is to deny to it the principle of growth that every other human faculty enjoys. Men grow in knowledge and understanding, in experience and insight, in emotion and aspiration; but the danger is that they may halt their religious development at the stage they reach in childhood. In all other things they are grown men and women; in religion they are still adolescents. Judaism was not completed at Mount Sinai nor did it fulfill itself with the closing of the last book of the Bible. The God of Abraham grows into the God of Moses, the God of Moses into the God of Elijah, the God of Elijah into the God of Isaiah, the God of the Prophets into the God of Maimonides and Spinoza and Einstein. Like every vital force, Judaism continues to expand and to express itself in higher concepts, in more beautiful ceremonies, in nobler codes of conduct, and in forms of communion of increasing richness and grandeur.

2. RELIGIONIZING THE SOCIAL ORDER

In reviewing the last fifty years I find that we have been engaged in the task of socializing religion. We have tried to socialize the congregation. This means that we have attempted to widen the social interests; to deepen the social sympathies; to cultivate and strengthen the social conscience of the members of the congregation and the community. We have endeavored to socialize the Synagogue, to bring it and society into closer contact. We have tried to make the Synagogue what it was meant to be and what it has been at its best, not only a house of worship and a seat of education, but also a religious center for community service, interested and active in meeting the social needs of the community and in building up new social programs. Most of all we have striven to emphasize the social implications of religion and of Judaism. We have striven to aid men and women to understand that Judaism contains not only creed and ceremony, but also codes of conduct; that the service motive and the passion for social justice are not only legitimate but necessary, even inevitable, expressions of the religious spirit. In the consecration of every prophet, communion with God converts the man into a protest against social evil and into a protagonist of social righteousness. I have given myself for fifty years to this task, not because I did not have other interests in the fields of literature and philosophy and science; but because it seemed to represent the greatest need in the field of religion. It has been an exacting but an absorbing task.

Now we face the greater task, not only to socialize religion, but to religionize the social order. This is after all the highest purpose of the Commandments, in biblical, talmudic, and later literature. In the classic passage from Deuteronomy which the Jew repeats daily, we are commanded: "Thou shalt bind them as a sign upon thy hand and they shall be as frontlets between thine eyes. . . . Thou shalt write them upon the door posts of thy house and upon thy gates." These are verses contained within both the *tefillin* and the *mezuzah* the Jews employs as symbols. Why? In order, we are told in the last verse, that we may remember the Commandments; and that we may obey the Commandments; but, and the third reason is most important, in order that our life may be sanctified and hallowed unto God.

In the Book of Zechariah, one of the minor prophets, there is a passage of major significance. Biblical scholars tell us that it is not by Zechariah, but whoever the author, the message is of the highest. The time will come, says the author and teacher, when the words "Holy unto God" will be inscribed upon the bells of the horses, and when the pots and pans in Jerusalem will be regarded as sacred as the utensils upon the altar in the Temple. The time will come when the lowliest things in life are lifted to the level of the highest and the holiest. It will come when all life is regarded as holy. The modern division of life into the secular and the sacred is not in accordance with Jewish teaching. The essential purpose of the Commandments, which means the essential purpose of religion, is to sanctify life. This is the teaching stated and reiterated throughout the literature of Israel.

I know that the word holy has different meanings in Hebrew, English, and other languages. The Hebrew *kadosh,* the dictionaries and etymologists tell us, originally meant to separate, to set apart. But for what purpose? The history of the word clearly proves that it means, to set apart for a sacred purpose. The English word "consecrate" expresses the idea and content, that is, to make sacred. The purpose of the Commandments is to separate, to set apart, to consecrate. Israel is consecrated, distinguished through the Commandments. Israel is consecrated to a way of life that is different from other ways of life, distinguished from the life of other peoples. But how distinguished and to what consecrated? Like all great words in the language, *kadosh* passes through various stages, and its content and connotation alter with the changing and unfolding conception of religion.

I know no higher reach of the spirit of religion to which men and women can consecrate themselves than in the Code of Holiness beginning with the 19th chapter of Leviticus. In this Code, that opens with the verse, "Ye shall be holy; for I the Lord your God am holy," Israel is separated, set apart, consecrated to a way of life that is high and holy. "Ye shall not steal nor deal falsely nor lie to one another." "Thou shalt not oppress thy neighbor nor rob him; the wages of the hired servant shall not abide with thee all night until the morning." "Thou shalt not curse the deaf nor put a stumbling block before the blind." "Ye shall do no unrighteousness in judgment; thou shalt not respect the person of the poor nor favor the person of the mighty." All these commands and many more are ideals. Ideals certainly. But Israel is old and experienced, more than any other people, and understands intuitively that ideals eventually prove to be the only realities.

Now let me indicate what I mean when I say that the next great task is to religionize life, our personal, family, social life. I begin with the circle of personal life. Human life according to the Jewish religion is sacred. It is so sacred that every law may be suspended in order that life may be protected and preserved—even the laws of the Sabbath. This is the meaning of the statement, "The Sabbath was made for man; not man for the Sabbath."

Let us imagine what a change would take place in most of us if we were to render ourselves sacred. It would effect the same change as in alloyed metal when we refine it into pure gold. We should purge ourselves of all impurities and imperfections. We should cleanse ourselves of all thoughts and feelings and fantasies that now poison the bloodstream of our being and darken and distort our vision. Prejudice, anger, hatred, cruelty—these are corrosive elements that desecrate our personal life.

One of the greatest tragedies of our time is that we have lost our sense of the sacred. We allow ourselves to live upon the purely secular level. We are doing much to protect our health and to lengthen the years of our lives. We are doing much to develop our minds and to increase our skills and intellectual power. But we are doing little to cultivate our moral sense and our spiritual strength. We are not only indifferent and apathetic; we are insensitive to the higher values. In our daily conduct and contacts, we are untouched by the spirit of reverence, which is the spirit of religion. We build no altars within our heart. We build no shrines within our home. We have forgotten the art of worship, its wonder and its awe.

Not all men and women, I find, appreciate the affect of wrongdoing upon themselves. I have often thought that an evil act may be compared to a little bag of poison dropped into a well of water. The bag sinks to the bottom and the ripples of water smooth themselves out and all seems as calm and innocent as before. But the poison oozes out of the bag at the bottom and spreads and contaminates the whole well. An act of evil cannot be isolated; it penetrates into all parts of our personality.

George Eliot has portrayed a classic example of this process in Tito, one of the principal characters in "Romola," a brilliant study of Florence in the age of the Renaissance. When we first meet Tito as a young man he is neither good nor bad. But he comes under the evil influences of his time and as the years advance and one evil act follows another, we see the corrupting forces at work. His whole life and personality are thoroughly poisoned, and this leads to moral disease and disintegration. Tito is a conscious and deliberate study of the action of evil in the human personality. George Eliot may have been psychologically and ethically incorrect in assuming, as she did, that some individuals come into the world as a *tabula rasa*. We now know that no one is born in this state. Every infant enters the world with certain predispositions, some of which are active and some latent. But George Eliot is correct in tracing so accurately the corrupting and disintegrating effects of evil acts. Her message is that of religion and of Judaism. Evil eventually and inevitably dies of its own poison.

To religionize our personal life does not mean merely to recite a creed; though everyone should know what his religion teaches in regard to the great and fundamental problems of life. Creed, as we have seen, is the intellectual expression of religious experience. It does not mean merely to observe ceremonies; though everyone should understand the symbols and find a joyous satisfaction in those that embody a religious idea. The idea of rebirth, for example, inherent in the vernal festival of Passover, is vital. Symbols and ceremonies, as we have seen, are an expression of the esthetic element in religion, an incarnation of religious experience in forms of beauty. Religionizing our personal life also does not mean merely to regulate our daily conduct and actions in accordance with a code or regime; though everyone should know what the codes command. Codes are an expression of the pragmatic factor in religious experience. But codes may be outgrown and in time become purely formal and lifeless systems of rules. Finally, to religionize our personal life means to eliminate from our life everything that is debasing and unworthy; to pattern our lives after the great religious teachers of the ages; to endeavor to live a hallowed life that is clean, clean in thought, in speech, in conduct. This may and usually does bring on a struggle, against forces within us and forces without. But the struggle is less difficult if we allow ourselves to be governed by the simple principles of sincerity and truth. The most religious men and women I have known have led the simplest lives and the most reverent. Simplicity, sincerity, reverence—these mark the religious man.

Now let me indicate what I mean by religionizing the circle of family life and family relationships. We know that during the last generation or two there has been a rapid, almost incredible increase in the number of divorces, annulments, desertions, and separations, legal and voluntary, and in the number of estrangements. At the present time there is one divorce granted to every three or four marriages performed in the United States. One fourth or twenty-five percent of families today are on the way to the divorce court. In a much larger percentage there are discord and dissension and the danger of disruption. This is a critical situation, as the family is the basic organization of society. To the extent that the family is weak, to that extent society is in danger.

In the course of my work in the field of marriage and family counseling, men and women often say, "Do you not think the principal trouble today is economic?" Or, "Do you not think the trouble is biological?" Or more recently, "Do you not think the

principal cause of distress is psychological?" No, I do not. I know
from experience and study and thought that the family in our
time is going through stages of change in structure, in form of organization, in our conception of function, and in the very foundations on which marriage and the family must be built. These
changes cannot take place without strain and stress, without contention and conflict. For they represent not conflicts between individuals, but between cultural patterns, that involve long-estab-
lished customs and that are often not only accepted intellectually,
but are, and this is most important, charged with emotion.

All this is true. And it is also true that not many men and women
understand fully the new foundations of marriage and the family,
that we have discovered in the social laboratories and that society
is more or less consciously constructing. I am constantly amazed to
learn that young men and women do not understand that there is
a legal foundation to their marriage. They do not even know that
marriage is a civil contract. A contract assumes certain conditions
in order to be valid. It assumes in New York State that the parties
to the contract are of legal age to marry, that they are free of any
syphilitic infection, and that they are mentally competent. But in
addition the marriage contract confers certain rights upon both
husband and wife, and also imposes upon both of them certain
responsibilities. What are their rights and what are their responsibilities? These things they do not know; in fact, they do not think
of them until conflict comes. But rights and responsibilities are
more than legal statutes; they are moral matters. A man has not
only a legal responsibility to protect and maintain his wife and his
children, but a moral responsibility to be a good father and a good
husband. When a man says to me, as one did in a conference not
long ago, "I owe my wife and children nothing. I want to live my
own life. I want to go and come as I please," he fails to realize that
there is a moral implication even in the legal foundation of marriage and family relationships. The only way in which I could explain his attitude and his conduct was by assuming that he was
morally undeveloped, ethically immature.

What is true of the legal basis is equally true of the economic.
The economic foundation of marriage and family life involves the

problems of income and expenditure, and especially preparation of the budget. But more than this, on the economic level marriage and family life are now a joint enterprise. This most young people will accept in theory, but not as a mode of practice and as a matter of morals. The failure to be perfectly honest in the question of income and assets, to observe scrupulously the terms, implied or open, of the agreement, are not merely economic matters, they are also moral concerns. It is surprising how often a person will not recognize this fact and how often refuse to admit or confess personal delinquency.

And what is true of the economic foundation is even more true of the biological. Under the latter we now include heredity and health and sex hygiene and contraception. These all seem purely secular or scientific or medical subjects. And yet each has its moral implication. How often it happens that a man or a woman conceals the truth in regard to heredity or health, and how often this concealment becomes a cause of misery or tragedy. Again and again I have heard the sad comment, "If I had only known the truth." No one in this field can question the statement that sex hygiene and contraception are moral as well as medical matters. The complaints that women often make underline the fact that the husband is not only indifferent to his wife's feelings, but that he does not realize that a woman must and should be approached with a sense of delicacy and tenderness and deep regard. More than one woman has said, "I always feel as if I am being assaulted."

What is true of the economic and biological foundations is unquestionably true of the psychological and the social. The psychological is the foundation we emphasize most at the present time, especially the factors of temperament, community of interests, development of personality, and cultivation of proper interpersonal relations. But each of these factors and all together are more than merely psychological; they are psychological factors with moral implications. The control of temperament is a moral matter; so is cultivation of common interests; so is development of personality, with due regard for others; and certainly the establishment of harmonious interpersonal relations between husband and wife and parents and children is all ethical endeavor. I find it impossible to consider the psychological factors without stressing the moral mandate under which men and women consciously direct their psychological life.

The same thing is true, I am convinced, of the social foundation. Education of the members in the ways of democracy rather than in those of dictatorship; activity in the advancement of social levels; participation in furtherance of social projects and social movements —are not merely social activities or attitudes of the family. They represent the obligation that every family should feel in building the social order in which they believe. The other side of the question is equally a matter of morals. Adequate food, proper housing, suitable clothing, reasonable income, and social security should be assured each family not only as a social program but as a moral social requirement. In truth, the absence of these social factors arouses our wrath and indignation because their lack signifies injustice.

What I mean by religionizing marriage and the family is implied in the Hebrew word for marriage, *kiddushin*. This is the term used as title of the tractate in the Talmud dealing with marriage, and it is employed in every Jewish code of law. *Kiddushin* is derived from the Hebrew word *kadosh,* signifying holy. We therefore translate it as "sanctification." Marriage sanctifies and hallows life. This is the Jewish concept. Translated into simple, everyday conduct it means that husband and wife and parents and children must learn to practice the simple and essential virtues in their relationships. They must learn to be patient, to be tolerant of each other's weaknesses and faults, and to be forgiving of failures. But they must also learn to be frank and sincere and truthful. Unless they are, they will not trust one another; and when men and women have no trust, their marriage is in danger.

But more than this, they must learn the meaning of sanctification or consecration. I often say to young people, "You have been in a synagogue or a church. You know that when you are there, there are certain things you must not do, certain things you must not say, certain things you must not even think. You must not desecrate its sanctity." Then I add, "The institution of marriage and the family is just as sacred as a synagogue or a church. We must do nothing from day to day, we must say nothing, we must think nothing, that would desecrate the sanctity of the marriage relationship." This is what I mean by religionizing marriage and the family; we must learn to lift marriage and the family to the level of the sacred.

Let me turn now to our social life and inquire what we mean by religionizing life in these circles. First let me take our cultural organization, on the local and national and international levels. This is a complex problem, but we must not allow ourselves to be misled by minor and extraneous issues. Essentially the problem in our cultural organization is this: How can groups develop their own peculiar genius and at the same time maintain amicable and cooperative relations? We must recognize at the outset, as every social scientist does, that groups do differ. They differ in race, religion, national origin and allegiance, language, customs, cultural development, and ambitions and aspirations. To ignore these differences is social folly. We must also recognize that we have entered upon an age when all these differences are being emphasized anew, and when group individuality is assuming strong and intense assertiveness. It matters little whether we call this movement racialism or nationalism or cultural pluralism—the fundamental concept is self-assertion and group development.

In some areas the emphasis is upon race, as in South Africa; in some upon religion, as in Hindu India and Mohammedan Pakistan; in others upon the nation, as in Germany and France; and in still others, upon language, as in the newly created state in Southern India where Telegu is spoken. But we must also realize that there are connotations and combinations that transcend the fundamental emphasis. The new Pan-Arabic or Islamic movement is a combination of race, religion, language, and cultural aspiration that has reached a point of intense and extreme fanaticism. In addition we ourselves realize that all these elements in Islam are associated with the oriental personality.

Is it necessary, is it inevitable that these differences between groups should lead to a "dislike of the unlike," to xenophobia, hatred of the stranger? I do not believe that it is. We have learned, in earlier pages, that prejudice is not an inherited characteristic, that we do not find prejudice among little children, that it is something we acquire from our environment. Dislike of the unlike, xenophobia, group friction, and hostility arise only when the alien offends, threatens, or endangers us; or when we come to feel ourselves superior to the alien and treat him as an inferior being; or when we find that he stands in the way of our ambition. It is also true, we know now, that we may mistreat the alien when we are in need of a scapegoat, someone upon whom to blame our mistakes or misfortunes. These causes or conditions are all moral matters and are not sanctioned by the highest teachings of religion. That groups can live with each other without developing friction and antagonism and hostility is evident on the local level in the city of New York. The population of the metropolis is composed of a variety of groups, racial, religious, national, linguistic, cultural. There are of course irritation and conflict from time to time and at different points. But these groups that make up New York do manage to live with one another. This may be due in part to the fact that the groups are to a degree segregated. It is impossible, however, to live there and to watch the groups mingle from day to day, and not come to the conclusion that group friction is here at a minimum, that men and women have learned to accept and respect each other, and to act in a spirit of amity and fellowship. New York is cosmopolitan in the real sense; it is a microcosm in proper group relations.

Upon the national level we are less fortunate, in the United States and in other countries. There is not only friction and hostility, but discrimination, restriction, and segregation, in all areas of life, social, educational, occupational, political, and even religious. We may say that these attitudes are due to the new nationalism, which is another name for the movement that demands conformity, or what the Germans called *Gleichschaltung*.

This is part of the truth. Some time ago the "Survey," now discontinued, published a series of issues entitled "Calling America." In the first appeared a cartoon that I recall clearly. It was a picture of a great hopper into which were being poured all the groups that make up America, racial, religious, national, social. Out of the bottom of the hopper marched a line of men all exactly alike, as much alike as a line of sausages. The interesting point to me was that the crank was being turned by an ape. This was evolution in reverse.

Evolution, as we learned long ago, is movement from the simple to the complex, or as we used to say, from homogeneity to heterogeneity. This means the development of differences. This also is what democracy means. Perhaps Israel Zangwill never made a greater blunder than to exploit the concept of the "melting pot." We cannot in our national life melt every individual into one mold or pattern, nor do we want to do this. Each group, as each individual, has a genius of its own, and we want each to make its distinctive contribution to the wealth and treasure of society. It is only out of a variety of instruments that can come the harmony and the symphony, the rich and highly developed social life. We do not want to lose even one element of culture; nor do we want to discourage any one group from cultivating its own peculiar genius.

On the international level there is today even less evidence of the principles of religion in operation. Let me cite as the most distressing illustration the land of India. When India won her independence and ended three centuries of British imperialism and exploitation, most of us rejoiced. At last that people was free. But to our dismay, India had hardly achieved freedom when the conflict began between two great religious groups, the Hindus and the Mohammedans. Thousands were slain and hundreds of thousands exiled. Now there are two states, India and Pakistan, and there is constant danger that more misery will overwhelm the lovely valley of Kashmir.

Why should two great religious groups not be able to live with each other? In this conflict we are taken back to the religious wars in Europe, between the Catholics and the Protestants. But India and Pakistan constitute only the most acute, tragic, and disappointing illustration of what is taking place in our cultural organization internationally. Racial, national, cultural differences have become sources of hostility and hatred, and make it impossible for us to establish harmony and peace. There is on every continent "dislike of the unlike," fear of the alien, hatred of the foreigner. We were innocent enough to believe that the peoples of Asia and Africa were free of the curse of xenophobia, only to discover that the bitterness of cultural groups in Asia and Africa is just as intense as it has been in Europe or the Americas. This distressing state is not a sudden outburst of these latter years. It is evident now that deep cultural antagonisms have existed for generations, that the worldwide movement of emancipation and self-determination has only uncovered age-old conditions.

All these irritations and antagonisms and conflicts in our cultural organization, local, national, and international, could be resolved and ended if these groups were to live up to the principles of religion which they profess. They all believe in the fellowship and brotherhood of humankind. They all know that the likenesses they have in common are more important, more fundamental, than the differences. But they do not practice what they profess to believe and what religion teaches. Even cultures, anthropologists are now agreed, have more in common than we once thought. It is not sufficient for us to know that the things we have in common, including our common welfare and common destiny, are fundamental and more important than our differences. Plato in his "Republic" expressed the opinion that the ideal state would be established when philosophers became kings and kings philosophers. This is Greek thought; but knowledge and wisdom are not enough. We need another principle and another ideal. This principle and ideal I find in Hebrew thought.

This teaches that Israel is to become not a secular state, no matter in what form; it is to be a kingdom of priests and a holy people. Consider the change if we were to invest the privilege of human relationships with the aura of sacredness. Think what a conversion in the cultural organization if we were all to take seriously the prayer the Jew has recited for two thousand years: "Fervently we pray that the day may come when corruption and evil will give way to purity and to goodness; when superstition will no longer enslave the mind nor idolatry blind the eye; when all created in the image of God will recognize that they are brothers, so that one in spirit and one in fellowship they may be forever united as one people in holiness." This is what I mean by religionizing our cultural organization.

The next circle of our social life is the economic system. This is one about which there will be most question and argument. How can the economic system be religionized? First, what does the economic system include? Agriculture, industry, commerce, finance, and all other factors involved in production and distribution or consumption, in meeting the economic needs of men; food, clothing, shelter, protection. Here we face at once differences in both theory and practice. There are many stages in the development of the economic system, and all countries are in different stages. European lands have passed out of the feudal stage of economic life; but Asia is now only in the midst of a feudal revolution; and Africa will not reach this stage for another generation. Some countries like India and China are still largely agricultural; others, like England and Germany and the United States, are highly industrialized. Not only are countries in different stages of development; they are today consciously and deliberately developing economic systems that differ in character and are in conflict with each other. Under communism the state takes control of the economic system and theoretically owns and operates the whole economic machine. It has endeavored to end private property, private enterprise, and private profit. Under fascism the state has organized the economic system in the form of guilds or corporations controlled by a dictator. Private property, enterprise, and profit are protected by fascist laws; but the laws are those of a dictatorship. Under capitalism private property, enterprise, and profit are maintained by the constitution of the country that presumably is a democracy. All these systems and their variations are today not only in conflict; they are competing for supremacy.

In every economic system, whatever the form or stage of development, there are evils and injustices. During the economic collapse of the Thirties, we were accustomed to say that one-third of the people in the United States were ill-fed, ill-housed, and ill-clothed. This was not rhetoric, but an understatement. Even today at the peak of prosperity, more than half of the peoples of the earth are ill-fed, have not enough to eat. In many countries great masses are improperly sheltered; in some they live in caves, and even in the United States, wealthiest of all, not thousands but millions dwell in houses unfit for human habitation. In some sections of the earth masses of people are destitute of adequate clothing; they do not know what it means to change dress. The standard of living is so low that it is impossible for the great majority of the people to maintain themselves in health and decency and self-respect.

These miserable conditions are not due to a lack of resources today. A generation ago Professor Simon Paton pointed out that we had passed beyond a deficit civilization and were now building upon a new basis of surplus. We have learned how to make three blades of grass grow where only one grew before. We have learned how to multiply the energies we need. We have learned how to draw from the earth, the sea, and the air the material wealth that mankind requires for an adequate and abundant economic life. The great injustice is that what is now available to us is wrongly and inequitably distributed; so wrongly that great masses of people today are without what they need while others have more than they can use. The great masses are in revolution; the revolution on every continent today is fundamentally on the economic level.

How can these evils and injustices be ended? What is the teaching of religion or Judaism in regard to the economic system? The Books of the Prophets and other prophetic writings contain many a law or commandment that is pertinent. But in back of all the laws is the religious principle, "The earth is the Lord's and all that is thereon." We are merely the stewards, custodians, and guardians of what we possess. We boast not the title of ownership, but of trust. In the Talmud there is a discussion concerning the well. The well of water in the East is essential to life, and the question that arises is this: Who is to hold title to the well? The conclusion states that the title should not be held by an individual, nor by a family or group. It should be maintained in trust by the community. It must be open and accessible to all, and without cost.

This law contains the principle that should govern the economic system. That which is essential to the life of the community should not be owned and controlled by any individual or family or group. The title of trust should rest in the community itself, and it should be open and accessible to every member. It is in accordance with this principle, I believe, that religion or Judaism should construct a social philosophy to govern our economic life. The title of trust is fundamental. Certainly this means the social possession and control of all social enterprises essential to life. It means the end of private property, private control, and private profit. It means that the vast resources of the earth are to be held in trust for the people, that the title is to rest in the people, and that the resources of the earth are to be developed for the welfare of the people and not for the enrichment of the few who may in some manner seize control.

It is interesting and significant to note that the rabbis of both the Reform and the Conservative groups have passed resolutions sustaining this teaching. In the report of the Social Justice Commission of the Central Conference of American Rabbis for the year 1934, we find the following statement: "The collapse of our economic system and the emergence of a new social order compel us to restudy and restate our position in regard to the principles and the ideals of Social Justice as they relate to the economic organization of society. Investigations and studies extending over a long period of time prove beyond any doubt that it is not safe for society to leave the basic social enterprises in the control of private groups that operate these enterprises for private profit instead of for service to the community." The Social Justice Commission then advocates the socialization of the following basic enterprises: the banking system of the United States, the transportation system and communications, the power plants, including coal, oil, water power, and electricity; and in the following year also housing. The pronouncement of the Rabbinical Assembly of 1934 is even more emphatic: "There are some social enterprises that are so completely essential to all economic activity that society cannot be content with efforts to regulate them. It must actually own them. We call for their socialization. We call for the public ownership of the following: (a) instruments of banking and credit, (b) transportation and communication system, (c) sources of power, such as water, coal, oil, gas, electricity." The bearing of these teachings upon the current action of Congress to transfer the oil resources and hydroelectric power to private corporations and to private control is too obvious to require comment.

Another item essential in our economic organization is income. In the report of the Social Justice Commission of the Central Conference of American Rabbis for the year 1934 we find the following statement: "The fundamental need at the present time is an increase in the purchasing power of both the wage earning and the agricultural groups, and also the salaried workers. The low purchasing power of the people is not due to a lack of income in the country as a whole. The trouble is that the national income is now unwisely and inequitably distributed. The Federal Government has established the principle of the minimum wage; but the minimum wage that is high enough to make a normal life possible depends upon the amount individuals with large incomes shall be permitted to retain. There is a point below which no wage should fall as a matter of decency and justice; and there is also a point above which no income should be allowed to rise, also as a matter of social justice and human decency. The minimum wage itself can never be high enough to be just unless the maximum income is low enough to make justice possible." The rabbis then advocated a radically revised system of taxation, and urged that it be employed not only for the purpose of raising revenue, but also for redistributing income. The statement of the Rabbinical Assembly on the social issue of wealth is just as emphatic. This resolution, that calls for a maximum income as well as for a minimum wage, was passed six years before President Franklin D. Roosevelt advocated the same program.

A third item in the economic organization that was especially important in 1934 was that of labor and employment. For a number of years the Central Conference of American Rabbis has emphasized the principle expressed in the following statement adopted thirty years ago: "The right to work is a spiritual necessity. Unemployment not only breeds poverty; it is a source of moral disintegration from which every man and his family must be protected." In 1934 the report contains the following statement: "The members of the Conference agree that relief is necessary to meet an emergency and to mitigate the suffering of the unemployed. But no government has the right to place ten million and more self-respecting workmen upon the rolls of relief and to assume that the problem is solved. What the unemployed want is work and wages. Work and wages for the unemployed can come only through a fundamental and comprehensive program on the part of the cities, the states and the Federal Government." The rabbis then present the following as parts of a program to reduce and probably to end unemployment: limitation of hours of labor to not more than forty per week; elimination of child labor through a Federal Child Labor Amendment; retirement of the aged with adequate old age pensions; unemployment insurance to cover the whole period of unemployment; and a construction program to include not only roads and bridges, tunnels, and harbor improvement, but also hospitals, schools, and, most of all, homes for the working people. In addition to the right to work the rabbis have also emphasized for many years the right of workers to organize and to bargain collectively through representatives of their own choosing for the purpose of advancing their social welfare. The rabbis also have endorsed and supported the program of social security from the time it was first considered as a government policy.

In the Social Justice Message of the Central Conference of American Rabbis issued in September, 1934, and entitled "Judaism and the Social Crisis," occurs the following statement: "Future generations will marvel at our mechanical inventions and also wonder at our lack of social creativeness and vision. Not one factor is missing today out of which to construct a world of social comfort and justice. We have natural resources so great that we are embarrassed by the very mass thereof. We have unmatched machinery that can operate with miraculous speed and precision and acres of it are rusting in idleness. We have armies of men trained to a high degree of skill and efficiency, and over ten million of these workers are walking the streets without hope and haunted by fear. We have vast reservoirs of wealth dammed up in vaults and banks and corporations and no one apparently knows how to wisely employ it. Most of all, we have great markets here and abroad, markets that are made up of a larger number of undernourished, poorly housed, and meanly clad families than we have seen in a century. Every factor of prosperity is present: material, machinery, men, money, and markets—we have a surplus of everything, even of suffering. The one thing we lack is the vision and the will to mould this unprecedented mass of riches into an order of social justice." From other statements of the Rabbinical Assembly it is fair to infer that in the opinion of the rabbis the real trouble today is that three of the five factors necessary for a normal economic life, material resources, machinery, and money, are owned and controlled by individuals and corporations. Until these are socialized and the title of ownership transferred to the people themselves there can be no recovery from our present economic collapse. This is what we mean by religionizing the economic system.

I turn now to the circle of the political order. It is necessary in considering the ways in which the political order can be religionized to understand the central teaching of Judaism. In Judaism religion is central to life. A study of religious organization among the Jewish people reveals a fundamental and determining principle. There is no intermediary between the individual and the Deity and no ritual of intercession. All men are equal in the sight of God; and every individual, no matter how humble or sinful, may approach God directly in petition and prayer. This principle establishes the equality of all men and is of the very essence of democracy. According to Jewish custom and law any Jew may perform any one of the many religious rites within or without the synagogue, even the marriage service. There is no distinction between laymen and leaders except that of learning. The efficacy of worship depends not upon the official position of a person, but upon the piety of the man or woman. According to an ancient law in the Mishnah, ten men are required for public prayer or worship. From this law derives the custom in Israel that any ten men may come together to form a congregation, to elect their own officers, to select their own leader, and to decide upon their own ritual. The congregation, in other words, is independent and autonomous.

In Judaism we do not believe that the State is supreme. We believe not in the supremacy of the State but in the supremacy of the moral law. Even in ancient times Samuel warned the people against the dangers of dictatorship. I quote from the First Book of Samuel, Chapter VIII, verses 1 to 18: "This will be the manner of the king that shall reign over you; he will take your sons, and appoint them unto him, for his chariots, and to be his horsemen; and they shall run before his chariots. And he will appoint them unto him for captains of thousands, and captains of fifties; and to plow his ground, and to reap his harvests, and to make his instruments of war, and the instruments of his chariots. And he will take your daughters to be perfumers, and to be cooks, and to be bakers. And he will take your fields, and your vineyards and your olive-yards, even the best of them, and give them to his servants. And he will take the tenth of your seed, and of your vineyards, and give them to his officers, and to his servants. And he will take your men-servants, and your maid-servants, and your goodliest young men, and your asses, and put them to his work. He will take the tenth of your flocks; and ye shall cry in that day because of your king whom ye shall have chosen; and the Lord will not answer you in that day." This speech put in the mouth of Samuel, biblical critics tell us, was probably written at a later date. The passage sounds suspiciously late, almost modern, even contemporary. If the supreme authority is not the State but the moral law, it is to the moral law in our time that individuals and groups must conform and not to a political pattern established by the State and imposed upon the people.

The concern of the rabbis today in the matter of political organization is clearly expressed in this passage adopted by the Central Conference of American Rabbis in 1935: "The democratic form of government is not only challenged but under attack even in the United States. The danger of Communism on the left and Fascism on the right is present through the activities of well-organized aggressive groups in our midst. In order that democratic principles and practices may be effectively safeguarded and democracy promoted in its development as our accepted social system, we urge the following measures: Freedom of speech, freedom of assembly, and freedom of the press, guaranteed to us under the Constitution, are threatened through both state and federal laws and their interpretation by officers of local, state and federal governments. Conservative and reactionary organizations are assuming authority without warrant, and in the name of patriotism are engaged in unpatriotic efforts to limit our liberties. We urge an investigation by the Judiciary Committee of the Senate of the United States, an investigation that will concern itself with the dangers that threaten us upon the right as well as upon the left. We urge that the committee be instructed to investigate the denial of rights of American citizens secured to them by the Constitution and the sources of un-American propaganda and activities directed against the exercise of such rights, and the organized bands of vigilantes interfering with the rights of workers and farmers to organize and to carry on their activities, particularly in relation to the guarantees of collective bargaining and the rights of labor as sct forth by law."

It is most important to emphasize the method through which the cultural organization, the economic system, and the political order are to be changed. Judaism repudiates outright the doctrine of force and violence and war as a method of achieving social change. I quote from the Social Justice Report of the Central Conference of American Rabbis: "Society as we understand it, is not static. Changes in social structure and organization must come with wider social experience, expanding social concepts, and a deepening sense of social justice. We believe that social change should be achieved through orderly and democratic procedure. Without equivocation, we firmly disavow the employment of force and violence in making the passage from the old social system to the new social order that we are confident must be established. We are convinced that force and violence once attempted as a method of social change cannot be limited to any one area of life and is wrong in all fields of social action. We are opposed to the method of force advocated and employed by Fascism on the right and we are also opposed to the technique of violence and force advocated and employed by Communism on the left. America must not allow our fear of Communism to drive us into Fascism, nor our fear of Fascism to drive us into Communistic methods of social change. We believe that the development of Democracy means the application of democratic methods of procedure to the solution of economic conflicts as well as to the settlement of national and international disputes."

This is the modern restatement and interpretation of the ancient biblical principle: "It is not by might and not by power but by the spirit of the moral law that man prevails."

The spirit of the social philosophy of Judaism is summed up, we believe, in the following statement taken from the Report of the Social Justice Commission of the Central Conference of American Rabbis for the year 1934: "At the present time three trends are developing in the political organization of America: Communism on the extreme left; Fascism on the extreme right; and a socialized democracy in the center. The danger is that the American people will fall into the trap of thinking that the choice is either Communism or Fascism. The either-or type of thinking is always dangerous and as a rule wrong. It is not necessary to limit ourselves to two choices, Communism or Fascism. In the judgment of the members of the Conference there is only one way in which the American people can escape the dictatorship and tyranny of Communism on the one hand, and the tyranny and dictatorship of Fascism on the other, and that is by establishing a thoroughly socialized democracy. This change can be achieved, the members are convinced, without force and violence and bloodshed and through the orderly methods of democratic procedure. We solemnly commend to the American people a social philosophy that is derived from the expanding democratic ideal that must henceforth be sovereign in our social life."

3. JEWISH INTERPRETATION OF LIFE

There is one advantage in living through seven decades and more of life. We are able to look back across the years and to see in correct perspective the different interpretations of life that have conditioned our thinking and that have controlled our conduct. We are accustomed to divide history into ancient, medieval, and modern times. Or, if we are speaking of western civilization, to divide history into the Classical Period, the Dark Ages, the Renaissance and the Reformation, and the Modern Period. But in every historical period there is a dominant power that we used to call the *Zeitgeist*. In the early centuries of the present era men and women were greatly influenced in their thinking by the neo-Platonic philosophy; in the Middle Ages their thinking was determined by the neo-Aristotelian philosophy. In the Dark Ages the conduct of men and women was controlled by the belief in demonology. Their treatment of disease is an evidence of this. In the Middle Ages the daily life of men and women was directed by their belief in astrology. Their fate was in the stars and not in themselves. The very word disaster proves this point. If men and women live under a dictatorship, they think and act in dictatorial ways. If they live in a democracy, they live and think in democratic ways. Even authors and musicians and artists are influenced in their expression by the movement of the period in which they write or compose or paint. They are identified as members of the Classical, or the Romantic, or the Realistic School. Only the great creative geniuses succeed in emancipating themselves from the spirit of the time in philosophy, in science, in art, or in religion.

Fifty years ago in the days of my youth, we lived under the spell of what were called the natural sciences, that is, physics and chemistry and biology. Thomas Huxley, Charles Darwin, and Herbert Spencer were the great and acknowledged teachers of our time. The laws of the natural sciences were the accepted laws of all life. All life's problems were thus interpreted. So much so that men and women thought of themselves and of the world and of the universe in terms of physics and chemistry and biology. I still have in my library books that interpret life in terms of physics; others that do so in terms of chemistry; and many that interpret all of life, individual and social, in terms of biology. Even religion and the spiritual life were thus adjudged.

One of the most widely read books fifty years ago was entitled "Natural Law in the Spiritual World," by Sir Henry Drummond. Here the author, a minister of the Church of England, attempted to explain our religious life and our concepts and even the creed of the church as expressions of the laws of the natural sciences. Not only was this book widely read, but men and women quoted the text as scientific support of their religious beliefs. They found great comfort in the teaching that science and the scientific spirit confirmed their theology. We are wiser now. We know that the laws of physics

and chemistry and biology do not operate on the level of our spiritual life. We no longer appeal for scientific sanction of religious
principles. We recognize that the material sciences give only a
partial and limited interpretation of life.

Twenty-five years ago we lived under the magic of the social
sciences, that is, sociology, economics, political science, and anthropology. In every college and every community men and women
not only studied the social sciences but were taught to interpret life
and the world and the universe in their terms. The so-called laws
of the Social Sciences were assumed to be the laws of life. Man is
a social animal governed by consciousness of kind and dislike of
the unlike. This was one of the constantly repeated formulas of
Professor Giddings. Man is an economic animal, controlled in his
conduct by the laws of production and distribution and consumption. We never thought of questioning this doctrine of Professor
Walker. Man is a political animal and instinctively organizes his
life in accordance with the laws of political science. This was the
teaching of Professor Laski and his school. Man is a creature of
culture, and as cultures differ, each is a valid law unto itself. So
we learned from the anthropologists. Many of us, even in our maturity, were captivated by these teachings and came to believe truly
that in the social sciences would be found the solution of all our
problems. They assured us of salvation. Even religion did not escape. Religious leaders everywhere interpreted religion in such
terms—"The Social Gospel of the Churches," "Christianity and the
Social Crisis." Graham Taylor, Walter Rauschenbush, Harry Ward
—these teachers are still invoked by our youth. We know now that
the laws of the social sciences are not necessarily the laws of religion,
that many of their so-called laws are themselves invalid.

Today we are living under the hypnotic power of the psychical
sciences—psychology, psychiatry, and psychoanalysis. Books and
magazines are crowded with the new doctrines and expositions of
the new dispensation. The literature of our time, novels, plays,
and poetry, is largely an endeavor to explore the subterranean
cellars of our subconscious life, personal and social. Most of us
have acquired the vocabulary though not all of us have come to
understand fully the content and implications of the terms. Men

and women are constantly diagnosing each other and allow themselves to make judgments that amaze the experts. "That man is a neurotic." "That woman is a paranoiac." "That child is a schizophrenic."

A few days ago as I stepped out of the Synagogue House, I saw a mother scolding a little girl. The child was crying bitterly. I ventured to ask the mother, "What is the matter with your little daughter?" She replied, "I think my little girl has an Oedipus complex." I looked at the child and remarked, "Your little girl looks to me as if she had a bad cold."

We ought to be more cautious in condemning and branding others as glibly as we do. Our diagnosis is not only evidence of our ignorance; it is all too often an expression of anger or, even worse, of wishful thinking. The best studies in the field of mental hygiene tell us that not more than ten percent of the population will ever be in need of mental or psychiatric care, and that only one out of eighteen or nineteen will ever need institutional care. In other words, ninety percent of us are reasonably normal. A distinguished psychiatrist once said to me, "Do not be so greatly disturbed about this mental hygiene problem. Remember that most men and women, even most Jewish men and women, are more or less sane." He himself was one of the sanest psychiatrists I have ever met.

Of one thing we are assured. We shall find salvation for all our problems in the psychical sciences, not only our personal, but family and social problems as well. Men and women no longer consult the minister or religion as they once did; nor lawyers nor physicians. They consult the psychologist or psychiatrist or psychoanalyst.

The guidance clinics of our day are staffed with men and women trained in the psychical sciences. Even large industrial companies and leading corporations are adding psychologists and psychiatrists to their personnel department. The problems of group relations also, group friction and group hostility, are to be solved thereby, especially through psychology. Even war itself, we are informed, is to be ended through the ministration not of diplomats and statesmen but through the therapy of psychiatry.

And of another thing we are assured; we shall find in the psychical sciences not only the solution of all our problems but the true interpretation of life and the world and the universe. Sigmund Freud considered psychiatry one of the divisions of medicine, just as are cardiology and endocrinology. He thought of psychoanalysis as a method of treatment, an instrument for exploration of the subconscious life, a means of draining and removing subconscious psychical abscesses and sources of subconscious infection. Freud would have been astounded to discover that his disciples or pseudo-disciples have expanded psychiatry into a philosophy of life, and that they delude us into believing that in psychoanalysis we shall find the secret of our being. We are evidently misunderstanding the meaning and scope of the laws of the psychical sciences as we misunderstood the natural and social sciences.

Religion, of course, has not escaped. "Peace of Mind" is only one avowed attempt, perhaps outstanding, to interpret religion and religious experiences in terms of psychology, psychiatry, and psychoanalysis. There is no doubt that the psychical sciences have aided us to understand better the origin and meaning of many religious customs and symbols. They have aided us to see deeper into the dark area of our subconscious life and to appreciate more fully the role that subconscious forces play in the concepts and in the conduct of men and women. They have developed techniques that assist us to relieve tension and resolve confusions that arise out of concealments or conscious misbehavior. They have added to our knowledge and equipment in understanding and mastering the material of human experience, just as the natural sciences and social sciences have added to our knowledge of the universe and our control of the factors in society. But this does not mean that we should make the mistake of assuming that the laws of the psychical sciences are the laws of religion. It certainly does not mean that we should make the incredible blunder of substituting them for religion. In fact, if I were a psychiatrist, which I am not, I should look with suspicion upon this current custom of interpreting religion in terms of the psychical sciences. I should come to the conclusion that there is a serious weakness in the convictions of men and women who are constantly searching alien altars for confirmation of their faith.

All these interpretations of the last fifty years are correct within the limits of their own fields. The laws of the natural sciences are correct in physics and chemistry and biology. The laws of the social sciences are correct in sociology, economics, government, and anthropology. The laws of the psychical sciences, as far as we understand them at all, are correct in psychology, psychiatry, and psychoanalysis. But these are not the laws of religion. There is grave danger in attempting to reconcile religion with every movement, every cult, every interpretation of life that emerges and asserts itself as the years pass. It is our duty to develop the inward genius of religion and of Judaism, to restate our faith from generation to generation in terms of our new knowledge and expanding experience.

It has been mentioned above that the rabbis asked why in the phrase, "Our God and God of our fathers, God of Abraham and God of Isaac and God of Jacob," the word God is repeated before the name of each patriarch. Why not say, "The God of Abraham, Isaac, and Jacob"? The word is repeated, they tell us, in order to teach that God reveals Himself anew with each generation. In Exodus, God says to Moses, "I revealed Myself to Abraham as God Almighty; but to you I reveal Myself as the Eternal." This principle of growth, of evolution in religion, even in evolution of the concept of the deity, is one of the most precious principles in religion and in Judaism. It has saved us from a static religion, from the rigidity of a formal and fixed creed. It has made religion, and especially Judaism, dynamic; a religion that broadens in horizon and deepens in insight as the ages increase. This principle of growth and evolution we must preserve. We must be free to reinterpret our faith in accordance with each new dawn of the truth.

We must remember something else. The laws of science, of the natural, social, and psychical sciences, are not unchanged or "immutable," as we once allowed ourselves to believe. What we call laws are after all only uniform ways of action; they are based upon our powers of observation. We observe that things act in a uniform way and we call this uniform action a law. Our powers of observation, however, are limited; and from time to time we learn to extend limits and to bring additional facts within the scope of our knowledge. These new facts sometimes compel us to change our concepts. The laws of physics certainly have been reformulated within the last fifty years. The textbooks we used half a century ago are completely outdated today. In view of this change in our concept of the laws, it certainly is hazardous to equate religion with the laws of the natural, social, or psychical sciences.

In the second place, we must remember that the philosophy of one age may be in utter conflict with that of a later era. The neo-Aristotelian philosophy of the Middle Ages certainly was in conflict with the neo-Platonic philosophy of the first century. Therefore to attempt to reconcile religion and Judaism with neo-Platonism, as Philo did; and to attempt to reconcile religion and Judaism at another time with neo-Aristotelianism, as Maimonides did—is to involve ourselves and religion and Judaism in contradictions. Religion and Judaism cannot be equal to two philosophies that contradict each other and still remain consistent. Let us therefore be cautious in our eagerness to prove that they are in keeping with the *Zeitgeist* or spirit of the time. The spirit of the time may be wrong, as has happened more than once in the history of human thought. Certainly the spirit of the present time, the interpretation of life today, is not final. It is too confused to be either consistent or correct or true.

The Jewish interpretation of life I find in the terms of the covenant which, according to tradition, God made with Israel and Israel with God. This covenant, in the latter chapters of the splendid Book of Deuteronomy, especially expressed in passages in the 27th, 29th, and 30th chapters, is not a social contract, not an economic treaty, not a political constitution. Neither is it a secular or scientific document. It is essentially a moral code. "Cursed is the man that dishonoureth his father and his mother." "Cursed is the man that removeth his neighbor's landmark." "Cursed is the man that maketh the blind to go astray." "Cursed is the man that perverteth justice due to the stranger, the fatherless and the widow." (Chapter 27) It is significant that the covenant is confirmed in the passage read on the most sacred day of the year, the Day of Atonement. Into this covenant, we read, enter all of Israel, the elders and the officers, the little ones and the wives, the hewers of wood and the drawers of water. Moreover, it is made not with one but with all the generations: "With him that standeth here this day and with him that is not with us this day." Nothing could be more impressive than these verses that describe its eternal character. (Chapter 29) Nor could any words be more profound than these that describe its nature. "It is not in the heavens, that thou shouldst say: Who shall go up to heaven for us and bring it unto us. Neither is it beyond the sea, that thou shouldst say: Who will go over the sea for us to bring it to us. But the word is very nigh unto thee, in thy mouth and in thy heart that thou mayest do it." (Chapter 30)

The pity is that we hear of this covenant only once a year, and that we learn so little of its content and so often forget its character. If there is any passage in our literature we should know well, if there is any part of our religion we should not forget, it is the covenant, fundamental to our faith, that binds Israel to God and God to Israel.

I find the Jewish interpretation of life not only in the covenant but also in the liturgy, in the daily prayers we recite in the synagogue and at home. The 613 commandments found in the Bible and those that comprise the later codes are given many explanations. Some are purely secular, and some pseudo-scientific. One explanation is that the commandments in the Bible and the codes are designed solely to set Israel apart from other nations. We have our own way of life, and this way we must observe in order that we may not be confused with others. Another explanation is a related one, that through the commandments and codes Israel is not only separated from others but is saved from assimilation. The commandments, the customs, the rituals, serve to protect and to preserve the identity and solidarity and uniqueness of the people. Without them we should soon become like all other peoples. A third explanation, and this applies particularly to the dietary laws and cult, is that the commandments are designed as health measures. Their purpose is to safeguard Israel from the diseases and the plagues that afflict and ravage others. These and other interpretations are all rationalizations. The true explanation, the true purpose of the commandments, I find in the clear and oft-repeated

sentence: "Thou hast sanctified us through Thy commandments."
I am aware that the Hebrew word *kadosh* has a history, that it has
passed through different stages of meaning. But the highest meaning (and why should we accept less?) is to sanctify. The highest
purpose of the commandments is to sanctify life, to hallow life, to
lift us above the secular and the scientific, and to teach us the sacredness of life, the sanctity of human relations, the holiness of religion.
Here is the Jewish interpretation of the laws we observe—to instruct us that life is sacred and that life is holy.

I appreciate fully that this is not an interpretation of life that
commends itself to the mood of our time. We are interested not in
the sacred but in the secular and the scientific, and now especially
in psychological interpretations. One of the salient symptoms of
our day is the search not only for outward but for inward content-
ment and peace. The widespread, eager, and almost morbid interest in every magazine article, every book, every movement that
promises inner peace is evidence not so much of the intrinsic worth
of these articles and books and movements, as of the hunger men
and women feel for spiritual sedatives, opiates, anaesthetics.

This hunger is not difficult to understand or to explain. It is in
part the normal reaction to the tensions and strains of two world
wars, the psychological aftermath that follows every war. It is in
greater part an expression and proof of the endeavor of men not
to solve their problems, but to escape the complexities, confusions,
conflicts, and convulsions that characterize our social, our economic,
and our political life, national and international. But in greatest
part this longing for mental rest and spiritual quietude is one of
the consequences of the disappointments, the frustrations, the losses,
the tragedies, and the anguish so many of us have suffered during
the past two or three decades. We discover that the problems of
today are too vast and too complicated for our capacities. We are
unable to cope with problems that have become worldwide in extent and infinitely complex in content and implications. Nowhere
do we find the leadership that is needed in times such as these.
We seem unequal to the "one world." This world has outgrown
us, to put it another way, and we have not grown in capacity and
in power with it. It is natural that we should seek to end the tur-

moil within as we would end the turbulence in the world without.

It is natural also that in their search for a solution of their problems and in their passion for peace, inner and outer, men and women should turn to religion and to religious movements. For they have always believed that out of religion should come the enlightenment and guidance they deeply need in a period of doubt and distraction; and also the wisdom that will reveal the correct solution of problems with which they wrestle from day to day. Out of religion, they hope, will come the courage and strength they need in the hour of temptation; the power to master evil forces; and also the counsel and the insight that will serve them when their steps falter and their own confidence fails. Out of religion likewise there should emerge the solace and sustainment, the comfort and consolation, they require in the hour of sorrow, when they are compelled to walk, as all men must, through the valley of the shadow of death.

Men and women reread the prayers of their religion; rehearse the teachings of the sages and the prophets, and restudy the principles and ideals of their faith, in the hope that out of the heritage of the centuries will come the inspiration to redeem them from the depths, to give them the faith to lift their eyes to the hills whence cometh their help, to vouchsafe the power to transform a world of wickedness and woe into one of peace and joy. In spite of all the secularism and the scientific spirit, of all the skepticism and cynicism, of all the disillusionment and bitterness of our generation, especially of the younger group, the churches and synagogues and mosques and temples still stand; and in them gather vast assemblages of people whose very presence testifies to their belief that somewhere in the sanctuary of religion there is a message that they need.

But let men and women not misunderstand the message of religion, and let them not mistake the methods of religion in this matter of outward and inward peace. It is not the role of religion to serve as a sedative. Symbols and ceremonies and rituals have a higher purpose than this. All the prophets emphasize this teaching. One of the best illustrations is found in the passage read on the Day of Atonement, from the writings of the great prophet of the exile called the Second Isaiah. In his time too men and women thought they could achieve peace of soul through fasting, bowing of the head like a bulrush, spreading upon themselves sackcloth and ashes. When these ritualistic methods failed they were disappointed and disturbed. "Wherefore have we fasted and Thou seest not? Wherefore have we afflicted our souls and Thou takest not knowledge?" It is necessary for the prophet to admonish the people, to remind them that this is neither the message nor the method of religion. Instead of sackcloth and ashes, instead of bowing the head, instead of afflicting oneself through fasting, this is what is acceptable to the Lord, the way that God has chosen: "To deal thy bread to the hungry; to bring the poor that are cast out into thy house; and when thou seest the naked that thou comfortest him; and that thou hide not thyself from thine own flesh. To loose the fetters of wickedness; and to let the oppressed go free. Then shalt thou call and the Lord will answer. Then shalt thou cry and He will say: Here I am." It is evident that the people of that far-off time completely misunderstood the meaning of religion. They had to learn that the ceremonies and rituals and symbols and the sacrificial cult could not in themselves soothe their consciences, that it is not the purpose of religion to serve as a spiritual sedative.

There are men and women today also who think they can achieve peace, inward and outward, through reading the ritual, the recitation of prayers, the beating of the breast, the incantation of the confession: "We have sinned, we have transgressed, we have acted perversely." But in spite of the appeal and power of religious symbols and ceremonies; in spite of the color and richness of much of the religious ritual; in spite of the moving tenderness and impressive passion of the classical music of church and synagogue, mosque and temple—these elements alone do not bring men and women the thing they seek. It is necessary to relearn the lesson the prophet teaches, that peace, peace of mind and peace of soul, can come only when our conduct is in accordance with the teachings and principles and ideals of religion.

I know it is the fashion today to say that the obstacles to peace lie within ourselves, that we suffer from complexes and compulsions and phobias and neuroses that disturb and destroy our peace. This is true of some men and women, and these undoubtedly are in need of psychotherapy. But it is not true of most of us. The source of the trouble is not a complex or compulsion, not a phobia or neurosis. It is the debased and perverted standards of conduct in which we allow ourselves to indulge. What we need is not the ritual of religion nor that of psychiatry, but the discipline of the moral law.

We may endeavor to excuse our conduct and to comfort our conscience through these pseudo-scientific explanations, as many men and women attempt to do. They are only deceiving themselves and misinterpreting the meaning of religion. They are ascribing to religion methods of healing and of help that prove what they really seek is not a solution of their problem but sedation, a magic formula that will soothe their pain. That is not the role of religion as we understand it.

As it is not the role of religion to serve as a sedative, it certainly is not to act as an opiate. In times of social distress, economic injustice, international intrigue, organized religion has often been accused of deceiving the people, of deluding them into the belief that conditions as they are, are as they ought to be. "God's in His Heaven, all's right with the world." What a sacrilege to take this one line from a lovely song Browning put into the mouth of a child on a holiday morn, and to distort it into a religious and social philosophy! Browning was too wise not to recognize the existence of evil in the world and the actions of wicked men.

The accusation that religion is often employed as an opiate we must acknowledge to be correct, as it was correct in the days of the prophets. Over 2500 years ago the people of Israel were gathered at Beth-El to celebrate a great national and religious festival. It was a period of apparent economic prosperity, of political expansion and military victory. In the midst of this religious assembly and national rejoicing, the prophet Amos suddenly appears. He sees through their prosperity and aggrandizement and triumphs. "Woe unto them that are at ease in Zion; and to them that sit complacent and secure in Samaria. For three transgressions and for four I will not revoke the punishment thereof. Because they sell the righteous for silver and the needy for a pair of shoes; because they pant after the dust of the earth on the head of the poor and turn aside the way of the meek and the humble." What is the response of Amaziah, the High Priest, and the rest of the priesthood to this accusation? The same that they have given in every age. "Amos has conspired against the king and the country." The prophet is always disturbing our peace and indicting our prosperity.

How can there be peace, inner or outer, in the midst of so much incompetence and corruption and crime, so much wickedness and evil? There is hardly a spot in our economic organization that is sound and wholesome, that is not full of festering and gangrenous sores. We say that waste is inevitable in every war program, that we cannot control every expenditure. But when we come to study the waste we discover that the trouble is not waste but wrongdoing, the giving and taking of bribes, unwarranted and illegitimate fees, even in high places of the government. We say that we must maintain the system of free enterprise, that we must recognize that the motive of private profit is essential in a democracy. But when we study the meaning of free enterprise and the motives that move men, we learn that it is not the profit motive that governs our economic life, but greed and extortion and exploitation.

This is the real explanation of the confusions and conflicts in our economic life today. The pity is that the conditions from which we suffer are so unnecessary and so inexcusable. For today we possess all the elements we need for a fair, just, and abundant economic life. We have all the raw material, the machinery, the money, the manpower, the markets we require. The real shortage in our time is not in commodities but in the conscience of men who control our economic organization. The root of the trouble is not in disregard of so-called economic laws, it is in the defiance of the ethical principles that constitute the organic process of our social life.

How can there be any peace in the midst of so much trickery and intrigue and treachery? The atmosphere of our international life is poisoned, with the venom and virulence politicians and statesmen pour out upon each other, which they call diplomacy. Not a meeting takes place on the international level that does not give evidence of this fact. The nations do not trust each other;

they are constantly charging each other with deception and false-hood and misrepresentation. In recent conferences of the American representatives with the President of Korea, it was perfectly clear that the representative of the Army said one thing and that the representative of the State Department said another. In the sessions of the Assembly of the United Nations it is perfectly clear that the delegates of the United States do not trust Russia and that the delegates of Russia do not trust the United States. We are assured that our government, even at its highest level, is engaged in open covenants openly arrived at, but we discover again and again that there have been secret agreements and commitments in closed executive sessions.

What are organized religion, the high priests, and the priesthoods doing to end this evil in international life? We have the same choice we had in every century—Amaziah and opiates, or Amos and the call to action against social evil. If we take our stand with Amaziah, as men are doing in many congregations, we shall have peace for a time, but we shall go down in disgrace with the very priesthood that has supported an order of iniquity and in-justice. If we take our stand with Amos, we shall not have peace, but shall at least prove that the blood of the prophets still runs in our veins. There can be no peace within as long as there is injustice in the world without.

If it is not the role of religion to act as an opiate, it certainly is not its role to serve as an anaesthetic. Yet many seek to solace and to save themselves through doctrines that are obsolete and dogmas empty of any rational meaning. No man who has emerged out of his adolescence and reached the stage of adulthood wishes to ease his agonies through teachings we have outgrown and doctrines that are dead. It will seem like heresy to some for me to say that the teaching expressed in the oft repeated Hebrew phrase, "This also is for the best," is outgrown and empty to thinking men. It is not for the best in any reasonable world that little children should be crippled for life and that their childish laughter should be turned into tears and that their parents should be compelled to suffer through years because of their children's affliction. It is not for the best in any rational world that six million Jews were murdered, that one third of the Jews of the world were destroyed in the charnel houses and death chambers of Germany. It is not for the best that the remnant of Jews in Europe were not only displaced and dispossessed but were herded in despair into concentration camps and sacrificed to the oil interests of Arabia, United States, and Great Britain. It cannot be for the best that within fifty years men have been so evil-minded that they have plotted three wars that have destroyed countries and devastated continents. It is impossible for any reasoning being to believe that if God were all-powerful as well as all-wise and all-good He would permit epidemics and disasters and weapons of war to maim and mutilate His children. What mortal father would not save his children if he knew how and had the power? Can we ask less of the Deity than we ask of man?

It will sound like blasphemy to many for me to say that the old theological doctrine that the universe is governed by a moral power is obsolete and untenable. It is contradicted by human experience. Our experiences prove that the only moral power in the world resides in the hearts of moral men and women, and that it expresses itself only in human relationships. How can we think of our personal experiences, how can we recall the losses and tragedies we have suffered, and still believe that a moral power governs the universe and directs the destinies of individual men and women? It is inconceivable that a moral power could commit so immoral an act as to allow a fatal disease to destroy the loveliest and most ethereal beings in our midst and to rob us of the fragrance and music and radiant beauty that made the very presence of our loved ones a benediction and the home in which we dwelt an altar of holiness. The heresy and the blasphemy lie not in discarding doctrines that are dead but in continuing to offer these doctrines as anaesthetics in our anguish. To continue to teach, as some religious leaders do, that we are living in a friendly universe—I use their own word—is not only an insult to our intelligence, it is a falsification of the facts and a sacrilege. We must recognize the bitter truth, that we are living in a world filled with hostile elements; we must accept the truth that we are at the mercy of forces themselves without mercy, that nature, as Tennyson long ago put it, is "red in tooth and claw." In the face of the facts of experience, both personal and historical, we must either surrender doctrines that are dead or surrender our reason. I prefer to keep my reason. The most ethical and ethereal life is no assurance of immunity. Nature has no regard for the most moral of men.

Hardly a day passes that does not confirm these statements. The intense and unprecedented heat wave through which we passed last summer not only ruined great areas of crops and destroyed thousands of cattle. It doubled the death rate, according to the reports of the Health Department, especially of babies under one year of age and the aged. Meteorology and morals do not coincide. A short time ago a little girl of five or six was stricken with cancer of the eyes. In order to save the child's life the surgeon had to remove both eyes. When the bandage was taken off, the child cried "I can't wake up, Mommy! I can't wake up!" Medicine did its utmost, but no medical care could make the blindness of the child or the anguish of the parents moral experiences. Last summer a nephew of mine, a brilliant young chemist who was working in a gas station at night in order to pay his tuition at the university, was bending over a machine early in the morning when a murderous assassin crept up behind him and shot him in the head. He left not only his parents and his sisters, but a lovely young wife and a baby less than a year old. What could I possibly say to the family of this young man when I officiated at the funeral? I could not bring myself to explain the tragedy. I could not explain it then and I cannot explain it now. These are only three experiences and they could be multiplied in the lives of a multitude of men and women. It is simply impossible for a rational man or woman to believe that a Diety Who is all-powerful and all-wise and all-good could permit these tragedies to take place. It is impossible to believe that a moral being could be guilty of an immoral act.

The failures and the frustrations, the miseries and the agonies of this one generation are enough to make men cynical and pessimistic. Disillusionment and disbelief are settling like a pall upon minds and hearts. The solution of our problem, our salvation, cannot come from religious sedatives, nor opiates, nor anaesthetics. It can derive only from learning to meet problems not as adolescents but as mature men and women. We must learn to face the world with patience, courage, and dignity. Our salvation will come only from recognition of the truth—and this is the most difficult lesson of all to learn and to accept—that nature and nature's forces are not moral in essence or in action, that the pure and ethical life ensures us no protection against the assault of nature and of the universe outside ourselves. It will come only from the solemn endeavor to make ourselves worthy of the sorrows and the trage-dies that have entered our life; from recognizing that it is our task to complete in our lives the unfinished symphonies in the lives of those who have joined the choir invisible, whose music is still the gladness of our world; from making our own the unconquerable spirit of heroic men: "It matters not how strait the gate, How charged with punishment the scroll," we must be masters of our fate, the captains of our souls. No man or woman is exempt from the inevitable vicissitudes of human experience. Judaism is too wise and too sincere in its teachings to deceive men with false promises; it has too profound a regard for the intelligence and the inward understanding of men to preach anything but the truth.

In the life of every one of us times come when we grow weary, weary of stresses and struggles, of separations and sorrows, of trage-dies and anguish. This is especially true when the years lengthen and our strength wanes and the burdens grow heavy, and the dusk seems not far distant. At these times all we seek is peace of mind, rest, the unconsciousness of endless sleep. That this is true I know only too well.

But in our better moments, in our higher moods, this is not what we seek of life nor what we ask of religion. In our better moments we do not ask that religion be a sedative to soothe us with its sym-bols; that it be an opiate to ease us with a false sense of content-ment; that it be an anaesthetic to deceive us with obsolete teachings and dead doctrines. In our higher moods we look to religion as an incentive to high resolve and to lofty action; as a passionate pro-test against injustice and evil; as a vital and victorious power to redeem us from disillusionment and despair.

What do I ask of religion? Not sedatives, not opiates, not anaes-thetics. I ask the understanding to face life with courage and the world with wisdom. I ask the power to overcome the forces of evil

and to establish the right. I ask the insight and the grace to trans-
mute my sorrows into sacred shrines. I ask the faith to lift my eyes
to the hills and to the horizons of the spirit; to throw the windows
of my soul wide open to the dawn of truth; to catch one fleeting
glimpse of the visions and glories of the coming day; to watch
patiently for the radiance of the rising sun. This I ask for myself
and this I ask for those who are near and those who are far off, so
that we may journey forth with new hope in our hearts, a new
song upon our lips, a new light in our eyes, to build the kingdom
of truth and justice and peace.

4. WATCHMAN, WHAT OF THE NIGHT

— GROUNDS FOR OPTIMISM —

Introduction

In the Hebrew anthology that we call the Bible, three books are
ascribed to Solomon. One, the Song of Songs, is really a love poem,
or epithalamium sung at weddings in ancient times; two, Proverbs,
which is part of our wisdom literature and contains the distilled experience of the Jewish people; and three, Ecclesiastes, the only
book in the Bible written in a spirit of gentle cynicism and patient pessimism. According to an ancient tradition of the sages,
Solomon wrote the Song of Songs in the days of his youth and romance; Proverbs in the years of maturity and understanding; and
Ecclesiastes in the period of old age and disillusionment. This tradition in itself is an interesting and illuminating commentary upon
the psychological development and the cycles of growth through
which the sages believed all men to pass. In other literatures too
we find that many of the poets and playwrights and novelists portray the period of advancing age as one of disappointment and in-
firmity, decline and dissolution. Even Shakespeare, who is among
the most wholesome of the dramatists, in his Seven Ages of Man,
pictures advancing age as a stage of weakness and despair. This
view is not shared by all poets and dramatists, nor is it an expression of the philosophy of many Jewish authors and thinkers. Rob-

ert Browning is correct in his exposition of the philosophy of Rabbi Ben Ezra:

> "Grow old along with me!
> The best is yet to be,
> The last of life for which the first was made:
> Our times are in his hand,
> Who saith, 'A whole I planned,
> Youth shows but half; trust God: see all,
>   nor be afraid!' "

If I were to accept the ancient tradition of the sages, I should at this stage of my life feel disillusioned, cynical, pessimistic. The pilgrimage through the years, it is true, has been long and often has been difficult. At times the journey has been dark and tragic. For I have been compelled often to walk through the valley of the shadow of death. But I am convinced that we must not allow our personal disappointments and disabilities, our own losses and sufferings, to determine or to limit or to color our outlook upon life. Life is larger than the personal experience of any one man; and we must learn to see life whole, if we are to see any one part in proper perspective. The danger is that we may and often do develop what might be called the microscope habit of mind. The microscope is a necessary and indispensable instrument in the laboratory, but it has two great disadvantages. In the first place, we can insert only a small fragment under the lens; and in the second, the lens magnifies the fragment out of all proportion to the whole.

It is not possible for every one of us to see the whole in cosmic outline. This is given to only a few gifted men, such as Aristotle and Newton and Einstein. But it is important to enlarge our vision and to expand the circle to include 360 degrees and all of life from the circumference to the center. We must not allow ourselves to be satisfied with segments, no matter how crowded and intense and vibrant these may be. When we try to see life whole we discover with ibn Ezra that there is ground for optimism, and that both human progress and social evolution are a reality. In spite of every lapse of the centuries man does move forward and upward. This century has been described as the bloodiest of all the ages; but it is only one stage in the historical development of mankind and the evolution of the human spirit.

Advance of Science

One ground for optimism I find in the growing understanding of nature and in the increasing control of nature's forces, both within and without. The poet is undoubtedly right; in the raw, "Nature is red in tooth and claw." But this is not the whole truth. Scientists are slowly and perseveringly advancing the frontiers of knowledge; they are slowly and persistently increasing our mastery over nature. The new understanding of disease and the control of epidemics that formerly decimated whole populations is one evidence of scientific advance. The health movement is now not a local or national program but world-wide. Through the World Health Organization of the United Nations we have progressed through three stages. The first is treatment of the sick. Medical, nursing, social, spiritual care are more widespread than ever before in the history of medicine. The second stage is prevention of disease. We have succeeded in reducing to a minimum or in eliminating altogether the plagues that formerly swept whole continents—cholera, smallpox, yellow fever, and malaria; even diphtheria and typhoid fever have been conquered. The "wonder drugs" that are multiplying in number under the title of antibiotics have robbed many infections of their power to poison the human body. Pneumonia has lost its terror, and scarlet fever and encephalitis and mastoiditis have become infrequent hazards of childhood and adult life. Through physics and chemistry and biology scientists are learning not only to understand nature; they are learning how to employ nature's energies for the protection of mankind and for safeguarding men, women, and children from disease. The third stage is the promotion of health. In this we are learning not only how to heal and to safeguard ourselves, but how to raise the health index through nutrition and a regulated regime, and how to increase the resistance of whole populations to germs and viruses we cannot control.

We have also learned how to make three blades of grass to grow where only one grew before. This means that we have learned how to increase and enrich our food supply. Through vast irrigation projects, conservation of natural resources, improved methods of planting and reaping and grafting and fertilizing, we are now feeding the people a more nutritious diet than they have ever before enjoyed. We have also learned how to improve housing. Our homes are not only better built; they are more sanitary and equipped with conveniences which only a hundred years ago were not even dreamed of. What is true of food and shelter is also true of clothing. Science has taught us how to manufacture fabrics out of raw material in the mineral and vegetable world, leaving us no longer dependent upon animals for wool and fur. Within a century transportation has changed not only the face of the earth but the relationship of peoples to each other. Time and distance have both contracted to the point where they tend to disappear altogether. We not only travel upon the earth and the sea, but through the air at incredible height and speed. Perhaps the most dramatic progress we have made is in our control over the sources of energy. Coal has yielded to oil as a source, oil has yielded to hydroelectric power, and hydroelectric power is now yielding to the inexhaustible supply of energy contained within the atom. The time is near when the atom will be employed not for weapons of war but for instruments of peace. But even this is not the end. The now unused energy radiated by the sun will in time be captured and controlled, and employed in the service of civilization.

One of the most promising movements, however, is control of the birth rate through scientific procedures. The uncontrolled and reckless birth of babies means an excessive death rate of children, a premature loss of mothers, destitution of many families, and all the human misery that comes with overpopulation. The scientific program we call birth control or planned parenthood means the birth of children through choice and not through chance, their spacing in accordance with the health of the family and the needs of society. We have come to realize that there is no human wisdom in bringing into the world more children than we can properly educate and maintain. If they are to grow into adolescence and adulthood and achieve health and the development of their capacities and powers and personalities, they require study and training and discipline that can come only when we place limits upon the birth rate. Not only have we succeeded in some countries in lifting the standard of living through control, but we have improved both the physical and mental health of the people. Today even Japan and India are opening their doors to this program. That they and a number of European countries, like Italy, suffer from overpopulation is clearly recognized by every social scientist. What the optimum population of countries should be is still to be determined. This we know, that if we are to escape the suffering that comes with too many children, we must learn how to limit the number of babies born, the size of families, and extent of the population, in accordance with social needs and social capacities. Havelock Ellis, in "The Task of Social Hygiene," a book that should be better known, develops the thesis that during the last one hundred years we have learned to cleanse the banks of the stream; and that now the time has come to control and to purify the stream of life itself.

Human Relations

A second ground for optimism I find in the changing attitude of nations and governments toward one another. It is true that during the last fifty years there has been a recrudescence of nationalism—political, economic, and religious. And it is also true that nationalism has led to war. But the wars of nationalism have been due in large part to a determination of colonial and oppressed peoples to emancipate themselves from imperialistic control. They have also been due to a growing and deep-seated desire of peoples in a feudal or semi-feudal state to develop their group consciousness and to assert their own particular group genius. These peoples are in various stages of revolt against political imperialism, economic exploitation, and cultural discrimination.

The emancipation and the enfranchisement of peoples all over the earth is inevitable. But at the same time men and nations are coming to see that cultures have more in common than they have in differences. They are also coming to realize that cultures cannot only co-exist, but can develop cooperative relationships. The old fears we include under the term xenophobia must in time fade into the past, and the ancient doctrines of racial or religious or national superiority will be unable to survive in the one world we are creating. In spite of everything that is happening today to the contrary, the doctrine of national sovereignty, to use a general term, is doomed as truly as the divine right of kings. This was the teaching of Harold Laski; and peoples and nations and governments are learning that truth on the cultural, economic, and political levels. The creation of the "Steel Community" by six nations in Western Europe, establishment of the European Council and the European Community, mean the end of the barriers that have shut nations out from each other. It is a slow process, but like an Alpine glacier it will continue to move forward.

There is an ancient Jewish legend which tells that God in the beginning created only one man. The sages ask why God created only one, why not ten or twenty? The answer is most significant. God created only one man in the beginning of time in order that all men might look back to a common father and realize they were all members of the same human family and therefore should treat each other as brothers. Peoples, it is true, differ in many ways; just as men and women differ in contour of body, color of skin, and texture of hair. But the League of Nations, and now the United Nations, emphasize the fact that all peoples have common interests, enterprises, and aspirations. The debates in the Assembly of the United Nations and the decisions of the Security Council may seem to stress opposing ambitions and to express nothing but discord. But beyond all the discussion and discord it is easily possible to see the common objectives. In time we shall learn how to appreciate our common aims and develop common procedures.

Even in the affiliated agencies of the United Nations we are discovering that we all have interests in common, such as the end of illiteracy, the expansion of education, increase of economic resources, and improvement of health. Through exchange we are learning from one another, and now realize that we must share not only our surpluses but our assets and resources. We are today sending not only money but boatloads of wheat to Asiatic countries in danger of famine and starvation. The Point Four Program means just this, that we are discovering that all men are brothers, and that we must do all we can to improve and advance our common welfare.

One of the best illustrations of the changed attitude of peoples is found in the Declaration of Human Rights formulated by a special commission of the United Nations. The Declaration is in a present state of eclipse, due in large part to the fears of certain groups in the United States. But the document was formulated by a commission representing all the sixty peoples in the United Nations. It emphasizes the rights the commission believes all men hold in common, including more than the Bill of Rights of the Constitution of the United States. The Bill of Rights, covering only civil liberties and political rights, expresses the political demands of peoples since the time of the Magna Carta. The Declaration of Human Rights, however, goes much further. It does stress the fact that all men should enjoy freedom of speech, press, assembly, and worship. But in addition, it expounds in detail what the commission believes implicit in "life, liberty, and the pursuit of happiness." The representatives agreed that in addition to civil and political rights, all men should possess economic and social rights. They must all have the right to work, to maintain themselves in decency and self-respect; the right to an education, to develop their powers and capacities and skills; the right to life, and a standard of living to maintain them in health and assure them a reasonable amount of leisure to enjoy life. They should be granted freedom of information. This means that the knowledge amassed by any group must be accessible and available to all groups. There is no doubt in my mind that we shall outgrow our present restrictions and limitations, and that the Declaration of Human Rights will be resurrected and established as a code for all peoples. We have come to see that civil liberties and political freedom are of little value unless men and women also enjoy economic and social rights.

A more immediate evidence of the changing attitudes of nations and governments, I find in the current statements of official representatives of the East and the West. Only a short time ago they were regarding each other with suspicion, mistrust, and antagonism. Addresses delivered in the Assembly of the United Nations

were filled with charges and counter-charges, accusation and vi-
tuperation. They created a state of international tension that
vitiated the atmosphere of the world. Today the former rigid and
inflexible attitudes of the East and the West are yielding to a new
approach and a new relationship. All the recommendations for a
Four-Power or Five-Power Conference and for meetings at the
highest level mean that the leaders are endeavoring to find ways to
reduce world tensions and transform international relationships.

Instead of making defense and the end of aggression the bases
of diplomacy or foreign policy, statesmen are changing their vocabulary and their outlook. They not only speak of co-existence
and non-aggression and international assurances, but are formulating policies and programs that would guarantee each nation protection, and safeguard the boundaries of every country against violation and invasion. The Locarno Treaty that guaranteed the integrity of the boundaries of Western Europe failed for the simple
reason that we were not prepared to think in these terms. Today we
are thinking in new terms, and more important, in broader terms.
We have grown to the point where we are now internationalizing
the principles of Locarno. I am convinced that the time is not too
distant when our attitudes toward one another will take on a new
complexion. Boundaries will continue, but instead of becoming
barriers that shut nations out from each other, they will prove
bonds to bind them together in a common program of world welfare. It is inconceivable that the United Nations should suffer the
fate of the League of Nations.

End of Armaments

A third ground for optimism I find in the conviction that the age
of armaments is coming to a close. This is, I realize, a strange statement to make at a time when nations are spending hundreds of bil-
lions of dollars in building armaments, on the earth, in the sea,
and in the sky. It is odd to say this when governments live in mutual
terror because of the implied threats of the atom and the hydrogen
bombs, when we seem to be in greater danger of complete destruction than at any other time in history. But there is increasing evidence that peoples and governments are coming to see that war,

as a means of settling disputes, is outgrown and futile as well as inhuman and outrageous. We have outlawed the duel between individuals. We no longer permit men to settle their personal disputes with club or javelin or dagger or pistol. We compel them to employ the court, in accordance with the law of justice. I am convinced that in the foreseeable future we shall also outlaw war.

The Kellogg-Briand Pact contained two main articles. In the first, the nations agreed to renounce war as a national policy; and in the second, to settle their disputes through peaceful means. The Pact failed because we were not ready. We were in Geneva at the time it was signed in Paris; and we knew then that the number of conditions, reservations, and compromises added by the several governments would nullify the Pact and make it impossible for the governments to honor their own signatures. But it will be resuscitated, and then we shall mean what we say when we insist that war is outmoded, and that nations must settle their disputes through pacific or peaceful means. It is true that the Disarmament Conference of the League of Nations ended in frustration and futility, and that the United Nations has not up to this time realized the high hopes expressed in the Preamble to the Charter. But the dream and the vision of a world without war cannot be erased from the hearts of men. We have come to see that in war today there are no victors, only the vanquished and the victims. The instruments of force today are so powerful and so destructive that they make war itself impossible as a means of achieving victory. We are coming to recognize its futility, and the stupidity of assuming that through force we can determine who is right and who is wrong.

We are turning to law and the court on the international level. We have established courts on the local, the state, and the national levels, and now are are establishing them internationally. Courts do make mistakes, for judges are human and influenced by their background and training and predilections. But they can and do reverse themselves. The Supreme Court of the United States has reversed itself a number of times. Courts change in composition and character, and the men who compose them review their decisions and revise their judgments. Men will agree that it is wiser to run the risk of a wrong court decision than of another war.

We can review and reverse decisions, and revise our judgments, but there is no way in which we can reverse the destruction and anguish and desolation that war brings. We shall also come to see that men accept court judgments not because the courts can enforce their judgments through arms, but because the peoples have learned the lesson of law and justice. The states do not accept decisions of the Supreme Court because it has the power to call out the Army and Navy and Air Force to impose acceptance. They accept because they understand the meaning of law and respect justice. Secession of a state in violation of a Supreme Court decision is inconceivable in America. The World Court will grow in prestige and power in the same way. Governments will in time accept the fact that in the judges of the World Court we have a group of men who are fallible but still distinguished for their learning, wisdom, international outlook, and sense of international justice. No one can watch the World Court in session and study its decisions and judgments without realizing that here at last we have the substitute for war.

I know that the Court is limited in its jurisdiction. According to the statutes that control the Court, it is able to consider only those cases that nations and governments agree to submit. Not many of the members of the United Nations have agreed to submit any of their disputes to it. In time, however, I am convinced that more and more nations and governments will decide it better to bring their grievances to the World Court for interpretation and for judgment rather than to go to war. We must expect differences and disagreements between nations as they arise between individuals, but it is not necessary that these lead to dissension and to a disruption of relationships. It is much wiser to employ all the machinery of negotiation and law. Through the centuries systems of law have been developing, from the simple and primitive little courts at the gates of the city, in which the judge was chieftain or magistrate of the community. Since the time of Grotius, or for about 300 years, law has attained a body of international jurisprudence that serves to guide the judges of the World Court. The Court, however, is limited to civil cases.

The first real attempt to develop a World Court to deal with criminal cases was made at the time of the Nuremberg trials. There is little doubt but that this movement will grow rapidly, and that the world will be able to try men and women for international crimes, such as are described in the Genocide Pact. I am convinced that as the years pass we shall shift emphasis from the Assembly and Security Council to the World Court, which will be recognized as one of the most important agencies to grow out of our world experiences. One of the most impressive moments in my experience was when I stood in the Peace Palace at The Hague with Mrs. Goldstein and our daughters, Eleanore and Beatrice, in the presence of the World Court. For I felt at that time, as I feel even more deeply now, that this is the Temple to which the peoples of the earth will come to settle their disputes by pacific means, and where they will learn the art of war no more.

Moral Mandate

The most important ground for optimism I find in the fact that men are coming to understand more and more clearly the laws in accordance with which they must learn to live upon the social level. Not the laws of the natural sciences, social sciences, nor psychological sciences, but the laws of ethics constitute the organic laws of social life. Ethical law, we are coming to realize, is just as powerful and inviolate as the laws of physics or chemistry or biology. If we wish to construct a house that will stand we know we must build in accordance with the laws of physics. Houses collapse, as did one recently in Westchester County, because the builders ignored or misunderstood the laws of physics. If we wish to produce a chemical compound that will work, we must compound it in accord with the laws of chemistry. It is because we disregard or misunderstand these laws that so many compounds fail to maintain themselves in industry and medicine. If we wish to cultivate a plant or animal that will grow normally, we must observe the laws of biology so far as we understand them. Our knowledge is still limited, and it is because of our limitations that we make so many mistakes in this area. If we wish to construct a social order that will survive and develop, we must construct it in keeping with the laws of ethics that operate upon this level of evolution. Sooner or later we shall come to understand that our social disasters are due to our failure, conscious or deliberate, to employ these laws. We shall realize that evil dies of its own poison. In religious terms, sin contains the seeds of its own destruction. I do not mean to say that the laws that operate upon one level are not at work upon other levels of evolution. The human body, for example, is so constructed that it operates in accord with physical laws when we lift our arms, with chemical laws when we digest our food, and with biological laws when we grow normally. But in addition we must recognize that we live and establish human relationships in accord with the laws of ethics.

The teaching that the laws of ethics govern our development at the human and social levels I find valid, certainly in our personal lives. Our behavior is due to somatic, psychological, social factors. But in my experience with men and women I find that the ethical factor is the most important. Those who have come to me for counsel and guidance are in difficulty chiefly because they fail to recognize and to live in accordance with the laws of ethics. The same thing is true of family life. There is no doubt that the family rests upon legal, economic, biological, and psychological foundations. But the discords and dissensions and disruptions are due largely to the failure of men and women to realize that marriage and the family must rest upon the moral foundation and be built in accordance with the laws of ethics. This is also true of our group relations.

The misunderstanding and friction, antagonism and hostility, that develop between groups is due to differences in background, in culture, and in outlook upon life. But fundamentally they rise from a violation of the ethical laws that should guide these groups in establishing community relations and community cooperation. This teaching is also valid, I am convinced, in the circles of our larger social life, in our cultural organization, our economic system, and our political order, whether we are concerned with the local, national, or international level. The laws of anthropology and economics and political science are valid only to the degree that they are in accordance with the laws of ethics. Wherever difficulties and conflicts develop in these areas I find invariably that they are due to the failure on the part of peoples and nations and governments to recognize their ethical relationships.

We are coming to see that the social order is not imposed upon us either by nature or by some higher power. It is our own creation and our own handiwork. We are the architects as well as the artisans of the social system we choose. It is true that we are limited by the land in which we live, by the soil and climate. If we live in the tropics, we develop a social order in accordance with torrid climatic conditions. If we live in the temperate zone, we develop a social order in accordance with the temperate climate. If we live in the arctic circles, we develop a social order determined by the frigid climate of the North or the South.

It is also true that the social order we create is limited by the resources of that section of the earth in which we dwell. The desert areas undoubtedly shape the civilization of nomads and desert groups. The land without mineral deposits is unable to develop an industrial civilization. It is not a matter of chance but of deliberate choice that large urban centers have been founded on large rivers and seacoasts. Even the resources of the sea make or unmake cities and civilizations. A simple shift in ocean currents may drive shoals of fish to other areas and deprive whole countries of a source of support. But it is also true that we ourselves decide whether we are to have a social order filled with incompetence and corruption and crime, or one that is efficient and honest and clean. We must recognize that if the social order is to survive and progress we must organize it in accordance with the laws of social ethics. This is why it is so important that men and women be trained in a democracy in an understanding of ethical laws. We cannot expect dictators to organize a social order that will be permanent and just, for the dictator is always moved not by ethical motives but by motives of power and prestige.

This, as I understand it, is the larger meaning of the unique and distinctive experiment we have conducted in the Free Synagogue during the last forty-six years. On the one hand we have been engaged in the task of socializing religion and the synagogue and of developing and emphasizing the social implications of Judaism. Our endeavor has been to relate religion and the synagogue more closely to our social life, and to stress our concept that the synagogue is a religious center for community service and social action as well as a house of worship and a seat of education. Fifty-five years ago, when I was a student in the University of Chicago I heard John Dewey deliver his great address on "The School and Society," the address that changed our whole concept of the content and character of education. Professor Dewey told us the story of the New England miller who wanted to sell his mill, but who offered it for sale at so low a price that everyone became suspicious. Finally one of his friends went to him and said, "John, what is the matter with the mill? I have examined the building and inspected the machinery and both are in good condition." The miller answered, "The building is in good condition and the machinery is in good shape. There is only one trouble with the mill; the mill-wheel stands just one foot above water." "That," said Professor Dewey, "is the trouble with the school. The mill-wheel stands just one foot above the water." And that, fifty years ago, was the trouble with the synagogue. During these fifty years our effort has been to bring the synagogue and society into closer contact.

But our greater task has been to religionize our social life. This means that we have endeavored to indicate in what way the circles of our social life must be reorganized in accordance with the laws of ethics if the social order is to survive and to develop—the circles, that is, of the family, the community, the cultural organization, the economic system, and the political order. It is true that we have been able to do only an infinitesimal part of what needs to be done. We have only touched some aspects of the major problems, in each circle of the social order. But our aim and objective has been to establish the pattern implied in the principles of our faith. I realize that the world is full of marvels, miracles, mysteries. I shall never cease to marvel at the simple and exquisite beauty of a snowflake; I shall never cease to wonder at the miracle of the birth of a baby; I shall never fail to be moved and awed by the mysteries that hover like visions of the dawn upon the horizon of life. But I also realize that in spite of marvels and miracles and mysteries the world is still an imperfect place. And here I find is the great challenge of life. What can each one do in his own field and his own way to improve and to perfect the world? We are all engaged ultimately in the same great task, ministers, teachers, physicians, scientists, to make the world a more livable place, in which human beings will be able to develop their capacities and powers for good to the utmost. This is what I mean by religionizing the social order in accordance with the moral mandate of Judaism.

This is the lesson taught us by the great teachers of the ages, and it is the lesson confirmed by our own experience. Amos, in the masterly address that opens his Book, indicts the nations for the social sins they have committed and predicts their destruction. In one of his great visions the prophet pictures God as dropping a plumbline into the social order of his time. To Amos God is the God of justice, and the law of justice is one of the laws of life. Among the Greeks Aeschylus is one of the most profound as well as deeply religious of poets and dramatists. In his great trilogy of Orestes he expounds the lesson, to use his own words: "Justice guides all things to their common goal." It is a mistake to interpret the teaching of the Greeks as the teaching of fate except in the sense that suffering inevitably follows sin. Dante in his "Divine Comedy" emphasizes the same lesson. The pictures of punishment he paints with such tremendous power mean that while earth is inadequate to deal with sin and crime, the sinful and the criminal cannot escape the consequences of their evil conduct. Shakespeare in his great tragedies, especially in "Hamlet," "Macbeth," and "King Lear," and more especially in "Richard III," stresses the same doctrine. King Richard tossing upon his midnight couch as his sins pass before him is a dramatic embodiment of the teaching that men cannot escape punishment for the evil that they do. This is also the teaching of Robert Browning, the greatest-minded poet of the last century. "The Ring and the Book" is not only his poetic masterpiece; it is also his ultimate statement upon the mandate of the moral law. Guido, the personification of evil; Caponsacchi, the warrior priest, the soldier saint; Pompilia, "the rose gathered from the breast of God"—all these illustrate and underscore the validity and reality of the moral law. No one understood this truth better than Richard Wagner, and no one expressed it with greater power in drama and music. "Tannhauser," "Parsifal,"—in fact, the entire drama of the Nibelungenlied—present in matchless and deathless musical form the doctrine that the laws of ethics are the laws of life and that only through these laws can salvation come to men.

What men need most in this world crisis is a rebirth of faith in the social ideals of Israel. Too many of the noblest visions born of the soul of our people have lost their lustre. In the Ryks Museum in Amsterdam the Dutch people treasure the masterpiece of Rembrandt called, incorrectly, The Night Watch. Rembrandt painted this picture three centuries ago. It was placed in the great hall of the tavern in which the Arms Guild met, and in time came to be covered with smoke and soot. The colors grew so dark and somber that those who gazed upon the canvas thought it portrayed the guard marching out at night to meet the enemy. Then someone cleaned the canvas and restored it to its original colors. Now we see it not a picture of the night but of the day, filled with glorious hues, flooded with sunlight, and glowing with noontide warmth and beauty—a picture reborn, the pride of Holland and one of the chief glories of the world of art.

We have allowed too many of our great ideals and visions to be covered with the smoke and grime of this Iron Age. We mistake them for pictures of darkness and despair when in reality they are brilliant with light and glorious with richness and power. The ideals of Israel, re-established in our heart and sovereign in our lives, will make us not the priests and protectors of the old order, filled with weakness and wickedness and woe; but the prophets and protagonists of a new world that is fair and strong and just.